MEDITATION
ON A
PRISONER

Towards
Understanding Action
and Mind

Edward Pols

SOUTHERN ILLINOIS UNIVERSITY PRESS
Carbondale and Edwardsville

Feffer & Simons, Inc.
London and Amsterdam

Library of Congress Cataloging in Publication Data

Pols, Edward.
    Meditation on a prisoner.

    Includes bibliographical references and index.
    1. Mind and body. I. Title.
BF161.P56   128′.2   74–22482
ISBN 0–8093–0679–4

Contents

Acknowledgments vii

1

The Prisoner's Views on Action and Causality 1

2

Action, Entities, and the Laws of Nature 28

3

The Originative Acts of the Prisoner: Introductory 69

4

The Originative Act and Its Infrastructure 101

5

The Hierarchy of the Infrastructure 140

6

The Mind of the Prisoner. Part One:
Materialism and Consciousness 176

7

The Mind of the Prisoner. Part Two:
The Autonomy of Mind-Becoming-Conscious 221

8

Mind, Action, and Infrastructure 274

9

From Act to Agent: Ontic Power 308

Notes 355

Index 363

Acknowledgments

Most of this book was written during the academic year 1972-73, when I was on sabbatic leave from my duties at Bowdoin College. I am grateful for that support and for its augmentation by a grant made to me by Bowdoin under the Ford Foundation Humanities Grants program. During that year, much of which was spent in the neighborhood of Florence, my work was often made easier, as on so many earlier occasions, by the hospitality of the *Villa I Tatti, The Harvard University Center for Italian Renaissance Studies.* I am grateful to its then director, Professor Myron P. Gilmore, and to Mrs. Gilmore. The atmosphere of that place is always life-enhancing, but I think never more so than in that year, the last one it was presided over by my friends Myron and Sheila Gilmore.

Quotation in chapter 1 from *Plato's Phaedo,* translated by F. J. Church, copyright © 1951 by The Liberal Arts Press, Inc., reprinted by permission of The Liberal Arts Press Division of The Bobbs-Merrill Company, Inc.

E. P.

Meditation on a Prisoner

1

The Prisoner's Views on
Action and Causality

ALMOST TWENTY-FOUR HUNDRED
years ago, on a day of which we know a great
deal because of Plato's extensive account of it,
Socrates rejected a certain view of the causes of
human action. It was in the year 399 B.C., and
the place was the Athenian prison where at sun-
set he was to drink the hemlock that would be
brought to him by the reluctant executioner. The oppor-
tunity to escape had been provided for him by powerful
friends, and it is supposed that the authorities had no wish
to make a martyr of him, and would have been glad if he
had taken advantage of his friends' offer. The story of his
refusal to escape is well known, and for my purpose it is only
important that he intended it as a moral gesture.

At one point in the long conversation with the group
of friends who had gathered in the prison to spend the last
day with him, he recalled the scientific and philosophical
preoccupations of his youth, and in particular his interest
in the teachings of Anaxagoras, to whom he attributes the
rejected doctrine. He had at first expected to find a quite
different view of action in Anaxagoras' book, one that was
based on the causal power of Mind, but he was disap-
pointed. "All my splendid hopes were dashed to the
ground, my friend," he said, "for as I went on reading I
found that the writer made no use of Mind at all, and that
he assigned no causes for the order of things. His causes

1

were air, and ether, and water, and many other strange things. I thought that he is exactly like a man who should begin by saying that Socrates does all that he does by Mind, and who, when he tried to give a reason for each of my actions, should say, first, that I am sitting here now, because my body is composed of bones and muscles, and that the bones are hard and separated by joints, while the muscles can be tightened and loosened, and, together with the flesh and the skin which holds them together, cover the bones; and that therefore, when the bones are raised in their sockets, the relaxation and contraction of the muscles make it possible for me now to bend my limbs, and that that is the cause of my sitting here with my legs bent."

It may be wise to interrupt Socrates at this point to remind the reader that the Greek word for cause is *"aitia,"* and that in its earliest appearances in Greek literature it was used in assigning moral responsiblity for human action. By the time of Plato and Aristotle, and in part because of the distinction Socrates was just about to make, it had come to have so many senses that to ask for the *aitiai* of a certain happening was to ask for a many-sided explanation. Our word "cause" inherits these ample overtones, but in scientific and philosophical use today it is often given a narrower sense, one that has, as we shall see later, some relation to the way Socrates has used it in the speech so far. At this point he introduced a different sense. "And in the same way," Socrates continued, "he would go on to explain why I am talking to you: he would assign voice, and air, and hearing, and a thousand other things as causes, but he would quite forget to mention the real cause, which is that since the Athenians thought it right to condemn me, I have thought it right and just to sit here and to submit to whatever sentence they may think fit to impose. For, by the dog of Egypt, I think that these muscles and bones would long ago have been in Megara or Boeotia, prompted by their opinion of what is best, if I had not thought it better and more honorable to submit to whatever penalty the state inflicts, rather than escape by flight. But to call these things causes is too absurd! If it were said that without bones and muscles and the other parts of my body I could not have carried my resolutions into effect, that would be true. But to say that they are the cause of what I do, and that in this way I am acting by Mind, and not from choice of what is best, would be a very loose and careless way of talking. It simply means that a man cannot distinguish the real cause from that without which the cause cannot be the cause, and this it is, I think, which the multitude, groping about in the dark, speaks of as the cause, giving it a name which does not belong to it."[1]

The English expression "real cause" translates two different Greek expressions: of one of them it is a tolerably literal rendering; the other would be more happily translated as "true cause." To remind the reader of that I shall for awhile give both words. I shall also use quotation marks whenever we are discussing "real (true) causality" both to identify the expression as an unusual one and to indicate that, despite my sympathy for what Socrates is saying, I regard the expression as not entirely satisfactory. For all its importance, the theme of causality needs to be supplemented by another and more fundamental one if the position Socrates was trying to establish is to be made invulnerable to attacks from modern versions of the rejected positon he attributed to Anaxagoras. This meditation will in fact be directed towards the development of what I take to be this more fundamental theme.

But despite these reservations, I take the theme of "real (true) causality" to be central to what Socrates is trying to say. It would not do him justice at all to suppose that the distinction he made between "causes without which the cause cannot be the cause" and the "real (true) cause" comes down merely to a distinction between the logical properties of statements in which the causes of an action are set forth and statements in which the reasons that motivated an agent are given. There is to be sure an important distinction of the latter sort: the two kinds of statements do indeed have different meanings, and the difference has been worked out in detail by a number of writers in recent years. But if the matter is not carried a good deal further, it is still open to those who hold modern versions of the position Socrates rejected to claim that a causal account is

3

more fundamental and more truly explanatory than the other one. Those who take this line will concede that there are reasons that motivate an action in the sense that the agent is more or less conscious of them and believes them to be efficacious in bringing about his actions, but they will maintain that an account of the actions in terms of the reasons will add nothing to a causal account. In the telling phrase that has become part of our vocabulary, all reasons whatsoever—and not merely the ones that disguise emotion or prejudice—are rationalizations of operative mechanisms of a more fundamental kind. On the face of it this is a preposterous suggestion, so preposterous that it is not often put forward directly, but rather hidden under such claims as that the reasons are identical with the brain states, so that a causal account in terms of the latter will not leave out anything essential that could be put into an account in terms of reasons. Socrates clearly recognizes the logical distinction between the two accounts, but he does indeed want to carry the matter further. He does not merely wish to contrast reasons and causes: he wants to claim that, when they are held by an agent, reasons themselves have power, efficacity, and explanatory value—in short, precisely what we might intend by calling them causes. More than that, he wishes to claim that an agent acting under reasons or principles possesses these characteristics in a deeper measure than do causes in the sense of the rejected doctrine. The idea of "real (true) causality" therefore combines the themes of power, agency, explanatory value, and fundamental authenticity. To bring the great dead into today's controversies we must always look to the tendency of what they are saying rather than to the literal formulation. Socrates says very little that would fall neatly into place in a technical discussion of agency today. But it is clear that he believes that man's physical nature provides only the conditions for his actions—"that without which the cause cannot be the cause"—and it seems no serious distortion to say that he takes the "real (true) cause" to be his own agency, an agency informed by the principles he holds. Agency, informed in this way and thus qualified by Mind, is a power that constrains other recalcitrant powers to keep him

4

there in prison. At any rate, it is that tendency in his speech that this meditation makes common cause with. How properly to conceive of that power, playing within other powers from which it can only be separated by abstraction, is its major task.

2

The dialogue the passage comes from is the *Phaedo,* and Plato there sets this profoundly important claim about human agency within a philosophic view of reality that has many ramifications. But the point he tells us Socrates made is separable from the doctine of the Form of the Good and the other Forms, the doctrine of the immortality of the soul, and all the other familiar doctrines of Plato, so that I shall not be concerned either to expound or to defend Platonism here. We need not be Platonists to see that Socrates supposed himself to be a moral agent and thought the point worth dying for.

The philosophic view he rejected is also separable from the archaic though vivid formulation he gives it. It was by no means a new view even in Socrates' time, and since then it has proved itself to be one of the most tenacious of human attitudes. Insofar as there is something of the scientific spirit in it, it is also one of the most profitable — certainly the one most capable of orderly and rational development. Indeed, if it were only the spirit of natural science that was at issue, it is hard to see why Socrates himself could have objected to it. He was troubled by a related but different matter. His complaint was directed not so much against the study, however extensive, of those things "without which the cause cannot be the cause," as against the assumptions, which often go with such a program, that there is no "real (true) cause" to be contrasted with the conditioning causes, and that these latter are the only ones that operate. When these assumptions are in effect we are not dealing merely with the scientific attitude, which tries to apply its complex method wherever it is both useful and interesting to apply it, but rather with a philosophy; and it does not make the least difference if the intellectual justification for it happens to be put forward not by a philosopher but by a natural scientist acting in a philosophic capacity. As a philosophy it has various names. It is depressing to run through any list of those terms with the suffix "ism" that mark out the strong points from which so much intellectual controversy is conducted, but in this case the names have been so commonly used that it will be both clearer and more convenient if I mention them and then fix upon one of them to use in this book.

The names most hallowed by time, "materialism" and "mechanism," are no longer very exact in the present state of science, but they are still heard often, and their very familiarity recommends them. Two other names, "physicalism" and "naturalism," are potentially more exact, but the first is not widely used except among specialists, and the second is ambiguous unless its use in other contexts is abandoned, a development that is not likely. A promising name is "scientism," since it implies a profound connection with science, and yet enables us to make the point that we are not talking about the scientific outlook but about a philosophic view that identifies the whole of rationality with science. But this last name has the disadvantage that it encourages the perverse, rhetorical, and almost deliberate misunderstandings that are common in intellectual controversy: any criticism of scientism may be taken to be a criticism of science itself, and thus dismissed as antirational. Besides, if we choose "scientism," we shall have no convenient label for a proponent of that doctrine except "scientist," which would produce hopeless confusion. In recent and current controversy another name, "reductionism," is heard more and more, and it is often used loosely enough to suggest that it is identical with the position Socrates was attacking. There is this much truth in the suggestion, that some writers who hold reductionist views also hold modern and more sophisticated versions of the position Socrates attributed to Anaxagoras. But if we are to be precise about it, reductionism is a doctrine with a more restricted range, being concerned primarily with the nature and proper objectives of science. Its basic tenet is that all the sciences are logically reducible to a perfected physics, and this tenet can obviously be held without inconsistency by someone who would not commit himself to the whole of the view Socrates thought so wrongheaded. For all these reasons "materialism," which can, after all, be given an exact sense not founded upon the view of matter that prevailed before the twentieth century revolution in physics, seems the best name to use. I shall try not to take it more seriously as a technical term than it deserves, and shall feel at liberty to use one of the other terms now and then if the context warrants it.

The conflict between Socrates' own view and the materialism he attributes — probably with less than justice — to Anaxagoras has taken many forms down through the ages. In our own times it has centered around a monumental effort to bring the study of man entirely within the scope of the natural sciences, and to do this in so thorough a way that there should be no remainder to be dealt with by other rational methods. That is why the term "scientism" had some attractions. This effort manifests itself in several fields: behavioristic psychology, the study of intelligence by means of brain physiology and the exploitation of the computer analogy, neo-Darwinian evolutionary theory, and biophysics — especially the further exploitation of the line of investigation that led to the discovery of the DNA helix. Any well-read child of this century can extend the list considerably. Despite the wide variety of interests comprised in any such list and the considerable differences in the methods used to pursue them, it has been an extraordinarily single-minded movement. Those who work these several fields in this spirit understand one another, they live in the same sphere of intellectual politics, and they look forward with equanimity to a day when an *ethos* still qualified by religious, moral, and artistic considerations shall have given way to one dominated entirely by science. Of course there are many workers in the same fields who do not bring any such philosophic bias to their work — but those who do carry on their work in that spirit belong to one magisterial movement that is by way of being the dominant intellectual one of our times. Carried along with it are many of

7

the major trends in the social sciences and in philosophy. Indeed, much of the work that goes on in academic philosophy today is designed to give a direct or indirect justification for it.

Dominant though it is, many philosophies that have at least something in common with Socrates' concern for the "real (true) cause" contest its steady advance, so that around the astonishing growth of scientific knowledge in our century two loosely organized philosophic parties can be observed in constant though ever-changing and often disorderly skirmish. On the one side, it is maintained that man is a responsible moral agent, and that no account of his nature and actions that is propounded either by an ideal and perfected physics or by a group of complementary but partially independent sciences will give us an understanding of his agency more profound than one we might hope to achieve by attending to it directly and expressing what we see in terms appropriate to its own nature. If my language seems vague, that is because it is deliberately general: it must encompass Socrates' complaint as well as the positions of many contemporary thinkers who treasure their differences from one another and from Socrates. On the other side, it is maintained that science is knowledge, that there is no other kind worth dignifying with the name in any exacting sense, and that therefore the only true understanding of man and his agency must be had through its methods; that if there is now something obscure about the nature of man as science understands it, the reason is that science still falls short of the ideal state towards which it is moving; that with time the progress of the physical sciences will provide a perfected understanding of nature and —because in principle there is no difference between the two —of human nature. Formulated in this way, the dispute is a metaphysical one; that is to say, a philosophical dispute about the most basic issues of philosophy—in a phrase of Plato's, about what is "really real" and about whether we have the capacity to know it.

Because of the unprecedented pace at which science has been developing, this ancient disagreement has taken an unusual turn. While remaining in a *de jure* sense as open as ever, it may well be settled in a *de facto* sense in favor of materialism in the near future. The natural sciences can now tell us so much about those things "without which the (real) cause cannot be the cause" that our knowledge of them is of an entirely different order from the vivid but naïve examples of scientific explanation that Socrates gave. The young absorb a steady stream of scientific knowledge from every organ of education and public information, and if things go on in this way, the stream continuing to increase, the alternatives continuing to dwindle, no dramatic and logically overwhelming demonstration of materialism will be needed, since the demand for alternative ways of understanding ourselves will gradually pass away. If once all the dominant organs of opinion and publicity in the culture should speak with a common voice on this subject, it would matter little if a few unheard intransigents continued to argue otherwise.

Materialists have proved better intellectual propagandists and politicians than their opponents; some of them, at least, are aware that to persuade people in large numbers it is more important to be constantly heard than to be absolutely right. Do computers really think? The late mathematician A. M. Turing, whose studies in computer theory played an important role in the rapid growth of the theory of artificial intelligence, was surely aware that, if they do indeed think, in any sense that closely approximates the way men think, neither he nor anyone else at the time he wrote had conclusively demonstrated that they do. In a *de jure* sense the situation today is no different. Yet he dismissed the question as not really important, remarking that when the word "think" and related words had been used about computers for a certain period it would no longer occur to anyone to contradict the claim that they do think.[2] A related question, can a computer be so constructed as to be conscious, has been dealt with in a somewhat similar way. The question has been much discussed, and a good deal of technical acumen has gone into the debate. Though it is not widely believed that a conscious computer is possible, a disinterested reader of the papers on the subject would have to conclude that in a *de jure*

9

sense the question is still open. J. T. Culbertson not only thinks that such machines are in principle possible but has also undertaken the daunting task of showing how one can be built.[3] His book is marred by what I take to be some unsound argument on fundamental points, and one or two of these are discussed later on in this book; but it is one of the more illuminating studies of analogies between the central nervous system and computers, and has besides some suggestions that, although they might not make out a plausible case for conscious computers, might nevertheless shed some light on how nerve circuitry subserves consciousness — "causes without which the cause cannot be the cause." But, questions of soundness aside, Culbertson has organized his book for maximum psychological impact, using many of the techniques of the programmed textbook. His thesis, which, by the way, is explicitly offered as a defense of materialism, might be totally wrong in a *de jure* sense and still promote in a *de facto* sense a metaphysical outlook in keeping with it. A student who conscientiously worked out all the exercises at the end of each chapter would become so imbued with the terminology of the book that he could scarcely entertain the thought that the doctrine conveyed by it was wrong. A more dramatic case is that of B. F. Skinner. His views about human nature, when they have been precisely and technically stated, have been refuted with precision time and again, sometimes with devastating effect.[4] But in a recent book [5] intended for wide circulation he simply takes it for granted that his position is unassailable, and directs his readers instead to that sunlit world "beyond freedom and dignity" that his position seems to make both possible and desirable. If his readers allow themselves to be diverted from the question of the soundness of his position to the question of the practical measures that might bring us closer to a world consistent with it, Skinner's cause will prosper. And if the steps are actually taken, what will it matter if the position is nonetheless, in a *de jure* sense, wrong? A world in which the terms "freedom" and "dignity" had lost all the positive resonance they still have would be in a *de facto* sense beyond freedom and dignity.

10

3

Although the dispute may not be an important feature of our culture much longer, it is still alive at the present time in both a *de jure* and a *de facto* sense. While this is so, it is worthwhile to try to express again, and in terms adequate to what we have learned since Socrates' day, what he was driving at. In one sense it is simplicity itself, and our common language says it as well as it can be said. He said, in effect, that no scientific account of his action could provide a more profound explanation of it than the statement that he *did* act, and that he acted in that way because he saw that it was right to do so. The simplicity lies, of course, in the ascription of all this to himself—and so far it is by no means clear just what that means—and in doing so with the help of the category of action. Any analytic procedure will reveal numerous complexities. Refusing to escape, for instance, is a complex action; and part of its complexity lies in the fact that seeing that it was right to do so can also be described as an action. But any complexities of this sort that we may find are perfectly compatible with what he was driving at: that an explanation that comes back to himself is final, satisfactory, and not to be set aside by any other. This means that it is also not to be set aside by scientific explanations that avoid the category of action entirely, and are couched instead in terms of entities, processes, functions, states, or events related under the laws of nature. Explanations of that kind have to do with what I shall call the infrastructure of an action—a concept that will be explained in some detail later.

To make Socrates' point persuasive we must manage to see the simplicity and explanatory finality of action more adequately than we do now. This means that we must also see the nature of the agent more clearly. If we succeed, no scientific account of the infrastructure of an action, no matter how subtle, precise, and detailed it may be, can undermine our confidence in the authenticity of act and agent. We should then see, more clearly than we now do, to what degree such accounts are abstract, and to what degree, accordingly, they are not competent to furnish a basis for the judgment of the ontological status of what in principle must escape their net. We could then get on with the fascinating business of science without being tempted to draw irrelevant conclusions from it. To put the matter in this way is to say that the status of scientific explanations in relation to action is not now well understood. Its application to the infrastructure of an action has a power and importance that even Socrates' naïve description of it concedes, and we must manage to understand just how it is related to the kind of approach he preferred. But so long as our attitude to it dissolves the simplicity and finality of an explanation like "Socrates acted in that way because he saw that it was right to do so," our understanding of it will remain inadequate.

4

In recent years a branch of philosophy called action theory has grown up around the study of human action and its relation to causality. The predominance of the method of linguistic analysis has, I think, prevented it from developing into the powerful alternative to scientific materialism it might have become, but a brief consideration of it may be of help in getting us started on our delicate task.[6] Philosophers working in action theory have studied in detail the logical structure of the ordinary language we use when we talk about action. If we had good reason to take seriously what our everyday, rather than scientific, language implies about the nature of action, it would be hard to take equally seriously a view of action in terms of scientific materialism. It is, for instance, a common claim today among writers on action theory that some actions of men can be causes and that some of these actions can not profitably be regarded as caused by still earlier actions. If I pick up a ball and throw it, my act causes the ball to move through the air, and there may be no prior act of mine, and certainly no mental act called a volition, that caused my act. It is also commonly argued that the concept of action is different in meaning from the concept of causality we employ in dealing with physical events, so that when I say I pick up the ball I express quite a different idea from the one I express when I say that an electrochemical event causes the muscles of my fingers to contract around the ball. The serious entertainment of such claims might well have awakened the suspicion among analytic philosophers that the category of action, when understood with appropriate qualifications, is more fundamental than the category of causality and that the latter can be derived from it. Indeed, after making relatively minor terminological adjustments, we might suppose them to be making a point as clearly antimaterialistic as the one Socrates made in the speech I quoted, even though the examples of action they work with are usually as noncommittal as they can find — moving one's finger, for instance — and the complexities of thought, decision, and moral principle inherent in the point Socrates was making are generally avoided.

The development of this suspicion into something philosophically trustworthy is of immense importance, for it would insure the finality of an explanation like "Socrates decided to stay, and he did so because he saw it was right to do so — that is, Socrates *acted,* and acted rightly." And the reference of the notion of causality back to action of this sort would then suggest a way of incorporating into such an account a subordinate account that would do justice to the "causes without which the (real) cause could not be the cause." The commitment to the linguistic method has prevented this development, for the rigorous analysis of our common, or ordinary, language merely brings us back to our commonsense understanding and to the commonsense experience that is its empirical correlative. Reliance on it persuades us that we have already done what still remains to be done. If there is indeed a simplicity to action that justifies the finality of explanations having the general form "Socrates acted," we can not merely appeal to the fact that we habitually use such expressions about him and about ourselves to authenticate the claim that this is so. We have not vindicated that simplicity by the mere fact that we use such expressions.

13

At a commonsense level, we all know that we act, but our understanding and experience of action at that level is precisely what that implies—a commonsense one. And although that is nothing if not direct and concrete, it is diffident and tentative whenever it is brought into confrontation with theory-laden but more exact kinds of knowledge.

Why there should be so widespread a commitment to the linguistic method in contemporary philosophy is a long story; whether it is told by friends or by critics it is also a tangled one.[7] Both will probably agree that where the method predominates there is in the background an old dogma that continues to make itself felt, even though it has long since been repudiated by the writers who once held it. The dogma is that the paradigm of knowledge is to be found in science, though not science as it is practiced by working scientists but rather a perfected science expressed in a language whose imperfections were to be removed by philosophy. Whatever the failings of the existing language of science, the philosophers who propounded this dogma nevertheless took it to be the nearest approximation of knowledge. They assumed that philosophy was an ancillary discipline that gave no direct knowledge of the real world but was limited to the analysis of language in the broadest sense. The dogma is the basic one of scientism, but recast under the influence of an epistemological and linguistic puritanism. While it was dominant, ordinary language was regarded as very deficient indeed. The overthrow of the dogma, due chiefly to Wittgenstein and G. E. Moore, consisted in the revelation—the word is appropriate in view of the language of mysticism that Wittgenstein came to use about it—that there is after all a profoundly important grasp of reality that we exercise when we use our ordinary language. The discovery did nothing to diminish the prestige of scientific language and of science as it is in fact practiced. How could it? That had never really been menaced by this kind of philosophy, and indeed there have been few periods in history when more basic discoveries were being made in science than in those days when empiricist philosophers were busy trying to construct the perfect language they supposed

14

scientists to be groping for. And in any case the revelation that ultimately came to philosophers of this sort, although it did restore their confidence in ordinary language, did not destroy their faith in science. Appropriately, it was a revelation that came to them in linguistic form, As they saw it, it was not the reflection upon ordinary language from the outside that restored their confidence in it, but rather a sudden awareness of how very comfortable a linguistic dwelling it was when one searched out all its corridors and discovered all its hidden amenities: the discovery was one, they thought, that was about their language, and thus it never disturbed their assumption that philosophy can not provide any direct knowledge of reality.

Insofar as action theory is based on a linguistic method in which the everyday language of action is explored, it can only bring our everyday understanding of it into confrontation with a scientific understanding that it is not equipped to challenge. It can not claim to provide a direct philosophic understanding of action while still supposing that the primary object of philosophic insight is the logic of the language in which we talk about our common world. If it can direct our attention to nothing but the logical structure of the language we use in talking about actions and causes, the suspicion that action is more basic than causality is more likely to fade as a cultural force than to grow into a reasoned conviction, for the respect we give our everyday language is subject to the cultural erosion exerted by science, which has a persuasive way of applying its own language to supposed actions. It is also a very direct way: science ignores what ordinary language labors to express, and goes instead for physiological processes and similar features of the infrastructure of the act. In dealing with the infrastructure it uses a language in which the mingled ideas of causality and law play so satisfactory an explanatory role that the ordinary language of action appears by contrast a prescientific place-holder, different in meaning only in the sense that when we use it we are less attentive and less exacting than when we use the language of science. We must not rest our case on linguistic analysis if we are to give an account of human action that will be both plausible to the contemporary mind and at least congruent with the view of action that Socrates was driving at.

5

If the mingled ideas of causality and law are central to the nature of scientific explanation, neither idea is totally clear. We can of course give examples enough. Some of the examples of causes I used in the previous section in talking about action theory will probably satisfy both the scientist and the man in the street. Setting aside the question of action, and setting aside with it what Socrates called the "real cause," the motion of my arm causes the ball to move through the air, and this example will then lead us naturally to the laws of mechanics in accordance with which both cause and effect operate. It is when we try to say what we mean by "cause" and "law" and try to establish an epistemological foundation for our knowledge of both that things seem less clear. I shall ignore these obscurities for the moment and say that the example I have given is an example of causality in the $C \rightarrow E$ sense. At the least this is intended to take account of the fact that in causality of this kind the cause occurs before the effect. Even this claim turns out to be somewhat obscure if one examines it closely enough, for the hand and the ball move together initially, and it is thus hard to see how the movement of the hand as cause can be said to be prior to the movement of the ball as effect. But we can presumably agree on this much: the motion of the hand and arm that is identified as the cause may have ended, while the effect, the flight of the ball, continues. A more clear-cut case is the one in which we understand the movement of one billiard ball to occur before the movement of another that it strikes, and thus call the first movement the cause and the second the effect. The laws of mechanics that are invoked to make the explanation of each of these $C \rightarrow E$ transactions persuasive stand outside the temporal sequence thus established: we suppose them to hold before and after these instances of $C \rightarrow E$ causality, and to be indifferent about whether they are used to explain these instances or different but similar ones.

If we try to be clearer than this, we encounter what I shall call the official philosophical doctrine of causality. It is official in the sense that although there are serious challenges to it, it is the one most often advanced by philosophers in general and philosophers of science in particular. It is also the version we hear most often from scientists who make philosophical observations about science. The official doctrine has many varieties, but most of them go back to Hume in one way or another. One recent example is this, which comes from an article on the mind-body problem by Jerome A. Shaffer.

> Very roughly, I understand by "cause of something" some prior event or state which, given the circumstances, is necessary and sufficient for the existence of the thing. If, given the circumstances, *A* and *B* are constantly correlated and if when we keep those circumstances constant, the occurrence of *A* is followed by the occurrence of *B* and the non-occurrence of *A* by the non-occurrence of *B*, then we have good *evidence* that *A* is the cause of *B*.[8]

Notice that we are talking of events or states, that the cause is temporally prior to the effect, and that there is a constant correlation between *A* and *B*. In the background, but not emphasized, is Hume's contention that we have no valid grounds for saying that a *power* in *A* *necessarily produces B*. That contention produces numerous difficulties, the chief one being the obscurity it introduces into the notion of law. That is a long and tangled story, and I shall not venture upon it except to say that I do not know of any Humean account of causality that has been reconciled with the idea of the laws of nature cogently enough to escape major challenges.

That is one, but I think not the only reason why there have been many contemporary attempts to introduce into this view of causality some surrogate for the idea of necessity that might be sufficient for the law-oriented proceedings of the sciences.

Some writers, however, go further and, while preserving the emphasis on events or states and on the temporal priority of the cause, claim that the relation of cause and effect is in fact one of necessity and power in somewhat the sense Hume excludes. E. M. Madden in a recent article [9] claims in effect that what we mean by saying that a group of conditions, f, g, h, and i, is the cause of a certain effect (C of E) is that they are sufficient to produce E with necessity and to do so by virtue of powers inherent in them. He points out that if we had some good reason for saying that the group was C of E and if the occurrence of the group was not followed by E, we should simply conclude that we had either improperly identified some of the conditions in the present case or had been wrong in the first place in identifying the group as C of E. What we should *not* conclude is that the group was indeed C of E and that E did not follow their occurrence. Madden claims that there is thus a conceptual necessity in the idea of cause represented by C (f, g, h, i)$\rightarrow E$; and this corresponds, he thinks, to a physical necessity in things, a physical necessity best understood in terms of the powers inherent in the various features of nature. He takes as an example an ordinary suction pump. E is the pouring of water from the spigot, and f, g, h, and i (jointly the cause) are such things as the pressure of the atmosphere (construed as a power), the vacuum in the cylinder (presumably brought about by the power of an arm or a motor), and so on. He thinks we do base causal explanations on the reality of such powers, and he believes we have direct experience of causal power.

I do not intend to argue the case between Hume and Madden here, although I think Madden certainly makes some telling points about conceptual necessity, at the least. But if the view he expresses here were sustained, it would make an account of science, in which the idea of law is at least as central as the idea of causality, easier than it has been for orthodox Humeans. The view, which is in effect Hume's with power and necessity restored, is probably very close to the version of $C \rightarrow E$ causality that dominates the man of common sense and the working scientist too—as distinct from the scientist concerned to put forward a guarded philosophical view of $C \rightarrow E$ causality. There is much to be said for this commonsense view: it is very useful, and all of us use it some of the time. Whatever its origins, its hold upon our belief is considerable, and Hume himself gives many indications that he believes in it in spite of the difficulty of giving a rational justification of it on the basis of the premises that govern his epistemology. No doubt most Humean philosophers believe in it when they are off duty. I shall therefore call it the *working view,* as contrasted with the *official view,* of $C \rightarrow E$ causality.

Some readers may object to my linking the working view with Hume. If anything, they may say, it would be more appropriate to link it with Kant's views about the way the understanding deals with the sensory world. But I am merely saying that what I am calling the working view was also Hume's working view, and that on that pragmatic level his thought is much like Kant's. It is perhaps worth a short digression to make this point. For both of them causality is a matter of temporal succession for the scientific intelligence, and for both of them a causal connection properly established by the scientific intelligence draws in the whole of nature. The assumptions about the world that confronts our senses are those of the eighteenth-century materialism that culminates at the very end of the century in the determinism of Laplace. For Kant the matter is beyond question: the world available to our understanding is one of substances in thoroughgoing causal reciprocity, in which the causal relation is one of necessary connections in a temporal order. For Hume, at the level of epistemological sophistication that yields the official view, the status of the "substances," the nature of the connection, and the regularity of the succession, are all of them matters of belief. But the belief is so powerful and unavoidable that there is no conceivable unbelief to oppose to it, and practically speaking (the working view) no exceptions are admitted. The belief once established *as* a belief, Hume shows himself to be as complete a believer in causal laws bearing on the regularity of temporal succession as Laplace himself was. Given a supposed aberration in a Laplacean analysis of a causal

19

sequence, what would Hume's reaction be? That a miracle had taken place? That someone had exercised free will? Hardly. He has carefully set aside, in arguments more persuasive than the epistemological premises from which they flow, any such possibilities, and has shown himself a believer in an entire regularity that no intellectual argument can, as he thinks, fully establish. The supposed aberration in a Laplacean prediction he would set down to a faulty analysis of the regularities antecedent to the moment at which the prediction is made. The working view goes back to Hume the man, confident that his dinner will nourish him, and that his trusted friend will not murder him. There is a belief, an unshakable one, that concedes practically to the sequence the necessity Kant seeks to establish rationally.

It only remains to be observed that Hume is not the only defender of the official view who draws upon the working view not just in his everyday occasions but in his philosophical occasions as well. There are few contemporary defenders of the official view who will not also defend some form of scientific determinism. I do not mean to say that the working view is inevitably deterministic: only that insofar as the ideas of power and necessity are vaguely present in it, it can, if it is *believed*, furnish the motive for construing the official view, in which there are no necessary connections, in such a way as to provide for necessity at the level of law.

Perhaps the working view, or at least some perfected and philosophically guarded version of it, will supplant the official view before very long. Indeed it is one subordinate purpose of this book to provide such a version, but I do not mean to concern myself directly with that issue just now, and so shall simply speak of $C \rightarrow E$ causality, without specifying whether the official or the working view is meant. But it should be understood that the official version is being questioned in many quarters. It is not even possible any longer to take it for granted that both C and E must be understood as events or states, since many writers, in philosophy if not in the exact sciences, are prepared to talk of C and E in terms of entities or their actions. Indeed, participants in recent discussion about the $C \rightarrow E$ relation agree upon so little that formulation of what is agreed upon must seem flippant. Certainly it is more or less canonical that, when the $C \rightarrow E$ relation holds, at least one factor of C is temporally prior to E, and its occurrence (or the occurrence of a group of such C's) sufficient for the occurrence of E. But can this mean any more than that the cause precedes the effect and causes the effect? Certainly if it is not settled whether the $C \rightarrow E$ relation is one of power and necessity or merely one of constant correlation, then precious little is settled.

In the sciences there is, despite all the conceptual difficulties, some further agreement about necessity, since science looks for causal regularities statable in terms of laws. The notion of law is indeed so important there that the causal relation is sometimes virtually absorbed in it. Since Russell's essay "On the Notion of Cause,"[10] there have been numerous philosophers of science who go so far as to claim that the word "cause" is not needed at all in the vocabulary of the exact scientist, since he is not concerned with causes at all but only with laws. Such views are no doubt extreme, and more characteristic positions are those in which the notions of cause and law are in effect treated as interdependent. David Bohm's statement of a widely held view is an especially clear one.

. . . in the processes by which one thing comes out of others, the constancy of certain relationships inside a wide variety of transformations and changes is no coincidence. Rather, we interpret this constancy as signifying that such relationships are *necessary*, in the sense that they could not be otherwise, because they are inherent and essential aspects of what things are. The necessary relationships between objects, events, conditions, or other things at a given time and those at later times are then termed causal laws.[11]

6

There are, then, difficulties enough about the nature of $C \rightarrow E$ causality, about the nature of law, and about the relation between the notions of cause and law. They are, however, philosophical difficulties, and if the history of thought teaches us anything, it is that philosophical difficulties can be ignored, especially if there is work to do that has some practical relevance. There is no doubt that science, working with the somewhat obscure notions of $C \rightarrow E$ causality and law, can give an impressive account of the infrastructure of what common sense calls, in ordinary language, an action of Socrates. And there is no doubt that the increasing subtlety of this account makes for the *de facto* advance of materialism. The account is by no means monolithic, and it would be more accurate to say that in practice there are a number of them, depending upon the interest of the scientist and also to some degree upon the philosophical view he holds about the nature of science; but they will be similar in that they all require the breaking up of the act into a number of units whose interconnections in terms of law and $C \rightarrow E$ causality are held to yield the only possible explanation of it. Some of these accounts sound very like the examples whose ultimate importance Socrates depreciates. A finger is crooked, an object grasped, an arm raised by virtue of a number of interconnected bones that move, as muscular forces are applied to them, in an order and sequence that exemplify the laws of mechanics and the $C \rightarrow E$ causality that, for all its philosophical puzzles, is taken for granted when we make use of them. An account of the contraction of a bundle of muscle cells and of the firing of the numerous motor and receptor nerves that play a role in its ordered contraction will be much more complicated, both because of the number of distinguishable units that are involved and because laws not relevant for the study of mechanical problems, including, for instance, laws governing electromagnetic forces, must now be considered. Once we carry the account below the level of the individual cell, and turn our attention to organelles, macromolecules, and even more fine-grained units, the intricacy of distinguishable units, distinguishable $C \rightarrow E$ transactions, and, perhaps, distinguishable levels of law is impossible to hold in the imagination. That we should in principle be able to carry the same kind of explanation downward indefinitely, stopping only where nature makes it un-equivocally clear, as it presumably does in the case of the quantum principle, that we have reached units within which no more fine-grained units can be found, seems to be generally agreed.

The status of the very many levels of units between Socrates and the lowest units of structure and function that can be found within the infrastructure of his action is, however, a matter of dispute, and in this, it might be thought, there lies some hope of interpreting scientific explanation in a way that would not undermine the finality of explanation in terms of the agency of Socrates. The dispute does not touch directly upon the meta-physical status of all these infrastructure units, however, since it is carried on chiefly in terms of the laws that govern the relations between the units. On the one side stand those working scientists and philosophers of science who hold that all science is in principle reducible to a perfected physics. On the other side a group, less numerous but nevertheless with impressive credentials in the scientific world, maintain that the sciences of life have a unique subject matter and unique laws not in principle reducible to those of physics. The exact sense the term "reducible" is to be given is itself a matter of complex and subtle dispute, but it seems to be generally agreed that biology would be reducible to physics if biological terms like "cell" could be given adequate definitions in which only such terms as "molecule," "atom," and so on appeared, and if from the laws of a perfected physics one could derive by a merely logical process the laws governing such matters as the replication of a cell, the propagation of a neural disturbance through the cortex, the orderly development of the embryo, or even, to cite the extreme case, the origination and development of life itself.[12] In any particular case the application of the laws of a perfected physics would naturally require our turning to nature to establish the physical parameters; but the reductionist would claim that, whatever experiments originally entered into the discovery of a law of biology, the law could have been deduced without experiment if we had had the laws of a perfected physics available to us.

23

The different ways of interpreting the behavior of water molecules in the vicinity of a DNA helix offer an interesting example of what is at issue between reductionists and their opponents. It has recently been observed that the water molecules that make up so large a part of any living cell reveal unusual properties when they are located within the space defined by the DNA helix.[13] Some of them that lie between two "threads" of the double helix are joined to the DNA by hydrogen bonds and thus lend the helix a structural support in addition to that provided by the molecular bond uniting the component parts of the DNA molecule itself. This is unusual for water molecules in the liquid state, and it at first appeared that the water molecules were behaving as they would in the lattice of an ice crystal. It now appears that only a monolayer of water molecules is tightly bound to the DNA in this way, and that this layer controls the secondary structure of these (relatively) very large systems. But this behavior is still unusual in the liquid state. If the hydrogen-bonding behavior of the water molecules were in fact what one would expect in the liquid medium of a cell, the large amount of water present in and around the helix would not reinforce the DNA structure but instead destroy the hydrogen bonds that also play an important role in tieing together elements of the four bases of the DNA itself. On the face of it, it would seem that an "abnormal," or "aberrant," hydrogen-bonding characteristic of water is vital to the structural stability of DNA, in which the "information" that controls the functioning and the genetic stability of the cell is "encoded."

The anti-reductionist might also point out that this is but one instance of many small forces that must be present together for a cell to exist, and that it is the law, principle of order, or system-principle, proper to the cellular level that operates to bring out a characteristic of water molecules not ordinarily present in a liquid and to combine it with a large number of other factors. A reductionist, on the other hand, will claim that there is nothing in the least aberrant about this mode of hydrogen-bonding: had we thought to ask in advance of experiment how water molecules would behave in the unusual boundary conditions of the helix, quantum mechanics would have told us that, given those circumstances, some of them must behave, when forming hydrogen bonds, as though they were in an ice crystal. What is unusual is not the behavior of the water molecules, but rather the constellation of delicate forces of which the hydrogen bond formed by the water molecules with neighboring elements of the helix is but one instance. And to explain this unusual constellation he will appeal only to the laws of physics, to chance, and to the vast periods of time over which chance has operated. There is nothing, he will say, in the behavior of the water molecules within the helix that we can not account for without having recourse to the biological laws that an anti-reductionist supposes to operate at the cellular level, and these "laws" are therefore dispensable in a pure and perfected science.

Whether it is true that, if it had occurred to us to ask the relevant questions, quantum mechanics would have enabled us to predict this certainly surprising behavior of the water molecules I am not competent to say. But even if it were true, it is not at all clear that it would settle the case between reductionism and anti-reductionism. The supposed prediction from quantum mechanics could mean no more than that the behavior of the water molecules was consistent with quantum mechanics, a point most anti-reductionists would concede in advance. Most of them seem to take it for granted that if any irreducible biological laws are found, they will be perfectly compatible with the basic laws of physics. They are intended, in fact, to supplement physics, and to do so by accounting, and in a way more rationally satisfying than an appeal to chance can do, for the curious fact that complexes like living things do arise and persist. The prediction of the odd behavior of the water molecules would therefore be beside the point. It takes for granted the living things the anti-reductionist seeks to explain, and in effect says that, given the odd circumstances represented by those living things, the odd behavior of the water molecules may be expected. But it is just those odd circumstances the anti-reductionist is interested in; to him it seems that they, or rather the principle that brings them about, elicits the odd behavior which, to be sure, the molecule must be capable of. What is *not* predictable from quantum mechanics is just this principle that brings about these odd circumstances.

When one expresses the attitude of anti-reductionist scientists in this way it might seem that they make common cause with Socrates against materialism, but I do not think this is really so. As scientists their major concern is with the autonomy of a number of sciences, chiefly those concerned in one way or another with life, over against the imperialism of physics. If the convergence of a number of complementary sciences upon the action of Socrates in prison should bring about an account of it as hostile as the reductionist account is to the finality and authenticity of the explanation that he stayed there because he thought it right to do so, I do not think the majority of anti-reductionist scientists would be troubled.

Some, of course, would: there is no doubt a tendency within anti-reductionist science that we can exploit to try to see Socrates and his actions in a light appropriate to them. It is best identified by saying that many anti-reductionist scientists are powerfully drawn towards philosophy. One can conceive of some of them as at least willing to entertain the suggestion that science is the exact quantitative study of aspects of real entities, real actions, and real processes, whose real unity is given to science by another discipline and is then refracted by science according to its own purposes. Socrates and his actions would be examples of realities thus refracted, but the class of such realities would be very large, and examples from all levels of nature would be found in it. No outlook that takes man's autonomy to be in irreconcilable contrast with all the rest of nature will ever be widely persuasive. But although we can conceive of some anti-reductionist scientists taking views of this sort seriously, the politics of the scientific establishment makes it hard for the working scientist to do so. Scientists who have ventured onto this ground, which is clearly philosophic ground, have usually had their careers as working scientists behind them, and their colleagues have not been above pointing this out.

What is at issue here is a certain conflict of impulse within anti-reductionist science. Unless we so exploit it as to bring out plainly the philosophic insight latent in it, we can not trust anti-reductionist science to justify and reformulate for our times Socrates' almost forgotten protest against materialism. At the moment anti-reductionist scientists are primarily working members of an establishment whose *Realpolitik* operates to bring the study of man entirely within the scope of the natural sciences. It may be better science in the long run if our understanding of Socrates in prison is parceled out to a number of complementary sciences rather than reserved for a perfected physics, but I think it will be small comfort if in the process we forget entirely what he was driving at. For, obscure and inadequate as his way of making this point against materialism may be, if we lose sight of it, we shall lose sight of him too—and he stands there as a representative of all of us. The only real comfort to be found is if we should make it clear in the very face of the united sciences that there really is no single scientific explanation, and no group of complementary scientific explanations, that can replace the simple explanation whose finality Socrates called attention to: "I have thought it right and just to sit here and to submit to whatever sentence they may think fit to impose."

2

Action, Entities, and the Laws of Nature

 A LAW OF NATURE EXPRESSES A certain constraint in the nature of things under which any $C \rightarrow E$ event takes place, a constraint so massive and pervasive that some philosophers have held the relation of cause and effect to be merely an expression of it, and thus to be dispensed with altogether in scientific explanation. Even if we reject so extreme a view, the importance of law in any scientific explanation can scarcely be set too high. That in the nature of things which we attempt to express in the laws of nature is appealed to by science as to an absolute, a stable and imperishable realm, exempt from the passage of the ephemeral events that it explains for us. The $C \rightarrow E$ relation is nothing if not temporal: this particular entity, event, or state of affairs is the cause, and it precedes that one, which is the effect. The laws of nature, though, are tentative formulations of what governs the relations, and this feature of things is exempt from time and from the particularity of place. In this sense, the laws hold before that particular $C \rightarrow E$ event, and they will hold after it; and as they reign here on earth, regulating the flight of a ball tossed by a boy, so they reign also where some unknown planet revolves around a distant star. They are attempts to express what is universal, necessary, and eternal, what reigns equably and everywhere as the very stability of "the nature of things." Even exceptions to law come some-

how within the sway of what we try to express in the laws of nature. The gravitational field within which a body moves may vary from place to place in Newtonian mechanics; the mass of a body may increase with its velocity in relativity physics; matter may in most circumstances be found in a gaseous, liquid, or solid state, and, where the circumstances are unusual, may take the form of plasma; but this very variability is ideally to be taken account of in a law of nature. We trust our formulations of them the more as they approach this ideal.

But to speak of the laws of nature as expressions of "the nature of things" is not to say that science regards its unceasing reformulation of the laws of nature as a gradual approach to a "nature of things" that has an ontological status quite distinct from law. It is not, for instance, usual in science to suppose that nature is based upon a power or powers more vital, concrete, and personal than the idea of law suggests, and to concede that the metaphor of law therefore distorts nature as it really is. It is indeed conceded that the laws of nature as science formulates them at any given time are tentative and, even at their most refined, only approximations. But it seems to be assumed that what they approximate to are *the* laws of nature, the laws of nature as they in fact are. They are essential aspects of what things are, these laws, and their status is to abide in the nature of things with all the impersonal and stable pervasiveness that the idea of law seems to carry with it. Or, to put it differently, if a little oddly, that in the nature of things which we aspire to express in any particular formulation of the laws of nature is itself lawlike in its ontological status. In what follows, then, I shall not labor to distinguish between the laws of nature and that "in the nature of things" which they are approximations of. I shall suppose that when scientists speak of *the* laws of nature they mean precisely that "in the nature of things" to which any *given* set of laws is an approximation. I shall be supposing, then, that according to science, these true laws of nature constitute the nature of things in some very fundamental sense. This supposition means at the least that they lie in nature with an absolute and impersonal stability that pervades all natural processes, and we may then use such metaphors as "control," "govern," and "regulate," as scientists indeed do in speaking about them, without being accused of a naïve anthropomorphism. In fact, the whole conception of the laws of nature as here developed is at the other pole from that of action, so that we can scarcely be said to impute any action to these laws when we speak of them as controlling, governing, or regulating $C \rightarrow E$ transactions.

The laws of nature, so understood, are independent of what is present and happening in any region that they govern. Just that independence and universality means that they may enter into and contribute to the $C \rightarrow E$ events that they govern, without themselves being in any way qualified by those events. A certain falling stone causes a depression in soft ground upon impact. Though it is precisely that stone that is the cause of that effect, still, like any other falling body, it must accelerate at a certain rate, and this, together with its mass, defines the kinetic energy it brings to the impact. It is "in the nature of things," it lies in the laws of nature, that this should be so. A certain number of photons falling upon an atom excites it to a definite higher energy state. Precisely those photons caused that effect. But like any other photons, these must be absorbed in just that way; and, like any other atom of just that sort, subject to just that much radiant energy, this one must absorb it by the movement of its electrons to certain shells and to no others. It is in the nature of things that it should happen in this way. The laws are so woven into the C that, knowing it to a certain degree of precision, and knowing the laws as well, we can calculate E to the same degree of precision, so that what was called materialism in the preceding chapter can just as accurately be called determinism.

As regards the degree of precision with which C and E can be established, it has sometimes been argued that the indeterminacy principle, which lays it down that regularities below a certain level of magnitude can only be given a statement in terms of statistical probability, means that the laws of nature are not deterministic. Others have argued that, except for the inability of science to give a $C \rightarrow E$ account of the behavior of entities like a single electron or a single photon, the laws are deterministic in the sense that from the state at time t_1 of a system involving large numbers of elementary particles the state of the system at time t_2 can be calculated. Those who incline to that view find nothing offensive in the idea of a statistical or probabilistic determinism operative at the microevent level. It is clear, however, that there is an important difference between a *statistical determinism* and a determinism involving *individual* elementary particles as well, which I shall call *neo-Laplacean determinism.* (There are, of course, no Laplacean determinists anymore, since a strict Laplacean determinism requires the belief that elementary "particles" are particles in the naïve sense that prevailed in the eighteenth century.) A neo-Laplacean determinism holds that our inability to calculate the behavior of an individual electron is merely a function of the interference, in a $C \rightarrow E$ sense, of a measuring technique of a certain magnitude with a physical event of a certain magnitude; and that, to a God-like intelligence that interposed no $C \rightarrow E$ interference with what it dispassionately observed, the behavior of individual elementary particles is as orderly as anything else in nature.

Someone holding a neo-Laplacean determinism could be said to give the statistical determinism of large numbers of microevents a *strong deterministic interpretation.* It would appear that both Einstein and Planck held some such view. It is also possible to give statistical determinism a *weak deterministic interpretation.* On the latter interpretation there is an indeterminism at the level of microevents over and above that which is a function of our measuring techniques: that is, there really is an ontological rather than merely epistemological contrast between individual microevent indeterminism and the statistical determinism of large numbers of microevents, upon which macroevent determinism is based. Those who hold the view that a microevent in the human brain can be used to establish the efficacy of free will, or at least of consciousness, must presumably give the statistical determinism of large numbers of microevents a weak deterministic interpretation. (This last matter is discussed in chapter 8.) I suspect that most scientists (*a*) incline towards a strong deterministic interpretation of the statistical determinism of large numbers of microevents, even though they may not put this preference in the form of an explicit neo-Laplacean doctrine; (*b*) accept a determinism at the macroevent level that is close to the view that Laplace actually held.[1] And even if they keep an open mind about whether there is a genuine ontological indeterminism of individual microevents, they will not usually concede that it creates any problems for macroevent determinism.

This general deterministic bias expresses itself in a pervasive, if sometimes vague and inexplicit, conviction that the ontological status of the laws of nature makes them the chief determinant in any physical situation. When this conviction is made precise and explicit, law can in fact be regarded as the *only* determinant, as in the view, touched upon in chapter 1, in which the $C \rightarrow E$ relation is absorbed into the notion of law. Indeed, though scientific explanation seems to take account of the causal power of just that stone, just that bundle of photons, the very existence of those causal powers is itself not exempt from $C \rightarrow E$ analysis under the same body of law. This is obvious enough when we talk about the origin of an object as accessible to ordinary perception as the stone is. But the distinction between an event regarded as a C and another regarded as an E can be refined to whatever tolerance is needful, even to that of point-events at point-instants, and though certain information may be lost below a definite degree of refinement, even the origin of a certain *bundle* of photons can thus be the subject of a $C \rightarrow E$ account under the same body of law that accounts for the effect of the photons upon the atom.

Do the entities—stones, photons, atoms, men—whose causal concourse is regulated by the laws, whose very coming into existence is but an exemplification of them, contribute in any way to their general sway? Are the laws of nature in any sense ontologically dependent upon other features of things, features of equal status with the laws, if not of more fundamental status? Although a question of somewhat this form has been raised by various philosophers,[2] I do not think that the question

32

ever arises in science qua science. The unexamined assumption that there is nothing more ontologically fundamental than a law of nature is very widespread. The tendency to absorb the causal relation itself into the texture of the law is simply an extreme version of this. When this tendency takes a precise form, temporality itself is simply incorporated into the structural scheme of the laws of nature, and, thus transformed into an additional structural property, is assumed to reign there as eternally and as equally as any more patently static feature.[3] In such interpretations, in which it is held to be theoretically possible to calculate from any state of affairs taken as a cause the state of affairs that follows it as an effect, causality loses whatever sense of temporal becoming it had, and time is transformed into a metric property of a static structure of which it is but one of the coordinates.

The language of action does not apply in any such materialist-determinist version of the laws of nature. The bundle of photons causes the heightened energy state of the atom, the falling stone causes the depression in the ground, yet neither acts to do so, but merely exemplifies the necessity expressed by the law. It is obvious that this should be so in the case of an inert entity like a stone. It is less obvious in the case of photons, which, being vibratory entities of some kind, seem to invite the vocabulary of action; but no more than in the case of the stone does this kind of explanation permit us to think of photons as performing actions. Given the cause, the effect follows in accordance with the laws. Nor is the ordering, regulating, or controlling feature of law itself thought of in terms of actions. The "nature of things" as expressed in the laws is utterly general and impersonal, and it would not occur to the modern scientist to think of a law of nature as imposing in any active sense the conditions it lays down for the connection between C and E, even though the law is understood to express a necessity such that, given a C of a certain sort, an E of a certain sort will follow it.

It is not surprising that the laws of nature should be elevated thus to a God-like ontological status. When the idea of laws of nature took shape in modern times it was frequently associated with the mind of God, and He was held to legislate for the physical world as an omniscient ruler might do. In this respect His active legislation held for awhile in science the role that formal and final causality had played in classical philosophy — causal forces, powers, orderings that stood outside the temporal framework of the material $C \rightarrow E$ connections that they regulated. Whatever sense of legislative activity, of attentive governmental guidance, once belonged to the idea of the laws of nature, it has not been a serious cultural force since Laplace's famous retort to Napoleon's inquiry about the role of God in his system, "Sire, I have no need of that hypothesis." When, apropos of the claim that the need to rely on statistical laws in transactions of a certain size argued for a certain indeterminateness in things, Einstein remarked that God did not play dice with the universe, and that although He was subtle — presumably in the laws He laid down — He was not malicious, he spoke rather for a certain view of the laws of nature than for a theology of an actively legislating God. The complete and universal rule has, in a cultural sense, long since displaced the ruler. The laws of nature are assumed to constitute an absolute and stable Being, and in their endless Becoming the observable and developing things of nature merely exemplify it.

2

When this line of reasoning is applied in detail to the infrastructure of a supposed act of Socrates, there seems no more reason than in the other cases to use the word "act" about it except in the easygoing way of common sense. The infrastructure is after all no more than an extremely intricate complex of $C \rightarrow E$ events under law. Whether we use the official or the working view of the $C \rightarrow E$ relation; whether we eliminate that relation entirely, absorbing it, together with the illusion of becoming it gives, into the eternal completion of the overarching law; whether we think of law in terms of classical or of statistical determinism; all this matters little, for the idea of the "real causality" of an action that pervades, unites, has its being in, and dominates a whole pattern of $C \rightarrow E$ relations in its infrastructure can in any case scarcely arise.

From the ideal of the laws of nature presented so far the speech of our prisoner recalls us decisively. Whatever else he tells us, it is clear that the "real causality" he spoke out for is intended to furnish a more fundamental explanation for what goes on in his infrastructure than general and impersonal laws of nature could do. The view of the laws of nature just sketched is a reductionist one. If only because it does not regard those laws as one single structure without a hint of internal pluralism, anti-reductionist science will give a somewhat different account of law.[4] Whether it is sufficiently different to permit us to take Socrates seriously it is one task of this chapter to determine. Certainly, seen as Socrates would have liked us to see it, the idea of human action suggests to us a different way of looking at the laws of nature than the one I have just described. Without in the least questioning the importance for the natural sciences of the idea of laws of nature, the fresh perspective urged upon us by the prisoner diminishes the overwhelming ontological status of the laws of nature. In contrast with the "real causality"of action it now seems possible to regard them as an abstraction from, and a codification of, the ordering power of entities whose ontological status is perhaps more fundamental than they are.

For a general application of this principle we shall have to wait until the last chapter. Meanwhile, though, it is worth hazarding a suggestion about how it might apply to an entity like Socrates. Seeing action with modern eyes, yet from the viewpoint he so steadfastly maintained upon it, the action of the prisoner seems to embrace, to gather together, to carry along in the sweep of its simplicity, an intricate pattern of $C \rightarrow E$ relations. It dwells in them, expresses itself in them, and they would be otherwise without it. With the finality of explanatory power that we are for the moment conceding it to have, it is the reason (sense 1) for the whole of the pattern, and there is no going behind that reason for a law or set of laws that would make intelligible some supposed obscurity in it. In using the word "reason" thus, I neglect for a moment any principles that might have motivated Socrates, and these are reasons in another and perhaps more usual sense (sense *2*). We may tentatively combine the two senses in this way: if the power of an action is so deployed in a pattern of $C \rightarrow E$ connections as to be the reason (sense *1*) for it, then it is the "real cause" of that pattern; and in that case Socrates' reasons (sense *2*) for acting as he did enter into and qualify that "real causality." As we set aside for a moment the ultimate explanatory status of laws of nature, another kind of law becomes relevant—moral law. But if respect for moral law is one of the reasons (sense *2*) for an action, it does not stand in conflict with the absoluteness of the laws of nature, since we are not now according them the ontological finality they are usually given when the contrast between a determinism grounded on the laws of nature and the freedom required by moral obligation is made in the usual way and erected into an antinomy. The "real (true) causality" of the act thus includes what Kant would have called the (noumenal) causality of the will, but it is not contrasted with a different and deterministic causality that reigns in nature. I am not, incidentally, arguing that Kant made laws of nature ontological absolutes: his claim that nature is phenomenal is at odds with such a view of law. But the Kantian antinomy is surely felt by many writers who would not accept the distinction between noumenal and phenomenal. At any rate, whatever conflict may be found between the efficacy of moral law on the one hand and a $C \rightarrow E$ account in terms of physical law on the other, there is no conflict at all between the efficacy of the moral law and the "real causality" of an act.

One reason for discussing this conception of action in the context of a description of the aims of anti-reductionist science is that if there is "real causality" of this sort, it would stand in somewhat the same relation to a pattern of $C \rightarrow E$ connections as a law, or laws, of nature would if there really were, as anti-reductionist science claims, irreducible laws of nature operative at this level. Suppose we set out to explain the movement of a certain molecule within a cell. Supposing also that we are anti-reductionists, we should not be satisfied with the perfectly intelligible account of it in $C \rightarrow E$ terms under the laws of physics and chemistry. They explain it well enough, but only if we take for granted: (*a*) all the forces within the cell that bear upon the molecule in a $C \rightarrow E$ sense, each of which could itself be the subject of a $C \rightarrow E$ account; (*b*) all the other features of the cell that can not be placed in a $C \rightarrow E$ chain with our molecule's adventures, owing to their being simultaneous with it, but that can nevertheless themselves be accounted for in some other $C \rightarrow E$ chain. But we do not want to take all this for granted, for the coincidence of all these factors is just what we think needs explaining. And we therefore look for some explanation of the totality of the $C \rightarrow E$ pattern, feeling that the adventures of the single molecule will not really have been explained until this is done. The higher-level laws that are the objective of anti-reductionist science are supposed to accomplish this, and they are thus being invoked for the same explanatory purpose for which, in our version of Socratic action theory, we are invoking the "real causality" of the act itself. The "real causality" of the act would, to be sure, only approximate the status usually accorded a law of nature. For one thing, the laws of nature are understood to be general: if they explain some particular pattern of $C \rightarrow E$ relations, they are able to do so precisely because they apply with equal rigor to other similar patterns. But our view requires us to suppose that the power of a given act explains just the particular $C \rightarrow E$ pattern of which it is said to be the reason (sense *1*) and "real cause" and no other. For another, our "law" is in becoming, while a law of nature is usually understood to be unchanging.

Whether anti-reductionist scientists can give any effective support to this view of the "real causality" of Socrates' acts depends upon the ontological importance they assign to the higher level laws they are looking for. If they should assign them so much importance as to interpret the expression "an act of Socrates" as merely a vague and commonsense way of referring to certain higher-level laws that pervade his physical structure, they will lend our view no support at all. The question does not seem to have arisen in their councils in just this form. But certainly the language they use in discussing their objectives suggests that they are aware of actlike features of the complexes they seek to bring under higher-level laws. The anti-reductionist movement, though, is a complex one, and before we can decide how much help it can give us in finding a contemporary expression for our prisoner's complaint, we shall have to look in more detail at its quarrel with reductionism.

3

Even if it should turn out that anti-reductionist science offers us little help in making clearly and definitively the point Socrates was driving at, the purely scientific credentials of its representatives are impressive. There is no doubt that they are making contributions to pure science that could not be made if the spirit of reductionism were strictly adhered to. It is inconceivable, for instance, that the brilliant work of Paul A. Weiss in biology would have been possible if he did not approach the study of the cell or the embryo armed with the positive heuristic principle that living things exhibit a hierarchy of ordering principles. It seems strange that they should march under so negative a device as "anti-reductionism," the more so as a more suitable name leaps out at us from the very language of their own discussions. Weiss and many others — Michael Polanyi, R. W. Sperry, Jerome S. Bruner, and J. C. Eccles — have made "hierarchy" so familiar a rallying cry that it seems only sensible to incorporate it in any label we give the movement. The idea of hierarchy is an old one in philosophy. Aristotle's conception of the scale of nature, in which any one level is form in relation to the matter of the level beneath it and matter in relation to the form of the level above it, comes immediately to mind — appropriately enough, since, like so many of these scientists, he thought naturally in terms of biological categories. Leibniz in the modern era is as good an example, perhaps a better one for our purposes, seeing that he is often very close in his terminology to science of this kind. But the long history of the idea of the Great Chain of Being, so brilliantly told by Lovejoy,[5] is full of other examples, and the historical importance of hierarchy, as both a metaphysical and a methodological principle, need hardly be labored. It is no worse for being of such ancient lineage, and it is certainly appropriate to the anti-reductionist movement. I shall therefore drop the negative label and from now on contrast *reductionist science* with *hierarchic science*.

If we now reformulate in terms of this contrast the issue that was troubling Socrates, we find that a reductionist will hold that a completely satisfactory account of the complex physical event that common sense calls an action of Socrates can not be given until the $C \rightarrow E$ events within it can be described in terms of the smallest units that can be found in nature, and until the laws that govern their transactions can be logically derived from the basic laws of physics. A biological structure like Socrates is on the face of it an unlikely enough event to occur in a situation governed only by the laws that a perfected physics might recognize, and it is not surprising that the reductionist must also have frequent recourse to the idea of chance to explain the phylogenetic origin of creatures like Socrates, if not their inherent stability. It is a familiar fact that reductionism makes common cause with neo-Darwinian evolutionary theory, which holds that the evolutionary process depends entirely upon chance genetic mutations, in this sense, that although most of them are deleterious, so that the carriers of such genes are eliminated by natural selection, some few procure advantages for their possessors and are thus perpetuated. The important role given to chance is justified by statistical reasoning of some complexity, and this whole line of thought is given a certain plausibility by the fact that statistical laws play an important role in at least those parts of the laws of nature that deal with very small-scale happenings. Once the obscure question of chance is set aside, we are left with the claim that the complex entity that common sense calls Socrates is in fact an assemblage of very small units bound together in $C \rightarrow E$ fashion under physical law, and that the complex event common sense calls his act is nothing but an assemblage of events understandable without remainder in an analogous way. And though there is much that is still merely programmatic in all this, the steady advance in biophysical studies lends considerable force to it.

To all this, hierarchic science responds with a vision of nature as a hierarchy of structure and function in which each level exemplifies certain laws that are appropriate to it and that govern the structural units and functional processes at the level immediately below it. The cell, for instance, exemplifies the laws of cellular order, and these laws regulate the behavior of such units as organelles and such functions as the synthesis of proteins. If we wish to understand the development and behavior of an organelle within a cell, we must bring in not only the laws of physics and chemistry, but also the laws of cellular order that bear upon the organelle. And the laws of physics and chemistry must be further qualified by the laws exemplified by the organelle in its relation to its own components. It is the biological scientist's job to discover the laws appropriate to the levels of cell and organelle and indeed to all levels above those of physics and chemistry.

Although it is natural to begin an account of hierarchic science with hierarchic laws (or rules of order, principles, regularities), the language hierarchic scientists use permits an alternative approach by way of the concrete and particular units that, in the above account, are said to exemplify hierarchic laws. Instead of laws, one speaks of the control, restraint, or regulation exercised by a certain unit upon the particular units in the level immediately below it: *this* cell, for instance, regulates the development and activity of just *those* organelles. From this viewpoint the controlling unit is understood as an individual, concrete, and functioning power, and the laws associated with it must presumably be understood to be generalizations founded upon the activity of a large number of such units—itself, its forbears, its relations, and its descendants. If the unit, say the cell, is a function of the laws, the laws would also be functions of the individual units; and the language of Socrates' doctrine of the "real cause" comes naturally to us as we discuss it.

A given level is irreducible, then, in one of two senses: (*1*) the laws in terms of which we understand the relation between a given level and the levels beneath can not be derived logically from the laws appropriate to any or all of the levels beneath; (*2*) any causal account of the level immediately beneath a given level can not be restricted to $C \rightarrow E$ relations discernible at any or all of the levels beneath, but must be supplemented by the "real causality" of the given level. These two ways of expressing irreducibility are in apparent conflict, but I shall not emphasize the conflict until sections 5 and 6, for hierarchic scientists express themselves in both these ways as they defend their viewpoint against reductionism, and it is only realistic to do as they do and, in section 4, draw upon both as needed in distinguishing hierarchic from reductionist science.

4

The most impressive work in hierarchic science, and probably the clearest accounts of it by working scientists, are to be found in biology. An example that is a conflation of the earlier one about the hydrogen bonds formed by water molecules with the DNA helix and an example given by Paul A. Weiss [6] will help to give us a sense both of the complexity of the empirical data hierarchical science deals with and of the difficulty of expressing without distortion the interpretation they have in mind. Consider, then, five levels of a biological hierarchy: organism, organ, cell, organelle, and molecule. Set aside, though only at the risk of oversimplification, the levels below that of the molecule. Set aside also the relation between the organism and its parents, even though our organism is an embryo in an early stage of development. This is a still greater risk: any control we try to isolate at the organism level will thus be ambiguous, for, on our hypothesis, there will also be some control exercised by the parent organism through the environment of womb or egg provided for the embryo. With this qualification, the topmost member of our hierarchy — the organism — will merit the title "system" without further qualifications. The next level down will consist of a number of units, each of which will be regarded not just as a system in its own right but also as a subsystem of the highest system. Throughout the levels below the organism then, the notion of system implies a merely relative autonomy. A unit at any level will exercise control over its multiplicity of subsystems, but it will itself be a subsystem under the control of a system at the level above it. Under this restriction of relativity, any level of systemic order is to be taken seriously. It is of course a corollary of this point that the sovereign control, restraint, or regulation exercised by a unit of any level upon units within its system is always exercised by way of the units at the level immediately beneath its own. If the organ controls organelles, it does so only through the medium of the cells it comprises. The number of units per level will increase as we go downward, the number at the uppermost level (in this case the organism) being 1, and the number at the lowest level we are here concerned with being unimaginably high. Some idea of the uttermost multiplicity of any organic system with many levels may be had from the approximate figure Weiss gives for the number of macromolecules in the brain: 10^{15} (1,000,000,000,000,000). The philosophical analogues of all this are familiar enough: hierarchic science is one more in the long series of attempts, going back to antiquity, to deal with the contrast between the One and the Many. Of all these, probably the philosophic idea closest to hierarchic science, expressing as it does a sense of the complexity of life in terms of unities that upon inspection disclose an endless profusion of other unities, is Leibniz's doctrine of the relation between a monad and the multiplicity of monads it dominates.

We might approximate the nature of hierarchies of this sort by calling them structural. For certain purposes hierarchic scientists also see their subject matter in terms of functional hierarchies. In the work of R. W. Sperry, [7] for instance, the functioning of the brain is understood in terms of a total circuit pattern that ramifies in sub-patterns that it dominates and controls. It appears to be implicit in this work that a function of this sort fits into a hierarchy of other physiological processes, and that it would occupy there a higher level than, say, the oxidization of haemoglobin or the digestion of sugar. The reconciliation of hierarchies like this with a hierarchy of structural units obviously offers some problems. The basic reconciliation — that of a structural hierarchy with a functional one — is presumably not insuperable: if a function is a process within a biological structure, a structure in its development is obviously a process, and its structural stability in maturity can itself scarcely be understood except in terms of reiterative processes disposed in a spatial order. In a less obvious way this last point seems to be true of physical structures below the biological level as well: even the impressive stability of a molecule can be so understood. The reconciliation of a functional hierarchy with the ramification of unity in multiplicity of Weiss's example is more troublesome, for if a total circuit pattern of the sort Sperry has in mind may in some sense be said to unify many subordinate patterns, it is not at all clear that one of the subordinate patterns in any way unifies the oxidization of haemoglobin, although it depends upon it, and although thought in general might be said to alter the rate of oxidization. But with some ingenuity the two schemes are perhaps consistent. One might, for instance, try to reinterpret any functional hierarchy in terms of the units involved in it. In digestion, for instance, stomach, liver, pancreas, and, directly or indirectly, a great many other organs are involved, and these are, in a reasonably straightforward sense, unified by the central nervous system. Consistent or not, though, the idea of a functional hierarchy is surely to be found in hierarchic science side-by-side with the hierarchy of units around which Weiss's example is built.

In our version of Weiss's example, level A will be an organism — an embryo in an early stage of development; it will be recalled that we are neglecting the influence of the environment in egg or womb, as the case may be. Level B will consist of four subsystems, B_1, B_2, B_3, and B_4, that at a later stage will become organs of the mature creature. Level C will be the cellular level, and it will naturally consist of a very large number of cells; but we shall consider only those in B_1, and we shall simplify our case by singling out only three cells, C_1, C_2, and C_3, for attention. Level D will be the molecular level, and the number of molecules in it will be vast; once again we shall consider only a set of them, those in C_1, and of these we shall single out only three, D_1, D_2, and D_3, which we shall suppose to be water molecules moving about in the cell C_1.

According to our introductory version of it, hierarchic science sometimes says that the cellular laws exemplified in C_1 control or determine what is left open, or indeterminate, by the molecular laws exemplified in D_1, D_2, and D_3; and it sometimes says that the cell C_1 controls, or determines, what is left open, or indeterminate, in D_1, D_2, and D_3. I shall work for awhile with the language of control, as that seems the most convenient way of getting at what is meant by the contrast expressed in the pairs "controls — leaves open" and "determines — indeterminate."

If we consider the movements of the three water molecules within the cell and do not refer to the behavior of water molecules in some other possible situations, it is hard to see anything indeterminate in them. If we analyze all the physical forces bearing on a molecule at any time t_1 our knowledge of where it will be at time t_2 will be an instance of the application to it of $C \rightarrow E$ causality and the normal laws that a physicist would bring to the study of molecular movements. Our knowledge of it will be relative to our capacity for analyzing the forces that bear upon it, and these will of course be very complex; but, given these reservations, its behavior will be no more indeterminate in the cell than elsewhere. If the molecule D_1 should in its wanderings finally pass between the "threads" of the double helix of DNA and there form hydrogen bonds that lend support to the DNA structure, it will violate no law of molecular movement to do so.

Evidently, then, if we are to find anything indeterminate, anything "left open" in D_1, D_2, and D_3, we must turn to some other situation in which such molecules might be found, and in which the control the hierarchic scientist attributes to C_1 is not operative. If, for instance, a beaker of water is poured into a beaker of alcohol and left to diffuse throughout it, the water molecules will eventually be distributed more evenly throughout the beaker than throughout the cell. If D_1 is one of these molecules, its career there will be analyzable in the same way as it was in the cell, and in that sense it is still determinate. If we want to find a sense in which the molecular behavior in the beaker is indeterminate, a sense that can be usefully contrasted with the situation in the cell, then we have to call just that evenness of distribution in the beaker indeterminate as over against the greater determinateness imposed by the cell.

All the water molecules together will form a distribution in the beaker more probable than their distribution in the cell, and, in a sense of "random" correlated with this sense of probability, a more random one. Molecule D_1 contributes to and takes part in the situation in the beaker just as any other water molecule would do: its role could have been played just as easily by D_2 or D_3. So that, when we consider D_1 in the cell C_1, we have to suppose that it and the other water molecules in the cell bring no more "determining" capacity with them than they had in the beaker. In this relative sense, and in this sense alone, we can regard their behavior in the cell as indeterminate and therefore subject to the further determinations—whatever they may be— that prevail within the cell. It is a sense of "indeterminate" perfectly compatible with the notion of a determinate physical progress through the cell, a progress in which no physical anomalies are discoverable. And recourse to it allows us to think of D_1, D_2, and D_3 as determined by the cell (or its laws), and as so determined because they were determinable. From the point of view of the cell, D_2 would have served as well within the helix as D_1 does. It is C_1 that determines D_1 in one way, D_2 in another.

From the point of view of the reductionist, the objection to our taking an action of Socrates seriously can now be brought forward in another form: the cell C_1 is constituted out of molecules D_1, D_2, D_3 and a great many others, and can therefore scarcely be said to determine or control them. Objections like this, one suspects, will make hierarchic scientists fall back upon the language of law: not C_1, but the *laws* of the cellular level, they may well say, bring it about that D_1 plays such and such a role and D_2 another. And if that is the line they take, the defense of Socrates can take little comfort from them.

Our cell C_1 was of course not utterly autonomous: it and two other cells we agreed to consider, C_2 and C_3, are controlled, or determined, by their inclusion in B_1, which was one of the embryo A's subsystems in development towards the status of organ. If we consider the embryo's development between times t_1, and t_2, the subsystem B_1 (we shall assume) retains the same position relative to subsystem B_2 and B_3. During the same period, however, the cell C_1 may have wandered considerably from its position relative to C_2 and C_3. The cells C_1 and C_3, for instance, may have crossed each other's paths and now occupy positions at the opposite end of B_1 from their original positions. To establish an appropriate sense in which C_1 is determinable and B_1 the determiner we can not now argue from the case of the molecules, for we do not have the behavior of the same cells in some alternate medium to appeal to without some elaborate contrivance. It is, however, perfectly clear that if a group of cells similar to C_1, C_2, and C_3 were released in a nutrient medium, their behavior there would be different from their behavior in B_1. It is of course not now just a question of position, for cells divide to produce more cells. Whatever the distribution of C_1, C_2, and C_3 in a nutrient medium, they will certainly not have the same developmental history outside the embryo as in. But the matter of development allows us to give a sense of "determinable" that does not require us to appeal to circumstances outside the embryo. It will, I think, be a clearer sense of "determinable." Let us suppose—what is frequently the case—that C_1 and C_3 were originally very much alike and their two situations in the embryo virtually indistinguishable. As the development goes on, however, their careers will be quite different, for they (or, more properly, their descendants) will differ not just in position, but in structure and function as well. That is simply the normal case for all embryological development: the gradual differentiation of cells that were more or less similar at the start is precisely the gradual determination of what was originally determinable.

Although I thought it worthwhile to work with an example that is cast in part in terms of one used by a distinguished hierarchic scientist who has thought deeply about what distinguishes his work from reductionism, I have expressed the contrast "determinate—indeterminate" in a way that he might not find acceptable. An *indetermination* in levels C and D, then, is here understood as simply a correlative of a *determination* imposed on them by levels B and C respectively; and to establish this sense of indetermination we have had to appeal either to some other set of circumstances in which C_1 and D_1 could be found or to a contrast between an earlier and a later state of development in which differentiation of roles that were originally similar takes place. If we do not make comparisons of this sort, the behavior of C_1 and D_1 is perfectly determinate in any set of circumstances in the trivial sense that, taking all those circumstances into consideration, no physical laws are violated. We simply interpret the total circumstance of the organism in its development as a supplementation of the determinations (or order) appropriate to C_1 and D_1 by the further determination of B_1 and C_1 respectively. Weiss chooses rather to think of any given level as determinate in contrast with the actual indeterminacy of the level below it, and he gives "determinate" the further sense of "stable."[8] This permits him to contrast the stability of one level with the relative instability of the units in the next level down, and to do so in a way that permits a quantification of the contrast. The wandering of the two cells C_1 and C_3 from their original position in B_1, while B_1 retains its position in the organism A, would be an example of this contrast. The difficulty with putting the matter in this way, and in speaking as he does of the "microindeterminacy" of the lower level, is that it suggests a greater freedom in the units on any subordinate level over against the determinateness of the level above. Yet, as both Weiss's assumption and my own require, these units are in fact less free, in that more complex determinations operate on them—precisely the determinations imposed by the level above.

Weiss proceeds in this way because he wants to establish the point that no "microdeterminacy" at the molecular level

47

determines the development of the cell, and none at the cell level determines the development of the embryo's organ subsystem. What Weiss means by the absence of "microdeterminacy" is that the cell is not the outcome of a set of individual molecular movements each of which is predetermined (or, as he says, "preset") in a $C \rightarrow E$ sense under only molecular laws to precisely that role in the cell and no other; and the organ is similarly not the outcome of preset cellular movements. Although the point is sound enough, I do not think it contravenes any claim a reductionist would make. After all, the presetting of a sequence of molecular movements under merely molecular laws would have to mean, if it meant anything at all, that some laws other than merely molecular ones were operative — precisely the laws of that ordering here identified by the vague notion of presetting. The differences between Weiss's formulation and my own are not, I think, irreconcilable, and though I have dealt with this example in my own terms, the example still gives a fair picture of the intent of hierarchic science.

5

There would appear to be a conflict between the two formulations of hierarchic science I began with. Let me repeat them in more precise terms. (*a*) For each level of a hierarchy there are certain laws (rules, principles, regularities), but though they are the laws *of* that level, the units of that level do not so much "obey" them as they exemplify them. It is the units of the level beneath that "obey" them or are determined, or controlled, by them; and this control, felt directly by the level immediately beneath, is consequently indirectly felt by still lower levels. The relation of the laws of one level to the laws of lower levels is one of supplementation rather than cancellation: lower level laws are thus qualified and not nullified. The laws proper to a level are general in two senses: (*i*) each of the of the units of the level in question *exemplifies* the laws; (*ii*) each of the units at the levels beneath *is subject to* them. Thus each and every cell exemplifies

48

cellular laws and those laws control all the macromolecules in all of those cells. From this point of view it would not be accurate to attribute to an individual cell the "activity" of controlling its macromolecules, unless we understood this to be merely an imprecise way of saying that cellular law controls those macromolecules. It naturally follows from this point that if there really are general laws of this kind operative at every level, however high or complex, then we could attribute activity to Socrates only in that same imprecise way. (*b*) Any particular, individual, concrete unit at a given level—some *particular* cell, for instance—directly controls (determines, orders, constrains, regulates) everything that is determinable in the behavior of the units at the level immediately below and indirectly controls everything that is determinable in the behavior of units at still lower levels.

There is no reason to suppose that (*a*) and (*b*) are utterly incompatible, but at any rate it is clear that there is a difference of emphasis, *general law* being decisive in (*a*) and *individual and particular control* in (*b*). Supposing that both aspects of things are real, a satisfactory reconciliation of the two will have to be searching enough in an ontological sense to allow us to give due weight to both generality and particularity. It is fitting that this book, arising as it does out of a need to express adequately the views of human action of a man who (at least as represented to us by Plato) was much concerned to honor adequately in his own very particular embodied life the highest demands of a general "nature of things," should eventually deal with this question. Anticipating that, I might say that the demands of the general side of things may not be adequately captured in the idea of the laws of nature as the physical sciences usually understand that idea. Here, though, we are still concerned with understanding hierarchic science and drawing from it—both from its insights and its possible confusions—something that may eventually help us in carrying forward these reflections. In this spirit it seems to me safe to say that hierarchic scientists have not pressed the matter to the point of a searching reconciliation of (*a*) and (*b*). Instead they seem to draw upon both (*a*) and (*b*) as convenient. In the rest of this section I shall suppose that, when pressed for a decision, they will generally take refuge in (*a*) and regard (*b*) as merely an unguarded and commonsensical version of (*a*). This is in part a device for demonstrating just where one version of hierarchic science will take us. I do not think, as will appear, that this version will give us much help in an attempt, however forlorn, to stem the *de facto* advance of materialism. But it is only in part an expository device, for it is probably fair to say that the practical organization as well as the polemics of the movement draw more heavily upon (*a*) than upon (*b*).

On the basis of (*a*), it is not the principle of $C \rightarrow E$ connections under general law that hierarchic science objects to but rather the principle that there is one level of law. We saw earlier that where the behavior of stones and photons is at issue there is no reason to attribute action to them when laws of nature — laws that in that case could be interpreted as reductive ones — can explain their effects. In a hierarchic context an emphasis on the generality of law leads to the same conclusion, not only about subordinate units in relation to their superordinate unit, but also about the superordinate unit as well. If, for instance, we asked for an explanation of the movement of a water molecule within the cell, an explanation over and above what a $C \rightarrow E$ account and the laws of physics would give us, and if in response we were offered some additional laws of the cellular level that also qualified those $C \rightarrow E$ relations, those laws would also lie, general and impersonal, in "the nature of things." If they were indeed hierarchic laws they would have to be equally explanatory of the behavior of other molecules within the cell, and not just severally, but also of their general and (on our assumption) orderly concourse. Their mode of regulation must therefore be very complex, since the several elements would be very different — as different, say, as a water molecule and a molecule of amino acid — and must have different careers according to their kind. If we then look for the "action of the cell" it will be hard to find, for it must encompass a multiplicity of $C \rightarrow E$ chains, and it is precisely this multiplicity that the general laws of the cellular level are supposed to be controlling. The "action

50

of the cell," then, is a superfluous notion; the cell is merely the exemplification of a general order that transcends it. The cellular order, on this hypothesis, operates with as much indifference to its exemplification in this or that cell as the principles of Newtonian mechanics are indifferent to their exemplification in the space of the solar system or in the space defined by a pendulum clock. It lies "in the nature of things," not only that a group of molecules of certain kinds, disposed in a certain way, behave together with cellular order, but also that they came to be so disposed in the first place. The unity of the components of the cell is given by a general cell-level law; and what by common sense might be called the "action of the cell" is nothing but the dominance of this law in a particular group of cell-components.

If, moving up through the hierarchy, the hierarchic scientist tried to understand the level represented by the individual man in the same way in which I have represented him as trying to understand the level of the cell, the result would be much the same. For though he would be looking for a general law, and though by definition the particularity of Socrates and of his predicament in prison would fall outside it, it would not fall outside it as some source of moral authority inaccessible to science, but merely as the particular physical complex to which the general law applies. Given the physical parameters of the biological complex just before what common sense or philosophy might represent as a moral turning point, they form to together a C which, under this biological law, yields as an E the physical parameters just after the turning point. A more general way of expressing this, however, is to say that a biological law (or laws) expressive of the level of the individual organism would exclude the "real causality" of its action as effectively as it would do in the case of the cell. This exclusion of action could perhaps be avoided if the hierarchic biological laws applicable to the total organism were held to be quite useless for the exact prediction of one physical state, E, on the basis of an earlier one, C, and to be, instead, primarily interpretative laws, whose predictive value was incidental and of a statistical kind — as, for instance, a law to the effect that cells divide after a certain period of time, and that when they do the chromosome material so divides as to provide a duplicate set for each of the resultant cells; or to the effect that organisms of the kind Socrates represents live for three score years and ten, more or less. This may indeed be the proper way to understand hierarchical biological laws, but if the biological wing of hierarchic science were to adopt it, I do not think they would necessarily concede that the inexactness of it left room for a "real causality" of action that lay in principle outside the scope of the scientific method.

All this is of course still speculative enough. Probably no hierarchic scientist would now maintain that even general cellular laws of an irreducible character have been successfully formulated. As for Socrates himself—the level of the individual person—no hierarchic scientist that I know of seems in the least inclined to formulate one set of purely biological laws that would apply to him. But that does not mean that they are not interested, when moved by (a), in bringing him fully within the scientific method. The tidiness I have, following Weiss, represented as a characteristic of hierarchic science—a smooth movement up through successive levels, the eventual discovery of the general laws of level after level—vanishes when we consider how that science deals with the study of individual organisms of any reasonably complex kind. But the interest in general laws continues, and the assumption seems to be that the understanding of a complex creature like Socrates will eventually be accomplished by the convergence of general laws put forward by several disciplines. These laws would not only not be reducible to physics, but it is conceivable that they would also be independent of one another—that is, Socrates may be the subject matter of several sciences unified neither under physics nor under any other unifying science of the future. The picture is an untidy one, and there is no point in trying to impose a tidy scheme upon it. But in the convergence of the laws of all these disciplines there seems no justification for looking for the reason (sense *1*) of his actions in precisely the "real causality" of the action itself. And there is consequently no justification for re-

52

garding the moral law as a reason (sense *2*) qualifying it. In principle the laws of psychology, sociology, and so on provide all the explanations that can reasonably be demanded.

The spirit of the biological wing of the cooperating hierarchic sciences may be seen from the "administrative sub-categorization" of the subject proposed some time ago by Weiss,[9] and since that time sanctified in some measure by the practice of government granting offices, foundations, and universities. It divides biology into "a hierarchical system of order according to functional principles in common to living organisms: Molecular, Cellular, Developmental, Regulatory and Group and Environmental Biology." It is interesting that this organization is partly in terms of structural hierarchies and partly in terms of functional hierarchies. It is notable that the level of the individual organism—the unity at the top of a ramifying multiplicity of structural subsystems—is left out. One goes from an understanding of an organism in terms of an aspect (e.g., Developmental) or a subsystem (e.g., Cellular) to the setting of the total organism (Group and Environmental).

The open level of the individual organism is perhaps a reflection of the fact that for biology all these categories are ways of studying the organism. It is a limitation, but in a scientific sense also a virtue, of biology that it seems to be most at home when it studies any subsystem as a set of subsystems—that is, when it concentrates on the multiplicity and the interrelation of the elements and functions rather than on the unity that, though it might consist in the *relating* of them, might be inscrutable to a scientific method. But if the level of the individual is in a sense left open by this organization of biology, the individual is nonetheless converged upon by a large number of other disciplines. Hierarchic science as a cultural force is a loose coalition of specialists. The biologists themselves are specialists of many kinds, their specialties ranging from brain physiology to biophysics, from embryology to evolution, from genetics to comparative anatomy. Naturally, the organization of biology favored by Weiss will not fit all the specialties that can be found in the catalogue of any department of biology at a large university.

And besides the hierarchic scientists who are, in some broad sense, biologists, there are psychologists, sociologists, psychiatrists, and not a few anti-reductionist physicists. If the concern of the biologists can be understood in terms of structural and functional hierarchies, the concerns of these other specialties are quite different. They seem to be concerned rather with certain *aspects* of Socrates, aspects that all include in one way or another reference to the cultural background against which he is studied. If, returning to Weiss's administrative categorization, we regard Group and Environmental Biology as being concerned with hierarchic levels *above* the individual, then these other specialties also bear, at least indirectly, on those levels. But there is nothing else that is peculiarly hierarchic about them, except, of course, that they claim to make intelligible to us certain aspects of things that no physics, however perfected, can cope with; that is, hierarchic scientists working in these other specialties pursue hierarchic science only in the sense that they hold the laws they are looking for to be irreducible ones. Their methods, though, will often be indistinguishable from the methods of their fellow specialists in the same field who take a reductionist line.

These converging specialties are bent on establishing generalities that shall be as lawlike as possible. We do not, fortunately, have to decide here whether it is plausible that they will ever achieve anything like the status we take for granted in the basic laws of physics. But there is no doubt about the objective when the version of hierarchic science formulated in (*a*) is the controlling one: it is a scientific objective, and it means to explain Socrates and his actions in terms of $C \rightarrow E$ connections under law. Though the attitude is less epistemologically puritanical than reductionism, with many irreducible and perhaps overlapping laws envisioned, the general mode of understanding proposed is at least congruent with that of materialism. If there is any aspect of Socrates left untouched by these laws, an aspect that the commonplace observation "Socrates acted in that way because he judged it to be right" expresses without distortion, it will have to be approached in a different way, for whatever personal views any of these specialists might have on this matter, the method of a specialty governed by the formulation in (*a*) leaves no room for it.

On the basis of (*a*), hierarchic science is first of all science and not philosophy. Although it holds that a science centered exclusively on the laws of physics and chemistry will not do for the study of man, it takes it for granted that there are other and equally scientific laws that will eventually do the job. Meanwhile, the status of Socrates' claim — "the real cause . . . is that since the Athenians thought it right to condemn me, I have thought it right and just to sit here and to submit to whatever sentence they may think fit to impose" — is as much a prescientific placeholder as it would be for a materialist. Though the movement, even as formulated in (*a*), is a salutary example for the natural sciences, which might otherwise be wholly governed by the dogma that all science should approach the condition of physics, it may nonetheless distort our understanding of Socrates' behavior in prison as seriously as a blunt materialism might do.

It may seem to the reader that half a loaf is better than none; that there is surely more comfort for the anti-materialist in hierarchic than in reductionist science. Up to a point I agree. If there are principles of cell replication, of organs and their functions, of embryonic development, of genetics, of evolution, of information processing in the central nervous system, of psychology, of language, of society, and so on; if none of these is wholly reducible to physics; and if Socrates in prison exemplifies all of them; then I am sure that the account of his actions that would emerge from putting all these accounts together would be closer to his full actuality than a reductionist account would be. But if we are to take an action of Socrates as seriously as he meant us to do, then we must think of it as a power that so unifies a multiplicity of processes and entities that all $C \rightarrow E$-like connections that we see in them as we attend to them severally are bent together into a pattern. The power unifying such a concourse would be, for each of the many causal chains, the "law-in-becoming" supplementing all subordinate laws we might find there. If hierarchic scientific laws were offered to us as abstractions from this order, we might be grateful for them. But they are seldom put forward in that spirit except by hierarchic scientists who are on the point of giving up a scientific outlook for a philosophic one—as Schrödinger, for instance, was doing in his later writings.[10]

If (a) represents adequately what hierarchic science is all about, the controversy between reductionist and hierarchic science is not about materialism at all, but about the nature and proper objectives of the natural sciences. The chief quarrel is between physics and the sciences of life, and the question is whether the latter have a domain in principle not accessible to the procedures of even a perfected physics. Metaphysical questions, it could be argued, need not come into it at all. It is true that many, and perhaps most, reductionists are materialists in metaphysics, and that many, and perhaps most, adherents of hierarchic science are anti-materialists. But it is also possible, if one is interested in metaphysics, to hold that in principle science can say nothing about metaphysical questions. Reductionists, like the rest of us, can think in compartments: they might without any inconsistency turn to "pure" philosophy for metaphysical answers, and might thus conclude on philosophical grounds that mind or spirit was the ultimate reality. And in the same way an adherent of hierarchic science might conclude that matter—construed to be sure in a sense suitable to hierarchic science—played that same basic role in the nature of things. Finally, if metaphysics need not come into it at all, it is also possible to conclude that it is not worth troubling about. I do not mean to suggest that hierarchic science has any explicit alliance with old-fashioned logical positivism. At the explicit level it is quite the reverse. But many of its representatives are dominated by a form of the same dogma that is so powerful in analytic philosophy and in reductionist science: that the natural sciences are identical with rationality in general. For those hierarchic scientists who accept this dogma there is an agreement with reductionism far more important than their disagreement about the sufficiency of the laws of physics. The dogma may not in the long run prevail within hierarchic science, but if it does it will make for the *de facto* advance of materialism, even though some hierarchic scientists might in their private metaphysics incline in the other direction, and even though (*b*) adumbrates a position which, if fully developed, might contribute to a *de jure* settlement of the issue in favor of a position more like the one Socrates was driving at.

6

In contrast with the monolithic ideal of reductionism, hierarchic science is an untidy enough movement. From the point of view of Socrates that untidiness must seem a virtue: whatever else he was driving at, he was surely making a distinction between a scientific and a philosophic explanation of human action. He would, I think, if he surveyed hierarchic science today, conclude that it is torn between a scientific and a philosophic interest in whatever it is studying—an organelle, a cell, an organ, or some particular man observed in a rational act—and might well also conclude that this tension, much to be preferred to a flat commitment to scientific explanation, is the source of all the untidiness in the movement. The contrast between the language of (*a*) and that of (*b*) is one symptom of this tension. If one takes (*b*) seriously, a unit at a given level is not understood to be merely an exemplification of a law or laws that transcend it, and its whole existence is therefore not identified with the regulation by those laws of the multiplicity of units at the next level below. Its ontological status is understood to be both more subtle and more fundamental than that. Though its unity is distinguishable from the multiplicity of the next lower level as the lawlike activity that controls them, the unity nonetheless expresses itself in just that multiplicity in just that order, so that the distinction is not of the kind that permits us to identify the unity as an entity or power independent of that multiplicity.

Assigning so fundamental an ontological status to the unit itself naturally raised problems for the generality of law, which the language of (*a*) takes for granted. But (*b*) can provide for a kind of generality of its own. The very individual control exercised, according to (*b*), by a superordinate unit over the multiplicity of its subordinates will have some resemblances to the way a general law would reign there. If the controlling unit is a cell, its power will be felt throughout the region occupied by its subordinate units: an organelle in one part of it will be as much subject to it as an organelle in another part, and in that sense its control is general throughout that region. Just that particular power of that particular cell reigns generally throughout that region. And if we choose some other particular cell its particular power will reign in the same way throughout the region of its own infrastructure. So also for any number of cells. And proceeding in this way, we can find generalities of a deeper kind, generalities about the behavior of organelles in cells in general. These will certainly be general cellular laws, but the status given the cell on the basis of (*b*) deprives laws of this kind of the ontological absoluteness that is implicitly given them in (*a*). The laws are, instead, ontologically contingent upon the power exercised severally by the cells about which they are generalizations. The constraint upon organelles within the cells will be no less general, no less predictable, and indeed no less quantifiable for that. But the status of these laws is that they are "in the nature of things" not absolutely and as engendering the very existence of individual cells, but in ontological dependence upon those individual cell-powers.

The principle of the ontological contingency of the laws of nature is consistent with the fact that the entities the character of whose environment is expressed by a law or laws of nature form part of that same environment. In a sense quite independent of our way of discovery or formulating it, the law is dependent upon the multiplicity of the entities in question. The individual electron, for instance, exemplifies certain regularities, not just in its behavior, but in its very existence: the electron is one of the packets in which energy, under certain conditions, manifests itself. But the environment in which such regularities appear is made up, in a significant proportion, of electrons: the individual, governed by the regularity, also contributes to it.

This inoffensively circular observation is of no help in the development of the next stage of particle theory, but it may help us to keep from hypostatizing the laws of nature. When the number of individuals is vast and the environment very pervasive, as in the case of electrons, it is impossible to single out the individual's contributions to the conditions expressed in the law. When the laws we are dealing with are less pervasive, as hierarchic laws expressing the order of living things must be in the economy of a universe not everywhere hospitable to their occurrence, the sense in which they are contingent upon the contributions of individual entities becomes clearer. The special environment in which a cell grows is at least partially characterized by saying that it is pervaded by life, and the contribution to that made by any individual creature is at least within the range of our imagination.

With some such view of the status of hierarchic laws of nature in mind we may return to consider the application of (b) to a cell. It is more implausible to look there for the kind of "control" that Socrates had in mind, but it is important to begin there rather than with Socrates. For one thing, if we begin with the cell without drawing upon what common sense tells us about Socrates, we can then extend the conclusion to Socrates without assuming what we wish to demonstrate. For another, having established an analogue in this way, we shall not, when considering Socrates, be tempted to represent his action as an anomalous intrusion into a nature that is regulated elsewhere by $C \rightarrow E$ causality under ontologically absolute general laws. We thus avoid a conflict like the one Kant found between the free causality of the will and the deterministic causality of nature, and do not have to convict nature of a phenomenal status in order to resolve it. If Socrates in action did indeed exercise "real causality," it is more plausible to conceive of it as a special case, though a grand one, of the general philosophic principle of individual powers exercising "real causality."

Why does it trouble us, as I am sure it does, to think of a cell as an individual and particular power whose influence is felt generally throughout the infrastructure of which it is also, in

59

some appropriate sense, constituted? I suspect it is because, when we look for scientific laws, and set it as a goal that we shall not be satisfied unless they are absolutely general, we simply take their ontological status for granted, assuming them to be necessary not just in the sense of being universal and without exception but also in the sense of ontologically necessary, that is to say generative of the entities or processes that exemplify them. From such a viewpoint we have no precedent for an individual and particular "influence" that pervades a multiplicity out of which it is, again in some appropriate sense, constituted. As such it appears anomalous, odd, an impossible "influence," while a general law whose "influence" lies "in the nature of things" and governs a host of $C \rightarrow E$ connections seems the most natural thing in the world. To get any help from (*b*), we must invert this habitual and, as I think, metaphysically lazy view of the laws of nature, and substitute for it a view of the ontological dependence of law that is no less hospitable to the search for laws that are as general as we can find. It is a view congruent not just with the view of Everyman about his own action, but with the scientist's own private view of his own responsible and intelligent action as he carries on his own search for law. Socrates' insistence on his own "real" causality and Kant's insistence on the free causality of the will are merely special cases of this.

Suppose, then, interpreting (*b*) in this sense, we take the hierarchic scientist as a potential ally, insofar as he is himself willing to take (*b*) seriously. How will the case of the cell, so much more implausible to our common sense than the case of Socrates himself is, appear to us? In the first place we shall assume that it is precisely the individual cell that controls the multiplicity of its infrastructure. We shall also assume, with the hierarchic scientist, that it can control the whole of that multiplicity only through the medium of the multiple units that occupy the next level. What this next lower level will consist of will itself be a problem. One plausible way of identifying it is to look for items within the cell that most resemble the cell—that is, that behave with something like the individuality and autonomy that we have to concede to cells in principle if only because there

60

are one-celled organisms. On this criterion the organelle is the obvious candidate. In the article from which the example of section 4 was taken, Weiss takes the organelle called the mitochondrion for an example. He points out both the structural role it plays in single cells of some complexity and also its functional mobility and power of self-transformation as it operates as a "power plant" bringing energy to places where it is needed for cell processes. In many important respects its structure and behavior are cell-like: it has, for instance, a surface membrane, and it is capable of movement.

Its own structure, when analyzed, reveals numerous macromolecular systems like enzymes, and it therefore seems that we have a plausible case for taking the level next below the organelle to be the macromolecular one. That is indeed Weiss's assumption. But not all macromolecules in a cell directly subserve organelles. At least one macromolecular structure—the chromosomal DNA in the nucleus—plays so key a role that a reductionist would regard it as the "cell itself" insofar as it made any sense to him to speak in such terms. But our point of view just now is that of hierarchic science understood in terms of (*b*), and from that point of view the power of the cell level could plausibly be said to deal sometimes with the macromolecular level directly and sometimes with the organelle level directly and, through that, with the macromolecular one indirectly. Additional evidence for this is the fact that a mitochondrion in the course of the transformations in which it carries out its energy-transporting function sometimes breaks down into macromolecular components, which are then later reconstituted into a mitochondrion. Since it will make no difference for our present purposes, we shall assume that to be the case.

Our example of the level immediately below that of the cell will be the movement of a mitochondrion from one point in a cell to another, its breakdown into macromolecular components, and its subsequent reconstitution. If we take for granted all the hierarchic controls that operate on it *below* that of the cell, it seems that we can give a perfectly determinate account of it in terms of $C \rightarrow E$ connections under these controls. Indeed we could dispense with all the hierarchic controls below cell-level and still give a determinate account of it by bringing in only the laws of physics and chemistry. Either way a determinate account does not require the introduction of a cell-level control. Without it the physical description of the movement, breakdown, and reconstitution will be complete and determinate in the sense already established in section 4. Given the structure of the mitochondrion, given an exact analysis of the boundary conditions at all points in the cell, the movement of the mitochondrion, its breakdown, and the participation of its components in energy-giving transactions elsewhere in the cell will conform completely to the control of whatever levels below that of the cell that we care to bring in.

Where, then, shall we look for the control exercised by the cellular level? Certainly not just by attending to this one $C \rightarrow E$ sequence, and certainly not by attending severally to other $C \rightarrow E$ sequences of the cell. Some of these, because of an appropriate spatial and temporal relation, will bear in a $C \rightarrow E$ sense upon our mitochondrion, and will then enter into the $C \rightarrow E$ account we have already given of it. The collapse of a vesicle near a mitochondrion or the passage of some molecules into such a vesicle may, for instance, bear upon the mitochondrion in a $C \rightarrow E$ sense. But, besides being factors in its career, they may themselves be dealt with in a distinct $C \rightarrow E$ account. There will be a vast number of other features of the cell that are separated spatially from the mitochondrion and yet simultaneous with it, so that one can not introduce them into the $C \rightarrow E$ account of its history; yet each of them will fit into a perfectly determinate $C \rightarrow E$ story of its own. It follows that we can analyze the total history of the cell in infinite detail, so long as we are willing to proceed item by item, and are prepared always to deal with any item that turns up in a given chain by analyzing it in a chain of its own; and so long as the item we are dealing with can always be refined by some appropriate measure device into still smaller items. None of the $C \rightarrow E$ chains will be anomalous when we neglect the cell-level control. In none of them shall we be able to find any control we can assign to the cell. The control of the cell, if real, must be exercised over *all* these $C \rightarrow E$ chains. It is the "reason" for the totality of them, the "reason" why an element in one $C \rightarrow E$ chain bears upon an element in another $C \rightarrow E$ chain, and also the "reason" why items in the cell that, because of their simultaneity and spatial separation, can not be in $C \rightarrow E$ relations with one another, are nevertheless in relations significant for the total structure and career of the cell.

All this means that the control exercised by the cell can not itself be understood in $C \rightarrow E$ terms. As a "real causality" it will pervade the total pattern of $C \rightarrow E$ causality, and will pervade it in a way having significant analogies with the way a law, supplementing lower-level laws, would pervade it. Weiss speaks of the structural regularities in the neighborhood of a mitochondrion in this way:

> The near-constant interval, for instance, between the collapsed cisternae or between the internal cross folds of a mitochondrion, reveals simply a rhythmicity in the interactions within such a group, which results in characteristically spaced crests and valleys of conditions favouring the aggregation and assembly of higher order arrays. We encounter here the phenomenon of the emergence of singularities in a dynamic system—"unique points," or lines or planes—comparable, for instance, to nodal points in a vibrating string.[11]

His language, which is reminiscent of field language, is appropriate enough to the way in which the "real causality" of a cell would pervade the cell like a field, and, like a field, determine $C \rightarrow E$ processes within it without itself being understandable in $C \rightarrow E$ terms. The lawlike character of it seems obvious when we think of it in this way. It is, however, a time-bound field: not only does it vary throughout its spatial span, but it is, besides, of the very nature of becoming, developing in its own rhythm, changing constantly any metric properties it may have. And if we are to take the language of control seriously we can not regard it just as a set of nodal vibrations in a medium, for nodes of this kind would be determined by the nature of the medium and the laws regnant there, but rather as the *active establishment* of a field. The field image of course breaks down at some points. Most physical fields are definable independently of some particular entities that might move within them. This field, though, is a field whose whole reality consists in the control of precisely all those cell components we have been assuming. It is so intimately involved with each and every one of the causal chains bound by it that there are grounds for calling it simply the unification of their multiplicity. It is the obsession of materialism to see this unity-in-multiplicity as an unqualified identity, to which the language of control would not be applicable in any case. It is the labor of this book to help liberate us from this obsession.

There is a curious relation between the cell and the organelle that may lead us eventually to the "real causality" of Socrates himself. Organelles as levels of control are ambiguous in that their whole function is by definition intracellular. They do not exist in nature as distinct entities forming the highest control level in their system, as some cells and some molecules do. This suggests that the application of (*a*) to organelles, with the consequent claim that there is an organelle-level of law, would be hard to support. An organelle-level law could prevail only in a situation where cell-level law (or control) prevailed. That is tantamount to saying that the "real causality" of the cell must be thought of as ramifying in the "real causality" we might wish to ascribe to the organelle. But the point is more important when we look upward rather than downward. Given any complex system, if we find in it a control level which would not be viable in nature outside that system, we must look upward in the system for the "source" of its "real causality." The relation between an organism and its organs will therefore be the same as that between a cell and its organelles. Outside the environment of an organism, or an artificial environment designed to duplicate that of an organism, we can attach no sense to an organ-level of control. And even if we were to revert to the law-oriented language of (*a*), we could attach no sense to an organ-level of law independent of the organism-level of law. The principle appears to be this: given any hierarchical system having levels some of which can not exist (in a natural state) independently of the uppermost level of that system, then the "real causality" operative at any of those levels must be ascribed to the "real causality" of the uppermost level.

The principle, though a natural outcome of taking (*b*) seriously, goes much further than I think any hierarchic scientist would press it. If we do press it rigorously, then any nonindependent unit exercising "real causality" within the unity of the system we call Socrates — say an organelle over its molecule, a cell over its organelle, an organ over its cell — owes its "real causality" to the unity of Socrates himself. The fact that the cells are here included as nonindependent is not in conflict with the fact that one-celled organisms exist independently in nature, because the cells now under discussion are not one-celled organisms. The only genuine independent units within the system of Socrates, if we follow the language of (*b*) rigorously, are such units at the molecular level and below as exist before and after their inclusion in Socrates. All the others owe their own "real causality" to that of Socrates, and it is therefore appropriate to regard his "real causality" as a unity ramifying in a multiplicity. In such a framework, "control," which we began to discuss in terms of cells, seems more properly attributed to entities than to actions. It is therefore the entity Socrates we are concerned with, so that, when we represent an action of his as binding in its power the pattern of all the $C \rightarrow E$ relations in its infrastructure, we must regard the "real causality" of the action as an expression of the "real causality" of an entity. Just how we are to understand identities of that kind is not clear at this stage. At this point the ontology we are beginning to develop is highly tentative: it is merely the ontology we seem to commit ourselves to if we take the claims of hierarchic science seriously, and if we interpret that kind of science in terms of the language of (*b*). Eventually, though, a consideration of an entity like Socrates in action may enable us to see our way more clearly: by the end of this meditation we may hope to have stated this ontology with more clarity. The concept of "real causality" is equally tentative. Just now it merely establishes a sympathetic link with the point Socrates was making; later it will suffer some absorption into the concept of entity, to the clarification, I trust, of both.

With these reservations, we may say that our interpretation of hierarchic science understood in terms of (*b*) brings us in sight of an ontological principle that is a plausible alternative to an interpretation in which (*1*) the unit at the apex emerges from a general law that engenders it as one of its exemplifications; and (*2*) the relation between the unit at the apex and those at the level immediately below it is identified with the regulation of those units, regarded in $C \rightarrow E$ terms, by that same general law. The principle will not be of much use to a hierarchic scientist qua scientist, but I hope that some of them will be receptive to it qua philosophers. The principle is that entities are organized hierarchically; that an entity at a given level exercises in its becoming a "real causality" on the $C \rightarrow E$ relations between units at the next lower level; and that this influence is lawlike — a kind of law-in-becoming. In the case of some hierarchic entities, however, we must look to the "real causality" of the apex for an adequate explanation of the real causality exercised by certain subordinate levels.

Socrates is a hierarchic entity of this type. As for his action, it is a special case of that "real causality": when he acts, he so unifies a myriad of entities and processes that make up his infrastructure that there is no better way of accounting for the totality of their concourse than by saying that he did indeed act in such and such a way. This means that his "real causality" bears as a law-in-becoming — better, perhaps, a law-that-becomes — on the $C \rightarrow E$ processes of his infrastructure. An analysis of those processes under the laws of nature, even the laws of nature as expressed in a perfected physics, will be of restricted significance, and this restriction will be of great importance to the hierarchic scientist qua philosopher.

This emphasis on the individual aspect of "control," of "real causality," is no doubt excessive. Wherever we can detect in nature a successiveness of entities of a given level analogous to the successiveness of organisms in the relation parent-offspring—and this analogy is applicable at most levels of nature—it is probably wise to regard any individual entity having "real causality" as the carrier of, exemplar of, or participant in, a "real causality" that transcends him and is in that sense general. Socrates, for instance, springs out of a biological stream that is general in the sense that it ramifies in all living things. The sharp distinction between individual and general, a distinction that makes us suppose that only concepts, universals, and that kind of thing are general, is thus blurred. The idea of the individual entity as participant in generality by the very exercise of his individual "real causality" might offer us some hope of finding within an ontology like this some appropriate, though derivative, status for general laws proper to levels above those of physics and chemistry. The "real causality" of Socrates might, for instance, be interpreted as laying down, with its forbears and descendants, general biological laws. The "laws" of organ development prevailing within his infrastructure would thus be laid down precisely by that individual entity Socrates, but he, as a carrier of a "real causality" that demands the category of generality no less than that of individuality, would not be laying down laws that were utterly private to him. And the issue of generality is naturally intensified if we consider also the involvement of his "real causality" with the generality of moral law and with the related generality of mind. We shall, however, not be in a position to do some justice to these last matters until the latter part of our meditation.

7

The language of (*b*) therefore makes hierarchic science a potential ally in the effort to understand Socrates' actions in a sense appropriate to what he was driving at. But it has already carried us into an ontology that is difficult, obscure, and, from the point of view of science, probably a hindrance rather than a help in the effort to explore and model mathematically the intricate forces that bear upon a mitochondrion, a cell, or an organ. The difficulty does not lie just in the particular ontology we seem to be drawn towards, but rather in the fact that we find ourselves talking ontology at all. Hierarchic science may be drawn towards philosophy, and even towards the more metaphysical kind of philosophy, but, while it feels the power of the ideal of explanation in $C \rightarrow E$ terms under general law, it is unlikely to take kindly to an outlook in which philosophic explanations are regarded as more fundamental than that kind. Whatever the outcome of the cultural struggle between hierarchic and reductionist science, some hierarchic scientists are engaged in purely scientific research of great interest, and there is every reason for them to devote most of their energy to that, especially since what they are interested in will probably be neglected by scientists of reductionist views. Whether any of them will wish to engage in a kind of interpretation that is not only primarily philosophical, but besides does not regard the findings of science as its only or even its principal subject matter, I do not know. But, in any case, this chapter has been designed to make common cause with what I take to be a profoundly philosophic instinct in hierarchic science.

3

The Originative Acts of the Prisoner: Introductory

 WE MAY NOW RETURN TO OUR prisoner and, dropping for awhile the controversy between hierarchic and reductionist science, see whether that famous passage can be used to advance a little the line of argument for which it was the original occasion. I chose the passage because it is about a moral gesture, and because the gesture is discussed in the context of an explicit rejection of materialism. Although that doctrine is applicable to nature in general, the gravamen of Socrates' charge is that it distorts our understanding of ourselves. His point is not just a theoretical one in which a discussion of the nature of moral action happens to occur, for the discussion is part of a moral gesture in which he sacrifices his life. The theoretical point, then, forms part of an explicit exemplification of a view of human nature opposed to the one he rejects. The practical framework — the framework of moral action — is the controlling one: while performing the act, the agent discusses it and represents it as responsible and free in the sense that causality of the $C \rightarrow E$ sort, while thoroughly permeating its infrastructure, can not be said to bring it about. When, at the end of this chapter, I introduce a number of acts and sub-acts of Socrates, with the purpose of considering both the relation between them and the "relation" between each act and its infrastructure, most of them will accordingly be drawn from the acts — exem-

plary, one now sees, in more than one sense of the word—of his last day in prison.

After the passage quoted, Socrates goes on to set his important, though perhaps in some ways obscure, claim about the true nature of human agency within a philosophic view of reality that has many ramifications. As I said at the beginning of chapter 1, I intend to neglect most of the philosophic framework of the dialogue; also set aside is the question how much of this framework comes from the historical Socrates and how much was provided by his disciple Plato out of his own developing philosophy. I shall pretend instead that Socrates is first of all concerned to make a point about the nature of human action, and that what he is saying can be reformulated so as not to imply the full panoply of the Platonic metaphysics. The Platonic Forms, for instance, are brought in shortly after the passage quoted, and they are then immediately connected with the idea of the "real cause," but I shall try to give an instructive sense to "real cause" that will not require us to suppose that there are Platonic Forms. Confining ourselves in this spirit to the passage quoted, we can represent Socrates as saying that although the infrastructure of certain human actions is made up of entities, forces, events, states, and structures linked together in terms of the $C \rightarrow E$ relation, these "causes without which the (real) cause cannot be the cause" can not in themselves provide a satisfactory account of the action. What else he is saying about such an action as his decision to remain in prison and drink the potion offers certain difficulties to the modern ear. I have already insisted that he is not merely making a distinction between reasons (sense 2) and causes when he speaks of "acting by Mind," or by "choice of what is best." A "real cause" is, we saw, a reason in another sense (sense 1), in that it furnishes an explanation for a total pattern of $C \rightarrow E$ relations, but there is no doubt that Socrates wants not just the force of the word "reason" (in either sense) but also the force of the expression "real (true) cause," with all its overtones of power, efficacity, and authenticity, and he wants it as an explicit antithesis to causality in the sense of the $C \rightarrow E$ relation.

Since we agreed not to consider the whole of the Platonic metaphysics, we are left with the suggestion that the totality of $C \rightarrow E$ relations in the infrastructure consists of "causes without which the (real) cause cannot be the cause," while the power-unity that is the *action* of choosing to do what is best (and using the mind in doing so) is the "real cause." This is not to make the disturbing claim that the "real cause" is the *cause of the action* of deciding to stay despite the wish of his limbs to be elsewhere. It is, rather, simply a device for permitting us to see that the unity of an action is so much an exercise of power on and with an infrastructure as to demand the force of the expression "real cause." The action, so understood, is not caused, but it *is* a cause in the sense of "real cause." Let us resist the temptation to say it is self-caused, and say instead that it is the "real cause" of the particular pattern of $C \rightarrow E$ relations in its infrastructure.

No doubt it is something of an anachronism to bring Socrates' protest against materialism into some useful conjunction with modern discussions of action and causes, but I think it is an instructive anachronism, and so shall go on with it for awhile. Brought into a contemporary discussion of the nature of human action, and confronted with the task of making his point clear without bringing in Platonic Forms and all the rest of the Platonic apparatus, Socrates might well have said something like what I began by saying, namely, that a category of action designed to accommodate such matters as choosing to stay is more fundamental than the category of $C \rightarrow E$ causality, and that one can not produce an adequate account of the former by confining oneself to an account of the infrastructure in terms of the latter. But I suspect that, wishing to retain the notion of "real cause," he would continue to run the conceptual risk of juxtaposing it, within the same conceptual framework, with $C \rightarrow E$ causality. I shall therefore suppose that he would have said something like this: "My choosing to stay was an act whose infrastructure consisted of a highly complex physical process taking place within the prison and more particularly within my body, where it involved all the distinguishable parts and functions of it: changes

71

at the molecular level, the growth and division of my body's cells, glandular secretions, the movement of complex electrical impulses within my central nervous system, the flexing of my muscles, the articulation of my bones, and so on. This complex physical process can be understood as a multiplicity of 'causes without which the (real) cause cannot be the cause'; that is, as an infrastructure, it is permeated by what you call the $C \rightarrow E$ relation. Perhaps it is also permeated by laws, either reductionist or hierarchical. In some sense I am sure it is, although I am by no means sure that science is very clear about the status of law. But all these are less fundamental than my act itself: they are unified by it, wielded by it, caught in its power. In that sense action is more fundamental than $C \rightarrow E$ causality. But I want to hold on to that expression 'real cause,' and I don't see why that should commit me to saying that I, the agent, am the cause of my acts in some objectionable sense. Obviously, I am not claiming that I cause them in a $C \rightarrow E$ sense, but neither am I claiming that I am the cause of them in some other sense that would radically distinguish me as cause from the texture of the actions that are mine, although I grant that my dualistic talk about mind and body is open to some such interpretation. Do not forget that before Plato and I began to use the word *'aitia,'* which you translate as 'cause,' in technical discussions like this, it was used chiefly to ascribe responsibility that might deserve praise or blame — indeed, that is the standard use in Homer and the tragedians. All I am saying is that the agent is responsible for his acts, and that any $C \rightarrow E$ account of them that obscures this fact is hopelessly abstract. This commits me to the further claim that the category of agent is more fundamental than that of action, although obviously inextricably mixed up with it."

2

Each of us, subjecting the infrastructure of one of his acts to even the most casual analysis, will be able to distinguish any

The Originative Acts of the Prisoner

number of distinct events and processes within it, and any number of structures and entities that play a role in it. As Socrates did, we can also see how they are linked with one another in $C \rightarrow E$ connection, and we may take it for granted that these linkages will be in conformity with the laws of physics, and perhaps, if hierarchic science is right, with other laws as well. If we take seriously the alleged "real causality" of the act, though, the importance of these connections is diminished, and we see them as $C \rightarrow E$ connections within the enframing power of the act; which, far from being the summation or outcome of all these linkages, now appears as a power that embraces all of them in its unity, carrying them along in its temporal sweep. Some it creates and sustains, as the act of thinking and writing creates and sustains a particular pattern of electrochemical activity in the brain that would not be there if I were sitting idle;[1] some it merely cooperates with, qualifies, insinuates itself among, as the beat of my heart, perhaps little altered in writing from what it would be if I merely sat looking out the window, goes about its business of sustaining the organism while I write; but all of them it embraces, unifies, and somehow qualifies. Though some $C \rightarrow E$ pattern will be found in any act, or in any state more quiescent than an act, the temporality of this act, directed to an end, if not always by forethought and plan, then at least by the very nature of act, seems to constitute the reason (sense *1*) why all of these $C \rightarrow E$ connections are precisely as they are, at least as much as they, in their assemblage, constitute the act and in that sense explain why it is as it is. So understood, the power of acts seems precisely the power of our own nature. By attending to them we single out that nature from what the body would be in itself if, for example, we were incapacitated to act because of drugs or injury. If it is not quite accurate to say that we *are* our acts, we may at least say that they express our nature, that it manifests itself in them, perhaps, even, that they spring out of it as out of a source. It will require this chapter and the next two, however, to fill out this sketch. It will not be brought to completeness, by relating the ontological status of agent and act, until the last chapter.

73

3

But, on the other hand, acts seem to depend in a very intricate way upon stable physical structures, and the status common sense or science give structures of that kind seems at odds with the preceding sketch of the autonomy of action. If there is a sense in which we *are* our acts, there is a very ordinary and everyday sense in which we also are the structures by means of which we act: the sense in which we act in and with our bodies defines a sense in which we are our bodies.

Not only does an act take place by means of a bodily structure, as when I move my hand in the rapid and intricate motion of writing, it may also simply be regarded as a disturbance *in* a structure; a disturbance, moreover, defined by the nature of the structure, as the disturbance that is writing is defined by the mechanical linkages of the joints of bones, of tendon and muscle linked to bone, and so on—in short all the structural side of Socrates' "causes without which the cause cannot be the cause." The structure remains, much as it was, when the action is past: I move arms, fingers, hands when I write, but when the paragraph is done, and I sit without moving for a moment, arm, hand, fingers remain as structures, at my disposal, as it were, for the next paragraph I write.

It is the same if we attend not to the act as an unanalyzed unity but instead to the components of its infrastructure—the rhythm of the volleying of the cortex, the impulses along the motor nerves, the contraction and relaxation of muscles, the circulation of the blood, the more minute happenings at the level of cell and below—all of them may be regarded as disturbances occurring in physical structures that persist after the disturbance is done. In act or in infrastructure, in gross or in fine, act and physical structure are correlated; and so much do the structures make the acts possible that one can see readily enough the force of materialism's claims that the body defines one's identity, and that physical events taking place within it in $C \rightarrow E$ linkage under law are identical with one's acts. Given the structure, given the appropriate stimulus to it, and the disturbance we call action is propagated through it.

It is interesting, and, from the point of view of reductionism, a telling point against hierarchic science, that most of the solid discoveries of hierarchic science can be interpreted as newly discovered structural complexities just as plausibly as they can be interpreted as newly discovered laws supplementing those of physics. The recent discoveries in biophysics of which that of DNA is the landmark are revelations, but the only thing that is beyond dispute is that they are revelations of highly complicated structures, and that some of the processes in which these are involved are as "mechanical" as the movement of a bone in its socket might be—consider, for instance, the aptness of the "template" image in the synthesis of proteins with the help of RNA. Even many of the processes themselves are naturally interpretable as the formation and persistence of such physical structures as DNA, RNA, enzymes, organelles, and so on.

The structures are relatively stable in themselves, but they give rise to a stability that transcends the individual unit, for many of them are reiterative, or self-replicative: parent gives rise to child, cells divide to produce new cells, organelles bud to produce new organelles, DNA gives rise to DNA. In this reiterative stability there is a regularity that, if less impressive than the regularities of physics—these structures have, after all, evolved, and are still in process of evolution—is nevertheless very impressive indeed. Such a massive stability of inheritance within biological structures large and small provides a regularity that operates much as "higher level" laws might do, even if it should never be demonstrated that "higher level laws" do indeed lie behind them. However we wish to interpret the fact, water molecules within the stable structure of the cell are subject to forces they are not subject to outside the cell, and these forces transcend the individual cell in the sense that they are perpetuated in offspring cells. Given that stable structure, much can be said about the "disturbance" within it that consists in the progress of a water molecule through it to this or that place, to participate in this or that chemical change. Much too can be said about the propagation through the cell structure of the "disturbance" which is the development of a mitochondrion and its subsequent actlike behavior. There are, in short, many regularities that are dependent upon structures, and if it is moot whether these go back to higher level laws of nature, they are regularities that are lawlike in their observable influences.

Suppose we try, in the light of this emphasis on structure, to express diagrammatically the view of action, so friendly to Socrates' intent, that was put forward in the previous section. There will be formidable difficulties. We wish to express the enframing power of an act, which supposedly embraces and carries along in its temporal sweep a host of $C \rightarrow E$ connections. But these connections take place in the body, which has a stability that in some sense makes the act possible, and may, on a materialistic interpretation, completely explain the supposed act. Let us represent the body's structural stability by a square made of unbroken lines. Since within it there will be happenings in some sense interpretable in $C \rightarrow E$ terms (e.g., the firing of some nerve cell under the excitation of others that are in synapse with it, or the angular movement of two jointed bones drawn by muscular contraction), we shall place the symbol "$C \rightarrow E$" within the square. It stands for all processes or events of this sort, thought of as coextensive with the structural order that comprises them. The act itself we represent, though tentatively, in view of the difficulties that can readily be foreseen, by a curved arrow sweeping through this structure: the thought is that in its unity it binds together, and indeed in some sense engenders, a host of such $C \rightarrow E$ connections.

All this takes place within the influence of the laws of nature. What those are (e.g., reductionist or hierarchic) we leave open for the moment. We represent their influence by the naïve device of a dotted square enframing the square representing the body. The similarity between the representation of structures and the representation of laws allows us to keep open the possibility that the regularity of biological structures can appropriately be interpreted in terms of higher-level laws. The diagram

76

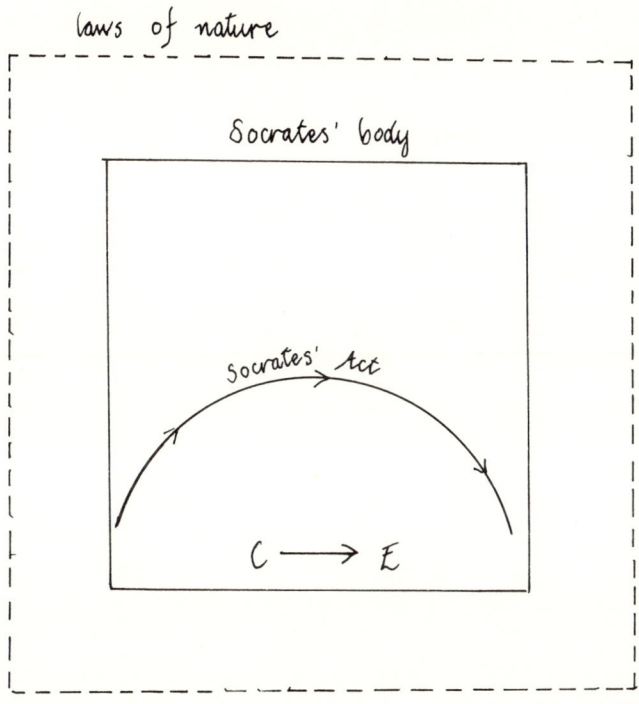

Figure *1*

appears as figure *1*. At any rate, $C \to E$ connections within Socrates' body that belong to this act are subject to the laws of nature, to the influence of that body (however interpreted), and also, on the hypothesis of the previous section, to whatever "influence" is brought to bear by the supposed act. But the erosion of this last "influence" is considerable as we follow out the logic of our naïve image. For within the structure of the body there are other structures, for instance the two bones supposed, in the example just given, to be in angular movement. And within these there are other structures, cells for instance. Our diagram immediately becomes a nest of Chinese boxes, and between those on the same "level" there will be $C \to E$ connections. The principle is represented in figure *1A*, but in highly

77

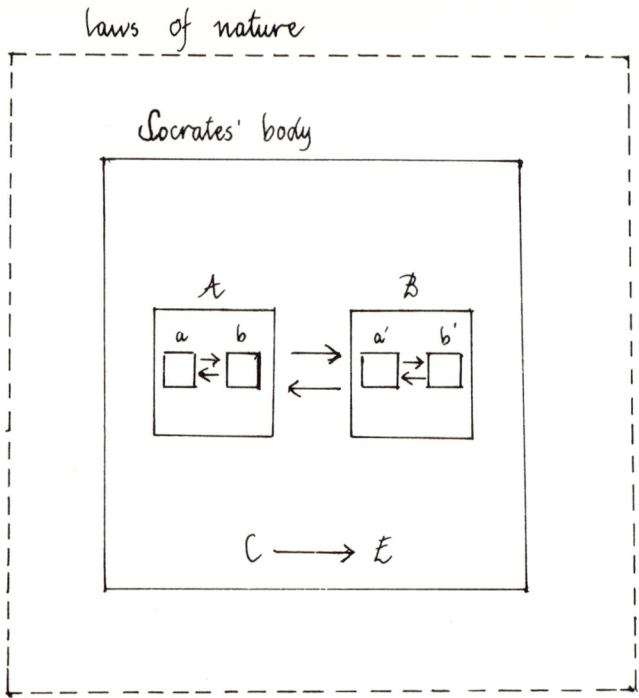

Figure *1A*

simplified form; the curved arrow is left out because it will turn out to be in contradiction with the developing logic of the diagram. Only three levels are represented in the diagram, though there will in fact be very many levels. It does not matter how we interpret the boxes so long as we are consistent about the levels. *A* and *B* might be two linked bones in movement, in which case *a* and *b* and *a'* and *b'* would be cells; *A* and *B* might, however, be cells—perhaps contiguous cells in the bones, perhaps two nerve cells linked in synapse—and *a* and *b, a'* and *b'* would then be two macromolecules in *C* → *E* relation. Since our elements linked in *C* → *E* fashion are not successive states or events, but persistent structures, the *C* → *E* connections are *inter*connections, and are accordingly represented by arrows going in both

directions. *Mutatis mutandis,* we are dealing with a group of entities in the thoroughgoing causal reciprocity that Kant had in
mind.

Between some of the boxes—those representing very sta-
ble physical structures that continue to exist after the $C \rightarrow E$
connections between them, as for instance, one bone pressing
upon another—the $C \rightarrow E$ connections will be patently like the
most commonsense version of the working view of the $C \rightarrow E$
connection. In short, they will be mechanical in a very usual
sense of that word, a sense congruent with that of the doctrine
Socrates rejected. Between other boxes the connections, while
still recognizably $C \rightarrow E$ ones in the broad sense laid down in
chapter 1, will be more subtle. Thus, if two nerve cells are
connected in synapse and the firing of the first causes the second
to fire, the $C \rightarrow E$ connection between them will also have to
be interpreted in terms of $C \rightarrow E$ connections of boxes of lower
level as well, for we have to provide for such matters as the
passage of ions across a physical gap. Yet other $C \rightarrow E$ connections may bear on the emergence of boxes of a certain level (e.g.,
macromolecules) out of the groupings of boxes of lower levels.
Some, at least, of the forces that bring about such groupings
could themselves be represented by boxes. In short, the $C \rightarrow E$
connections between boxes may range from the patently
mechanical to those in which the mechanical aspect, though less
obvious, can be found by correlating $C \rightarrow E$ connections at
several box levels. So long as we confine ourselves to boxes—
structures—that do not fall below the size at which the very
notion of stable structure grows ambiguous, as the notion of
particle becomes ambiguous below a certain magnitude, a discussion of Socrates' body in terms of structures linked in
$C \rightarrow E$ fashion is very plausible indeed. Below that level the
$C \rightarrow E$ relation can be retained (certainly in the official version),
but only if we think of it as linking states, or events, within which
we have to forego a $C \rightarrow E$ account of the fate of individual and
unambiguously persistent structural entities. This last reservation is an important one, for it seems to call in question the
ontological finality of the whole system of persistent structural

entities in $C \rightarrow E$ connection that is in some sense built upon it.

Setting aside this last point, since the whole framework presented in terms of figures *1* and *1A* was provisional, and was, furthermore, only advanced to make clear some of the difficulties that the model of a disturbance in a persistent structure presents for our "Socratic" view of action, we may continue with the model for a moment. So long as we stay above the critical level of magnitude, a recognizably "mechanical," though very complex and subtle, $C \rightarrow E$ account of a supposed action of Socrates can presumably be given. And even below that level the account is a defensibly $C \rightarrow E$ one, though not a mechanical one. So much is this the case that the lawlike role I envisioned a moment ago for any structure that enframes another and smaller one begins to break down. The "laws" imposed upon its components by a cell-structure, for instance, suddenly dissolve in a flurry of little "boxes" in $C \rightarrow E$ affiliation under the (reductionist) laws of nature, as when for instance, one attends to the purely mechanical way in which the templatelike structure of messenger RNA links onto and carries along some other structure that fits it. Our concrete understanding of any such transaction in $C \rightarrow E$ terms is not remarkably different from our commonsense understanding of a causal connection between Socrates' body (a "box") with some other "box" in the environment, as when, for instance, he raises the cup of hemlock to his lips. Despite the breakdown of mechanism at the level of the very small, there are therefore many contemporary attempts by writers with scientific backgrounds to devise, at least in principle, mechanical and reductionist accounts of human nature, including, of course, the component of mind; in all of these the theme of persistent physical structures is naturally very important.[2]

4

An act, or more generally, a process, is a disturbance in a structure. There is some truth in the image, enough truth so that any account of Socrates' acts that does justice to what he was driving at must, if it is to be plausible, come to grips with all the "mechanical" $C \rightarrow E$ links in his body. Surely, though, the emphasis is wrong. For one thing, these structures we have been talking about are themselves in process. They are in process in gross, as in the case of the development of an organism from birth through maturity to death, or in that of the parallel cycle of an organ; and they are also in process in fine, as in the life cycle of cell or organelle, or as in the cyclic formation and destruction of macromolecules like enzymes and amino acids. The static image of a nest of Chinese boxes gives way to that of a nested dynamism more hospitable to the desired image of Socrates' act. The stability of my arm, wielded now in writing, is of that dynamic sort: from the first laying down of tissues in the embryo up through maturity to decline, it is a stability of process in which spatially disposed components — tissues, cells, macromolecules, and so on — reiterate themselves in multiple life cycles isomorphic with the cycle of the whole. From this point of view the dynamic cycle that is the arm wields the multiple dynamic components, and though neither arm nor cell nor macromolecule is an act in the sense we are attributing to Socrates, there is more similarity between the dynamic cycle of arm, cell, or macromolecule and the dynamic cycle of act than the word "structure" allows us to notice. And the "mechanical" linkage of bone with bone, though real enough, depends ontologically upon these dynamic facts.

If there is a sense in which an act is a "disturbance" in a physical structure, there is also a sense in which all such physical structures are sustained by component units that are actlike in their dynamism, as an organ is sustained, for instance, by the reiterated life cycles of any number of cells, or the cell sustained by the reiterated "life" cycles of constantly renewed populations of macromolecules. But these component units, reiterated in their spatial disposition, can not be said unequivocally to sustain the larger structural units within which they exist, for they fall into place in their dispositions, and are held there and used there by the overarching dynamism of the growth of the larger structural unit itself, which is in that sense sustainer no less than sustained. Sometimes the life cycle of larger units is as reiterative as that of the smaller — cells within an organ are renewed constantly, as are their component organelles and macromolecules. Sometimes it is less so — in higher animals important organs are not strictly speaking reiterative. But the single dynamic life cycle of the organ embraces the long sequence of cell life cycles no less so for that. Moreover, in many cases, the organ, as over against the embracing life cycle of the organism, expresses its very existence in rhythmic, and in that sense reiterative, processes. Rhythm, of course, runs all through biology, and many smaller units are thus "reiterative" in a sense that supplements the reiteration of their life cycles: the regular firing of nerve cells, the regular expansion and contraction of muscle cells are instances of this.

But the main theme here is that from this point of view any organism is a nest of dynamic processes in which one process that enframes others is not only sustained by those others but also sustains them. We are back again with the language appropriate to interpretation (*b*) of the intent of hierarchic science: the language in which we speak of control exercised by individual units on their subunits.

Representation of these dynamic relationships that sustain the stable spatial relationships we call structures is difficult indeed. Any mode of representation designed to bring out the temporal and reiterative status of the units composing a structure will be somewhat at odds with the structural feature. Thus, though a cell is (whatever else it is) a dynamic process deployed in three dimensions, if we try to represent the life cycle of, say, three cells sprung from a single one by successive division and to relate this to the life cycle of the organ within which it exists, we must neglect for the moment its spatiality — the very thing that makes us think of it as a structure, and that made the representation of it by a box, in the diagrammatic terms of figures *1* and *1A,* a plausible one. Let us represent, in figure *2,* the life cycle of both organ and cell by directed curved lines; the diagram does not imply that the comparative lengths of life of cell and organ are as they are in nature, and it takes account of only one unit resultant from each division. Comparing this with

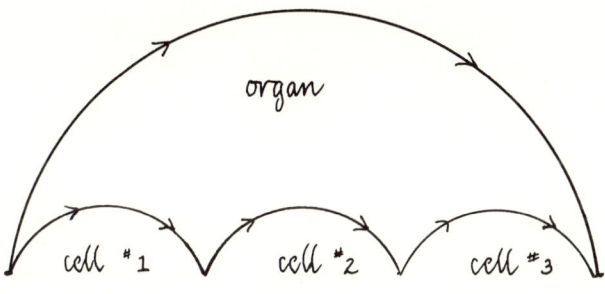

Figure *2*

figure *1A*, one notes that although our representation is purely temporal, the relation between cell #*1* and cell #*2* bears some resemblance to the $C \rightarrow E$ relation between little boxes in that figure. At least, the event which is the splitting of cell #*1* gave rise, on our assumption, to cell #*2*. On the other hand, by definition cell #*1* is "gone" when we decide to identify one of the offspring cells as #*2*. The structural identity of our little boxes in figure *1A*, however, is usually more clear-cut, until, when we go below a certain level of magnitude, we reach a situation for which our present dynamic diagrams might be more helpful. There is another important difference between figure *1A* and figure *2*. In view of the conflict between hierarchic and reductionist science, we left open in the case of figure *1A* the question what laws, if any, in addition to the laws of physics, qualified the $C \rightarrow E$ relations. But the conventions of figure *2* require us to assume that the $C \rightarrow E$-like relations between cell #*1*, cell #*2*, and cell #*3* are qualified by the dynamic power of the life cycle of the organ here represented as embracing them in a temporal unit. The conventions of the diagram also permit us to assume—what it is one of the labors of this book to make evident—that the identity between the organ and its component cells is not an unqualified identity. The overarching dynamism is identical with the other three only in the sense in which a power-unity can be identical with the multiplicity of its infrastructure.

Figure *2* is flexible enough to be turned to many represent-

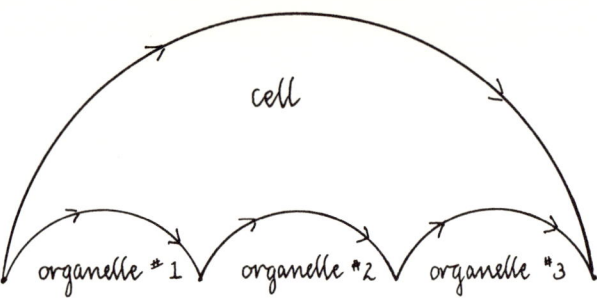

Figure *2A*

ative purposes. In cell #*1,* for instance, there will be a large number of organelles throughout its structure. If we suppose only one to break down into its macromolecular components and then to reconstitute itself, and to do this three times, we have a reiteration that we may perhaps call, neglecting some no doubt important problems about identity, organelle #*1,* organelle #*2,* and organelle #*3.* This gives us figure *2A;* once again, we neglect the spatial factor—the movement of the organelle(s) in process of breakdown and reconstitution. One could also do something of the kind by relating either cell or organelle to the constantly renewed population of macromolecules within it. We might also use a diagram of this sort to represent the relation between the life cycle of an organ and the reiterated elements in its rhythm: the life of the heart and its many beats; the life of the brain and the many complex patterns of electrochemical activity within it; the life cycle of Socrates and his many actions. The relations between the overarching line and those enclosed within it—relations which will be taken up in the following chapters—might be subtly different in each case. If we go to a high enough level in the hierarchy, we must produce a diagram of nested dynamisms of enormous complexity if we are to show the relations between it and, say, the level of the macromolecule.

No doubt both kinds of figures—those, like *1* and *1A,* that emphasize stable spatial structures, and those, like *2* and *2A,* that emphasize temporal relations whose spatial significance is still obscure—are needed to make sense of an act of Socrates. As to figures *1* and *1A,* to use his own language, his body really is "composed of bones and muscles . . . the bones . . . hard and separated by joints" and so on; and science can carry the account down to relations between the structure of his DNA and his snub nose; and in principle perhaps even to habitual circuit patterns in his brain that may be facilitated by changes at the molecular level, and that may, moreover, play some role in the things he habitually talks about and habitually attends to. But if a really searching account of structural features can not be established without showing them to be dependent upon dynamic relationships of the sort as yet merely adumbrated in figures *2* and *2A,* then the image of action—wielding, by virtue of its "real causality," a pattern of $C \rightarrow E$ relations in a structure; embracing and sustaining those as well as innumerable other $C \rightarrow E$-like relations in the unity of its power—is not necessarily at odds with it. The sweep of the curved arrow that appears in figure *1* and is dropped in figure *1A* was not really in radical conflict with the rest of figure *1,* for though there is a sense in which an actlike unity may be regarded as a disturbance in a structure, it is also true that very many dynamic units that we can distinguish may be regarded as energetic sustainers of structure. From this point of view all structural regularities depend upon the reiteration of actlike units. We shall not be in a position to develop this matter in detail until the last chapter.

5

There are no doubt formidable problems for the view of action adumbrated in this chapter so long as we attend to the massive stability of structure in which it takes place. Even if, as I claim, it is ontologically dependent upon the dynamic powers whose reiteration sustains it, the stability is massive indeed. Knowing it, knowing at least some laws of nature that are of profound importance, one knows in general what to expect from a man in certain circumstances, as every critic of the doctrine of free will since Hume has been quick to point out. That familiar snub-nosed, bald, popeyed figure had been going about Athens for many years, and his habits of thought and action were well known. If the stability of its structure should be ontologically dependent upon the kind of ramified dynamic system that I have suggested, the reiterative pattern of that system is stable enough—stable enough to support what to common sense is simply a structure. At the moment we encounter him, this dynamic system, we must suppose, has inherited a pattern not only from its own individual past but also from his ancestors. Genetics can tell us a good deal about the inheritance of the familiar bodily pattern, and we can conjecture that in the future it may tell us something about the inheritance of attitudes and ways of thought as well. Anyone equipped with what both common sense and science could tell him about the pattern inherited by Socrates from both his individual and his ancestral past would scarcely have expected him to give way under pressure of the kind that was put on him. Though more in keeping with figures *2* and *2A* than with *1* and *1A*, the reiterative impetus of our nested dynamisms becomes itself a problem: macromolecules, cells, organs, including the vital one of the brain, have at any age their "habits"; and what we call habits in the usual sense are related to these: Socrates will "choose" and "act," we may expect, much as he has done before. Can we, then, really think of one of those "acts" in prison as "a power that embraces and sustains all these ($C \rightarrow E$) linkages, carrying them along in its temporal sweep"?

Well, yes, provided we have regarded his past life in somewhat the same way. We have only to suppose that inherited physical structures, sustained by dynamisms isomorphic with the acts we attribute to Socrates, may always have stood ready for an act of Socrates to wield them. Even the earliest acts of the infant Socrates as he ran about in play wielded them: the temporal unity of the act of running bound together, we may assume, an intricate nest of dynamisms isomorphic with the act itself, and all of these pervaded, possessed, and wielded the structurally linked young bones. And we have only to suppose that acts of this kind, like the past dynamisms with which it is isomorphic—dynamisms which, if we take them far enough back, either in a phylogenetic or an ontogenetic sense, have laid down those bones—can leave behind them new structural stabilities. The infant Socrates as he ran presumably brought about by those acts molecular changes in his brain, just as he certainly strengthened his muscles. Young and old, Socrates in act forms habits, and interfused with those are the deep changes in the body's "habits"—the structural stabilities that result from and further the power to act.

All of this rests on our taking seriously that arguable "relation"—the reason for quotation marks will be introduced later—that on our assumption pervades the nested dynamisms of our diagrams: the "relation" between an act and its infrastructure, between any level of an infrastructure and those beneath it, between an organism and its organs, between an organ and its cells, a cell and its organelles, and so on. Everything is tentative now and must remain so at least until the further development of the position in the next two chapters. But if the position should prove persuasive, the presence of a reiterative dynamic pattern sustaining structural regularities that further the habitual repetition of an act is not in itself a refutation of our "Socratic" view of action. Our view supposes that the ability to perform the intricate bit of fingering needed to play a certain phrase in a Beethoven sonata is based upon certain neural circuit patterns that have become regularized in virtue of certain structural changes, perhaps at the molecular level; but it also supposes that the development of the circuit patterns, and therefore the production of the molecular changes, rests upon the successive acts in which the playing of the phrase was perfected. Eventually the playing of the phrase moves from the level of labored attention to that of unconscious mastery, but in our view this movement is based upon a series of acts each of which had the unified dynamism of our diagrams, and each of which contributed to the structural changes that made possible more accomplished successor acts of the same kind.

The image of a computer sub-program, so often brought forward in discussions of subroutines of this kind, blurs the more difficult and less mechanical sense in which the new act wields the mechanical—i.e., structurally stabilized—residue of its predecessor. One way of reminding ourselves that the nested dynamisms of action persist despite such structural stabilities, and persist as the mode in which the agent possesses and wields those stabilities, is to note that the performer, at the point of having mastered some phrase, is still usually laboring at the mastery of the whole sonata. Even if the mastery of the phrase were now to be understood as a complexity of parallel $C \rightarrow E$ steps in which each step is exhaustively accounted for by its predecessors, all of this taking place by virtue of stabilized changes in the neural and muscular systems, the total act of the playing of the sonata can still be said to embrace and carry along these $C \rightarrow E$ steps and to bind them together with many new $C \rightarrow E$ steps not yet so stabilized at the structural level. But in point of fact this way of considering the playing of the whole sonata, together with our way of considering the acts in which the perfected playing of the phrase developed, is at logical odds with the conditional clause of this hypothesis. Even though the playing of the whole sonata should at length move to the level of unconscious mastery, with concomitant structural changes, we are at no point confronted with a number of sets of purely mechanical subroutines linked in a mechanical master program, for the whole account of the achievement of mastery contradicts this conception.

I suggested earlier that the very structural reality of the physical elements—bones, muscles, nerves—linked mechanically in any routine are sustained by actlike dynamisms that pervade them. It would be more precise to say that the reiteration of some of these dynamisms under the dynamism of the whole *is* that structure. Our present discussion is concerned with a different but closely related point: with the apparently $C \rightarrow E$ events or processes that constitute the routine. Some of these, at least, are of a highly mechanical sort on their surface (e.g., the movement of fingers), and the assumption is that their fine-grained sub-events (e.g., neural circuit patterns ending in motor connections) are facilitated by fine structural changes that have become stabilized, and that in that sense have some important features in common with the patently mechanical surface events. But our assumptions about the dynamism of the acts that precede mastery and have brought about the fine-grained structural changes is that they advance towards mastery *pari passu* with the structural changes. It is this that seems logically incompatible with the supersession of this act-dynamism, after mastery, by a mechanical process of parallel $C \rightarrow E$ steps within a stable structure. It would seem that even when the structure is stabilized, the calling of the process into play, and into reiterated play, must require an act-dynamism isomorphic with those that engendered the fine-structural changes that now facilitate reiteration. The mechanical *aspect* persists, as indeed some was there from the very start: fingers, muscles, nerves interact in a series of steps that can be mimicked by a suitably constructed automaton. But we have to think of the mechanisms as possessed in operation by act-dynamisms isomorphic with those that created at least some of the fine-structure features of them. How such nested dynamisms should permeate structures in some sense mechanical it will be the task of the next two chapters to show. We must obviously lean heavily on the view that structures are created and sustained by actlike dynamisms, and this in turn means that this "Socratic" view of action must have consequences for the way we interpret those "mechanisms," "programs," and "sub-programs" in less developed organisms that are sometimes advanced as arguments for a mechanistic view of human nature. The wasp sets out to entomb in a burrow a paralyzed insect, having first implanted in it an egg from which a larva will eventually emerge to feed on the still-living insect. Interrupted in her routine, she must begin again at the beginning, and reperform tasks already completed in order to reach the end of the task she is intent upon. But even so stable and simple a structure as the nervous system of that wasp, one that may leave little or no room for freedom or creativity, may be possessed and moved in its operation by a nested dynamism isomorphic with those that—in an evolutionary sense—laid it down. This example of the wasp, incidentally, which is so often quoted in defense of mechanism, should probably not be taken so seriously as it once was. Some recent ingenious experiments seem to reveal an unexpected "creativity" in the frustrated wasp.[3]

If I turn now to myself, doing all the things one does when one writes, fiddling with the pen, moving papers about, idly twirling spectacles as I stare out the window, where, at the beginning of winter, darkness gathers, and the wind blusters down the slopes of Monte Pilli and tosses the massed ilex outside the window, is it not true that I am trying to *wield* the forces and structures of the body—brain, heart, muscles, finger tips and all the rest, so that at last some clarity should come in the slow unfolding of a sentence? The long, slow growth of structural stability going back beyond my particular life to my ancestry, the long slow growth of habit, custom, and convention in myself and in the society in which I live may facilitate or betray the enterprise, as the case may be. If the structural stability and regularity depends upon the reiteration of actlike units, the stream of structure in which I now stand poised to act can itself be interpreted as a "habit" engendered by those reiterations. The poised act may be hindered or facilitated by the "habit" which is structure, by the "habit" which is convention, and by habit in the usual sense of that word. But the image we are working with does not on this account make the unifying power of the act unreal—not for Socrates, and not for me.

6

The claim I have put in Socrates' mouth can be made more economically in the language of power than in that of causality: the power of the agent permeates the infrastructure of certain acts in such a way that an account of it in terms of $C \rightarrow E$ connections under the rule of reductionist or hierarchic laws is highly abstract, though profoundly interesting and important.

90

It is abstract in the sense in which models, theories, and other conceptual or symbolic structures are abstract as over against the concrete, existent, developing and changing reality we try to understand or manipulate with their help.

In this book I shall argue that the category of action, understood as including this sense of power, is more fundamental than that of $C \rightarrow E$ causality, and that the latter can be derived from it. But I shall not appeal for justification to the logic of the language in which we talk about actions and causes. I shall instead call attention to certain features of action that, while they are no doubt consistent with the ordinary language of action, are by no means evident to us by the mere fact of our using that language. The features are there to be attended to, but they are not fully evident to us in the mode of attention usual to common sense, nor can they be made evident merely by turning a philosophic mode of attention upon the logic of our language. The philosophic mode of attention I propose is to be sure language-bound: we can not practice it without creatively deploying and enlarging our linguistic forms, nor can we deploy our linguistic forms in this way without practicing it. But when we do, our attention is directed not upon language but, through the medium of language, upon the full concreteness of action itself.

It is difficult to attend to action or indeed to anything else in this way, and it is accordingly difficult to talk about this mode of attention without seeming to fall into obscurantism. It may clear the air if I say that the spirit of this meditation has nothing in common with the many contemporary obscurantisms that appeal to the wisdom of the feelings or the wisdom of the blood over against that of the mind. My intent is rather to celebrate our rationality. But the fulfillment of our rationality is not necessarily to be found either in common sense or in the natural sciences, even though both of these are expressions of rationality — so much so that they conspire together to make themselves the whole of it. Common sense begins in taking actions of Socrates or anyone else at their face value — that is, it begins by taking their unity for granted. Yet the same capacity that allows common sense to isolate an act of Socrates and Socrates himself

91

from their context and then to connect that act and that entity with all other units that it can distinguish in the world, can also be focused on an act of Socrates or on Socrates himself. That is one of the meanings of "analysis." Thus an act is analyzable into a multiplicity that is not that act, and an entity—for instance, the one we call Socrates the agent—is analyzable into a multiplicity that is not that entity. Moreover, acts in general are analyzable into multiplicities that are not acts, and entities into multiplicities that are not entities—for instance, into events or states.

Analysis is as familiar as common sense itself. Science, which is much more closely tied to the commonsense world than one would at first suppose, simply carries this process as far as mathematics, the experimental method, and the limits of technology permit. The elements into which act and entity are resolved then find place in a synthesis of another kind, a synthesis dictated by an interest in the measure properties of what is investigated. Now our commonsense understanding of act and agent also has a feature that is sometimes called synthetic, although this involves a serious distortion. Synthesis is first of all the putting together of distinct elements, and the concept of synthesis does not entail that the whole that results from this process has any other reality than that conferred upon it by the act of putting the elements together. The end product of synthesis may be, and very frequently is, something artificial. If we tend to think of synthesis in honorific terms we say that it is creative, and regard its end product as something fresh, new, not thought of or made before—as, for instance, the view of material nature as a four-dimensional field of which time is one of the dimensions. If we think of it in pejorative terms, stressing the discreteness of the elements and the fact that the end-product is indeed artificial, there is a pejorative sense of the term "synthesis" ready-made for us, for in one sense what is synthetic is precisely meretricious, specious, inauthentic. (It is not usually observed that a synthesis creative in one sense may be inauthentic in another: the most ingenious expression of the laws of nature may be inauthentic if the activity that made it is taken to be coextensive with the whole of rationality.)

I do not think that an act of Socrates or the entity Socrates out of which common sense understands an act to spring is synthetic in the sense of being inauthentic—an artifice of the synthesizing intelligence. No doubt when they are subject to some powerful mode of analysis—either a scientific analysis resolving them into events, states, elementary particles, and the like; an epistemological analysis resolving them into a set of sense data, a set of impressions, or simply into a sensuous manifold; or a linguistic analysis that does something similar with the ways we talk about them—they may seem inauthentic. To my mind, act and agent as understood by common sense are authentic enough. The first problem for philosophy is to hold on to what is authentic in them in the face of the most subtle forms of analysis and resynthesis. The second problem is to deepen our grasp of them, to comprehend them, to conceive of them more adequately in the mode their own authenticity demands.

For that reason, I prefer to avoid supposing that the polar activity to analysis is necessarily synthesis. I prefer to say that the essence of rationality is its capacity for *recognition*—a term I have elsewhere given what I hope is an exact technical sense.[4] Our intelligence is equipped to recognize unities that are authentically unities even though analysis may find a variety of multiplicities within them. The principle preservative of a unity so recognized is that some elements, at least, of the resulting multiplicity, may themselves be recognized to be unities as authentic as those within which they find place. The status of the hierarchies discussed in the last chapter depends upon this point. The view of action and of the agent-entity towards which our meditation on Socrates' speech is moving is intended to deepen the recognition already present, authentically enough, in common sense. I propose a philosophic mode of attention that shall reveal the unity of an act, and consequently the unity of an agent, to be a power pervading the multiplicity of an infrastructure, and to be distinguishable *as* a unity *from* that multiplicity to just the extent that its power *unifies* that multiplicity. It will not in the least detract from the authenticity of this power that it will also be seen to consist in the pervading *of a multiplicity:* the interdependence of act and its infrastructure,

of agent-entity and its infrastructure, is profound. The power
unit, exercising itself in multiplicity, is so refracted that one can
see why some philosophers prefer to give up the effort to see
it as it is in favor of calling the unifying power and the unified
multiplicity identical. One way to define materialism is to say
that it is so obsessed with the interdependence of acts and entities on the one hand and their infrastructures on the other as
to take it for an unqualified identity. It is not surprising that the
most influential kind of materialism abroad among philosophers
at the moment is one whose major tenet is that mind and body
(brain state) are identical.[5]

7

Assuming for awhile no more than a commonsense knowledge of Socrates as an entity capable of action, we shall in the
rest of this chapter and the two following ones focus on his
actions. But an account of action is not self-sufficient, and our
only reason for beginning there is that we may be able to see
there in greater relief certain features that belong to Socrates
the agent. Our meditation will eventually return from the category of action to that of agent, and thence to that of entity, with
the intent of showing that progression to be from the less to the
more fundamental. The discussion so far should in any case
have warned us that the view of action towards which we are
moving can not be made quite clear by restricting ourselves to
the category of action. The massive structural-mechanical features of the body, for instance, are difficult to reconcile with the
"real causality" of action unless they are seen to be ontologically
dependent upon reiterated entities like organisms and cells,
which, in their nested dynamism, exhibit a becoming congruent
with that of action.

Consider now a number of acts that will be called, without
any formal justification, acts of Socrates. It is arguable that one
might simply take the concept of a string of acts as ontologically
fundamental, and that introducing an entity called an agent to

94

whom they belong or out of which they come is unwarranted. The justification for the presence in the argument of a presumptive agent will later be found in certain features of certain of these acts. We shall suppose the acts to have these characteristics: (*a*) none is caused in a $C \to E$ sense by prior acts of Socrates; (*b*) none is *wholly* caused (in any sense of "cause") by virtue of a network of $C \to E$ relations within its infrastructure. I shall call the acts *S–1, S–2, S–3* and so on, the sequence indicating, so far as possible, the temporal order in which the acts begin. When two or more acts begin at the same time they will be given distinct numbers in accordance with the order in which they are considered. As I shall consider later on in the argument an act that begins earlier than the sequence, I shall call the first act to be considered *S–2*. He (*S–2*) sits up on the prison bed, (*S–3*) bends his leg, and (*S–4*) rubs it with his hand. While he is rubbing, (*S–5*) he takes the gradual cessation of the pain in his leg as the occasion for some connected remarks about the relation between pleasure and pain. If we arrange these acts in a sequence in which each of them appears as a curved arrow representing both its temporality and the unity by which we identify it as a distinct act, we get the schema of figure *3*. Except for the temporal overlap, each item in the schema appears as a simplicity or unity. What I have called its infrastructure will be a complexity, or multiplicity, of unimaginable intricacy. Our presumptive agent is "in" each of the acts, and is "everywhere" in the infrastructure of each, but neither of these claims is to be justified just now, and the second is not even under consideration. Although on our hypothesis none of the acts causes a later act in the series in a $C \to E$ sense, no matter which of the current meanings we give the $C \to E$ relation, we may assume

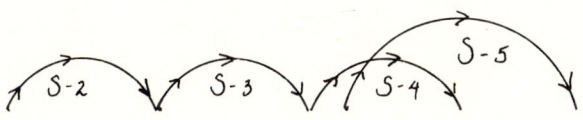

Figure *3*

95

safely that some acts may make contributions to later acts. Thus no doubt *S–2* contributes in some sense to *S–3*, and *S–3* to *S–4;* and no doubt *S–4* contributes to the easing of the pain (which does not appear in the diagram) and thus to *S–5* (the speech about pleasure and pain). It would be unwise, however, to take this contribution to be an example of the $C \rightarrow E$ relation, but except for that cautionary observation we shall have to set that question aside until the last chapter. On the basis of the first supposition, (*a*), about them, the acts are what have been called basic actions.[6] But the further supposition, (*b*), makes me prefer to call them originative actions.

Consider now the long argument for immortality that is the principal conceptual framework of the dialogue. For the sake of simplicity I shall take it as beginning just where *S–5* began and I shall call it *S–6*. It is a complex argument, and an important part of it is an almost equally long sub-argument about what Plato calls opposites, the word "opposite" being understood in one sense towards its beginning and in quite another sense towards its end. I shall call this sub-argument *S–7* and shall suppose it to begin where *S–5* and *S–6* begin. It is of course *act S–7,* for although arguments can be analyzed logically to yield a number of logical steps, we are concerned now only with the sense in which the argument has the unity of an act of Socrates. Within *S–7* there is a special unity to the little intellectual autobiography from which I took a fragment to get my discussion underway; call this *S–8*. We thus arrive at the schema that appears as figure *4*.

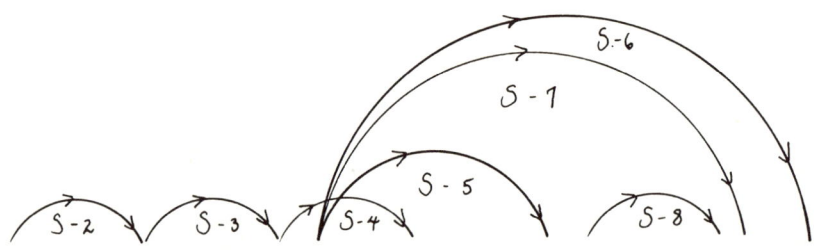

Figure *4*

Because of the suppositions we have made about them, we can attribute a number of further features to originative acts. (*c*) An act like *S–6* that temporally embraces other acts (*S–5*, *S–7*, *S–8*, and part of *S–4*) will not simply be a collective designation for that group and whatever other acts it embraces, but will have whatever originative properties we ascribe to each of the members of that series. If we regard each of them as unifying (in a sense that awaits clarification) a set of physical processes that makes up its infrastructure, then *S–6* will function in the same way. And, since the physical processes that make up the infrastructure of *S–5*, *S–7*, and *S–8* will also form part of the infrastructure of *S–6*, there will also presumably be a sense in which *S–6* will unify the acts *S–5*, *S–7*, and *S–8*. This will be the originative feature of it that distinguishes it from any merely collective way of describing that group and whatever other acts *S–6* temporally embraces. It will be plain, then, that although there is much that is obscure in the relation between *S–6* and the group *S–5*, *S–7*, and *S–8*, we are attributing to it an influence over them — an influence which must be compatible with the fact that it is in some sense identical with the group it unifies. (*d*) It will also follow — it is in fact a somewhat different way of making the same point — that an originative act may ramify in other originative acts. Although it may be difficult and perhaps impossible to identify originative acts that are simple in the sense that they do *not* ramify in sub-acts of this sort, there seems no reason why we can not find sub-acts in some of the supposed originative acts so far considered. The act *S–5*, for instance, being a set of connected remarks, can plainly be analyzed into sub-acts consisting of several individual remarks. It is important to note again that all this leaves us still in the realm of originative acts; we are not yet considering the relation of *any* act to its infrastructure, in which we shall eventually find a multiplicity of a different sort. (We are also deferring until later the possibility of analyzing an originative act into a multiplicity of qualitative factors, as when, for instance, we should distinguish several nuances of feeling that might qualify any originative act as it is performed.) But if we suppose that originative acts can ramify downward into sub-acts of the same sort, we have also been supposing, (*e*), that a new originative act, capable of unifying and making subordinate other subsequent sub-acts, may begin anywhere, as we assumed *S–6* to begin in the course of time-span *S–4*.

With all this in mind we may now amplify the schema of figure *4*. It is plainly very abstract, since it leaves out a large number of trivial and perhaps unrelated originative acts that begin and end in the course of it, as well as many other acts in which Socrates formulated the many other sub-arguments of *S–6*. At the end of the day Socrates (*S–9*) raises the cup of hemlock to his lips and drinks it; (*S–10*) just before dying he uncovers his face for a moment to tell Crito that he owes a cock to Asclepius and to ask him to repay it. Finally, we go back well before the beginning of *S–2* and consider the unity of Socrates' total action in defending himself at his trial, refusing to escape, conversing with his friends on the last day, calmly taking the hemlock and then lying down to let it have its way with him. Call this action, which embraces everything we have so far considered, *S–1*. There will of course be sub-actions lying between *S–1* and *S–2* that we do not consider. The schema for all this appears as figure *5*.

Although we are still in the realm of supposition, where it is not at all clear whether there can be originative acts of this sort, our suppositions—especially (*e*)—have allowed us to ascribe to the agent some of the features commonly looked for in an agent and fewer of the deficiencies he has in accounts that

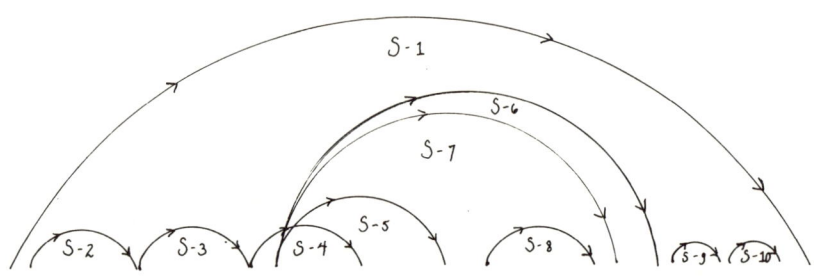

Figure 5

98

must construct him out of atomic units—memories, impressions, events, bodily states, or whatever—that are taken to be more patently authentic than the agent himself. Suppose any act that ramifies in sub-acts that it unifies, and that act will stand to each of the sub-acts much as an agent would stand to a set of successive acts we attributed to him as to an entity with an ontological status more fundamental than the acts themselves. For the unification of sub-acts by an act is not, on our supposition, a conceptual one that we make after the fact, but one that also consists in the emergence of these same acts. The point is perhaps clearer as we think of a new act (*S–6*) beginning in the midst of another (*S–4*) that "occasions it," or "contributes to its emergence," but that on our supposition does not cause it in a $C \rightarrow E$ sense; and think also of *S–6* as unifying in its course a set of acts (*S–5, S–7, S–8*) that in some sense constitute it but that also have their own status as originative acts.

The point also applies to much longer acts that embrace many more sub-acts. We have been supposing *S–1* to begin much earlier and to embrace, or unify, the group *S–2* through *S–10* in precisely the same way that *S–6* embraces, or unifies, the group *S–5, S–7*, and *S–8*. Each originative act, no matter how long, has an absolutely seamless unity as over against the sub-acts it unifies. Indeed, the supposition that it unifies is precisely the supposition that its unity over against what it unifies is seamless: we do not, on our suppositions, give an adequate account of our superordinate originative act by enumerating a sequence of subordinate originative acts. In that sense the identity between an act and its sub-acts is an asymmetrical one. Such seamless unity, if real, is all the warrant we need for taking the whole of Socrates' life as a single "act" having that same seamless unity. A unity of this kind would, to be sure, be qualified by the vast number of distinguishable originative sub-acts that are, in an asymmetrical sense, identical with it. But in making these last points we have simply moved from the category "act" to the category "agent" and thus to the category "entity" as well. That, I suggest, is exactly what we are assuming when we suppose that there are indeed acts of the kind I have been describing. The ontological feat of an originative act ramifying in sub-acts that are themselves originative acts is appropriately attributable to a subject-entity whom we appropriately call an agent. To be sure, when we began this chapter we were using a commonsense language framework that required us to attribute acts to agents like Socrates, but we did so without any serious scrutiny of the ontological status of the "agent" thus named. An act-ontology in which "Socrates" was merely a name for a succession of related acts is at least a possibility once that commonsense framework is no longer taken for granted. The argument is now advanced only in the sense that *if* there are originative acts having the status we have attributed to them on our suppositions, then it would appear that there are agents that have an ontological status appropriate to the performance of them. But this movement back to the category of entity will not be completed until the last chapter, and it is only at that time that we shall be able to see how $C \rightarrow E$ causality is ontologically derivative, if not precisely from originative action, then at least from the same power in an entity that, in an important class of them, expresses itself in action. Whether there are originative acts of this sort depends upon a "relation" between acts and infrastructures that has so far merely been sketched.

4

The Originative Act and
Its Infrastructure

 WE LEAVE NOW FOR AWHILE THE topic of the relation between originative acts — both the relation between antecedent and successor acts and that between superordinate and subordinate acts. We shall return to it eventually, since it is central to our effort to understand Socrates in a way that is consistent both with what science can now tell us about him and with the intent of his remarks about "real causality." An act-ontology in which acts are originative, in which they may ramify in sub-acts that are themselves originative, and in which they may be subsumed under superordinate acts that are also originative, is an agent-ontology. It requires us to conceive of the agent as being so lodged in "the nature of things" that originative acts emerge from him as from a source. No doubt this way of putting it is too metaphysical and vague, and it certainly suggests an unwarranted independence of agent from acts. But it has the advantage, at least, of pointing out that "he acted in such and such a way" is not simply a rough and everyday way of expressing something that could be more profoundly expressed in the language of the natural sciences, either now or later.

There can be nothing more fundamental to an agent-ontology than the "relation" between an originative act and its infrastructure, and it is to this topic that we now turn. We can not take an agent seriously if we can not see, in the

face of scientific $C \rightarrow E$ explanations, how he can act originatively, and we can not take originative action seriously unless
we can see its "relation" to its infrastructure clearly enough to
see how its power can be expressed there. If we see that, I
conjecture, we shall see in it an exemplification of that feature
of nature that gives rise to new ordered, persistent, and reiterative structural patterns. And though this will not lead us to any
new laws of nature, it may put us in a better position to interpret
the status of the laws of nature. But if there is an authentic power
"relation" of this kind, nothing is more fragile and evanescent
under our analytic scrutiny. Habituated as we are to the causal
explanations of science, there will always be an illuminating
scientific explanation of any portion of an infrastructure that we
can isolate and establish the parameters of by observation or
experiment.

Before we begin, then, it is well to remember that the unity
and power of an originative act is accessible to a mode of rational activity we are all master of. We do not need to have
recourse to some recondite procedure for putting together a
complexity out of simple elements, and indeed if we did "syn-
thesize" an act out of such elements it would in that measure
be inauthentic. The notion that genuine unity and power are to
be found only in entities or processes at the limits of analysis
and the parallel epistemological notion that the authenticity of
our cognitive claims about complex entities and happenings
rests upon their rational constructibility out of data at the limits
of analysis are what we must guard against. To attend to Socrates in action is not to attend to the infrastructure, or at least not
to attend to infrastructure items severally, but to a power that
gives that infrastructure nothing more mysterious than the unity
common sense calls Socrates acting. When I wish to put the
matter in a way that will maintain its authenticity in the face of
a variety of scientific or epistemological analytic procedures, I
may say that it is a power that develops to completion in a
time-unit that is coextensive with it, and that this development
is the domination of a spatial region during that time unit. But
this abstract saying does no more than express, in a way suited

to the fact that Socrates is also a complex entity, such concrete matters as that Socrates raised the cup to his lip or lifted his cloak from his face to speak to Crito. There is no mode of insight more fundamental or authentic than the one in which we recognize acts of that kind. And it is one circular feature of this meditation — not an offensive one since it involves no deductive circle — that we also exemplify the principle of originative action in our very recognition of it.

2

I have been using the word "infrastructure" so far in a way that emphasizes its connection with the ordinary physical sense of the word "structure." There is some justification for this. If Socrates acts originatively, he wields the physical structure of his body to do so, and in the previous chapter we looked at some consequences of this fact. The concept of infrastructure, though, is a more comprehensive one. It also includes all the functions and processes that take place within the persistent physical structure of the body and, it may be, alter it in one way or another. The process in which a neural cell fires and the more complex one in which a sequence of cells fire belong to the infrastructure of an act. So also do the contraction of a muscle, the movement of a bone, the circulation of the blood, and the production of secretions by ducted or ductless glands. Processes that are of more obvious structural-functional import in that they consist in the production and breakdown of structure — the building up and breakdown of the complex molecules of proteins, hormones, RNA, and the like — form part of the infrastructure. And minute processes like the ionization of atoms and their movement across a synapse or through a membrane play an important role in it. In short, the concept of the infrastructure is that of a spatiotemporal manifold that includes massive structural stability, but also many processes and functions that, though they may be given a structural interpretation in a different context, go on within this massive stability, contributing to and limiting its becoming. We shall take it for granted that an infrastructure consists of levels, and that the theme of unity-in-multiplicity runs through the various levels.

The multiplicity has a spatial sense: abstracting from the temporal feature, we shall be able to detect in any given region structural unities containing structural multiplicities. An organism discloses distinct organs, organs disclose distinct parts or tissues, these distinct cells, and these in turn macromolecules. It will have a temporal sense, also arrived at by abstraction: an act expresses itself in a time-unit, and the time-unit will embrace many distinct happenings that are also time-bound, though not perhaps in the same way: the beat of the heart, the firing of a nerve, the movement and structural breakdown of an organelle, the collapse of a cell vesicle, and so on. The spatial and temporal aspects can not be radically distinguished from each other: the units whose spatial disposition is what we mean by structure are sustained by dynamic units whose temporal aspect of unity-in-multiplicity was touched upon in the earlier discussion of nested dynamisms. On the other hand, the temporal processes that course through them course through spatial regions; and the nested dynamisms themselves possess certain spatial regions.

It will be obvious from all this that if the act endures for a certain time-unit, then some features of the infrastructure are enduring structural features that existed before the act and will exist after it; and that other features are temporally coextensive with the act and are gone when it is gone. In this chapter the term "infrastructure" will include both features, but it will be understood that we are concerned only with that temporal part of the enduring physical structure that is coextensive with the time of the act. In less technical language, the infrastructure of the act includes the body to the extent that the body is wielded in the act, but only that portion of the body's history that coincides with the history of the act.

The reader will recall that, on our supposition (b), which was introduced at the end of the last chapter, one of the features of an originative act—it is clearly the indispensable feature—is that it is not wholly caused (in any sense) by virtue of the

$C \rightarrow E$ relations within its infrastructure. I say "not wholly caused *in any sense*" because it is plain that anyone urging that Socrates' acts were caused by, say, the physiological processes within his body as he seems to perform the act could not reasonably claim that the physiological processes caused the supposed act in a $C \rightarrow E$ sense, since the act would be simultaneous with those processes and indeed in some sense identical with them. But this same restriction holds for the "real causality" we thus ascribe to the act as over against its infrastructure. By definition it stands in no $C \rightarrow E$ relation to the processes of the infrastructure, but is simultaneous and in some sense identical with them.

But in what sense is the act identical with its infrastructure? It will be an odd sort of identity, since we are claiming that there is a power "relation" between the unity of the act and the multiplicity of the infrastructure: we represent the act as a power so permeating the spatiotemporal manifold of the infrastructure as to unify it — the unification being precisely the full concreteness of the act. This may be expressed in a number of other ways: the power of Socrates' act orders, disposes, uses, deploys, shapes, binds together, wields the multiplicity of the spatiotemporal elements that make up its infrastructure. Nonetheless, all the reasons that make the identity theory of the mind-body relation persuasive to so many intelligent people still operate to make for some sort of identity, however odd, between act and infrastructure. Not only is the act exercised by means of the components of the infrastructure, it is also inseparable from them and subject to them. If they are different, the act, and therefore the agent, is different; if their course is difficult and their outcome tragic, the agent suffers accordingly, for he is defined and distinguished by what they in the end have been. If the act shapes the infrastructure, it is also the outcome of the career of the infrastructure; and if the act is a function of an agent, then an agent is also the outcome of his acts.

But whatever the identity may be, it is different from what is called for by the identity theory of mind and body. It is a defining feature of that theory (and, with appropriate changes, of materialism in general) that an exhaustive account of an act of thought can be given in physical terms and that this account will also be a sufficient account of what is sometimes ascribed to mind. Any $C \rightarrow E$ account of the same act that introduced reference to mental entities or events, or to any sort of distinct mental "level," can be reformulated, according to this theory, entirely in physical terms. The identity consists, then, in the fact that the explanation in physical terms is entirely adequate. Alternative accounts in terms of mind only seem to be dealing with something distinguishable, and their inadequacy becomes patent as soon as we produce the account in physical terms. Indeed, the only excuse for the nonphysical account is that there are still lacunae in the physical account. Gradual progress in neurophysiology is therefore in effect construed as confirmation of the identity theory. In this book I am not yet contrasting mind and body but rather act and infrastructure. Transposed into that key, the identity theory would hold that an account of the infrastructure is an adequate account of the act, and that they are therefore identical. On our view the dynamism of the act stands in a "real causal," or power, "relationship" to the infrastructure, and an account of the infrastructure in $C \rightarrow E$ terms would simply leave this out.

The identity between an act and its infrastructure, though real enough, is qualified by this "relation," and as it is a power "relation" between a One and a Many, let us say that the identity between act and infrastructure is one of *asymmetrical identity*. The act "is" its infrastructure by being "in" it, by exercising its power on and by means of the infrastructure, by unifying the infrastructure in a power-unit. The infrastructure, on the other hand, "is" the act by being the multiplicity that is unified by it. It is an identity dismissed in advance by the identity theory propounded by central state materialists. But it is indeed an identity of a kind, and that fact is enough to assure us that the "relation" between an act and its infrastructure is *sui generis,* a fact I shall try to keep before the reader by continuing to use the word in quotation marks in this context. Though *sui generis* it is anything but odd: this "relation" between One and Many is the defining feature of all those hierarchical entities in which nature is so rich.

3

The establishment of this "relation" is the first and most important step in showing the category of originative action to be more fundamental than that of $C \rightarrow E$ causality. It will be obvious, in view of the metaphor of nested dynamisms — and so far it is only a metaphor, that what we must do is to distinguish the becoming of the originative act from the becoming of the multiplicity it is said to unify. And since time, whatever it may be — perhaps a measure of becoming, perhaps our way of apprehending it, is at any rate a necessary concomitant of any discussion of becoming, we must distinguish the temporal unity of the originative act from the temporality of the multiplicity of the infrastructure in which its "real causality" is operative. If the distinction is tenable, then any "identity" between the temporality of the unity and that of the multiplicity must be qualified and asymmetrical. The temporality of the act will be asymmetrically identical with that of the infrastructure in the sense that it pervades it and unifies it, and the temporality of the multiplicity will be asymmetrically identical with the act in the sense that it is unified by it and lends it support. The fundamental contrast established by this asymmetry is between the one temporal unit of the act and the many temporal units of the infrastructure.

A view of time appropriate to the becoming of an act will be radically different from the one associated with the measurement procedures of common sense and science, and it will at first appear strange. There are, however, some precedents in philosophy for certain of its features, and when the initial strangeness is overcome, it will, I think, show itself to be closer to our natural intuitions than the time of event-ontology as that is understood in philosophy of science. Let us consider the latter first. The view of time I have in mind will then be clearer by contrast.

An event-ontology in which the notion of event is given a sense exact enough for the purposes of science is a powerful alternative to the agent-ontology to which we shall eventually be led by the idea of originative action. It takes the expression

"Socrates' agency" to be no more than a primitive and prescientific name for a complex of events of unimaginable intricacy held together by $C \rightarrow E$ relations governed by the laws of nature. Even before science turns the notion of event to its own exact purposes it is a completely flexible notion, flexible enough, certainly, for us to apply it to such different things as the fall of a leaf, the birth of a child, a thunderstorm, the firing of a neuron, or the jump of an electron from one energy state of an atom to another. We apply it to things that presumably have some sort of inherent formal unity, but also to things whose formal unity is in part a function of our interest—the movement, for instance, of an especially striking pattern of light on the ground as the wind moves through the leaves of a tree. This flexibility makes it a ready candidate for quantitative abstraction: whatever inherent unity is to be found in any physical event, it is always open to us to break it up as we will and to call any component of it an event just as readily. We are thus drawn towards an arbitrary and linear sense of "event" in which whatever happens in any determinate region between any time t_1 and any other time t_2 can be so called.

This sense of event carries with it a sense of time that is equally linear, and these combined notions are lent considerable force by their appropriateness for $C \rightarrow E$ analysis. On the basis of what I have called the working version of $C \rightarrow E$ analysis—a version, it will be recalled, that is close to common sense —it is natural to suppose that a nascent event is produced by events in its past. The time in which this takes place is accordingly understood as a directed continuum in which the nascent moment exhibits the same kind of dependence upon moments that are in the past with respect to it. The two events related in $C \rightarrow E$ fashion are in some sense continuous, in some sense distinguishable; so with time past and time present. There is a dependence of the second event upon the first that is intimate, primordial, and difficult to elucidate; so with the relation of the second of two moments of time to the first. There is no reciprocal dependence of the cause upon the effect, and none of the present upon the future. On this view past time is dead, but its power appears in time present, past events are dead and gone, but their power lives in the present events they have produced. Future events do not yet exist and hence exert no power; and future time is therefore unreal in a sense more radical than that in which the past is unreal. It is a view of time in which time either consists of events arranged in a linear way or is the measure of such events.

The Humean, or official, version of $C \rightarrow E$ analysis naturally lacks the theme of the production of the present moment by the past moment. But as we allow the theme of production to recede, the purely linear character of time is heightened. If events are in some sense continuous and in some sense distinguishable, we need only suppress the theme of production to be able to make the distinction between events anywhere we choose. This is the conception of both events and time that is dominant in the philosophy of modern science,[1] and the time-feature of this kind of analysis is strictly linear. The flow of events is a directed line, and any portion of the line we choose, however small or large, can be considered an event. Choose any point on this directed line and that point will partition the line into a "cause" (or earlier) part and an "effect" (or later) part. If it suits us, we may also consider the partitioning point itself to be a point-event.

The expression "act" is not appropriate to an event-ontology of this extreme kind, and what I have been calling the infrastructure of the act would be construed in it as a pattern of events. It is not surprising that an analysis in these terms makes it impossible to find something that can be identified as an act, and therefore impossible to find *Socrates,* gathering the whole of his being into the well-remembered gesture I have been taking as my paradigm for originative action. The consequences of hunting for agency in this way are familiar. We set about looking for a decision, a choice, a volition, a resolve, or something else of that kind that might have initiated a purposeful course of activity. If we locate the desired item (or think we have), then the method we have used implies that it has the status of an event or set of events in that same configuration.

109

But if it is to be the cause of events subsequent to it in the configuration it must also be the effect of events prior to it. No matter how much we are bent upon finding a "free," or "real," or "true" cause, with the mode of attention characterized by event-ontology, linear time, and $C \rightarrow E$ analysis we seem to be able to locate only "causes without which the cause cannot be the cause" — causes, furthermore, that we must also take to be effects. There are, of course, additional complications that I am neglecting. It might, for instance, be thought essential that any event that should qualify as an instance of agency should be a mental event, and the identification of this and the establishment of its place in a series of events, most of which would be physical, would seem to be insurmountable within an event-ontology of the kind just described. Even if found, however, it would be no more a "free," or "true," cause than any other in the chain.

Looked for in this way, the act eludes us. If this is what we mean by "somewhere," then the act, and hence the agent, must be nowhere. Philosophers have put considerable ingenuity into avoiding this consequence, but without much success. The interest in action theory today is the most striking symptom of a general conviction that it is a philosophical dead end to think of an agent in these terms. But it does not follow from this that the agent is unreal. It does not even follow that there is nothing mental about an act of an agent just because mental events conformable to this sense of event can not be found and would be stultifying if they could be found. In that sense the ingenuities of those who labor to demonstrate an identity theory of mind and body by attempting to show that a complete $C \rightarrow E$ account can be given without introducing mental events are in vain.

Let us take the fact that the act of an agent is nowhere to be found in a field discriminated by this mode of attention as a helpful clue to the nature of the agent rather than as a refutation of his existence. He is nowhere to be found in a nexus of events linked in $C \rightarrow E$ terms in linear time because his act is everywhere and at every time in the manifold of an infrastructure understood in other terms.

110

4

The unity (or simplicity) of an originative act expresses itself in a time radically different from the linear kind that is appropriate to event-ontology, and the "relation" between the act and the multiplicity (or complexity) of the infrastructure can accordingly be understood only in terms of that distinctive temporality. Though it is not in the least foreign to our everyday intuitions of time, it is difficult to speak clearly about it; here, even more than in most philosophical discussions of time, St. Augustine's famous saying — if no one asks me about it, I know; if I wish to explain it to an inquirer, I do not know — is not likely to be forgotten.[2] It is also by no means foreign to the intuition of philosophers. Much of what I shall have to say about it has been said before: there are affinities with James's doctrine of the discrete character of time, with Whitehead's epochal theory, which owes so much to James, with Bergson, and even with Heidegger. These writers by no means agree on this topic, but there is something common in what they labor to express, and I shall labor to express it again. The differences between their views and the present one will be clear enough by the end of the chapter.

The simplicity, or unity, of an originative act means that it is exercised in a unit of action that requires a corresponding time-unit for its realization, and that it can not be identified as an exercise of power unless we take the whole time-unit into consideration. Any present "moment" that we might single out by abstraction within the time-unit will have some of the features of the Bergsonian *durée*, although a Bergsonian *durée* does not consist of discrete units. Any such "moment" carries the past of the unit with it, which qualifies it as it develops towards its own completion. On this view, power lies in the *present* of the originative act, although it is no immediate help to say this, since the present itself is ill understood. As the "locus" of power the present has a vitality and "reach" to it that is difficult to elucidate but extremely important: the power is "in" the present but only in the sense that, being exercised there, it is also exercised

111

through what is earlier and later in that unit. Confusing spatial images present themselves: one is tempted, for instance, to speak of the temporally "elsewhere"; and no doubt that kind of talk only obscures the issue. What I have in mind has really very little in common with reaching out from some spatial location to other distinct locations. But the spatial image may at least help to suggest that a present "moment" in the temporality of an originative act bears the whole of that unit's past and future in it, bears them not as their respective register and container, but as the focus of their enactment.

The time of the action is just as isomorphic with the action itself as this suggests: indeed there is no time of the action that is distinct from the action in a way that might make the enacted unity an anomalous violation of the condition established by time's equable flow. (If there is another sense in which time does flow equably and continuously — and I think there is — it need not concern us just yet.) The exercise of power is temporal only in the sense that its time is one feature of it — a feature quite inseparable from the content of the act. The becoming of the action is precisely a unified becoming and its temporality is merely that unit of becoming considered in a certain way. The order we distinguish within it as we apprehend it in terms of earlier and later is given by the present exercise of power. But it follows that this holds for any present "moment" of the action we consider: each of them is the enactment of that same order. If we regard each of them as interpenetrating with all others of that action unit, then every one is an exercise of the power of the originative act. If we regard each as thoroughly distinguishable, isolatable, its whole essence "gone" as soon as we can distinguish another "now," then none of them can be regarded as an exercise of power. It is of the nature of the power of an originative act that it reaches throughout a span distinct as to its limits and ordered within those limits both as to content and temporality. Thus, if we represent the time of some particular action by a curved arrow from beginning to end as in figure 6, any present "moment" in it that the artifice of analysis might distinguish "reaches out" to, or is "in," every other "moment"

112

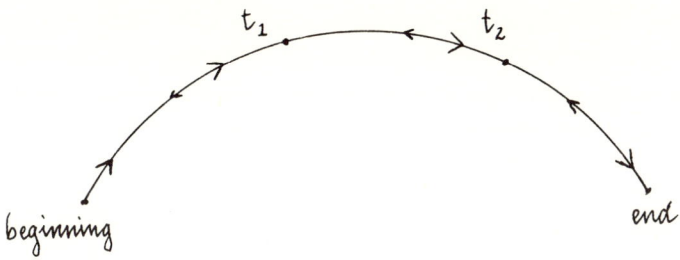

Figure 6

in a mode appropriate to the order of the action. We represent the "direction" of time (its anisotropic character) by the large arrowheads pointing from left to right, which incidentally also serve to indicate its "reach" in that "direction"; we represent the "reach" of any "moment" towards the past, by smaller arrowheads pointing in the other direction. The "moment" t_1, regarded as some present moment of the power, reaches out to t_2 in such a way that t_2 is "in" it in the mode of the future; and t_2, similarly regarded, reaches out to and sustains t_1 in the mode of the past. The very distinctness of t_1 and t_2 is blurred, for the order of earlier and later in terms of which we distinguish them is laid down by the exercise of the one power that has enacted itself *in* them.

An originative act therefore transcends the linear time of an event-ontology. If we consider figure 6 in terms of point-events distinguishable as t_1 and t_2 are, there is no exercise of power "at" t_1 or t_2, none in the interval from the beginning to t_1 and none in the interval from t_1 to t_2. The power is exercised only throughout the whole sweep from beginning to end. But if we interpret the diagram in terms of the vitality of the present of an originative act, then neither t_1 nor t_2, nor for that matter any "point" that analysis might distinguish, can really be regarded as an event that can be precisely *located:* any creative present of this sort "reaches back" to the beginning and to all past "phases" that lie between it and the beginning, sustaining them in the mode of existence appropriate to the past; and it

113

"reaches forward" to the completion of the action, holding future "phases" in its anticipatory grasp in a mode of existence appropriate to the future. It is the very mode of existence of the present that it should "reach out" thus in two "directions," sustaining the past and anticipating the future to complete the act. In that sense *any* "moment" of the unit we might consider is an exercise of power.

Let us call this view of time *act-temporality*. It is obvious that if we insist on analyzing an originative act into earlier and later moments, or earlier and later phases, and if we wish to think of such moments or phases as concrete units, rather than as those "moments" whose "reach" justifies our treating them as abstractions from the utter unity of the act to which they belong, then our analysis will deal either with sub-acts, which are not considered in this chapter, or with units of the act's infrastructure, which are. It will also be obvious that a sub-act will have its own act-temporality, as seamless as that of the superordinate act. It is not as yet obvious, though it is at least plausible, that there will be some units in the infrastructure that will have an act-temporality of their own, analogous to the act-temporality of the originative act, and so we shall set that question aside for awhile. But the central point about act-temporality is that no "moment" distinguishable within it will have the kind of unity attributable to a unit of act-temporality taken as a whole. The becoming of an originative act, considered as a power-unit "related" to an infrastructure, can not be analyzed into concrete units that are "parts" of the act-unit.

When we apply the language of causality to this view of the time of the originative action we find it gives rise to paradoxes. Any present of an originative act carries its past with it as qualifying it, but it is just as accurate to say that the present exercise of power causes that past as that the past has caused the present. Any present exercise of power brings about the future, but it is just as accurate to say that the future causes the present exercise of power as that the present causes the future. Some other traditional senses of causality (e.g., formal or final) might conceivably be used to supplement $C \rightarrow E$ causality and thus

114

do away with the paradox. No doubt other conceptual difficulties would then arise. Certainly some supplementation of $C \rightarrow E$ causality would be needed even to state the paradox intelligibly, for clearly the future can not be operative in the present in a $C \rightarrow E$ sense. But the paradoxes will not appear at all if $C \rightarrow E$ causality, together with whatever is of permanent worth in the other three Aristotelian senses of cause, can be derived from the concept of an originative action, and thus, ultimately, from the concept of an agent.

The view of time here presented is that time consists of the discrete units of the becoming of act-temporal units and that *within those units* there is a continuum both primordial and *sui generis*. It presents itself as "real," "underived," "unconstructed," and it is folly to seek to supplant it with a model that is "clearer," more "well-defined," more "intelligible," if the adequacy of such a model can only be judged by asking how well it reproduces the characteristics the unit-continuum itself discloses.

This is not meant as a criticism of models of a continuum —a continuum transcending such discrete units—that are devised for some purpose other than the understanding of becoming. It may well be that the event-ontology prevalent in today's physics requires that the scientist and the philosopher of science work with a temporal continuum understood as a "dense" structure of an infinitude of point-instants. But that is a continuum from which the time in which an action *becomes* has been left out, a point that has been conceded by Grünbaum.[3] There is no "reach" to the point-instants of such a structure: its continuity consists precisely in a denseness in which there are distinguishable elements, each precisely its isolatable self, each assignable to just that location in the continuum and to no other. And though the continuum is intricately dense, so dense that there is no nearest neighbor to any given point, it is also inert: in its frozen *staccato* each point is held aloof from every other. Indeed, the same principle that makes for denseness makes also for aloofness, for the continuum is defined by the possibility of choosing one and only one point that we may characterize as a *now* and use as a Dedekind partition to divide all other points of time into the two classes of past and future, to neither of which the chosen point will belong. It is an instance of the "no nearest neighbor" principle that when the "points" of time are ordinally arranged and thus partitioned there will be no greatest member in the class of the past and no least member in the class of the future, and though this might be seen to be the essence of the mathematical model of the continuum, mitigating the isolation of any one point, it is no more the essence of it than the principle that makes for the awful isolation of the partitioning *now.* For the theoretic purposes it was designed for, it is an admirable model. But the elegance of its infinite *staccato* misses the characteristic of action that, in the literal sense of *legato,* binds the development of a unit of action together in a continuum—the temporal "reach" of the creative present.

The artifice of an analysis of time in terms of point-instants has its dangers for $C \rightarrow E$ analysis as well, or at least for a working version of $C \rightarrow E$ analysis used as a version of becoming. The only way we can make $C \rightarrow E$ analysis even plausible as a version of becoming is to keep our understanding of it vague and commonsensical, as it is in what I have been calling the working view. By some unexamined recourse to a *legato* connection between the C and the $E,$ the working view of $C \rightarrow E$ causality might allow us to think in terms of a becoming initiated somewhere in the past and continuing into the present. The "reach" of any present "forward" into a future, which would thus play a role in the development of the power, would however remain an impossibility. Only the past would be efficacious. There is some, but only a very limited, justification that can be given for such a commonsensical understanding of $C \rightarrow E$ analysis, and I shall eventually try to give one. But when we turn to an understanding of it in terms of the event-ontology of physics, the linear character of $C \rightarrow E$ analysis is pressed to its ultimate conclusion, and we are in the more Humean atmosphere of the official view. An event has whatever temporal and spatial size we find it convenient to specify. What is important is that the event taken as the cause be so locatable that when

116

the laws of nature are invoked it should be possible to determine what event or events will succeed it as the effect. The concept of event is more and more purged of becoming as our purposes require us to locate an event with more and more temporal precision. To the degree we succeed in isolating it as taking place at a temporal point t, we deprive it of any tie with a succeeding event beyond the fact that the succession is an infinitely close one. However "dense" a structure one then provides for the time of such events by resort to the analogy between any moment t and any point in the continuum of real numbers, it is hard to see how a *legato* suitable for becoming can be contrived.

Since on the present view the power exercised in an originative act is the prototype of concrete becoming, the associated view of time is that time is either power in this sense or the measure of it. Action is a temporal thing, understandable only in terms of time, but on the other hand it is as much necessary to explain time as time is necessary to explain it. It is in that spirit that one may attribute to act-temporality the same characteristics one claims to find in an exercise of power. The unity of an action fixes upon the end and still retains the beginning at the end, and so with the time that in one sense lies at the base of the action and in another sense is a creation of it. The end of the action "influences" the beginning, although it is not yet there; the future "influences" the present, although it is not yet there. The beginning of the action "influences" the end although it is already "gone"; the past "influences" the present although it is already "gone." Present, and present for the whole time of the action—present in the sense that the time of the action-unit has its source in it—is the power of the originative action.

5

The discreteness of act-temporal units is, I have claimed, characterized by an internal continuity of a unique sort. It "reaches" in both "directions"; which is to say that within it we can not find other units analogous to the act-temporal one, unless, to be sure, we turn our attention away from the power of the act to the multiplicity (either of subacts or of infrastructure-units) that is subject to that power. How many and what kinds of units in the infrastructure exemplify a temporal unity analogous to act-temporality is not at once clear. It does appear that the smallest entities accessible to the indirect observation of physics do indeed exercise it. It is well known that below a certain magnitude the idea of a particle, which is to say the idea of a continuously enduring physical body, becomes inapplicable. Entities of this size have a spatial existence that is not constant but develops in a changing pattern that requires a time-unit for its realization. Their very occupancy of a spatial region is not continuous but develops, then recedes, and is gone, to be succeeded by another such pattern. Entities of this sort can not indeed be said to occupy a spatial region, though they might be said to possess it for a time. And their very status as continuous entities is ambiguous, so much so that Whitehead, who was the first to give the physics of the very small a concrete interpretation of this kind (although not exactly this one), regarded each distinct time-bound pattern as a distinct entity, called in his terminology an "actual entity," whose existence was over and done with when the pattern had been expressed. The continuous entity that physics takes for granted, as when it supposes that it can identify the track of a given electron in a cloud chamber, Whitehead interpreted as a succession of time-bound entities—a "society," or "route," of "actual entities." The time-bound character of entities of that kind is the fundamental doctrine of his epochal theory of time. No doubt William James, so much admired by Whitehead, furnished the original suggestion, with his claim that the temporality associated with subjective experience consists of discrete units or droplets. The theory of act-temporality has obvious resemblances to Whitehead's doctrine, but this fundamental difference, that I take it for granted that an act-temporal unit can embrace in its span countless numbers of such vibratory, or wavelike, happenings, and

118

that, though a discrete unit itself, it is utterly continuous over against the discrete successiveness of the units it embraces. Whitehead's epochal theory is based upon the opposed atomistic assumption that discrete time-units are of the smallest possible size only.[4]

If the clearest parallel within the infrastructure of an act to its own act-temporality lies in the temporality of the smallest units that can be found there, there are other plausible cases at a higher level of the infrastructure. Each of them has, however, some difficulty or ambiguity about it. A given pattern of neural activity in, say, the associational part of the cerebral cortex clearly has act-temporal features of a significant kind. The pattern spreads through an intricate spatial manifold defined by the ramifications of the neural net through which it courses, and its existence is a temporal one — that is, the pattern is not complete, and its role in mentality thus presumably ineffective, until the temporal period needed for fulfillment is completed. Yet, though such complex patterns, insofar as they have some originality to them, may be novel as to the exact neural pathways traversed, the preexistence of *some* more or less enduring pathways of the central nervous system is a precondition for it. Other plausible cases are the firing of a nerve cell, the contraction of a muscle cell, the contraction and expansion of the heart, but these are even more tightly bound to the existence of more or less persistent physical structures. These examples will come up later in another connection. Meanwhile, it is clear that the time of an enduring physical structure can not be exhaustively interpreted in terms of the discrete elements of act-temporality. Before turning to that, though, it is worth remembering that all biological structures in their cycle of growth and dissolution can be construed as patterns whose deployment in space, whose very existence in space, requires a time-span for its realization or enactment. In that sense they clearly have something important in common with the minute vibratory entities that lie at the lowest identifiable level of their infrastructures.

The theme of the continuous endurance of physical structures is a convenient one for introducing the continuous aspect of time. Below a certain level of magnitude, where wavelike features are important, the spatiality of a unit and its act-temporality are one. A unit at that level has no continuous space-filling character, though it may possess a spatial region in a growing and receding pattern that develops in the time-unit appropriate to it. It is, in short, a spatiotemporal pattern, and not a spatial entity that endures for a time. But the structure of entities above that level consists of a multiplicity of distinguishable units in more or less stable spatial relationships. This is true of atoms and molecules, and it would remain true of them even if we later found some grounds for supposing that the power that holds their component units in a continuing spatial order was a periodic and act-temporal one: for the spatial order *as* persistent, *as* stable, *as* continuous, can scarcely be regarded as act-temporal. And *a fortiori* this is true for larger biological structures whose components are molecules and atoms. Considered purely as stable structures made up of a multiplicity of units, there is an element in them that resists act-temporal interpretation, even though act-temporality should turn out to pervade them and perhaps even to play the major role in sustaining them. The temporal correlate of this mode of being is the continuous time in which they persist, are moved about, form combinations, and so on. There is, in short, a mode of becoming different from that of acts and from that in which, as we may suppose, an entity like an agent develops. The temporality of this becoming is that for which the metaphor of continuous flow is roughly appropriate: these structures, considered precisely as structures, are passive within the passage of a continuous time. The ontological ground of this continuity may, as I suggest, be a multiplicity of discrete units. But when we look at becoming not in terms of the discrete contribution to it by an act-temporal unit but rather in terms of the massive temporal environment in which such discrete contributions take place, becoming is continuous, and so, therefore, is time. Within it any given act-temporal unit will be *after* some act-temporal units and *before* some others.

If we regard act-temporal units as ontologically fundamental, this continuous aspect of time must be regarded as derivative in the sense that the massive temporal environment in which any act-temporal unit takes place is made up of a vast multiplicity of other act-temporal units. This is a conception congruent with the interpretation of an enduring physical structure as a multiplicity of such units. Each act-temporal unit is to be understood as making a discrete contribution to this aspect of time, but their infinite variety in length and their intricate overlappings make that temporal environment for any one of them a continuum as real as the internal continuity of act-temporal units themselves. Each originative act, each act-temporal power, enacts its time-unit, and in doing so it contributes to both a general temporal environment and a general environment of power. Though ontologically derivative, the aspect of temporal continuity is thus no less real for that. It is the time in which more or less persistent physical structures exist continuously, though sustained by actlike units that become in an act-temporal measure. Time "flows" all around us whether we act as persons or are at rest, and our bodies, as more or less enduring physical objects, belong to that flow. When we act, we enact our time; when we do not, we undergo the time of other entities, our bodies then being included in that category. But, even as we enact our time, we do so only in and with a temporal environment that is continuous and just as objective as the fact that reality includes an aspect of multiplicity. The continuity of time is as real as the multiplicity of the discrete act-temporal power units that contribute to it.

6

But the argument seems to have carried us too far. Faced with this seamless unity of an originative act, one wonders what has become of the complexity, or multiplicity, that it was said both to unify and to be in some sense identical with. The originative act now seems a One as indivisible as Parmenides' great sphere of Being, although no doubt less static than that. Where is the Many that seemed also to belong to Socrates' act?

Well, in one sense it has been before us all this while, for the seamless unity represented by the sweep of the curved arrow is, if real, an ordering unification of precisely that complexity. That same unit of action, quite seamless when we think of it as a unit of becoming, so intimately pervades the spatiotemporal multiplicity of what it unifies that we can not identify it except in terms of its "relation" to them. Indeed we can not specify the unification except in terms of its pervasion of a particular multiplicity. Consider any of those originative acts we tentatively attributed to Socrates — say his uncovering of his face towards the end to make his last request to Crito. Though we suppose the act to have the time-binding unity here proposed, it is so much "related" to the persistent physical structure in which and by means of which it is carried out that it is identical with it in the asymmetrical sense that it is what it is only in giving unity to that complexity.

This physical structure is a multiplicity in a spatial sense — a structure of many interlinked parts, and its existence has developed over a period of time within which multiple events can be distinguished. It is permeated constantly by processes, or functions, in which its structure is maintained and in which it expresses itself. Whether we approach it from the point of view of space or of time, the number of units that analysis can reveal in the infrastructure is enormous, so much so that if we think of the unification of infrastructure by act in terms of the flat contrast between the unity of the originative act and the uttermost complexity of the physiological processes that form part of its infrastructure, the consequences are preposterous. In what sense, for instance, does the act of uncovering his face *unify* the several heartbeats, the multiple firing of some single nerve cell or of some neural chain, the vast number of chemical changes in each of his cells, and all the other minute incidents that take place within the time-span of the act? Some of them plainly would have been little or no different even if the act we are speaking of had been quite different. It is all less preposterous, however, when we remember that the contrast between the unity of an originative act and the uttermost multiplicity of its infrastructure is a mediated one. It is mediated in a sense for which we have been prepared by the theme of control exercised by subsystems, which was developed in our discussion of hierarchic science; by the idea of "nested dynamisms" proposed in the previous chapter; and by a number of classical philosophical precedents mentioned earlier, among them Aristotle's doctrine of the relativity of the distinctions between form and matter, and Leibniz's doctrine of the dominance exercised by a given monad over subordinate monads by way of intervening monads. The topic of mediation is, however, a complex one, so let us set it aside for awhile in favor of an attempt to represent the temporal and spatial aspects of the multiplicity (or complexity) of the infrastructure that we have set in contrast with the unity (or simplicity) of the act that pervades it.

A power temporal in the sense we have been discussing expresses itself in and unifies an infrastructure one feature of which is a spatial multiplicity—an enduring physical structure, a body—of great complexity. With this in mind, I repeat an earlier formula with modifications: an originative act of Socrates unifies, orders, disposes, binds together an unimaginable multiplicity of subordinate powers; but it is also subject to them, suffers them, is their outcome, and is asymmetrically identical with them. It is an abstraction to consider this complexity in purely physiological terms, but as there is likely to be more agreement about clearly physiological features of the infrastructure, let us begin there.

The physiological complexity of the infrastructure occupies a spatial volume and it has a history, some aspects of which we can register in a variety of ways. Any one way, say the polygraph or the electroencephalograph, may be important for some special purpose, but it will only scratch the surface of the underlying complexity. If we put together the results of a number of techniques, the register is probably still superficial. If the originative act has the characteristics claimed for it, then these various aspectual records fit together in the form of a complex history for the recording of whose totality we have no observational device. Indeed, given some ideal register of that complexity, we should not be able to recognize in it the unity of the single act we began with. There is no reason why we should, for what we are registering is the complexity of the *infrastructure*. If we assume the complexity to be under the power of an act-temporal order, then any present "moment" for it that we might isolate by abstraction will consist of a multiplicity of spatially distinct elements. Let us represent the spatial aspect of an act at such a "moment" by a bounded plane passed through the curved line

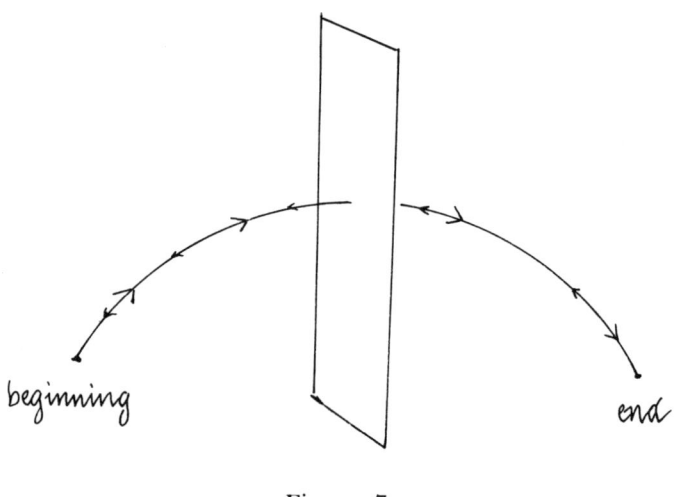

beginning   end

Figure 7

of act-temporality at right angles to it, as in figure 7. There are certain difficulties about the diagram. *(1)* Since the plane and the line intersect at a particular point we seem to be locating the "now" of the line at some particular point in the spatial complexity of the act's infrastructure. This is of course not intended. The intersection of plane and line means merely that any present "moment" of the act that we might single out from some abstract viewpoint is the present "moment" of an entire spatial configuration. *(2)* There is the additional obscurity that the three dimensions of ordinary space are represented by a plane. We shall have to remember that any given point on the

124

plane corresponds to some particular point in a three-dimensional space — say, for instance, some location in the cortex — and that other points on the plane are elsewhere not on a plane but in that same three-dimensional space — say some other location in the cortex, or some location in the thalamus, heart, or liver. Taken as a whole, the plane is meant to represent the full spatial complexity of a temporal slice through the whole action. *(3)* The final diagrammatic obscurity is that the power of the originative act seems to operate at a point-instant and to pervade a three-dimensional spatial region of elements simultaneous with it. We have already seen, in discussing the "reach" of any present "moment" of the action-unit, that this will not do: the power of the act is exercised throughout the whole time span, although it is exercised by the "reach" of the creative present. To the degree that the power relationship pervading the spatial region is an act-temporal one, and to the degree that there are some elements in the infrastructure that share this act-temporal character — and it would appear that, at the least, happenings at the quantum level share it, any interpretation we give a "simultaneous" spatial slice must exclude the idea that it is defined by a point-instant. I shall say that the plane identifies a set of spatially distinct elements that are in *act-temporal simultaneity* but are nevertheless bound together by power.

This term is to be taken to mean that the notion of simultaneity becomes ambiguous in a context where at least some of the temporal units involved in the infrastructure have themselves the "reach" of act-temporality. In figure *7A,* for instance, the concentric circles represent nested three-dimensional spatial regions some of which might be permeated by act-temporality in a way analogous to the permeation of the *total* region by act-temporality as in figure *7.*

We shall not attempt to be clearer about the nature of act-temporal simultaneity than this. It will mean at least this much, however, that the spatial region represented by the plane is permeated by a power which, though in essence act-temporal, has a spatial "reach" that is not elucidated by this sense of temporal passage, nor indeed by any other, and to which, ac-

125

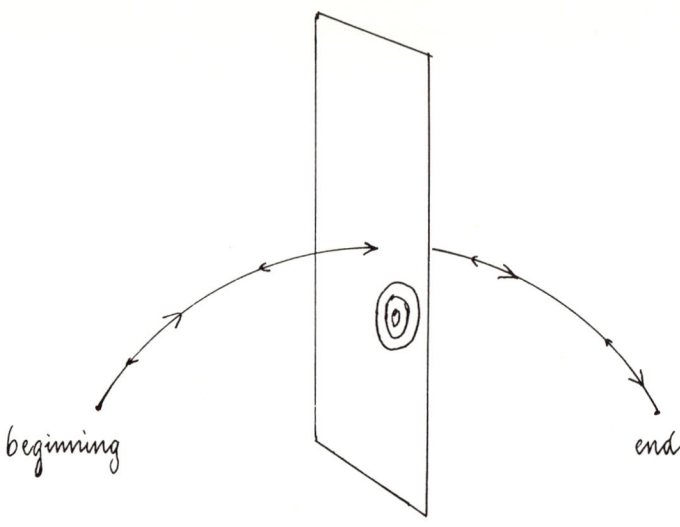

Figure 7A

cordingly, the idea of $C \rightarrow E$ causality, tied as it is to temporal successiveness, it especially irrelevant. The spatial "reach" of the power is not being interpreted as acting *from* some particular location, *at* a point-instant, *across* a space, consuming time in the transaction. Therefore even if the idea of simultaneity here employed were tied to the notion of the point-instant, the claims made for the spatial "reach" of this power would not violate the physical principle that excludes $C \rightarrow E$ relations between events defined as simultaneous. The point is rather that there is a spatial aspect to act-temporal power: it is pervasive of space in a way analogous to its pervasion of a time-unit, and we do not elucidate this aspect adequately by referring it to temporal becoming — not even to the temporal becoming of act-temporality, and certainly not to that proper to $C \rightarrow E$ causality.

The idea of the (act-temporal) simultaneity of the spatial region represented by the plane is however of vital importance, for what it means in terms of act is that there are influences pervading a spatial region and binding the elements of the re-

126

gion together in a power relation, even though some of those elements can not significantly be said to be earlier or later than any of the others. Stated in this way the power relation seems puzzling if not incredible. It is easy to dismiss it by pointing out that simultaneous entities or events can in no way influence one another and therefore can neither support an act nor be developed by it; and to point out instead influences that are nonsimultaneous, and that can therefore be dealt with by some version of $C \rightarrow E$ analysis. There are really only two ways of doing this. *(a)* We may, for instance, take particular influences and deal with them seriatim. The blood that passes through Socrates' heart now, we may insist, will later be at some other point in his body; and, if his heart should fail now, his brain will be affected later. *(b)* We may instead consider the total simultaneous spatial complexity represented by our plane as a total state at a point-instant and relate it to a later state in $C \rightarrow E$ terms, setting aside the relation between the simultaneous elements of both states as in no way significant of any power aspect that is missed by our analysis. Proceeding in either way, however, we simply refuse to assign any ontological authenticity to the *act* of uncovering the face, except as a summation of such particular $C \rightarrow E$ influences or as a succession of such total states.

Puzzling and obscure though they are, the simultaneous power relations represented by figure 7 must be taken seriously if we are to take an originative act seriously. The representation is no doubt defective, yet it has the virtue of making it clear that an originative act, if real, is among other things the act of an entire spatial region. If Socrates moves his hand and uncovers his face, his act is the wielding of all the elements of that spatial region. As in acting he does not act before the act to cause the act, so we can not without loss, resolve the act itself into a set of particular $C \rightarrow E$ relations within the spatial region. The act ripples like a wave through the whole of the spatial region, but if it is indeed an act, then the wave is a shaping of that entire spatial region over a time-span that has its own unique temporal "shape."

Some simultaneous power relations are not in the least

127

mysterious: they simply go unnoticed because they are so taken for granted. These are the powers that bind together persistent structural features, as, for instance, those that make up Socrates' body. Its elements are by definition simultaneous, bound together by the forces that make them one structure and place them, so to speak, at the disposal of the agent who is asymmetrically identical with them. Nature is full of examples of structural stabilities held together in simultaneous array by powers that consume no time to traverse the spatial regions they pervade and govern. The cells at the base of the tree trunk support cells in its crown that are simultaneous with them, even though analysis of any change taking place at the base will show its effects reaching the crown somewhat later. A nucleotide in a DNA helix supports and is held by the total structure simultaneous with it — that is indeed part of what we mean by such a helix — and this point is not in the least turned by noting that a happening in which an impact on a component of the nucleotide produces a mutation, and thus changes the total structure, must take up some time. Nor is it turned by the fact that the measurement of any such simultaneous force must be by way of a technique that will involve a $C \rightarrow E$ transaction. The point is generalizable to the various forces in nature that bind together any one of those patterned becomings that we think of as stable structures: gravity, the chemical bond, the hydrogen bond, the immensely stronger forces that hold the atomic nucleus together are cases in point; for the elements bound are indeed bound, and the entities they are bound to, and the forces they are bound by, are simultaneous. At least, there appears to be no sense we can attach to the idea that the forces that bind them take time to traverse the space between them. The entities so bound may be temporal entities — indeed, I assume that they are — and the forces that bind them may be inseparable from these temporal features, but that does not mean that these forces traverse the space between them in, say, the way that light does. If we try to set aside this curious feature of things, claiming, perhaps, that any structure in nature consists of an assemblage of units, and that the only power relations discernible in nature are the nonsimultaneous effects of these subunits upon other subunits of the same sort, we shall find that that same curious feature of nature reasserts itself in each of the subunits: if they are themselves structures or even patterned activities, then they also have infrastructures consisting of simultaneous spatial complexities bound by power relationships that can not be analyzed in terms of a time required for their exercise.

Though simultaneous forces of this sort enter into the power exercised in an originative act, they are only one factor in it. As the originative action develops through its act-temporal unit, it uses or wields forces like those in using or wielding the physical structure at its disposal. As it does so, the totality of simultaneous forces permeating the body and constituting the full spatial "reach" of the act's power will change continually throughout the course of the act. That is the way in which the unity of the temporal "reach" of the act makes itself felt throughout the multiplicity of the infrastructure. This pervasion of the spatial region of the infrastructure by the power of the act-in-becoming does not permit us to single out the $C \rightarrow E$ influence of one spatial element upon another one that is simultaneous with it, for there is no such influence. The only "influence" is the unifying one of the act, and it consists only in this, that the multiplicity of distinguishable elements disposed simultaneously throughout the spatial region behave in concert. In and with the multiplicity of his structured body, in and with everything that the physiologist seeks to discover, Socrates *acts,* and the multiple elements move together in an infinitely complicated concord in which at any point there will be an act-temporal simultaneity of elements bound by his power.

The diagram of figure 7 is thus too simple to capture the complexity of the "relation" between act and infrastructure. Socrates' act-temporality "shapes" the spatial region in a temporal order, shifting spatial emphasis in the realization of the becoming of which it is the unity. Socrates' whole body is involved, though in the act that is our present example he is lying still throughout it: he raises his arm, bringing his hand to his face to lift the cloak, and, this done, he moves his lips in speech.

129

The spatial region "shaped" thus by the unity of the act will also submit to $C \rightarrow E$ analysis as we look back from any "moment" at which analysis intervenes: the firing of the motor nerves involved in the speech movements of larynx, tongue, and lips comes after the firing of the motor nerves involved in the lifting of the cloak from the face. Though it would be odd and unilluminating to say that the cause of the speech was the lifting of the cloak, the whole chain of physical events will nevertheless display a sequence of unbroken $C \rightarrow E$ continuity, and any neural or other physiological event that analysis seizes upon will be intelligible as the E, under law, of some prior event or events taken as a C, and the C (or one of them) of some subsequent event taken as an E. But in this way we merely pick out seriatim certain causal sequences that we isolate from their backgrounds. Focusing on any one such event we ignore if not all, then at least most of those that are in act-temporal simultaneity with it, and it is this total pattern that we must regard as being wielded by the originative act if we take the act-temporality seriously. It is in the total pattern of a spatial "region" that the "real causality" of an originative action is felt, but, so far from being at odds with $C \rightarrow E$ analysis, this very claim requires that any "subregion" of it be intelligible in $C \rightarrow E$ terms. There will be no way we can "measure" or otherwise calculate the power that spatially pervades an act-temporal simultaneity, for intervention of that kind relies upon the $C \rightarrow E$ relation between the situation measured and the measuring instrument, and there is no $C \rightarrow E$ successiveness in the way that power pervades such a simultaneity. The act-temporality of the originative act we therefore suppose to be wielding elements not relatable in a $C \rightarrow E$ sense, and wielding them by virtue of a power not intelligible in $C \rightarrow E$ terms, in a total complex process whose aftermath can certainly be illuminated to a degree by $C \rightarrow E$ analysis.

It is worth pursuing a little further the question why we can not measure or otherwise detect in a direct physical sense the power by which an act-temporal unit pervades a spatial region. We saw earlier that a hierarchically ordered structure (like Socrates' body), when it persists and is reiterated in the usual biological cycle, plays somewhat the role that a hierarchic law is said to play by hierarchic scientists. An act-temporal power, pervading such a structure and supplementing the regularities it lays down, also bears some resemblances, or so I claimed in chapter 2, to the way in which a law might be said to pervade a region. But there are some important differences. An act-temporal "law" is as much in becoming as any of the entities and processes in the infrastructure it is said to govern by its "relation" to them. If we attempt to isolate its "influence" upon a certain spatial region, trying, perhaps, to determine just how an act Socrates is engaged in "influences" in a law-like way some area in his cerebral cortex, we shall get a null result. On our hypothesis, an analysis of this "influence" must involve the whole spatial region that is in act-temporal simultaneity with it; but if we set out to determine just what this means in terms of the physical forces or states prevalent throughout the region, all we have to investigate are the *ad hoc* physical parameters of the structures and processes that constitute the region. The only way to do this is to abandon the act-temporality we are trying to comprehend and turn instead to the continuous time relevant to the $C \rightarrow E$ analysis of physical events, for we must place our instruments in some sort of $C \rightarrow E$ relationship with whatever we intend to measure with them. That is a familiar problem in all physical meaurement, but if we are using such procedures to detect a law or a structure that is by definition a stability that transcends the moment and place of measurement, it offers no problems, and indeed can be turned to some advantage. In a particle reaction, for instance, the measurable energy gained or lost may be taken as a clue to the nature of the relative stability of the structures involved in the reaction, and this stability may then be interpreted in terms of the laws of nature or may be used to make adjustments in existing laws. But as we deal now with the permeation of a spatial region (Socrates' body) by the act-temporal unity of the becoming of his act, the unique nature of this act-temporal "law" prevents such a move. Our attempt to give a physical account of it turns out to be a physical account of something else—most likely, in this case, an account of the particular boundary conditions under which known physical laws operate.[5] If, aware of this difficulty, we insist that what we are really interested in is the *simultaneous* slice of spatial elements represented by our planes of the diagrams in figures 7 and 7A, we find not only that we have no physical way of analyzing the very simultaneity of that slice, but also that we can in principle detect no influence of one spatial element in it on another spatial element.

Our helplessness about this last point may, however, be used to illuminate the curious nature of the power I believe myself to be calling attention to: one such spatial element *has* no such influence on other elements in act-temporal simultaneity with it, for it is the originative act as a whole that "influences" the total spatiotemporal region in which it develops and with which it is "related." Its pervasiveness is *sui generis:* it pervades the infrastructure by being responsible for (the "real cause," or "true cause," of) the fact that all the elements in the simultaneous region are together in a concourse within which there are no $C \rightarrow E$ influences.

To put it differently, the act *is* that concourse of elements in act-temporal simultaneity, a simultaneity including but not limited to the simultaneity of the persistent physical structures involved. And, beyond the role played by the stability of the laws of nature (however interpreted) there is simply no other reason why the concourse is as it is. No wonder, then, that the idea of chance, or random, configurations is so often brought forward to "explain" what are from one point of view the arbitrary or *ad hoc* parameters of a physical situation that in all respects is lawful, since these parameters do nothing if not exemplify the usual laws of nature.

The application of the idea of law to the way the act-temporality of an originative act commands the spatiotemporal region of its infrastructure is therefore only a metaphor. It is a persuasive metaphor perhaps only when act-temporalities of this sort make for the reiteration of their own most general features in subsequent acts. A habit of Socrates, engendered by past acts of Socrates, exhibits a lawlike regularity that may be interpreted in this way; and any physical changes at the level of circuit patterns made permanent by structural changes at the molecular level would be the physical correlatives of such lawlike regularity.

With all this in mind, we may now see an authentic sense in which, when Socrates raises his hand, every molecule in that hand not only supports the action in which he raises it but is also used, moved, deployed by that action. Indeed the action is identical with the multiplicity of the infrastructure in an asymmetrical sense of "identity" related to our use of words like both "support" or "use." Though analysis will reveal important non-simultaneous $C \rightarrow E$ relations between molecules in his fingers and those in his cerebral cortex, it would appear that we can not even begin such analysis except in a context of simultaneous relations that are taken for granted. Difficult to elucidate as they are, they may be the key not only to action but to all entities whatsoever that our intelligence is capable of grasping.

Returning to figure 7, we shall assume that any plane transecting the curved line represents a three-dimensional complexity of elements that, although simultaneous, are held in a power relation by the originative act represented by the curved line, and that any such slice will "reach out" temporally to every other such slice that we might pass through our curved line of act-temporality. Consider now some particular element in such a slice, say a "moment" in the firing of a single cortical cell in the associational area. Let us suppose that our discussion so far has made it plausible that there is a "reach" of any "moment" in its firing to any other "moment" in the same firing, a supposition we shall have to qualify in the next chapter. But the interpretation just given of the entire act of Socrates in terms of figure 7 now requires that we regard the entire firing of that cell as "reaching out" to all past or future firings of the same cell, or even of quite different cells that lie within the scope of the act we are considering. The importance of this will be seen if we suppose, what is surely sometimes the case, that a given cortical cell in the associational areas may fire many times in the course of some given act of Socrates that involves speech or thought, perhaps under a somewhat different set of synaptic stimuli each time. The "reach" of one firing to another firing under the unifying temporality of the act would then be an important expression of the unity of the act. But a "reach" of this kind is quite a different matter from the "reach" of some moment in the firing of a cell to some other moment in the *same* firing. So too with the even greater "reach" we must ascribe to any molecular or submolecular happening within such a firing as it "reaches out" to molecular happenings in some quite different firing. It is possible for us to take these "reaches" as seriously as the view here presented requires us to take them only if we suppose them to be mediated by the "reach" of the subordinate powers that intervene between the utter unity of the act and the final complexity of the infrastructure. This topic of mediation, so important to this whole view, we shall however continue to defer awhile in favor of the completion of the account of the multiplicity of the infrastructure. Having emphasized the spatial multiplicity of the infrastructure in this section, we turn now to the multiplicity of its temporal aspect.

7

Though the act-temporality of an originative act is seamless, the temporality of its infrastructure is not. I have already suggested that at the level of the smallest magnitudes accessible to the indirect observation of science, which, so far as we can tell, is the level at which the infrastructure reaches its uttermost multiplicity, there are entities whose very existence appears to consist in the reiterated realization of a spatial power-pattern that is absolutely inseparable from the time-unit required for its completion. The reiterative character of these patterns made it so questionable to think of a sequence of them as a continuous entity that Whitehead's suggestion that each distinct pattern should be regarded as an entity (an "actual entity"), and a sequence of them as a "route," seemed to have something to recommend it. Without attempting to settle the question

whether the metaphysical terminology he put forward is a satisfactory one, we may still say with some show of plausibility that
the uttermost complexity of the infrastructure calls for interpretation in act-temporal terms. Our earlier and purely temporal
diagrams may now be used to represent the "relation" between
the act-temporality of the whole act and this lowest level. In
figure *8* the overarching curved line represents the temporality

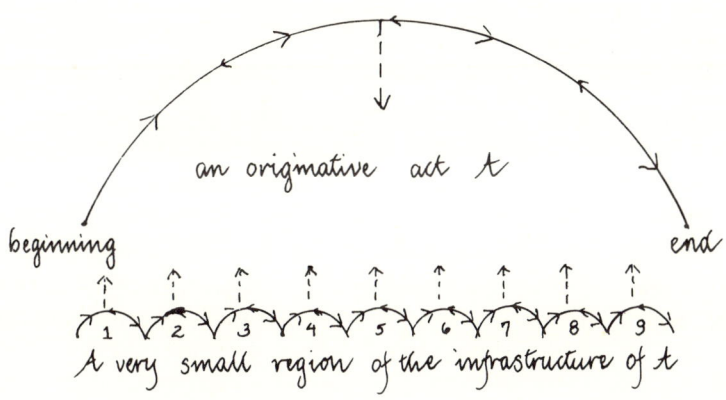

Figure *8*

of the act, which in its becoming realizes a power-pattern
throughout the whole of its spatial region, and the small curved
lines represent the act-temporal reiteration of a sequence of
units at the lowest level, which in their becoming realize successive power patterns in some extremely small component spatial
region. The vertical dotted lines indicate that there is a nontemporal power "relation" of an asymmetric kind between the two
levels. The lengths of the overarching curved lines and the
smaller ones are absurdly out of scale, and all other component
happenings of the same size in different regions are omitted: the
diagram conveys only a schematic "relation" between unity and
multiplicity. If we once again passed our plane through the line
we should then also be representing an unimaginably large

number of distinguishable spatial regions in which similar and equally repetitive patterns would be carried out. That there is a sense in which this feature of the infrastructure is independent of the act needs merely to be mentioned in passing. Electrons (whether entities or regular sequences of events) outlast acts. But the whole concourse of powers of this kind that form the base of the infrastructure is another matter. It is, at least according to the previous section, very much in the grip of the act, and of course it contributes to the act. The vertical dotted lines remind us of this.

It will now be clear that although we can not distinguish concrete moments within the act *A*, but only "moments" that have a "reach" that is not in keeping with the idea of an exact temporal "location" within the act, we *can* distinguish distinct moments correlated with the distinct spatiotemporal power-patterns within the infrastructure. In figure *8* act-temporal unit *3* at the lower of the two levels in unambiguously after act-temporal unit *2* and before unit *4*. In that sense, and in that sense only, the internal continuity of the time of the originative act is susceptible of analysis in terms of discrete units: what we are thus analyzing is the infrastructure, not the act.

Let us now suppose that there is at least one level of act-temporal power-units mediating between the unity of the act *A* and the uttermost multiplicity of the infrastructure. We shall not attempt to identify it, our discussion of mediation being still suspended, but shall suppose merely that it consists of a succession of power-patterns in a spatial region larger than that of any of the units *1–9* in figure *8*. Since our diagrams are fundamentally temporal, we are only dealing with the reiterative temporal character of the pattern in one spatial region of this kind. The length of the line indicates merely the duration of each mediating act-temporal unit. This now appears as figure *8A*, in which the three levels are identified as *A, B,* and *C.* The "relation" between *A* and *B* and between *B* and *C* is now analogous to the one we previously supposed to exist between *A* and *C.* The vertical dotted lines, indicating a power "relation" of a nontemporal sort between the levels, reflect this fact.

136

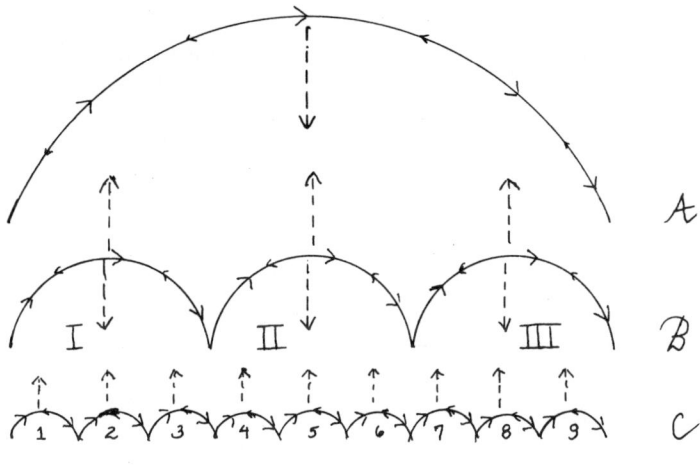

Figure *8A*

8

But in these diagrams we have neglected the more patently mechanical features that are obvious within the infrastructure to the extent that it consists of a persistent physical structure that precedes and, usually, outlasts the act. Somewhat earlier, I associated mechanical happenings within the physical structure with a continuous time, which was not understood to be an abstract time based only upon a measurement procedure, but a concrete, though ontologically derivative, time. In the course of an originative act there will be a number of events in which persistent physical structures take part. There will, for instance, be the overt physical movements of bodily structures in which the hand moves to raise the cloak and the lips move in speech. There will be the underlying contraction and expansion of muscles and the movement of bones secured together in mechanical linkage. And there will be important mechanical features to the neural "sub-programs" involved in all this: the successive events, for instance, in which an impulse is conveyed from a receptor nerve to a sensory area of the brain by the successive

137

firing of neurons fixed in persistent structural array, the whole succession being correlated the while with motor impulses moving outward from the brain along motor neural pathways to the muscles.

In figure *9* such a series of events is represented as taking place in a time coextensive with the act-temporality of the originative act. In that we are now concerned with persistent

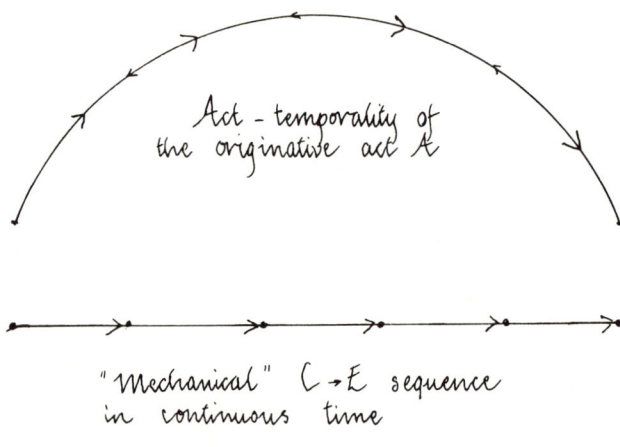

Figure *9*

physical structures, the linear sequences below the curved line is not devoid of spatial significance. That is to say, the successive events are not necessarily to be construed as taking place in the same spatial subregion, a construction that we could put upon figures *8* and *8A*. The sequence might represent the propagation of an impulse along a neural chain by the successive firings of its components, or it might stand for a sequence of movements of several muscles and bones. But the spatiality is not directly represented, and the diagram deals primarily in the temporal successiveness of the events involved. Nevertheless, insofar as the sequence of events that succeed each other are understood to involve a sequence of movements passing through a persistent physical structure, it is readily interpreted as a $C \rightarrow E$ sequence, and one moreover of the kind that the working view is quite at home with. Setting aside the sophistications of epistemology, a mechanical $C \rightarrow E$ sequence of this kind is in fact one of the clearer examples of the working view of that relation. If we are to take the originative act seriously we must think of it as wielding not just other act-temporal sequences like those represented in figures *8* and *8A* but also $C \rightarrow E$ relations of the sort represented in figure *9*. We must therefore try to show how the nested dynamisms of act-temporality can pervade spatial regions in which there are many structures exhibiting mechanical $C \rightarrow E$ sequences.

5

The Hierarchy of the Infrastructure

THE ACT—TEMPORAL UNITY OF an originative act, we are assuming, expresses its power in the multiplicity of its infrastructure, but the power is effective on the uttermost multiplicity of the infrastructure only through the mediation of many subordinate levels. Yet even if our assumption is sound, it is no easy matter to distinguish these levels and establish their order in a definitive way. However subtle the analysis, however complex and detailed a set of levels and individual units it should reveal, the end-product will not be the one and only infrastructure of the act. We are not only limited by our own shortcomings in perspicacity and industry, for when we are dealing with an act-temporal unit, any analysis we make will be relative to our purposes. What we bring out in one kind of analysis we suppress in an alternative version. It is not that the multiplicity of an infrastructure is unreal in the sense of being only a by-product of analysis. The multiplicity we attend to when we try to understand the infrastructure is real enough, but it is a multiplicity held in a power unity, and that unity is what frustrates a definitive analysis. The same principle that makes it impossible to give an adequate account of the act in terms of the infrastructure—the principle of the asymmetrical identity of the power-unity of the one with the multiplicity of the other—makes it impossible for us to exhaust analytically all the ways in which the unity of the act possesses the multiplicity

of the infrastructure. The analogue of this in epistemology is
that there can be no analysis in terms of discrete empirical data
that can furnish either the equivalent of, or the justification for,
our rational awareness of either a commonsense entity of the
world or so commonsense a thing as an act of Socrates. All this
is just another way of saying that any analysis of the mediating
levels of the infrastructure of an act must preserve the distinction between the unity of the act and the multiplicity of the
infrastructure. The unity of an act, if it has the character we are
assuming it to have, is so "related" to the multiplicity of an
infrastructure that we can always distinguish some additional
way in which it possesses and uses some units of the infrastructure—and this then becomes an additional feature of the infrastructure.

We begin, then, with the scheme of figure *10*, which provides for a number of infrastructure levels without identifying
them and without establishing the kind or the number of units
that each level comprises. We may suppose it to represent a

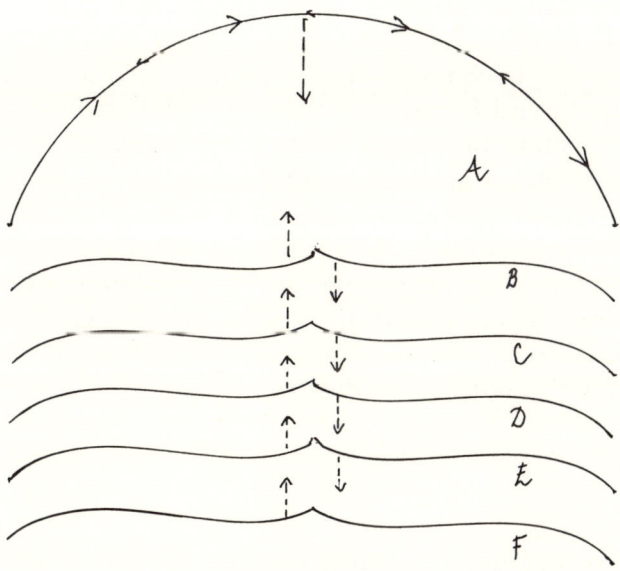

Figure *10*

141

selection from the levels that could emerge from one of the possible ways of approach to the infrastructure. As the act *A* develops through its act-temporality there will always be these infrastructure levels that it unites and that lend it their support. The level of act *A* is represented by our usual device, which has a merely temporal significance, although the act itself is a three-dimensional becoming: whatever else is involved, Socrates does move his hand to raise his cloak and then moves his larynx, mouth, and lips in speech. The brackets representing the lower levels do not have as yet any specifically temporal or spatial representative value, although each unit in these lower levels will also be a three-dimensional becoming. A given level may be diffused throughout the body, as it would be, for instance, if we were to interpret level *F* as consisting of all the time-bound three-dimensional happenings of the magnitude of an electron taking place within the time of the act, as in figures *8* and *8A*. But it may well be more local, as it would be if the principle of our analysis required us to interpret some higher level, say *B*, as the processes taking place in the complex three-dimensional structure of the cerebral cortex. But all the levels of the infrastructure would be spatially coextensive with the whole of the body in its becoming — both the large-scale movements of the externally visible parts and the more subtle movements and processes within the body — through the course of the act. As the diagram makes more obvious, the temporal spans of *all* the infrastructure elements are coextensive with the act-temporality of *A*. The main point of the diagram is that the power of the originative act *A* is felt throughout the spatiotemporal multiplicity of its infrastructure, but that the power is exercised mediately: on *C* through the mediation of *B*, on *D* through the mediation of *B* and *C*, and so on down.

2

If it is legitimate to construe some of these levels in act-temporal terms, it is nevertheless absolutely necessary to construe some others in terms of $C \rightarrow E$ impulses whose character is determined by the persistent structural features of the entities through which they pass or between which they take place. These impulses are of the kind we usually call mechanical, and their temporality is linear rather than act-temporal. Our problem then, is to reconcile two distinct kinds of mediating levels that appear to be in conflict. In this section we shall be concerned with the two kinds understood in a pure form and without regard to the reconciliation of them. The next section deals with the reconciliation of them in a single originative act.

(*a*) If all the levels of the infrastructure were themselves composed of act-temporal units, each of them would be distinguished from the originative act itself by being one of a spatiotemporal multiplicity. The act-temporal power of the originative act *A* would by contrast be a unity, and it would be responsible for (the "real cause" of) their precise spatiotemporal relations, calling them into play in this or that spatial region and in this or that temporal order. The complexity of organization of an infrastructure level made up of act-temporal units would be very great, no matter how we might identify the particular units. There would be an important aspect of successiveness to the complexity, as for instance the electron-units of figures *8* and *8A* were successive. But even at higher and less populous levels there would be many spatially distinct successive arrays in varying spatial arrangement. If level *C* were the level of the firing of single neurons, and if the firing of a single neuron were an example of act-temporality (as, without important qualifications, I think it is not), there would be in level *C* many such temporally sequential arrays in different places. They would naturally come under the power of act-temporal units of *B*, whatever those might turn out to be. But if we regarded each unit of this multiplicity of *C* as an act-temporal one, each of them would have an infrastructure comprising some units in level *D*, and this one-many power "relation" would then be repeated down through the infrastructure. There would be no going behind this "relation" for a more fundamental kind of explanation: no mechanism, no $C \rightarrow E$ complex cast in mechanistic or in other terms,

143

could furnish an explanatory account of the total act more adequate than this scheme of "nested dynamisms" supplies. The complications would increase enormously as we descend in the hierarchy, but the principle would remain the same. A diagram in principle like figure *8A,* but much more complex, would apply.

Despite the striking possibility of explaining the lowest level accessible to observation by an appeal to the fundamental nature of the act-temporal unit, it is obvious that such a system will not do in its pure form, even if we should find that there are other levels that exhibit act-temporality. Its chief failing is that it does not account for the fact that some of the supposed act-temporal units — indeed, among them the firing of a single neuron, which was just offered as an example — take their distinctive character from the persistent physical structures in which they take place. Not only is the neuron a persistent physical structure that defines what we call its firing, but it also fits into well-defined, if flexible, neural routes, along which run impulses innervating in their course muscle cells whose function is in turn defined by the character of their own persistent structures. How are we to reconcile the supposed act-temporality of the originative act with the fact that the orderly sequence of neural impulses along certain motor channels plays a vital role in Socrates' lifting of the cloak from his face, and that another sequence of the same kind *after* this one, and therefore later in *A,* plays just as vital a role in his speech to Crito? Sequences of this kind in the course of the alleged originative act will be very numerous, and they may be plausibly interpreted in "mechanical" $C \rightarrow E$ terms. If there should be originative acts, there must nevertheless be a sense in which the play of their power through an infrastructure is mediated at least in part by physical structures of this kind. A hierarchy formed exclusively of act-temporal units will not do.

(*b*) Once we concede that there are within the infrastructure of an originative act some $C \rightarrow E$ processes determined by the nature of persistent physical structures, we raise the possibility that the supposed act can be reduced entirely to events of this kind. There are, first of all, the gross and obvious structural

144

stabilities of internal organs and of the skeletal, muscular, neural, and vascular systems. At a level of more refined observation there are much more subtle structures, many of which are well understood. I have already used as an example the neural loops, so like those of artificial servomechanisms, that connect receptor and motor organs to the cerebral cortex, and that, together with their interconnections with structures that terminate in the spinal column or in phylogenetically older parts of the brain, play so important a role in enabling Socrates to lift a cup to his lips or reach for and grasp the cloak that covers his face. Among the organs whose gross structure is well understood, the brain stands out as one the fine-grained structure of which is full of many subtleties of this kind and of many more whose significance is ill understood. No one questions its vital role as a control center whose function depends on just those only partially understood fine-grained structures. The story can be continued in endless detail and can extend to the development of structures no less than to the functioning of fully developed ones. The DNA macromolecule is a highly stable physical structure, and it plays a key role in the development of the embryo, and in this way is the bearer, though no doubt not the only bearer, of the phylogenetic stability of all the other physical structures. In short, there is the whole familiar structural complex of a living system, with all its analogies, familiar at least from the eighteenth century on, to machines in the older sense of that word, and with many recently exploited analogies to machines in a wider sense that includes computers and computer dominated automatons.

One kind of structure should be singled out for special mention, as it has certain features that will help us a little later on in reconciling act-temporal levels with mechanical ones. I mean the structures that are code-bearing, information-bearing, or meaning-bearing, structures of which DNA itself is the leading example. It is an interesting oddity that, on the one hand, the stability of their structure, the simplicity of their components, and the complexity in which these components are united, are what make them capable of carrying meaning, while, on the other hand, these same features make their operation, in which the information actually becomes effective, a mechanical one. An impulse passively received causes an RNA molecule to move; the stable nature of its structure in movement constitutes a pattern that is transmitted; by way of a structural fit the pattern is later duplicated. The mechanical feature, so patent in operation, considerably erodes the normal sense of the word "information" when it is used about such structures. At first a useful metaphor, with many connections with our own capacity to make or discern order, or to achieve an objective by way of a temporally ordered sequence of movements, it has been so altered by its association with structural-mechanical features that a whole generation seems ready to believe that information structurally stored in this way can have arisen by chance, a linguistic development that means that we are not really talking about information, but only about "information" in the sense of a complex and stable structure. To keep alive the sense in which such structures can be the vehicle for meaning, I shall avoid that worn term when possible and call structures like DNA *meaningful control structures.* I hope in this way to keep salient what is too easily forgotten, that the presence of such structures in nature is a major problem for any materialism. But I shall try to exploit that point later. For the moment I am concerned only to show that if we allow our attention to wander from the meaning of structures, they offer some difficulties for the concept of originative action. If we consider them *only as persistent physical structures,* they form a major support for any attempt to understand our hierarchy of mediating levels in terms of a pattern of $C \rightarrow E$ relations determined entirely by the laws of physics and by the structure of the persistent entities in which they take place. It is of the essence of any meaningful control structure that it *is* a persistent physical structure, and as such can engage in physical interaction with other persistent physical structures to which its own structure bears certain relationships — to which, that is, its structure is "encoded."

How DNA came to be so significant a bearer of the order

of embryonic development, and how DNA and RNA came to be bearers of the order of the building of proteins are questions that hold some mysteries for those—and their number is increasing—who do not feel that they have been enlightened when they are told that both the gross order of the living creature and the "encoding" of that order in DNA came about by chance. But the operational role that DNA and RNA play together in the building of the proteins is in principle a matter of the linkage of physical structures that fit each other in a way for which the "template" image so often used in describing these processes is a tolerably good one. Neglecting the notion of the significance we attach to codes, we can attend instead to the structural fit of the macromolecular units that take part in the process. When we do so we regard these highly meaningful structures not as the bearers of a *telos* but as paradigms of a mechanical and deterministic $C \rightarrow E$ relation.

There are many other structures in the body that, like DNA, can be interpreted either as coded and meaningful or as transmitters of, or participants in, $C \rightarrow E$ relations that, because they depend upon structural stabilities, are mechanical and deterministic in their actual operations. But their coded or meaningful character is not usually emphasized. Presumably the facility with which DNA can be regarded as a genetic "code" written in a "language" having an "alphabet" encourages scientists to single it out from all other ordered structures in the organism and deal with it as though it were the only example of "encoding" to be found there. But it is only the extreme case, forcing itself on the attention of the investigator because so much "information" is packed into it. Unlike DNA, these other "coded" entities are more obviously concerned in the manifest operations of the organism, and this makes it easy to attend to them purely as transmitters of $C \rightarrow E$ processes that traverse them or as participants in $C \rightarrow E$ relations mediated by structural features. Oscillatory circuits consist essentially of neural loops whose size governs the time it takes for an impulse to traverse the loop, and this structural feature, together with their threshold level and recovery time at the point where the circuit is innervated produces a timed output that regulates the beat of the heart in lower animals. Though the structure of the loop is "encoded" for the heart's rhythm, the carrying out of the "meaning" of the "code" is identical with the $C \rightarrow E$ process that traverses it. So with the numerous programs and sub-programs that are to be found in the human central nervous system. The sensory-motor loop that enables Socrates to reach for and take hold of the edge of his cloak is "encoded" for a variety of tasks like that, but the "encoding" is physically identical with the structure that enables it to carry out, by virtue of the $C \rightarrow E$ impulses that traverse it, a task that is itself understandable in structural-mechanical $C \rightarrow E$ terms. Once we decide to set aside the question how the significance, or meaning, gets into the structure, once, that is, we set aside the ontological significance of a structure that carries a "code," we need only consider the structural-mechanical $C \rightarrow E$ processes in which it is involved. "Coding" is thus reduced to the adjustment of structure to structure, and in this sense we may speak with as much justice of the "coding" of the hand for grasping, of the heart for pumping, of its blood vessels for the lungs, as of the "coding" of DNA and RNA for the building of the proteins.

Proceeding in this way an opponent of act-temporality need only call attention to the structures and maintain that in principle all the gross and fine-grained structures of the body form a mechanism congruent with, if more sophisticated than, the one rejected by Socrates. He might then go on to arrange these structurally based mechanisms in a set of levels that, though it preserved the principle of hierarchy, would reveal no act-temporalities either in subordinate levels or at the apex. The apex he could then construe as a persistent structure like all the rest, its control exercised by $C \rightarrow E$ impulses traversing it, much as the control section in a computer shares with the logical circuitry and the memory banks it calls into ordered play the character of being a physical structure passively traversed by $C \rightarrow E$ impulses. And in fact elements of such a reductive program have been carried out in detail for portions of "man the machine" ranging from the biophysics of the very small up through the detailed study of the motor or receptor neural networks of the brain itself. The philosophic case for the program has generally been made in more general but sophisticated works addressed to a nonspecialist but educated audience.

In this approach an action is treated as a number of distinct operations, each under the domination of a control system, or sub-program, several of which are gathered together in an operation of higher order under the domination of a still higher order control system. It is important to this view that an operation at any level is supported by persistent physical structures — bones, muscles, organs, nerves, cells, DNA — and that, despite the obeisance to hierarchical principles, the whole "act" is understood in terms of $C \rightarrow E$ operations determined by stable structures. This applies both to the substantive task (Socrates moves hands, larynx, mouth, lips) and to any control operation (the servomechanismlike neural loops that guide hand to grasp and lips to move) that governs the substantive operation. So with higher levels of control: a control center in the brain that might integrate several such operations — whether in the cerebral cortex, or, as some now think, in the mid-brain — is capable of control because its distinct physical shape permits it to take part in $C \rightarrow E$ operations and to be traversed by $C \rightarrow E$ impulses. For yet higher levels of control this approach must become more speculative, but the speculation is of the same kind. If Socrates, taking thought, decides upon this or that line of conduct, it will be taken for granted that his assessment of the likelihood of achieving a certain objective; his estimation of its goodness, its relation to other objectives, and the like; and the degree of consistency that pervades his thought are the outcome of $C \rightarrow E$ impulses passing through fixed circuitry. No less than the control exercised by lower programs that integrate several sensory-motor activities, control at the level of taking thought will be understood to be based on fixed structures. And though the proponent of this doctrine may be willing to ascribe "encoding" features to these structures, it is just as easy at this level as at lower ones to maintain that the key to the matter is the structure that determines a pattern of $C \rightarrow E$ events under

149

the laws of nature. In the background a doctrine of evolution that sees the origin of these structures in chance, and their persistence in the genetic advantage they confer, makes it all the easier to dismiss the consequences of the metaphor of "coding" and to concentrate serious attention on the $C \rightarrow E$ happenings governed by the structures.

3

The presence in Socrates' body of *some* programs based on physical structures offers in itself no difficulty for an interpretation of them as subject to the control of act-temporality — or at least no more difficulty than is raised by the idea of act-temporality itself. Once we admit the "relation" between the utter simplicity and unity of an originative act and the spatiotemporal multiplicity it controls, we admit also that it can "control" discrete units here and now and other discrete units now and later. The temporal and spatial "reach" of its power will not be made more evident to doubters if the units it reaches out to are act-temporal ones rather than subroutines embodied in persistent structures triggered in some temporal order. What is essential to a reconciliation of act-temporality and mechanism is that there should *not* exist at the apex of the hierarchy a physical structure so "encoded" as to activate, under suitable environmental stimulus, a selection of sub-programs of a mechanical nature, and to do so because the $C \rightarrow E$ impulses that traversed it were uniquely determined by stimulus and by the precise paths that the impulses in fact traversed. If there were, for instance, one and only one neural path that could be activated by some given complex environmental stimulus, and if the activation of this then called into play, say, all the sub-programs I have conceded to play a role in Socrates' raising of the cloak to speak to Crito, we should have no reason to introduce the theme of act-temporality. But the presence of some physical structures and some sequence of $C \rightarrow E$ events within them — say precisely those we may presume to have taken place in the course of that action of Socrates'—does not in the least support this claim. That out of the immense number of spatiotemporal patterns of neural excitation possible in the complexity of the brain some one did in fact take place and did bring a certain set of sub-programs into play tells us nothing more than that the structure was capable of being traversed by that pattern among others. We can recognize this and still suppose that pattern to be a multiplicity that arose by virtue of an act-temporality that, even when the first subroutine involved in raising the cloak was activated by the pattern, was "reaching" towards a completion that required the later activation, by some later part of the pattern, of the subroutines involved in speech. In that sense the act would have wielded in its service a subroutine that might in the past have been wielded in a variety of different ways by other acts.

What appears to be essential to an act-temporal interpretation is the *absence* at the uppermost level of a persistent structure, energized by the electrochemical energy of living things, and operating inflexibly so as to control a set of subroutines each of which is inflexible in its operation once activated. If there were any such ultimate control structure, it would presumably have a form analogous to a computer's control center into which a program has been punched. Such a program is of course a code, but it is one embodied in a structure—in the punched cards or magnetic tapes on which the symbols of the machine "language" take a physical form, in the punching of keys, in the initial state of the computer's circuitry—and its control then consists in bringing into play successive subroutines in a determined order that needs no act-temporality for its explanation. For the purposes of the example I set aside the question how the structure of the machine and its programs came into being, a gesture that also sets aside, though in a different spirit from that in which writers committed to the computer image of human nature make the same gesture, any possible act-temporality in the makers of the computer and its programs. There seems no empirical reason for supposing that somewhere in the brain there is a control unit of that kind, despite the large number of

151

structures that can be interpreted on the basis of sub-programs. There seems considerable reason to believe that the superabundance of alternative neural patterns in the higher centers of the brain points in a rather different direction.

It will I trust be clear that I am not claiming that the presence of a large number of alternative pathways in the brain, and especially in the newer areas of the cortex, in itself demonstrates act-temporality. In that case we should be compelled to ascribe it to a sufficiently complex computer. Even if we were able to show that the structure of the brain was not deterministic — show, that is, that it was not the case that, given a certain stimulus and a certain initial brain state, one and only one brain state could succeed it — we should not have demonstrated the reality of act-temporality, but merely the minimum conditions for its compatibility with an infrastructure some mediating levels of which consisted of stable structures traversed by $C \rightarrow E$ impulses. The point is entirely negative, and no conclusions can be drawn from it about artifacts designed to be indeterministic. Thus certain modern students of computer circuitry have concluded that deterministic computers can not duplicate the capacities of human intelligence, and they have tried to endow computers with a "free" and "creative" capacity by incorporating within them a radium driven randomizer. The thought was that the radioactive decay of radium, being governed by the indeterminacy principle, lifted the burden of determinism from the instrument. Even if this line of investigation were successful in the sense that we could justifiably regard the machine as indeterministic — and many scientists think that this is not so, and that the laws of nature are no less deterministic because they incorporate this principle within them — we could not regard such a device as capable of doing what we here ascribe to act-temporality. The computer is indeterministic, if at all, only in the sense that an event at the quantum level arbitrarily determines whether a given circuit is to be open or closed. The microevent thus determines part of the total circuit-pattern of the macroevent. Act-temporality, if real, is indeterministic in the sense that the total unity of the act expresses itself in the total spatiotemporal pattern assumed by its infrastructure, and in that sense the total spatiotemporal unity of the neural circuit pattern determines whether a given circuit is to be open or closed. If we wish to use event-language about this, we can say that the macroevent of the total circuit pattern determines what the microevent will be.

Though the preceding discussion of brain circuitry is concerned only with the absence of structures that would *exclude* act-temporality, the richness of alternative channels in the brain gives us reason to suppose that we may find spatiotemporal power units operative there that are clearly act-temporal and that nonetheless subserve the superordinate originative act. Such units, if they exist, would require a time-unit for their complete realization and they could not be said to be caused in a $C \rightarrow E$ sense by the particular neural pathways they in fact course through and by the physical brain state immediately preceding them. We have already seen, at the lowest level observation can deal with, time-bound happenings of which something similar could be said: the successive power-patterns we are accustomed to thinking of as a single electron are clearly not dependent on a continuous structure, and the $C \rightarrow E$ relation does not seem to give a very helpful interpretation of the relation between one such power-unit and its successor. It would clearly make the act-temporality we are attributing to the act itself more plausible if we could find similar units up towards the apex of its infrastructure and show how they might control routines more inflexibly tied to structures. These matters are pursued further in chapter 8.

4

There are some striking parallels between the body's structurally based "mechanisms" and the act-temporality I am ascribing to Socrates' actions. If they can be made apparent, the mingling in the infrastructure of both act-temporal and "mechanical" levels of mediation will seem less strange. In particular it will be easier to see how act-temporality might guide them without being overcome by the "mechanism" that is surely one aspect of them.

Suppose that *a* is a structurally based routine that has to do with vision and more particularly with that attentive kind of vision in which one discriminates some particular and rather small item from a larger field, as just now I picked out among the dense grey-green foliage of the ilex outside the window a particular sprig with its group of leaves. I can easily perform that act of attention, and presumably I might have employed the same routine, if I were closer to the tree, to pick out some particular leaf. We shall suppose it to involve a complex including the musculature of the eye, the receptor nerves at the back of the retina, the optic nerves and chiasma, the several layers of the cortex in the visual area, the vertical columnar bundles of neurons and axons that bind the levels together,[1] and no doubt a great deal more. Since we are talking about a conscious act of attention, we do not by any means isolate its full physiological basis by isolating *a*, but since we are not now analyzing the total act but merely one of the routines in its infrastructure, that is no great matter. Now suppose *a* to contain at least two neuromuscular subroutines, *b* and *b'*, one of which might be concerned in the movement of the whole eye, the other in the change in focus of the lens. There will no doubt be other subroutines, but we shall not consider them. Both the subroutines will form a closed loop with the environment, so that there will be a feedback that is an integral part of each subroutine.

If we now consider any particular happening in the course of the routine, either in *b* or *b'* or elsewhere — say the firing of some single neuron — we shall find it linked in $C \rightarrow E$ connections with other happenings, certainly, in this case, with other neurons with which it is in synapse. There will be no single happening in that hierarchy that, considered purely in terms of its place in *a*, will not be interpretable in that way. Shift our attention to the whole pattern of the routine *a*, however, and some oddities emerge. Suppose there is a single-neuron event in *b* that is spatially separated from and temporally either simultaneous with or slightly before or after one in b'. We shall so choose our events that there is no immediate $C \rightarrow E$ connection between them, or at least none that is relevant to the carrying out of the two subroutines b and b', and, in part because of the time factor, no mediate $C \rightarrow E$ connection by way of other structures in a. In short, we consider the firing of one cell in b that, even if it is before the given firing of another cell in b', is not in synapse with it and not in a position to exercise even indirect excitation upon it. The events in b and b' will however be significantly related to each other in that the two routines to which they make their separate contributions will together make possible the focus of the eye upon the sprig to which attention is being directed. This significant relation, and indeed the whole sequence of events in both b and b', will be explicable only by reference to the total temporality of the routine a: both make their contribution to the full sweep of the routine, but both occur as they do precisely because of the nature of the total routine. The routine a is, however, a spatiotemporal pattern, as indeed are the subroutines b and b', and its temporality is bound and circumscribed by the nature of the structure within which the process takes place. The total pattern of a is, in other words, the reason for the pattern of b and b' and therefore the significant temporal relation of the two events in b and b' is given by the temporality of a.

The materialist will find nothing unusual in this. And indeed, if we merely attend to the fact that the physical relations between the many structural elements in a are responsible for the relation between the given event in b and the one in b', we shall have to agree. Yet the coursing of the impulses through the structure of a consumes a certain time and follows a certain order. Though the spatial structure does indeed define this order, it is the total temporality of a—the temporal unity of the whole of it—that lends significance to our two events. And by "lend significance" in this case I mean precisely the coordination of them in the common task—the focus of the eye upon the sprig of leaves. The *significance* of the structural arrangements of a only appears, then, in a unit-temporality analogous in its function to what I have claimed to be the act-temporality of an originative act. The temporal relation of our two events is absolutely essential to the coordination of b and b', and it is a unit defined by the total temporality of a that is responsible for this. The significant temporal relation between the two events can not be expressed in terms of linear time but becomes apparent in the unit-time necessary for the completion of a, and in that sense the temporality of the spatiotemporal routine a mimics act-temporality.

The situation is much the same in the relation between program and sub-program in a computer, but though similarities between man and computer have been advanced to urge the complete adequacy of $C \rightarrow E$ causality, when used in conjunction with an adequate grasp of the laws of nature, to explain the workings of human nature, it is hard to see why this should be so. Within the computer highly significant structures define discrete and nested units of temporality that qualify each other in much the same way as I have represented our routine a to qualify by its temporal unity the temporal unities of b and b'. There can surely be few things more telic than a computer. Indeed the computer reinforces at more than one point the analogies we have considered between physically based routines and act-temporality. We need only concede act-temporality to the scientists who made the computer to see the whole of its structure as a static counterpart of act-temporality.

The theme of the act-temporal significance encoded in the physical structure of a routine can be developed in an even more striking way by considering the time needed for the effectiveness of a routine, that is, the time taken to achieve its "end." Our routine a subserves, we have supposed, the conscious act of attention. At what point in the time taken for the completion of the routine may we say that the subject manages to attend to the sprig of leaves? Plainly we can not give a satisfactory answer even in principle without bringing in a great deal more than this one routine. Let us simplify it somewhat. At what point has the routine made its contribution to the act of attention? Here we shall probably be on safe ground if we say that the whole of the routine must be completed before this can be done. The eye must indeed focus on the sprig, a pattern of excitation, itself involving many subroutines, must take place in the receptor neurons at the back of the retina, and this, being considerably processed on the way, must be led by its elaborate divided and rejoined route to the visual cortex, where there takes place a pattern of excitation involving an ordered region whose several successive layers are tied together by a vertical organization housing the columnar feature mentioned before. Those whose life work is devoted to investigations of this sort seem in little doubt that the whole of a considerable region in its three-dimensional organization must be activated before it can be said that there is a neural counterpart of what the eye has focused upon. And for some time now it seems to have been taken for granted that the temporal order of the excitation plays just as important a role as does the excitation of a given three-dimensional region.[2] The conclusion seems inescapable that a time-unit associated with the whole of the three-dimensional structure of a is essential for it to make its full contribution. Indeed some experimental evidence related to our conscious awareness seems to lend some support to the belief that there is some minimum time-unit necessary for a neural event to have any consciousness at all associated with it. Quite apart from the question whether our psychological experiences come, as James thought, in quanta, there seems some ground for supposing that the neural events that subserve consciousness must be of a certain length before we can be conscious of anything at all.[3]

The structures that support routine a and subroutines b and b' belong to the class called meaningful control structures in section 2, and it will now be clear that the temporal correlate of their significance is a time-unit having act-temporal features. The time of an act-temporal structural unit is accordingly *meaningful time,* and our inability to isolate within it "moments" that can be divested of their reference to the whole of it is an analogue of the reference of any part of a meaningful statement to the rest of it.

When $C \rightarrow E$ processes are interpreted in this time-bound way their mechanical features recede, and it seems less strange that they should operate under the control of an originative act, the more so as we are not dealing with inert structures energized from outside, but with living things whose time-bound processes are quite inseparable from the energy that sustains the structure itself. The number of persistent structures in the body which thus mimic the time-bound character of originative action is very large, and it is impressive even in areas where we find it difficult to relate one time-bound process to another existing as a hierarchical component within it.

The most important general character of these processes is that they are cyclic or reiterative — a more patently time-bound feature than that of the routine just discussed. The heart "acts," if not precisely originatively in the sense we attribute to Socrates, then at least in a time-bound way, for it "acts" through a period of time the whole of which is necessary to perform what, if it were simply a pump in a man-made machine, we should have no hesitation in calling its telic task. Moreover, the rhythmic cycle that is inherent in the very muscular and neural structure of the human heart expresses itself in subsidiary time-bound units of which the auricular and ventricular systoles are the most obvious examples. These two time-bound processes are thus bound in a more complex sequence. Within this total complexity many more fine-grained units like individual nerve and muscle cells echo, as they express their own structural significance in the time-bound units of firing and contraction, the time-bound nature of the whole. From this perspective the whole of the heart and each part of it seem residues of phylogenetic "acts" that gradually formed the human heart, and each cyclic process within these structures seems to reiterate the power of those "acts." Besides all these examples of structures whose stability lies at the basis of time-bound impulses and functions, there are many examples of structural development that mimic act-temporality, the most obvious example within the fully developed organism being the cycle in which a mitochondrion breaks down and then reconstitutes itself.

158

In all these cases a time-bound structure that, in the language of teleology, "provides" at any point in a cycle for the completion of a unit of becoming necessary to the whole of the organism is nonetheless fraught with mechanisms in the sense that when we isolate any event and consider its relation to antecedent and successor events it turns out to be a $C \rightarrow E$ relation that is mechanical in the sense that it is determined by a structure. So long as impulses of appropriate strength arrive at the afferent synapse the single neuron will continue to fire in a volley whose frequency is proportioned to the strength of the impulse; so long as the integrity of its structure is preserved and blood supply continues, the heart will continue to beat, mimicking in its cycle of systole and diastole the completeness and unity of an originative act. Structure makes this so, but if we take seriously the temporal significance of the structures, they seem nothing if not congruent with the originative acts I have supposed to command them.

5

That there are indeed originative acts will, however, be a more plausible claim if we can find in the infrastructure at least one level whose spatiotemporal units are act-temporal without qualification.

It seems probable that in the course of an originative act there exist in the brain power-units of a true act-temporal kind. To develop this claim adequately we must look at an act of Socrates from a somewhat different perspective from the one we have adopted so far. From the very beginning we have taken it for granted that any description of an originative act sufficiently concrete to distinguish it from another original act must make reference to a multiplicity. The act-temporal unity in which an act dominates an infrastructure is not, qua unity, distinguishable from any other, and when we identify some particular originative act, like Socrates' lifting the cloak from his face to speak to Crito, we must make at least implicit reference to

159

a multiplicity. However summary our description of this action may be, it will clearly include implicit reference to hands and lips, both of which belong to the infrastructure. We have until now considered an act of Socrates only in this way, as it presents itself objectively to a sympathetic but external observer. But there is a good deal more that is implicit in our identification of an act, and if it occurs to us to make some of it explicit, we come to a multiplicity of a different sort, one that belongs to what has been called mind, mentality, consciousness, awareness, subjectivity, thought, and intentionality, and no doubt has been known by a great many other names as well. The reader is free to reject any or all of these terms. I am not interested just now in persuading him of the soundness of this or that philosophical terminology, but I think this feature of action will be familiar enough to him. The multiplicity that goes with it is also familiar, though once again there will be no agreement about what terminology is appropriate to it. Descartes expressed both the "mental" aspect of action and the inner multiplicity of it by saying that we are thinking beings, and then giving some content to this claim by a familiar catalog: "What is a thing that thinks? It is a thing that doubts, understands, conceives, affirms, decides, wills, refuses, and that also imagines and feels" (*Meditations,* II). Without trying to settle just now the ontological and operative status of mentality and what we find in it, let us merely say that there is an aspect to Socrates' action that is difficult to formulate but nonetheless qualitatively rich and complex, and that it is familiar enough, even though our language so far only draws attention to it in a rough and ready way. That familiar aspect is part of the actions we are trying to understand. Action therefore has an ontological dimension for which "internality" is no doubt a poor word, but in any event we miss it utterly when we attend only to what is overt in it. The denseness of this dimension will contribute to any "real causality" exercised by the action it qualifies, and if we take it seriously we must suppose it to share in the unity of the act-temporality of the originative act. That to the introspective glance a passage of that subjectivity is characterized by a multiplicity of ideas, impressions,

160

feelings, and whatever else we take to be the furniture of it, no more detracts from the unity of the act's power than the fact that we identify the act as the reaching for the cloak, the raising of it, and the uttering of an enigmatic sentence or two to Crito.

We must expect that this dimension of the act will express itself in infrastructure elements of considerable complexity. It is the brain we turn to for this, and it is there, I suggest, that we might expect to find power-units which, in their act-temporality, stand as vicars for the unity of the originative act under consideration.

We may now attempt to represent in principle the "relation" between the level of Socrates' originative act, A, which we now assume to have this "internal," or "subjective" aspect, and some group of act-temporal power units belonging to a level B immediately below it. This level of Socrates' agency, A, will of course have only one member. The act may have sub-acts, but these do not belong to a different ontological level, because they are also originative acts of Socrates, and we therefore set them aside. The one act we are considering will include a train of thought, although perhaps not a momentous one, and we shall assume that it "comes into" consciousness as it is expressed, or at least partly expressed, in the words Socrates speaks to Crito. It is, however, important to note that we are considering a total act that has a conscious component and not merely a passage of subjectivity without resonance in the world of overt activity.

I shall not attempt to identify the whole of level B, but shall assume that it includes the electrochemical processes of the whole brain, some not very adequate indications of which are given by the electroencephalograph and other recording devices. We shall suppose that this is a patterned activity that lasts as long as the single act at level A, but, unlike the act-temporality of A, falls into a number of temporal units. Without an exact understanding of the detailed physiological events presumably summated in the wave patterns of the electroencephalograph, it would be unwise to identify these hypothetical temporal units with units in those wave patterns. We shall therefore merely suppose that the whole brain is permeated by a spatial pattern

161

whose unity is accomplished in a certain period of time, and that several such patterns take place in the course of the act *A*. There will presumably be differences in each of the spatial patterns, for to ascribe each pattern to the whole brain is not to say that all neurons fire in the course of it: a given neuron might fire in one pattern and fail to fire in the next; another neuron might fire as a member of one sequence in one pattern and as a member of a different sequence in the next. The chief point is that the realization of one pattern requires a certain temporal duration. To speak of the patterns as successive does not mean that one of them must have finished before the next starts. The spatial relations are so complex that one neuron or sequence of neurons, having fired in one pattern, might well then fire as a member of a distinct pattern before the first pattern had been fully realized.[4] In figure *11*, in which only temporal relations are shown, I assume this more complicated case, and represent each of the patterns in *B* as act-temporal. If there are such time-bound units possessing the whole brain, it would appear that neurophysiology is very far from being able to give us a spatio-temporal map of them. It has, however, been a commonplace in neurophysiology since the pioneer work of Sherrington [5] that temporal integration of the three-dimensional impulse pattern of the central nervous system plays as much importance in its

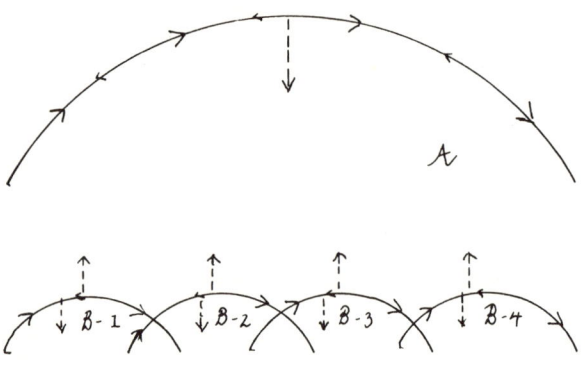

Figure *11*

functioning as the spatial relations of the neurons involved. That this feature plays an important role in subjective experience both of the passive and active kind seems reasonable. Even the most sustained effort to show in principle how a conscious computer might be built, that of Culbertson, takes it for granted that an integration over the dimension of time is of the first importance. More to the point, perhaps, are the views of Sperry, who is more interested in the relation between brain and consciousness. We shall return to the views of both of these scientists in our discussion of the mind of the prisoner in chapters 6, 7, and 8. We have already noticed that at least one recent study seems to offer quantitative empirical evidence for the view that even a simple act of perception is time-bound in the sense that the emergence of something into consciousness can not take place in any time short of a certain period.

If we represent each unit of level B in figure *11* as act-temporal we are ascribing its unity, which could in principle be represented in a three-dimensional model incorporating movement, and which would then display an order visible to the intelligent eye, to its act-temporality. But the power of that act-temporality, although thus displayed in the multiplicity to which it is "related," would itself be a simple unity, not representable by anything in which we might distinguish parts. This act-temporality would be distinguishable from the act-temporality of A in the sense that there are four distinct patterns in B that are unified by A's power; on the other hand, the four units with which A is asymmetrically identical would each of them be a vicar for the act-temporality of A itself, since each of them has its unity and its power by virtue of A's power. Although we can not define the act-temporality of any of these units in terms of the neural circuitry it possesses, we must, as noted earlier, assume that the connections in the brain are rich enough so that we need not regard any one spatiotemporal pattern as necessitated by input and by the spatial structure of the network through which it courses, except in the trivial and innocuous sense that it does in fact course through it. The channels are there, together with a great many others, but the power of any unit, say $B-1$, is

163

expressed in its possession of just the channels it does possess in just the order in which it possesses them. Indeed, a unit of that kind may be unique in the sense that in no other instance will just those circuits be activated in just that order. If it should be said that the energy gradients throughout the physical structure during the time of *B–1* will play a role in what the pattern in fact is, we may concede this with the reservation that what we mean by the act-temporal power in *B–1* expresses itself *also* in those energy gradients. We regard *B–1* as a *power*, not as a symptom of boundary conditions set by the nature of the structure and the energy state within it, and of the laws of nature. Nor would the situation be any different if we introduced chance into this group of conditions, although it should be conceded that, to a conceptual outlook that precludes the idea of act-temporality, what is not explained by that first group of conditions *will* seem to be explained by the addition of chance.

Supposing that the first level of the infrastructure of Socrates' act includes total brain-patterns of this sort, it is plain that within any single spatiotemporal pattern, say *B–1*, a large number of sub-patterns could be distinguished. We were, in the case of *B–1*, concerned with the whole brain, but now, in subdividing it, we shall have to consider not just a temporal succession, *C–1*, *C–2*, *C–3* . . . *C–n*, that takes place in the course of it, but also a division of the pattern in terms of spatial regions. The complexities of all this would be a matter for experimental neurophysiology and psychology, and we can expect that they will be considerable. The practical difficulties are so great that even if this approach should be a sound one, the complexities of the sub-patterns and their further ramifications will probably never be laid out in detail. It should be recalled that the full concreteness of the act itself is very complex. The simplicity we have ascribed to any originative act belongs to the unity of the power that expresses itself in the infrastructure, and we have seen that this unity is refracted in the objective multiplicity — the movement of hands and lips, the articulate speech — that allows us to distinguish it from others. It may be subjectively complex as well. Simply as an example of the regional complexity that might be involved at a hypothetical level *C* let us see what sort of counterpart in the infrastructure such qualitative subjective complexity might have.

We can suppose that as Socrates uncovers his face he is aware of the promise he made to Asclepius and feels that he ought to call Crito's attention to it; that is, we may suppose that awareness, feeling, evaluation, and intention characterize the act although they do not precede it and cause it. Besides the general purposeful, or intentional, tone of the act, there may be the specific intention, which also characterizes it qualitatively, to make the point that some critics have attributed to him, namely, that death is a cure for the soul's disease, embodied life, and that in that sense he has a debt to Asclepius the physician-god. And the whole act may be qualified by other concomitant attitudes that we may describe in a noncommittal way as evaluative-emotional. If we suppose ourselves to be dealing with a single originative act having a unitary time-span, the qualitatively various features of it are either compresent throughout the whole of the act, or at least related in their succession by the same "reach" of temporality we have already discussed. At the risk of considerable oversimplication, we are assuming that the sequence *B–1* through *B–4* includes, in its subordinate units, support for this qualitative complexity, and that therefore the subunits of *B–1* will be analyzable accordingly. On the basis of current research it seems clear that several distinct cortical regions and several distinct regions in the older part of the brain stem function simultaneously in support of the qualitative complexity of any act. In the cortex the speech centers, the motor centers, and the integrative-attitudinal centers of the frontal lobes will mainly be important; in the older parts of the brain, the cerebellum and the emotion-connected centers of thalamus and hypothalamus will be deeply involved. There will also be ways in which the act will wield $C \rightarrow E$ connections between the regions.

On the basis of all this, we may suppose that *B–1* will be analyzable into several simultaneous sequences, each of which might have an order analogous to that of the sequence *B–1* through *B–4* in figure *11*, but each of which would belong to a distinct spatial region of the brain. I shall give each of these sub-pattern sequences a number thus, C_1, C_2, C_3, etc. We thus get several simultaneous sequences, as follows:

$$C_1–1, \ C_1–2, \ C_1–3, \ C_1–4;$$
$$C_2–1, \ C_2–2, \ C_2–3, \ C_2–4;$$
$$C_3–1, \ C_3–2, \ C_3–3, \ C_3–4.$$

There is no reason to suppose that a unit from one sequence endures just as long as a unit from another sequence, but the

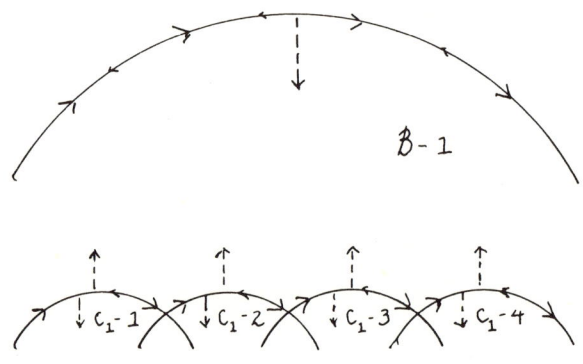

Figure *12*

endurance of each of the sequences would coincide with that of *B–1*. In figure *12* I represent the "relation" between *B–1* and just one of the sequences C_1 through C_3. Call the sequence C_1 and suppose it to be a sequence of spatiotemporal sub-patterns in one of the temporal lobes. I suppose the sequences C_2, C_3 . . . C_n to be taking place at the same time. Figure *12* thus stands for a much more complicated one which would achieve detail only at the expense of perspicuity. In other respects the form of the representation is the same as that of figure *11*. The representation is exceedingly schematic. The relative length of *B–1* and C_1–1 may, for instance, be absurdly out of scale; nor is there any reason to suppose that all members of the sequence C_1 should be of the same length. Each of these units will be, whatever else it is, a neural event, and perhaps one of considerable spatial complexity, involving very many neurons, but we do not here consider in the diagram either the multiplicity of the neurons or the fact that some single neuron may fire several times in the course of the unit. The diagram also does not allow us to represent what might well be an important feature of some of these units: the simultaneous firing of distinct and spatially separated neurons that nonetheless play a role in the total character of the unit.

As in the case of the previous diagrams we suppose that the act-temporality of B–1 is expressed in the act-temporality of each of the units of C_1 and indeed in each of the units of the sequences $C_2, C_3 \ldots C_n$, which are not represented. The principle of mediation requires that as B–1 was vicar for the originative act A, so now each of the act-temporal units of C is vicar for A as well. If figure 12 gives some sense of the unification of levels B and C by act A, it also conceals a considerable complexity. As we go down our ladder and add successive levels, this soon exceeds our capacity to imagine it. Any particular act-temporal power at any particular level will stand as a unity of action over against a multiplicity of subordinate powers that it unifies, orders, makes use of, and is identical with in an asymmetrical sense. Even if we continue for the moment to concern ourselves only with distinguishable spatiotemporal circuit patterns in the brain (ignoring those that are inflexibly tied to some sensory or motor function), it would appear that the units of C may stand in an act-temporal relationship to sub-patterns within each of them. Figure 12, then, would serve with appropriate relabeling to represent the "relation" between a unit of C and a unit of a lower neural sub-pattern level D.

At length we come to levels in which, as we saw earlier, act-temporal features are more inflexibly confined by persistent physical structures; and in which $C \rightarrow E$ features, which are of course present throughout any act-temporal unit, since it wields some particular complex of them, now seem more prominent and "mechanical" in that much of their course is dictated by the fixity of the structures they move through. In chapter 9 we shall turn to the origin of these structures in the act-temporality of the entities they depend upon, and we shall try to complete in that context the reconciliation of "mechanism" and the "real causality" of acts that this chapter has sketched out. But clearly, to the extent that the partial determination of $C \to E$ patterns by the nature of the structures they take place in—neural loops, single neurons, muscles, bones—increases as we descend through the levels of the infrastructure, these levels are heavy with the weight of mechanism. We do not encounter a pure act-temporality again until the level of the very small—the level that too much, as it seems to me, preoccupied Whitehead.

6

A consideration of the way in which $C \to E$ causality does not apply to act-temporal units and the way it does apply to at least some features of their infrastructures may help to make it clear how structural-mechanical features in an infrastructure can mediate the power of an act-temporal unit.

Consider first the relation between successive act temporal units. On our assumption, the act A is act-temporal, and each of the units in the subordinate sequence $B-1$ through $B-4$ (figure 11) is also act-temporal: indeed we described each of the units in the sequence as a vicar for the originative act A. Passing then to the infrastructure of the single unit $B-1$, we also considered its subordinate sequence C_1-1 through C_1-4 (figure 12) to be made up of act-temporal units. The very successiveness of the members of the two sequences immediately suggests to us that within each sequence the relation between a unit and its successor has much in common with the relation we try to capture with the help of the idea of the $C \to E$ connection (understood in either the working or the official sense). It would appear that $B-1$ contributes in some way to the character of $B-2$, and

168

B–2 to B–3, and so on; and the same point can be made about the sequence C_I–1 through C_I–4. I think this resemblance is deceptive, but even if the contribution were indeed a $C \to E$ one, it could not be adequately understood merely in terms of the laws of nature interpreted as a reductionist might interpret them. If we suppose both A and B–1 to unify their respective subordinate sequences by way of an act-temporal power "relation" to them, we must also suppose that their influence supplements the influence of the laws of nature so interpreted. Any contribution made by one unit to its successor would be subject to the influence of the superordinate act-temporality that pervades the whole sequence and that, in virtue of its temporal "reach," makes the relation between the members of the sequence different from what it would be if an adequate account of it could be provided in terms of a continuous time unqualified by act-temporality.

But the relation is not a $C \to E$ one. There are some very obvious difficulties in the way of interpreting the two sequences B–1 through B–4 and C_I–1 through C_I–4 in terms of the working view. An interpretation of that kind would ascribe, no doubt in a vague way, the occurring of one member in a sequence to the power of the previous member. On our diagrams, the temporal overlap of the units makes this hard to establish, but even if we suppose one unit to have ended before another begins (as in all of the earlier diagrams), there would be an obscurity to the working view's interpretation of the relation. Our diagrams are temporal, but there is a spatial aspect as well to our patterns, and the rhythmic nature of their pervasions of a region gives us no assurance that the spatial region where we detected the *last* trace of B–1 and C_I–1 would be the same one in which we detect the *first* traces of B–2 and C_I–2 respectively. That is, if we establish a temporal sequence such that B–1 and C_I–1 are clearly finished before the start of B–2 and C_I–2 respectively, it is by no means clear that we can establish the spatial connection that the naïvety of the working view seems to require.

The case is no better if we turn to the official view and restrict ourselves to some notion of the $C \to E$ relation in which regularity of succession plays the predominant role. It would surely beg the question to use this version of the relation to try to establish the sufficiency of a unit of B or of C_1 (regarded as cause) for the succeeding unit (regarded as effect). For there will always be *some* understanding of such a sequence that can be had by disregarding the act-temporal "relation" of A and $B-1$ to the two subordinate sequences B and C_1 respectively in favor of attention to $C \rightarrow E$ connections *within* the subordinate sequences. And even if A were different, and if through its power the subordinate sequence $B-1$ through $B-4$ were different, there would be precisely the same possibility of interpreting the sequence as a $C \rightarrow E$ one as there was before.

It is open to the critic to suppose that, given the boundary conditions, the sequence could not have been different without anomalies in the laws of nature. He might claim, for instance, that we can suppose that Socrates, instead of uncovering his face to speak to Crito, might have moved his hand in a simple gesture of farewell only if the group $B-1$ through $B-4$, which would then differ from what it is now, were to exhibit aberrations in the laws of nature. Any really determined attempt to discredit a unification of the series by A must presumably take this line. But to do so it must introduce deterministic metaphysical assumptions that are neither required nor justified by the practice of science. Such an attempt would naturally not be content with a consideration of supposed $C \rightarrow E$ relations within the group $B-1$ through $B-4$. Indeed it could scarcely take the level B any more seriously than it took A. It would fasten instead upon some supposed fundamental level, governed by laws in principle accessible to a perfected science, and upon the boundary conditions defining the physical state of the total biological system. The total state of the system at a time t_1 would then be held to yield in principle the state at t_2, and the supposition that Socrates could have acted otherwise than he did would thus be refuted. But it is hard to see how the boundary conditions, no doubt in any case impossible to establish in the desired detail, could be set without arbitrariness at the confines of the body:

presumably the state to be considered at time t_1 would have to be a quasi-Laplacean cross section of the entire universe. The implausibility of such a program does not of course demonstrate the truth of the view of action here presented, but it does make more plausible the claim that unification by an originative act A of an infrastructure series like $B-1$ through $B-4$ is not in the least inconsistent with the usual kind of scientific analysis of the level B. Science is normally concerned not with the total state of such highly complex systems, much less with a cross section of the entire universe, but only with relatively small regions of them. And its normal concerns are not pure ones in which there figure only events or states of the kind proper to a deterministic ideal, but rather impure ones that also take for granted entities like neurons and macromolecules; entities which, though they might in principle be understood otherwise, are in practice dealt with as though they constituted distinguishable levels of some sort within the systems the biological sciences are concerned with.

Some of the preceding discussion of the analysis of the two sequences $B-1$ through $B-4$ and C_1-1 through C_1-4 assumes that our critic has attacked our assumption that A and $B-1$ respectively are act-temporal. But if we insist on that assumption, which of course also provided for the act-temporality of *all* of the units of the two subordinate sequences, it is obvious that a $C \rightarrow E$ analysis of the two sequences would be very unenlightening. Each unit, except A, in both of the diagrams is a vicar for the act-temporality of A itself: it is part of the definition of these units that they can *not* be caused in a $C \rightarrow E$ sense. Within the persistent structure of Socrates' body we shall find an abundance of events that submit to $C \rightarrow E$ analysis, but we can not apply this analysis either to the successiveness of his acts or to the successiveness of any act-temporal units that there may be within the infrastructure of an act.

On the other hand, $C \rightarrow E$ sequences may indeed be found within the infrastructure of an act-temporal unit, and some of these may be in part determined by persistent structures. These may mediate the power of the act-temporal unit, and by doing so introduce into it the weight of mechanism mentioned at the end of the previous section.

Consider, for instance, some level lower down in the hierarchy than levels A, B, and C. Suppose our new level to be one that includes all firings of single neurons. The level will then subserve at least the following: (1) act-temporal sequences like those in B and C, which are by definition in our brain; (2) sequences in neural structures that form part of neuromuscular loops—for example, in the structures that control coordination of the turning of the eye with changes of focus in the lens; (3) sequences in neural structures of a more inflexible kind—for example, in a reflex that does its work independently of direct cortical command. Now neurons in any of these situations will fire whenever impulses reaching their afferent synapse from other neurons attain a certain strength, provided that inhibiting impulses from other neurons in synapse with them do not prevent this. Although we may not yet be in a position to say just how the $C \rightarrow E$ relations should be interpreted, the relation between the inciting neurons and the firing neuron seems a clear example of it. In case (1), where the neuron plays a role in an act-temporal unit, our assumptions make us ascribe the energy state of a given neuron and those in synapse with it to a pervasive act-temporal power. But with that reservation, there is no difference between (1) the firing of a neuron in an act-temporal complex, (2) the firing of a neuron in one of the neural loops that act-temporality might command in the act of attention, and (3) the firing of a neuron in a reflex arc. In the second case an impulse that may have been act-temporal in origin is now confined in the less flexible structure of the loop that mediates its power. In the third case the flexibility is gone. But if we discuss the reasons why certain $C \rightarrow E$ influences bear upon a neuron and consider only the fact that the influences *do* bear upon it, we can find no differences in the behavior of single neurons in the three situations. The pervasion of a spatiotemporal region by the power of an originative act does not cancel $C \rightarrow E$ connections but rather makes use of them.

7

The flat contrast between the utter unity and simplicity of an originative act and the uttermost complexity of its infrastructure is thus mediated by intervening levels some of which share the act-temporality of the originative act, and some of which merely reflect that act-temporality in the "telic" and time-bound nature of the persistent structures of which they consist. So long as this mediation is taken for granted we are in a position to state once more the otherwise preposterous sense in which the unity of the act A can be distinguished from the complexity it supervenes upon. Every element within the complexity, however spatially distinguishable, stands in a power "relation" with every element in act-temporal simultaneity with it within the complexity of the total infrastructure; and it is of the nature of that power "relation" that all the elements bound together in it stand in a temporal relation (of the sort proper to an action unit) with every other element outside that simultaneous time-slice but within the time-span of act A. All this must be qualified by the fact that any simultaneous slice through an act-temporal unit can not have the clear and unambiguous sense it would have in a linear time associated with the measurement procedures of physics.

The complexity of the infrastructure is therefore a unified one, and the counterpart of the unified complexity is the unifying act we call A. As we thus make our distinction the act remains identifiable by a description that includes some reference to the complexity of the infrastructure. We can not discuss the act without bringing in the complexity: Socrates' act is precisely the uncovering of his face and the speaking of the words to Crito, and any detailed analysis of this leads immediately to a complexity of the kind we have just been discussing. The considerable persuasiveness of the family of doctrines of which mind-body identity theory is just now the most influential representative depends upon an obsession with this point, combined with a total inability to see that the asymmetric and enigmatic "relation" of One and Many that we find everywhere in nature can sometimes be a power relationship. The unity of the act is everywhere and nowhere in the multiplicity of its infrastructure, and its pervasive presence is the presence of a power.

This chapter may appropriately close with a summary of the "relation" between an originative act and its infrastructure. An act like the one at level A uses, disposes, unifies the multiplicity represented by levels B, C, D, E, and so on; it is also subject to them and asymmetrically identical with them. The units at some of these levels have, furthermore, important features in common with A, features that make the terms "action-unit" and "act-temporal" more appropriate to them than the term "event." At others, the theme of $C \rightarrow E$ events in persistent structures becomes more prominent, though such events are wielded and controlled by A. The "relation" between A and its subordinate units must be consistent with the unity of its power through its act-temporal time-span. Its becoming is characterized by a temporal "reach" of power, in which all "parts," or "phases," of a time-unit are qualified by all other "parts" of the same unit. The complexity of the infrastructure of an act is also a spatial complexity, in which distinct and simultaneous elements are linked in a power nexus. In the sense that the elements are indeed so linked, we have to suppose a power that takes no time to permeate a spatial region, a spatial region represented somewhat abstractly by our diagram of a plane that transects the curved line of the time-unit. There is thus a spatial "reach" of power that is a correlative of its temporal "reach": the power of the originative act at A "reaches" throughout the spatial complexity that is at any moment act-temporally simultaneous with it. But though this power takes no time to permeate that spatial region, it is in another sense temporality itself, seeing that the permeation of the spatial complex is accomplished by virtue of the act's own development through the whole of the temporal unit proper to it: Socrates does indeed raise his cloak from his face and move his lips in speech.

The unity of an originative act is therefore nowhere and everywhere in a complexity of powers that it orders, disposes, unifies, and, in an asymmetrical sense, is identical with. (*a*) The "reach" of it is felt throughout a temporal span, but it is not exercised at or from a particular temporal locus. Although its power does not exist in temporal independence of its subordinate levels, it is neither before nor after all the units in them and it is neither before nor after any one of them. (*b*) It is exercised throughout a spatial region, and its "reach" is felt throughout that region, although by no means uniformly. Although it does not exist in spatial independence of the units of its subordinate levels, it does not exercise itself at or from a particular spatial locus, but only throughout the total volume, though with regions of emphasis here and there; and in this spatial "reach" no temporal span is involved. The parallel to the principle that the superordinate act is neither before nor after the units at its subordinate levels is the principle that the act can not be located at the place of one of its subordinate units. The power is exercised simultaneously in many widely separated spatial locations, but not from a distinct spatial source. In that sense, the "simultaneous" exercise of its power offers no offense whatever to any principle of physics. Indeed, it can now be seen as a mere instance of the principle that there can be no $C \to E$ influence between the power of an originative act and its subordinate levels, just as the notion of the temporal "reach" is an instance of the principle that there can be no $C \to E$ influence from one "phase" of an action-unit to a later one. If Socrates acts, he is nowhere and everywhere in the full complexity of the act in which he exercises his power.

6

The Mind of the Prisoner. Part One: Materialism and Consciousness

 THE MOVEMENT OF THIS MEDI-
tation is designedly circular, and it will return
at length to consider the agent, whom we took
at the outset to be the source of the acts I have
called originative. But before we can do that we
must turn our attention for awhile to the topic
of the mind, for if there are originative actions,
the most important of them appear to be those in which our
minds play the leading role. Socrates himself, in his protest
against the materialisms of his time, took it for granted that
what we should today call his mind was central to the
responsibility and authority of his actions. Indeed, he went
much further, for if we follow his text strictly, we notice that
what I have been calling the "real causality" of his actions
he himself identifies not so much with the action itself as
with what he thought he saw by using his mind: the realm
of the Forms, with the Form of the Good regnant in it. Since
we are not contriving here a defense of the particular
philosophy developed in the *Phaedo* and the other dialogues
of Plato, we shall not follow him so far; but we are at the
least committed to the view that mind may play an effective
role in originative action, and that in some cases—and the
"action" of standing fast in prison is one of these—its role
may be decisive.

There are still other cases that are perhaps best defined
simply as actions of the mind, since they have no other goal

176

than seeing things exactly as they are. That is in fact the aim of this meditation: to see the human agent and its action for what it is. And that is yet another reason for taking up the question of mind at this point. An action of this kind—an action on the part of the mind—is a reflexive one: intent on seeing action as it is, and the role of mind in action for what it is, it has also the obligation of assessing its own adequacy to a task of this kind.

The unity of the topics of mind and action will be apparent from these preliminaries, even if it is as yet by no means apparent what mind is. Certainly, if one conceives of mind as a species of originative action, one is obliged to show it to be "related" to an appropriate infrastructure. When we take up that topic again in chapter 8, the reader will see that the question of the "relation" between an "action" of mind and its infrastructure is dealt with much as though it were the old question of the relation between consciousness and its physical basis. That does not mean that mind and consciousness are taken to be identical. It does, however, mean that consciousness is taken to be a state, function, or activity—let us keep the terminology open for awhile—that belongs to mind, and belongs to it in so essential a way that without some reference to it the topic of mind remains totally obscure. To the agent that "performs" it, an action of mind takes the form of mind-becoming-conscious, and every attempt to disembarrass himself of that fact in the interest of a more "objective" or "scientific" approach to nature only leaves him more firmly committed to it. When we begin to philosophize, the action in which mind-becomes-conscious has, at one level, already been accomplished for us by phylogeny, ontogeny, and maturation; but thereafter every effort at attentive awareness as well as every effort at conceptual understanding includes the aspect of mind-becoming-conscious and revealing itself as such to the agent who concerns himself with such matters.

Since Descartes this theme has been taken up again and again by philosophy, but never, I think, with the clarity it demands if it is not to deceive us utterly. Today more than ever one takes it up at the risk of being understood to say that our

177

first certainties are those about our consciousness, subjectivity, or mentality. It is not enough to say—as I do—that this is not what one means. The risk is there anyway, inherent in the delicacy of the theme and also in the cultural situation that will be touched upon at various points in this and the next chapter. I shall take the risk anyway, because I think that clarity about mind-becoming-conscious is in many respects prior to the theme of the "relation" between act and infrastructure, since it confers upon mind a self-conscious autonomy from which it is capable of judging the authenticity of that latter theme. The reader is asked to consider this and the next chapter as examples of originative acts of the mind that would be no less effective if taken in complete ignorance of the "relation" between act and infrastructure. In this chapter I shall focus upon a negative point: that materialism is committed to a program that denies the efficacy of mind-becoming-conscious but nonetheless implicitly relies upon it. The next one makes the positive point: that clarity about mind-becoming-conscious brings with it an autonomy that consists precisely in the awareness that it can not be caused in a $C \rightarrow E$ sense or in any other. We shall then be ready to return to the theme of its own "real causality."

2

Although we might find ourselves at a loss to give an exact definition of mind and a precise account of the role mind plays in Socrates' actions, most of us probably take it for granted that it does play an important role. Imagining ourselves there in prison with him, we can identify a number of different acts and describe them in terms of the overt movements of his body and the words he uses as he speaks to us. But we suppose all this to be accompanied by awareness, consciousness, thought, feeling, and a number of other things we associate with mind. No doubt we attribute these things to him in part because we find them in ourselves. As we listen to what is said—the eloquent, complex, and, as it might well seem, often sophistical arguments

178

of the *Phaedo*—we see him, we hear him, we are engaged in thought as we try to follow him, we understand or are puzzled, and we are moved, each in his fashion, by what is said and the situation in which it is said. But we are also aware, or conscious of, these things, and as we make this point in these words, it also is borne in upon us that we are self-aware, or self-conscious. The word "mind" comprises these things and more, and confronting Socrates as observers with minds, we attribute mentality to him as well. All this is too abstract, and without giving any such reasons, any observer of Socrates will simply take it for granted that he has a mind, and that the nature of his action displays that as clearly as it does his possession of hands, feet, and lips.

Even if we have no particular sympathy with Descartes, most of us will be willing to grant that any account of the overt feature of Socrates' actions—of his behavior, as some might prefer to say—may be usefully supplemented by an account of everything that he is aware, or conscious, of—everything, that is, that passes through his mind—as he performs the actions. And under "everything" we might list at least as many things as Descartes did in the definition of a thinking being I have already quoted: "What is a thing that thinks? It is a thing that doubts, understands, conceives, affirms, decides, wills, refuses, and that also imagines and feels" (*Meditations,* II). The word "consciousness" is not, as it happens, in that list; yet, armed with post-Cartesian cultural equipment, we might feel that the idea of a thinking being presupposes consciousness, and we might wish to supplement the list with an account of what consciousness is. Despite the influential aridities of behaviorism, this, the century of Proust, Joyce, Virginia Woolf, Freud, Jung, and Husserl, has been remarkable for its introspective exploration. It is only natural to be as clear as we can about what has so fascinated us. In any case, we have only to glance at contemporary discussion of the mind-body problem to find that we can not take part in it without talking about the nature and role of consciousness in our own nature.

If we begin by trying to define it we are hampered by its utter familiarity and also by its thoroughgoing involvement with

179

the very act of formulating a definition: it seems that when we try to define it we can well be said to be trying to become articulately and precisely conscious of the nature of consciousness itself. If we insist on making the attempt anyway we can say, I suppose, that consciousness is a state or mode of being in which we sometimes find ourselves when we are passive and sometimes find ourselves when we are active. But then we must also notice that "finding ourselves" means "being conscious of ourselves." We may express this in a negative way by saying that consciousness encroaches upon any effort to formulate it. But a more positive way of putting it is to note that, in us at least, if not with other animals, consciousness is always *self*-consciousness. Many writers since James have agreed with him that it is not an entity, and that we have no right to identify it with the Self or the Ego or the Subject or the Soul or the Person or a Substance—there is no need to fasten upon any one of these terms since there is no generally accepted way they have been used either in this or in other connections; and they have followed him in calling it a function or an activity.

State, mode of being, function, activity—no doubt they all fit it in some of its manifestations, and the last two will plainly be useful in connecting it with the general theme of this meditation. Hardly a definition, though, unless we qualify these terms in a way that puts us right back where we started: conscious state, conscious mode of being, conscious function, conscious activity. Maybe it will help to dwell upon its familiarity: who is not conscious of being conscious? Yet its familiarity is of an odd kind, for it consists in its being the basis of our familiarity with anything else. I am *conscious of* the tree outside the window and the chaffinch singing in it, I am *conscious of* the pen in my hand. And to say this is to make consciousness elude us once more: it is a state, function, activity that is so neutral and transparent that much play has been made in this century with its being *nothing* in itself. In the moments we are most familiar with it we are familiar with it as presenting the quality of *what we are conscious of.* Thus though pain is private and subjective and the trees outside my window are not, that fact is of no help whatever to

180

me in any introspective attempt to isolate "consciousness it-self." At best I am limited to noting that I am conscious of pain, or conscious with pain, or painfully conscious. Indeed, the tend-ency to think of our awareness of pain as more "subjective" than our awareness of the tree probably should be really attributed to the fact that it brings home to us, more immediately than our awareness of the tree does, that we are conscious in and with our bodies.

If consciousness should be thought of as a "medium" — and I think this metaphor, though useful, misses at least one impor-tant feature of it that I shall deal with later — then it is a medium in which the tree is found no less than the pain, and in that case attending to the pain is no more revelatory of the nature of the medium than attending to the tree is. The body, mediating consciousness, qualifies the medium and makes it seem less neutral than it is to just the extent that, being conscious in and with the body, we are also conscious *of* it. But the reflexivity of consciousness is full of paradoxes, for to note that the metaphor of a medium has some uses and to go on to say that the medium is neutral or transparent is probably to say something true about consciousness. Surely it escapes definition, but watching it do so is to learn something about it. And even if we could propound an acceptable definition, the definition would contribute to our heightened and more accurate *consciousness of* the thing defined; besides which, we should also be *conscious of* our definition, con-scious also that we understood it or not, agreed with it or not.

State, medium, quality of our being, function, activity: what-ever it is, it admits of degree. In sleep we are either unconscious or conscious in a limited way, and under anaesthesia we may be totally unconscious. But even the relative intensity of conscious-ness can scarcely be measured except by the clarity and order, the vagueness and confusion, of *what* we are conscious of. And, given a certain degree of intensity — as my own state as I write — there is also the matter of focus. I am aware of a plane passing overhead, the voice of a mason working on a wall outside, the rustle of papers in the next room, a bird in the tree outside the window, but all of them are, except for the purposes of this example, peripheral to what I am trying to say. They come to focus as I use them in the example, and then fade again as what I am trying to say becomes the focus of my awareness, my consciousness, my sentience. Trying to say! One is reminded at once that to speak of it as a quality, a medium, a state, even a function, that admits of degree, that is capable of focus, is to miss something of great importance. It is only when I succeed in saying what I wish to say, am trying to say, what I am only half aware of as I try to master it by the power of an act, that I can at last be said to be fully conscious of it. From this perspective the only one of the notions we have been toying with that appears to fit consciousness is that of activity—a notion, to be sure, that is close to that of function but that threatens to bring back with it the agency William James meant to exclude by describing it as a function. Conscious of something or other, something I am not clear about, I aim at becoming clearer about it, and the outcome of the effort is successful: it is an achievement of a more adequate consciousness. Presumably even while invoking the term "act" we can not disembarrass ourselves completely of the terms "state" and "medium." It begins to become clear that we can scarcely speak of this feature of mind with any adequacy by relying only on such words as "consciousness" and "awareness," since we seem to be concerned with a movement towards, an achievement of, consciousness. But the effort, the exercise of power, springing as it so often does out of a prior and less satisfactory state of consciousness, now illuminates that ordinary or habitual state, giving it too an air of achievement.

It is usual to think of an expressive act of the kind I have been discussing as an act of understanding. So it is, but if we dwell only on that aspect of it and take our everyday sensory awareness of the world as a paradigm of consciousness, there arises a false and confusing opposition of conceptual understanding and consciousness. By approaching it as I have done I hope to make it clear that understanding is a heightened mode of awareness of what we thus understand. It is true that when we complete an act of expressive understanding we do so in and with the set of symbols—words, images, formal symbols—to

182

which we give an ordered structure. These too we can be conscious of just as, for that matter, we are conscious of the meaning of any set of symbols we can understand, whether or not we take them as guides to the nature of the real world. But, in their role of mediating understanding, symbolic structures are properly as transparent as "consciousness itself" — they should, that is, mediate our awareness of the real objects or features of things that they are "about."

I have piled up so many terms that have at one time or another been associated with mind that I trust it will be clear that I do not think it is wise to fix upon one or two technical terms to discuss this important feature of action. One notable term that has had a curious history is absent from the list — "subjectivity." It must eventually be introduced, though with great caution because it inevitably drags with it the polar term "objectivity." But if we set that difficulty aside for the moment and refuse to entertain preconceptions about "objectivity," it may be the best general term for this important feature of Socrates' actions. It includes without strain a whole realm of affect — emotion, feeling, passion — and of valuation that the word "mind" is sometimes thought to be unsuitable to; and it can include comfortably as well many features that are unconscious and yet contribute to either the quality or the content of consciousness.

What role, then, does mind play in Socrates' actions, taking mind to include all those features of Socrates' nature we have touched upon in this section, and especially consciousness and subjectivity? The answer will depend on whether we take it seriously as what it purports to be: clearly as Socrates acts or as we ourselves act, we *seem* to be *aware of* our world around us, and this seems to be vital to our behavior even at the level of physical orientation within that world; and clearly, in complex kinds of actions involving moral decision, scientific discovery, and artistic creation, the *bringing into consciousness* of what we were at best vaguely or confusedly aware of seems to play an important role. And all this is compatible enough with the "relation" between act and infrastructure that is so laboriously emerging

183

in the course of this meditation. If we take the agency of Socrates to be a "real cause" we must suppose that his mind, his subjectivity, his capacity for consciousness, is an important factor in it. Most of us make this supposition habitually, and one suspects that out of office hours many materialists do too. But on the other hand we have only to dismiss, with the materialist or reductionist, the reality of originative action, to alter the picture profoundly. What we have been calling the infrastructure of the act will be called instead the physical structure of the body, and this, operating as a $C \rightarrow E$ complex under known laws of nature, will be regarded as sufficient, if understood in sufficient detail, to explain the complex event we have chosen to regard in another light. The "real causality" of mind regarded as an aspect of the "real causality" of an agent — regarded that is, as an aspect of an originative act — goes with it. It is not surprising, then, that the contemporary scene abounds with materialist explanations of mind in which subjectivity, consciousness, and the seeming "act" by which with considerable effort we bring something into consciousness, perhaps deploying as we do so act-temporal units of immense complexity within the physical structure of the nervous system, are set aside as, at best, irrelevant, except as symptomatic of underlying physical processes of deeper import and, at worst, illusory.

The task of this and the next two chapters is to bring the mind-body problem under the rubric of the "relation" between originative act and infrastructure. There that ancient and intractable dualism may be more easily subdued, the more so as the asymmetrical "identity" we have found in that "relation" is no dualism at all — at least not in the sense we associate with Descartes or, for that matter, with the *Phaedo* itself. But before that we must look at at least some of the more materialistic interpretations of mind that hold the field today. Some of these views come from scientists in the field of computers. More, and perhaps more extreme, views come from philosophers who follow these matters, as I do, as conscientious amateurs who know something in a professional way of symbolic logic, of which the modern computer is a prodigious offspring. The physiologists

184

are, as we shall see, more circumspect, and from some of them, at least, we have drawn some, and will draw other, illustrations congruent with the theme of originative action.

3

We have grown accustomed, after a quarter century of astonishing progress in the theory and design of computers, to think of these devices as electronic brains. Their achievements are already so great and their future promise so intoxicating that we no longer find any exaggeration in the name. Indeed, their capacities exceed those of our own brains in so many important respects that we scarcely suppose ourselves to be flattering the computers by this comparison. During the same period there have also been great advances in our knowledge of the structure and function of the brain, although they have been neither so spectacular in a practical sense nor so satisfying in themselves as computer discoveries. The brain remains more difficult to understand than a computer, which is not surprising, since we have not constructed it. The analogies between computers and brains are obvious enough on a superficial level and they have been and are being pursued at deeper levels by a vast troop of biologists, physicists, mathematicians, and philosophers. The circuitry of computers and of computer-dominated automata has often furnished illuminating models for some aspects of the central nervous system—especially the servomechanisms already mentioned. Sometimes, although less frequently, the study of the central nervous system has led to some suggestions about possible lines of development for electronic brains. The compactness of the animal brain, and especially that of the human animal, is a marvel that no computer made of hardware even begins to approach. As progress is made in the study of the "machinery" of the brain one would expect the impact upon computer development to increase. It seems at least possible that structural changes in the RNA molecules of the nerve cell's nucleus play an important role in certain forms of memory, although Hydén's theory to that effect has found some formidable critics.[1] These molecules are very complex; they are also, although large for molecules, very small by most standards. A more compact form of "memory bank" than these minute intricacies, with their vast range of combinatory possibilities, can scarcely be imagined. Another area in which brain physiology may be of more immediate help to the computer engineer is in the development of new computer relays incorporating the flexibility and adjustable thresholds of the neuron.[2]

In these circumstances it is not surprising that the mind-body problem, which has never really ceased to interest the philosopher, should now enjoy a wider vogue. It is a notoriously intractable problem, so intractable that it is difficult even to state it in a way satisfactory to all parties to the dispute, let alone solve it. The very way one party will state it will look like at least the outline of a solution to another, and may indeed look like a total denial that a problem exists.

Many computer scientists and their philosophical allies maintain that we are already well on the way to solving it, if indeed the progressive success of this line of investigation can not be said to have solved the problem already. They think they see a gradual improvement, to which they see no limit, in the simulation of intelligence and cognition by the computer, and this persuades them that the secret of mind consists entirely in the organization of a set of physical events analogous to those which, within the computer, enable it to perform its wonders. There are, to be sure, important dissenters, and it is not entirely surprising that some of them are workers in the more advanced kind of programming. But in this field it is orthodoxy to hold that consciousness, which one might well take to be the heart of the problem, is nothing of the kind. Perhaps a complicated enough machine can produce it as a kind of queer by-product of its problem-solving efforts; perhaps it is an irrelevance not worth discussing whether we are dealing with men or with machines. Even if, as some computer men concede, consciousness might play some positive role in either men or machines, it must still be regarded as *produced,* or *caused,* by the physical events in

186

the machine or the organism. But the general attitude engendered by computer studies is that it is chiefly by attending to the physical structure of the computer and the central nervous system, to the analogies between them, and to the outward behavior of machine and man that we may hope for an adequate understanding of the capacities we usually sum up under the term "mind." The practical achievements possible within this framework are so impressive that those who work within it are generally willing to ignore the fact that it is not completely satisfactory and to assume that, whatever its defects, there is no alternative way of understanding mind available to us. To pursue the problem in this way is to lean towards a solution for which we have used the names "materialism," "mechanism," "reductionism," and "physicalism"; we may now add "epiphenomenalism" and "behaviorism" as names designating the application of this general attitude to the particular problems of mind and body. If one undertakes to *make* consciousness, he presumably advocates this solution in an extreme form; if, like the behaviorists, he thinks we can simply ignore it, the positive investigatory procedures he advocates will nevertheless bear out the main lines of this solution.

Most of the discussion of consciousness-making has revolved around the question whether an appropriately contrived physical structure can cause, bring about, or produce consciousness even if that physical structure is inanimate. Although it has often been highly technical it has not really come to grips with the difficulties that lie behind those innocent expressions "cause" and "bring about." We may suppose that some version of the $C \rightarrow E$ relation will be assumed to prevail within the structure of the machine. One suspects that in the construction of computers the working view is taken for granted: if a certain circuit is closed the *power* of the current flowing through it will *cause* a certain relay to close; but no doubt if pressed on this matter the philosophers, if not the engineers, involved will take refuge in the more circumspect official view. But to say that such a very complex pattern of such $C \rightarrow E$ happenings will produce, cause, or give rise to consciousness is to suggest a relation

187

between the total complex and consciousness that is itself hard to construe in $C \to E$ terms even if one is committed to the soundness of the $C \to E$ view of causation.

At any rate the question under consideration requires that we replace the image of the human body and its brain with the image of an appropriately constructed machine. The word "machine" if of course taken in a very wide sense, so that any piece of electronic apparatus can be considered a machine. In particular, the question concerns the machines usually called robots — machines that are under the control of a computer in much the way in which a body is said to be under the control of a brain, and that also have appropriate sensory and effector, or motor, organs. Can such machines, when their construction is sufficiently intricate and their performance sufficiently impressive, be said to doubt, understand, conceive, perceive, affirm, deny, will, reject, imagine, learn, want, decide, feel, and do all the other things we have associated with human minds ever since Descartes first produced his familiar list as a definition of a thinking being? Is it possible that, whenever a machine carries out a set of physical operations whose end-products, or, to use computer-jargon, whose outputs, are like the end-products, or outputs, of human thought, at least a trace of consciousness accompanies these physical operations? The question is put precisely enough, and it would not do to confuse the issue by supposing that it depends upon the obvious analogy between electrical impulses in a computer and electrical impulses in the brain. The logic of the problem would be unchanged if we supposed our machine to be constructed, like the famous Analytical Engine planned by Charles Babbage in the early nineteenth century, of gears, levers, pulleys, and other such old-fashioned hardware, although the machine would have to be much bigger in that case.

To answer the question affirmatively, it would seem, is to accept the classical solution to the mind-body problem that holds that consciousness is caused by, or is epiphenomenal upon (an "appearance on top of"), an underlying material organization. Yet even if one admits the presence of consciousness in a machine, and grants that it has been "produced" by the machine, it is by no means clear that epiphenomenalism has really won the day and that the other classical solutions are immediately excluded. Setting aside as unsporting the obvious objection that it would in fact be the (conscious) *maker* of the machine that had produced consciousness, there are still a few things to be said in favor of the solution called interactionism, which was given its formulation — at least for the modern era — by Descartes. He separated mind (thinking substance) very radically from matter (extended substance), and described each of the two substances in such a way as to suggest that happenings within each of them were in principle self-contained. His position thus gives rise to the possibility of a set of mental happenings understandable in $C \rightarrow E$ terms and a set of physical happenings understandable in $C \rightarrow E$ terms, and there seems on the face of it no reason why one such complete $C \rightarrow E$ account should require reference to the other. Yet his account of man, whom he takes to be a composite nature involving both substances, requires that the two $C \rightarrow E$ sequences do interact. The logical difficulties are enormous. Modern defenders of interactionism, who generally think of the interaction as taking place between mental events and physical events, rather than between substances, inherit these difficulties. And the difficulties are compounded, since their adherence to $C \rightarrow E$ analysis is more complete than the adherence of Descartes, who stands at the beginning of the development in which a more complex traditional sense of "cause" is gradually reduced to the $C \rightarrow E$ sense.

A modern defender of interactionism who, in defiance of all difficulties, wished to make his point in terms of machines might well argue that if consciousness is not present in machines of a low degree of organization and behavior, but is present after a suitable degree of intricacy of organization and behavior is reached, the possibility can not be excluded that consciousness, produced by the machine, then becomes efficacious *upon* the machine. If pressed to define just what he meant by "efficacious," he might say that if there are some internal physical states of the machine that are not predictable on the basis of its earlier physical states, and if, further, what is otherwise inexplicable in these physical states becomes explicable on the hypothesis that the intervention of some particular conscious state produced them, then a prima facie case has been made out for interactionism. But if such a machine were constructed, we could not understand it in $C \to E$ terms unless we also assumed some aberration in the physical laws that go with $C \to E$ analysis. One startling consequence would be the impossibility of giving an account in purely physical terms of the physical operations of the machine, for one physical event would not follow from another in $C \to E$ fashion in accordance with the laws of physics alone, but only in accordance with them as supplemented by a happening in consciousness. And the intervention of this happening would have to be consistent with its own concatenation, in $C \to E$ terms, with similar happenings in consciousness. The intercalation of the two series would also seem to require some anomalous interstices in physical time, for the $C \to E$ intervention of a conscious happening in a series of physical happenings would have to take place *after* one physical happening and *before* the next one in the series.

There are of course many who feel that we can make no inferences from the behavior (or output) of either machines or organisms to consciousness. For these the dispute between epiphenomenalism and interactionism does not arise, nor does it make sense to turn to some other solution. According to this view, epiphenomenalism, interactionism, parellelism, and contemporary alternatives to these classical positions suffer alike from a fascination with that will-o'-the-wisp, consciousness. According to Watson's classical formulation of behaviorism,[3] consciousness is merely something whose existence we assume. It can not be seen, touched, smelled, tasted, or moved, and accordingly has no place in the scientific study of human behavior, for which the laws of physics and chemistry suffice. It should be banished from our scientific vocabulary along with the other subjective notions that have been used to talk about it, notions like sensation, perception, image, desire, and, above all, pur-

190

pose. Even the the notions of emotion and thought are to be tolerated only after appropriate redefinition. To introduce consciousness either in the spirit of epiphenomenalism or in the spirit of interactionism is unscientific and medieval. Those who do it are guilty of what Watson calls vitalistic or spiritualistic leanings: it is quite as bad as if they had tried to explain behavior by talking about the soul. Despite some changes in it since Watson's day, behaviorism still holds, in effect, that the scientific study of behavior is only obscured by talking about consciousness. Although it is now willing to talk about "intervening variables" in the physical account, these variables are dealt with as mere placeholders, temporarily intractable strong points against the advance of the physical account, which are bypassed for the moment by the progress of the method, but which by the same token furnish convenient objectives for future mopping-up operations.

One historical curiosity that bears upon this point should be mentioned, if only because it makes the pattern less tidy. As we have seen, Descartes held that consciousness (thinking substance) was acted upon by the body (matter, or extended substance), and that in its turn it was capable of altering the course of the physical happenings in the body. He supposed, however, that this kind of interchange took place only in the case of man. Indeed, he denied that other animals possessed any consciousness at all. In this limited respect, then, he sounds like a behaviorist. With respect to man he is, naturally, the very reverse of a behaviorist, for the entire structure of his philosophy — including even what he has to say about animals — is based upon a scrutiny of the contents of our own consciousness. It is clear, however, that he felt the force of at least one premise of behaviorism, namely, that if we consider behavior from the outside only — as a set of physical operations, so to speak — then however "intelligent" that behavior may appear to be, we have no reason whatever to associate consciousness with it. Indeed, we can make complete sense of it in terms of the laws that operate in physical operations. Far from being constrained to attribute consciousness to the intelligent behavior of machines, we have no need to attribute it even to the intelligent behavior of organisms other than man.

4

The claim that consciousness can in principle be produced in machines is often associated in contemporary controversy with the name of the English mathematician, the late A. M. Turing, who published in 1950 an influential essay called "Computing Machinery and Intelligence." [4] The association of Turing with the issue of consciousness is not quite exact. His chief claim, which is supported by an exact analysis of the "discrete state" kind of computer, is that if a machine could be so constructed as to take the place of a human being in a game the point of which is to deceive another human being (call him Simon), and if the machine managed to carry out the deception so that Simon was indeed deceived, then it would be difficult to say that the machine did not think. The point of the game (now often called the imitation game) need not concern us here; it would seem that Turing has, in his wish to be rigorous, made it more complicated than it need be. But on the hypothesis that Turing entertains, Simon is deceived, not only in the sense that he never guesses that his opponent is a machine, but also in the sense that he fails to guess the identity assigned to the machine by the conventions of the game. The machine does as well as a human being does at the game, and also does not give away the fact that it is a machine. It is at least a plausible hypothesis that such a machine could be constructed. It should not, however, be supposed that Turing intends us to think that the machine is conscious. It would appear, rather, that he thinks the question of consciousness is not an important one. His solution to (or dissolution of) the mind-body problem is in short the familiar solution of behaviorism. Let us confine ourselves, whether machines or men be our theme, to the question of intelligent behavior, which is (so he appears to say) the only question worth considering anyway. The instinct of those who attack Turing as though he were defending the epiphenomenalistic view that consciousness can be caused in a machine, is, however, sound enough in a practical sense, for behavioristic solutions depend upon an acceptance of the chief premise of epiphenomenalism, namely, that the only data worthy of serious scientific attention in the psychological sphere are observable physical happenings.

Turing was of course at once brought under fire from several quarters. One attack, especially interesting because the author later reversed his own opinions, came from Michael Scriven in an article called "The Mechanical Concept of Mind."[5] In that article Scriven argues that the evidence of behavior is never sufficient to prove that an artifact is capable of consciousness. This does not seem to be an effective argument against Turing if I am right in assuming that Turing is advocating a behaviorism for which the issue of consciousness is irrelevant. It does, however, seem a sound enough criticism of the position against which Scriven explicitly directs himself. In a later article called "The Compleat Robot: a Prolegomena to Androidology," Scriven sums up his earlier disagreement with Turing in this way:

> Now, the substance of my disagreement with Turing was that a machine *might* be made to duplicate sensation-behavior without having the sensation, i.e., the designer could fool the interrogator.[6]

Playing the imitation game, then, is not a conclusive test. But Scriven came to believe that there are better tests, and he proposed at least one that, if successfully passed by a robot, would give at least the same grounds for attributing mind or consciousness to it as we have when we are dealing with people. Scriven is not, if one understands him, a behaviorist. Certainly he maintains, in the later of the two articles, that there is an irreducible nonbehavioral element in mind and identifies that element as "a compound of the possession of sensations and the possession of personality." Assuming, then, that in all the outward signs of intelligent behavior the robot's output is indistinguishable from that of a man (in Scriven's terms, that it has "all the performatory abilities of humans"), we need only determine whether this missing component is present.

The test he suggests for determining this is ingenious. Its essentials are as follows: the robot is taught English; it is taught to use "subjective" language where appropriate in referring to men ("Scriven is in pain") and "behaviorist" language in referring to itself and to other robots ("Robot 289 has been subjected to an overload current"); it is taught that the subjective language *might* be applicable to itself as well; it has fed into its memory banks "the complete works of great poets, novelists, philosophers, and psychologists"; and, finally, it is given circuitry that prevents it from lying. Scriven has such an offhand way with formidable difficulties that in reading him one finds oneself taking it for granted that providing such a liberal education for a robot is a trifling technical consideration — something that can be left, so to speak, to the engineers. And it may not even occur to the reader to wonder whether, in assuming that we can provide a robot with circuitry that makes it incapable of lying, we are not in fact already assuming that our robot is conscious. What is lying but being *aware* of one version of the facts and reporting another? And not being able to lie, then, is presumably being aware of the truth without being able to report something false. We should never say of something or someone that it could not lie unless we assumed that it *was* conscious — not, at least, if we meant the word "lie" literally. At any rate, Scriven asks us to assume that all these difficulties are taken care of, and that our robot is now ready for the test.

The test turns out to be a simple one: the robot is asked whether it has feelings, and if the answer is yes one half of the part of the mind that is not reducible to behavior must be ascribed to it. The ascription of personality then appears to follow easily, although the arguments for it are based rather on the convergence of evidence than on logical necessity. What aspect of human personality has the machine failed in? Well, it is hard to fault the robot, whom Scriven calls R. George Washington;

but it does seem that in describing the test and the provisions leading up to it he has in fact been saying something like this: "If we can construct a robot that is as intelligent as a human being, and that is moreover conscious, then we ought to ascribe mind and indeed personality to it." And with this proposition we might well agree, and yet continue to wonder whether the issue had been settled for us. We might also feel that Scriven relies too heavily on that familiar refuge, the phrase "in principle." Certainly the programmatic side of his test is so vast that we might find his argument unconvincing even if we could overlook the question-begging side of it.

Presumably the question remains open, for those who took it seriously in the first place, but the debate of which Turing, the earlier Scriven, and the later Scriven are fairly representative makes it clear that for many people the mind-body problem seems soluble by the tour de force of so constructing a machine (an artificial "body") that it will have mind. It would then be at least plausible that the answer to the mind-body question that holds consciousness to be an accompaniment, and only that, of a certain kind of physical organization (epiphenomenalism) is the true answer.

5

Perhaps the most ambitious assault on our problem from what would appear to be this angle is to be found in James T. Culbertson's *The Minds of Robots*.[7] At least Culbertson is concerned with establishing the principle that it is possible to build a conscious robot, and with telling us, moreover, how to go about building one. That the angle is a little different is plain from his rejection of the label "epiphenomenalism." It will be instructive to follow his argument some little way, both to see how illustrative of an epiphenomenalistic position it is, in some important respects, and to see why, in spite of what would appear to be the demands of logic, he refuses to be considered an epiphenomenalist.

195

His central claim is that a subjective sense experience will occur when impulses pass through either a suitably contrived "neural" structure of a robot or a suitable neural structure in an organism. This claim he calls "physicalism"; and he defines it, by reference to dictionaries, as the doctrine that human thought and action are determined by physical organization. A little later he also describes his position as "pure materialism." [8] The terms "physicalism" and "materialism" are certainly interchangeable enough, and if the former term is used more often recently, it is probably to avoid the association between the latter and the too-naïve conception of material that prevailed before the twentieth-century revolution in physics. At any rate, one expects a physicalist, or materialist, to be an epiphenomenalist. Culbertson defines epiphenomenalism, acceptably enough, as follows: "the point of view that consciousness results from neural activity but has no influence on neural activity." [9] He holds not only that it is in principle possible to construct robots that are conscious in the sense of epiphenomenalism, but also that an insignificant and trivial form of consciousness accompanies "any machine activity where impulses are connected together while passing through the machine." [10] Epiphenomenalistic robots are of little interest, as such a useless form of consciousness would have no survival value and hence could neither arise in nature nor throw any light on behavior. He maintains, however, that a more interesting type of conscious robot, in which the consciousness would *direct* the behavior, can also be constructed. And he believes that man's consciousness is of this more interesting kind. It is incredible, he thinks, that epiphenomenalism should be an adequate theory of man's consciousness. For one thing, consciousness has a survival value for men; for another, it permits a much more economical brain structure than would otherwise be possible for an entity having so complex a behavior pattern. [11]

It would not be surprising, then, if we found Culbertson also maintaining that in men there is an interaction, if not of two distinct entities, mind and body, then at least of two distinct kinds of events, mental (or conscious) and physical. He does not in fact do so, and this rejection of dualistic interactionism [12] is presumably what leads him to believe that he is successfully maintaining a physicalistic position despite his insistence on the efficacy of consciousness and the rejection of epiphenomenalism that follows from this. I doubt whether the position as he states it is a consistent one. There are indeed other physicalist positions that are not—at least according to those who have devised them—epiphenomenalist, the most prominent being those forms of the identity theory that are clearly materialist, or physicalist, in their bias, as their alternative name, central state materialism, implies.[13] Yet these, while they agree with Culbertson in denying the existence of distinct mental events, also deny the efficacy of consciousness, since they ascribe all efficacy to a single reality—the physical one with which they hold mind to be identical. Whether their position is really distinct from epiphenomenalism, seeing that, of the two names said to be applied to the identical thing, one is plainly taken more seriously than the other, does not concern us here. But at least their physicalism carries with it a usual consequence of physicalism, namely, that consciousness has no efficacity whatever. Culbertson seems to combine two principles that are in conflict: (*a*) consciousness is efficacious in a sense different from the efficacity of physical processes, even though it is not an entity or event that is distinctly mental rather than physical; (*b*) it is nonetheless caused—entirely caused—by physical processes.

His book has, it seems to me, two real virtues: it wishes to take consciousness seriously and does so to such an extent that it often seems in conflict with its own materialist premises; and —as we shall see shortly—it takes very seriously the matter of the temporal relations within a pattern of brain impulses. The commonsense conviction that our capacity for consciousness really does enter into our getting things done has a lot to recommend it, so much so that we might well prefer Culbertson's doctrine to run something like this: "There *is* an important physical basis for consciousness, so important that there is no consciousness without it. This has been the subject of penetrating and profitable study by the physical sciences, and if current

197

progress continues, we may before long see *how* that physical basis contributes to consciousness. Nevertheless consciousness is not a superfluous phenomenon, and the physical account of it may for all we know be in principle incompletable; and if it is, so be it; we shall have to devise a theory of causation in keeping with that odd fact." I do not know what we should call an attitude like that, but I am sure it would not be a physicalism. But neither would it be the interactionism he is so concerned to avoid.

Culbertson does want to say that consciousness is (wholly) caused by the passage of impulses through a certain kind of physical structure, and that is what makes the impact of the book a physicalist, or materialist, one despite the inconsistencies within which the physicalism is set. His view seems to be that the book must be physicalist in philosophy if it is to be scientifically sound. But the result is a picture of consciousness difficult to take seriously, for all of our sympathy with the things he has to say about the importance of consciousness. It seems beyond any ingenuity to make clear the nature of a consciousness that is totally caused by physical events; that is not sufficiently distinct from the physical to be called mental; that is nonetheless efficacious upon the physical in a way distinct from the way in which the physical is efficacious upon the physical.

Culbertson's is not the only ingenious doctrine whose natural development is hampered by a dogmatic scruple. D. M. MacKay, who shows in many ways that he takes the efficacity of consciousness seriously, nonetheless allows a materialist premise to control his argument at every vital point. His view of the mind-body relation is a "double-aspect" one, consciousness being the "*internal aspect* of the total human activity, of which brain (and body) activity is the complementary 'external' aspect." [14] Like Culbertson though, he is struck by the usefulness of consciousness, and to that extent shows some signs of distinguishing his view from the more patently materialist versions of identity theory. In reading his discussion of a postulated metaorganizing system (he takes it to be in the midbrain rather than in the cortex), which organizes "internal action upon the behavioral organizing system itself," [15] and which has conscious experience as its correlate, one almost expects him to propose that of the two aspects the conscious one may be causally dominant in the sense that we—no less than the internal observer himself—might turn to it for an understanding of why the physical processes of the metaorganizing system are as they are. But from the beginning of the essay MacKay's controlling premise has been what he calls the "physical determinacy in the linkages of the cerebral information system," [16] and he interprets this, not just as we have done, as meaning that *some* set of $C \to E$ connections would manifest themselves in any circumstances, even those where the controlling factor was the "real causality" of an originative act, but rather as meaning that there is a succession of states in which the later ones are predictable on the basis of earlier ones. For an external observer, at least, we are dealing with a physical system only, and one understandable in almost Laplacean terms; in principle, future conscious experiences are predictable because they depend upon cerebral states that are themselves predictable on the basis of past cerebral states.[17] The ingenuity with which McKay then labors to reinstate the significance of the mental aspect that is thus diminished suggests that he could help us more with the riddle of consciousness if he freed himself from the dogma of physicalism.

To return to Culbertson: it may be useful to follow his argument a little further if only to see how he uses the word "cause" as he tries to answer the question how consciousness can be caused in automata, and thus, by analogy, how consciousness is caused in men. We shall be concerned only with what he has to say about a passive, or receptive, consciousness, although in fact his argument goes much further. His answer is an ingenious one. It depends first of all upon the obvious analogy between circuit components in a computer—for simplicity's sake, let us say a switch that upon receipt of an electrical stimulus of a certain intensity will transmit it along an attached wire —and a neuron, or nerve-net cell. Culbertson is interested not just in the spatial path of a given "neural" impulse to a certain part of the machine, but also in the time taken by such an impulse and its temporal relations, in turn, to a whole group of similar impulses. The point is, roughly, that the physical basis of consciousness lies not merely in the reception of certain impulses in a certain location, but in the integration over the dimension of time of a complex of impulses moving through a three-dimensional space. He therefore describes the impulse through a neural net in an automaton in terms of a "world-line." A world-line (the term is derived from relativity physics) is the path of a body, particle, or impulse, through a four-dimensional "space" of which time is the fourth dimension. Such a line is, strictly speaking, not representable, although various dodges have been employed in the past to make more vivid to the concrete imagination a conception that can readily be handled, as can, for that matter, "spaces" of n dimensions, by modern geometry. One can make a stab at representing it by first reducing the spatial dimensions to two and then using the third dimension in a solid (or perspectival) model to represent time. One then simply assumes that the third spatial dimension is present as an additional complexity.

Culbertson employs this diagrammatic device to represent that variety of world-line he is interested in — namely, the movement of a neural impulse through the three dimensions of a brain (or an automaton), which movement "takes up" a certain amount of the fourth dimension, time. He calls these world-lines CT lines, or lines of causal transmission, and it seems clear that they are in fact what I have been calling $C \rightarrow E$ sequences moving within persistent physical structures. In representing them on a page, in his most simplified procedure, he simply uses the *direction* of a CT to stand for the three spatial dimensions and its *length* to stand for the temporal dimension. It is interconnected groups of such CT's that concern him and, in especial, groups that have the general structure, in his diagrams, of the inverted branches of a tree. Where mathematical analogies can be established between such a "tree" and the spatial structure of some sensory quality of things, a patch of color for instance, the neural happening of which the "tree" is a model is held to yield in the machine a consciousness of that sensory quality.

200

Does the consciousness *follow* the completion of the tree, so that we can thus establish a *CT* line, or a $C \rightarrow E$ connection, between the whole of the tree and the event in consciousness? It would be difficult to maintain this, especially if, like Culbertson, one does not wish to introduce mental events distinct from the physical events. It seems to follow that the sense of "cause" that applies to a *CT* line—the sequence of physical events in which an impulse is transmitted—must be radically different from the sense we should have to give the word if we said that the existence of a neural "tree" causes consciousness. Culbertson does not appear to have noticed this.

This is an oversimplification of but one part of a very complicated argument. At least one aspect of it would appear to have considerable merit. That is the claim that consciousness involves an integration over a time-span of impulses coursing through the complexities of a nerve-net, and that therefore the image of consciousness in terms of messages moving along nerves to a certain "place," where note is taken of them, is an inadequate one. The inadequacy does not mean that localization does not play an important role in consciousness, as, for instance, in awareness of sensory qualities. Brain physiologists can locate with considerable exactness areas concerned with sight, sound, touch, and smell. All this, however, is perfectly compatible with the claim that consciousness of data locally received involves an integration over a time-span. The claim is, however, not a new one. It is one of the main themes of that classic of brain physiology, C. S. Sherrington's *The Integrative Action of the Nervous System,* and that great physiologist also gives it eloquent expression for the nonspecialist in his *Man on His Nature;* [18] insofar as it is persuasive at all, it is because it does rest on physiological evidence. It is an insight by no means tied to physicalism, and indeed it can be given a most natural interpretation in terms of act-temporality.

In Culbertson's book the elaboration of this and other basic claims has a dogmatic air, however, and the discomfort this provokes in the reader is aggravated by the book's organization, which is that of a "programmed" textbook. At the end of each section there is a set of questions or problems designed to make one learn the terminology and theories so thoroughly that they become second nature. Failing any feasible experimental proof of the doctrine, one gathers, the truth of it is to be established by the ineradicable thought habits generated in those who read it with attention. For those whose aversion to programs prevents their being indoctrinated in this way, there is also suggested an experimental test for the theory, but it has its grave difficulties. Some of them are logical ones, such as plague Culbertson in his discussion of epiphenomenalism, interactionism, and such matters: that is, it is not at all clear that the experiment if successful would prove what Culbertson wants it to prove, namely, that the machine is indeed conscious. Others are physiological, surgical, and moral ones, for the experiment would require a coupling of the machine with the receptor organs of a man—say his optical nerve—in such a way that those organs might never again be put back into their original state. On the part of any volunteer for the experiment we should have to assume a dedication to the theory so complete that we might hesitate to trust the poor fellow's report of what he was aware of when coupled to the machine.

6

Dean E. Wooldridge, in his *The Machinery of the Brain*, takes a line more unequivocally physicalistic than Culbertson's. His book is intended as a summary of what is now known about the structure and function of the brain, but it is a summary couched almost entirely in terms of the analogies between computers and brains. This approach fits Wooldridge's conviction that "a competent theory of intellectual processes will come from the physical scientist, with the aid of clues supplied by natural organisms." [19]

As the title of the book suggests, Wooldridge prefers to call his philosophy mechanism rather than physicalism or materialsim, perhaps a sound enough choice since his emphasis is clearly on the role played by persistent physical structures. Throughout most of the book mechanist (and hence epiphenomenalist) views are merely implicit in his clear exposition of what is known about the neural "mechanisms" that subserve the automatic, or unconscious, control systems that operate in the brain. The problem of consciousness is naturally related to a number of important topics he devotes himself to — the speech centers of the cortex, for instance — but for most of the book it is kept, as he says towards the end, well in the background.

When he finally confronts the problem directly, in two concluding chapters, he becomes more explicit about his commitment to mechanism and epiphenomenalism. He concedes that the qualitative attributes of "the subjective phenomenon of consciousness" make it impossible to account for "by any combination of physical principles known today." This would be disastrous for "mechanistic models of brain function" if consciousness is indeed "an active and directly controlling part of brain function." In such a case the "mechanistic explanations are not likely to be in accordance with the observed facts of behavior." But if "consciousness is purely a passive property, a kind of window through which we can observe a small part of the workings of the brain without interfering with the orderly operation of the machinery we are watching, then we can hope for pertinence of our models to conscious as well as to unconscious activity." [20] He goes on to say that in the course of the book he has been implicitly subscribing to the passive theory of consciousness and will continue to do so. He thus finds it possible to regard consciousness as a clue to the workings of an underlying mechanism that is in fact of deeper import, much as an engineer, in analyzing the construction and function of a new and unknown computer, would take due account of any flashing lights, cathode ray oscilloscopes, and meters he found on the control panel, without supposing these to be more than symptomatic of the real operative principles of the strange machine. Consciousness, then, he is prepared to regard as a "display device" rather than as the most essential operative feature of the human mind.[21]

203

The present state of knowledge of the brain, however, is so fragmentary that Wooldridge is willing to concede that it is logically consistent that some small degree of control is exercised by consciousness. We are not now in a position to detect such conscious control if it does exist, and so are justified in proceeding on the assumption that our present methods are adequate. He takes it for granted that the exercise of any control by consciousness would involve a small perturbation, or aberration, of the physical principles established by science.[22] In doing this, he is of course assuming that mind would have to be efficacious in the admittedly anomalous sense of Cartesian interactionism. That consciousness, or indeed any function "higher" than those that operate in the inanimate world, should be efficacious by cooperating with, or making use of, these principles is a possibility he does not even consider. Presumably there operates here, as generally in materialisms, the Laplacean notion that the physical state of any system, however complex, at time t_1 will enable us to predict the physical state at time t_2, a notion that does not arise where act-temporality is taken to be more fundamental than linear time.

Why the Laplacean dogma should be so persistent is hard to see. Its origins are connected with the perfection of celestial mechanics (taking "mechanics" here in the restricted Newtonian sense rather than in the more general sense implicit in Wooldridge's use of "mechanism") in the late eighteenth century, and in principle a mechanical state is only one aspect of a total physical state. What exactly one might mean by "*total physical state of a brain at time t_1*" is in itself obscure, and if it were clarified it would no doubt be even clearer than it is now that it eludes all practical measurement. The notion of an unqualifiedly total physical state at some time t implies in any case the unqualifiedly total state of the entire physical universe at the same time — a conception to which we can attach no clear meaning. Act-temporality offers an alternative to this dogma. The application of predictability to it is qualified by the fact that the only "state" we can point to that does not distort the reality of the act is the "state" of the whole infrastructure under its dominance for the whole time-unit in question. We can no more describe this total spatiotemporal pattern in detail than we could a Laplacean slice, but what we are pointing to is different in character from such a slice. A spatiotemporal pattern of this sort does not of course exist in isolation, but the only restriction under which it develops is that it can be in conflict neither with the unity of any wider spatiotemporal frame within which it exists nor with the unity of the spatiotemporal systems it comprises.

Alternatives of this kind are congruent with an analysis of a neural pattern after the event that is complete in a $C \rightarrow E$ sense and implies no anomaly in the physical laws — unless indeed it is an anomaly that the interpretation of the pattern as an expression of act-temporal power excludes in principle a *prior* Laplacean analysis of it, an analysis that would in any case have been precluded on practical grounds. Wooldridge, having entertained no such alternative, takes it for granted that any efficacity on the part of consciousness will be an anomalous intervention of mind in the lawful operations of matter. Thus, if any opponent should maintain that the conscious entity's efficacity will not ever be adequately explained in physical terms by way of the gradual progress in the investigation of the brain's mechanisms, Wooldridge must convict him in advance of entertaining an outmoded Cartesian image of mental activity, an image that elevates the anomalous interference of mind with matter into a metaphysical principle. Wooldridge, then, expects the view that the mind is nonphysical and that it makes use of the brain as an agent for some of its activities, a view which he calls the "dualistic brain/mind concept," to continue to lose ground to the advance of science. And he supposes that advances in this sphere are due not only to electronic computer developments, but also, and perhaps to a greater degree, to the success of the traditional physiological approach.[23]

Wooldridge, like Culbertson, devotes considerable attention to the many analogies between brains and digital computers — computers, that is, that are constructed to solve extremely complicated problems by means of a large number of component steps, each of which may be thought of as taken by virtue of a "yes or no," or "true or false," decision whose physical counterpart is a switch that is either on or off. His physicalism nowhere appears more clearly than in this part of his exposition. He makes the point — soundly enough, one might venture — that the analogies between computers and brains are more profound than those that are most frequently cited, namely, the electric nature of the impulses in both computer components and brain cells and the digital character of both computer switching components and brain cells and nerve synapses. He points out that research is now going forward into "electronic neurons with variable-summing and adjustable threshold features" and that the narrowly digital character of our digital computers is probably not here to stay. The essence of the modern computer, he thinks, lies rather in its capacity to break "complex computational and logical operations" into simple processing steps. And this, he maintains, "would appear to be a valid description of the essence of brain function." This point is of course debatable, but the chief premise of physicalism — that the laws operative in the smallest components are the real laws of nature, and that laws operative in more complex contexts are derivative from these — is here clearly applied to the philosophy of mind. And it is this clarity of application that leads him to make common cause with Culbertson at least about the possibility of constructing a conscious computer. Because his physicalism is more consistent than Culbertson's, it appears to Wooldridge that this would yield us a mechanistic, or epiphenomenalistic, solution to the mind-body problem.[24]

7

In the preceding section I have taken it for granted that a physicalist, or materialist, account of mind has the following features. (*a*) Consciousness — more accurately, mind-becoming-conscious — is irrelevant to the achievements of an intelligent person or machine. This is a point about which behaviorists, epiphenomenalists, and those who hold an identity theory (in

206

the sense of central state materialism) would agree. Culbertson and MacKay would not, and I am taking this to be inconsistent with the physicalism both are concerned to maintain. (*b*) Where present, consciousness may be regarded as entirely produced, or caused, by the physical processes it is correlated with. Those who make this claim take it for granted that the analysis of the physical processes is to take place entirely in terms of $C \rightarrow E$ relations determined by physical structures; they usually leave vague the nature of the causal relationship between the physical processes and the conscious experience. If it is assumed that that too is a $C \rightarrow E$ relationship, then the conscious experience is an epiphenomenon taking place *after* the physical event that produces it. If it is not, one might suppose the conscious experience to be a simultaneous epiphenomenon, the causal relation between physical event and conscious experience then being mysterious—at least from the point of view of materialism. (*c*) Conscious experience may alternatively be regarded as identical with physical processes in the central nervous system. The question of any causal relationship between the two things identified naturally does not arise, nor can we, strictly speaking, consider one of them to be the epiphenomenon of the other. On the other hand any account of the sequence of conscious experience adds nothing of any explanatory value to the account of the sequence of the neural events in $C \rightarrow E$ terms.

Culbertson, MacKay, and the growing number of workers in both computer science and physiology who take the efficacity of the conscious mind seriously stand in need of a philosophy other than materialism to interpret their most creative insights. One suspects that an interpretation of that kind would not only be satisfying in itself, but would release besides an imaginative power that now seems much hampered by the materialist dogma. As it is, a strict materialistic interpretation deprives conscious experience of any genuine explanatory value. And this sets a very strange goal for physiological investigation. It is so implausible a goal that simply stating it clearly may lead us to look again and with unjaded eyes at what most of us take for granted most of the time—the importance of consciousness.

Where the dogma of philosophical materialism operates in

computer research it is assumed that, whether or not consciousness should be attributed to machines, we must be able to explain their operation without bringing consciousness into the explanation. To the extent that neurophysiological investigations are conducted under the dominance of the same philosophical dogma, it must be taken for granted that the intelligence with which the organism operates must also be explained without including as part of the explanation the fact that the organism is conscious. And as it could be said that it is precisely because we do not need to draw upon the notion of consciousness that we understand machines so well, so it could be argued that we shall not really understand human intelligence until we can deal with it in the same way. Each step the machine takes in solving some problem can be understood by electronic analysis and its place in the succession of similar steps can be plotted. A computer scientist who works through the operations of the machine in detail will understand just why it produces the answer it does produce; and, assuming that the problem was stated properly to the machine, he will understand that the answer is the correct one. He does not suppose that a consciousness presides effectively over any single step the machine takes or indeed over the whole sum of them. He sees instead that the throwing of a certain switch has been caused by a current flowing through a certain complex of circuits; he sees the throwing of the switch causing current to flow through another circuit complex. These physical events lead to others, these to still others, and so on until the physical events in which the machine types out an answer.

So far, we have a classical application of the structurally based $C \rightarrow E$ relation to a physical interpretation of mind. But that is not the whole story. We do indeed understand the course of the physical events in $C \rightarrow E$ terms, but we also see that each step is justified by the previous steps and contributes to the justification of later steps. The point is not that a physical operation like the closing or opening of a switch in itself justifies anything. It is rather one that is frequently made about computers and indeed historically lies behind their development, namely, that the physical structure of a computer is an analogue of a formal logical system. As J. R. Lucas puts it, "it is of the essence of being a machine, that it should be a concrete instantiation of a formal system." [25] We have to consider not only the physical structure of the machine, and the nature of the physical impulses coursing through it: we also have to consider the meaning of its structure and the meaning of the impulses. This point is sometimes expressed in a distinction between the machine state and the logical state or between electronic analysis and mathematical analysis. If we consider the demonstration of a theorem in logic, it is neither the writing down of the steps nor the succession of physical shapes on the paper that constitutes the valid demonstration but the meaning of the steps and the shapes. And so here it is our understanding of the meaning of the structure and operation of the machine that makes it clear to us why the answer given was the correct one.

On the other hand, though we as observers might distinguish between the physical process in the structure and the meaning of it, between the machine state and the logical state, between the electronic and the mathematical analysis of the machine, it is at the same time clear that we do not have to bring the meaning of the machine's operations into any account of the way it operates. Still less do we have to bring consciousness into it. I am not, I hasten to add, confusing the meaning of a structure or a process with a possible consciousness in the structure or process, although I think MacKay does so in the essay cited earlier.[26] Even if we did have to bring the meaning of the structure in, the question of consciousness would not arise. If one were to write out in conventional mathematical symbols — no doubt in a very large number of pages — the successive steps in a computer's solution of a problem, one would have on the paper a physical structure that carried a meaning, but one would not attribute consciousness to that string of symbols. The point is rather that for the observer of the computer the account is *causally* completely satisfactory in purely physical terms and therefore excludes any recourse to consciousness as a causal factor.

We are therefore in a position to make an important point about the kind of physiological evidence that is necessary to make physicalism tenable. Let us suppose that brain physiology has been perfected sufficiently for us to state with exactness the physical counterpart of any conscious state (or, if you prefer, the physical state with which the conscious state is identical). On this supposition, we can understand and plot the course of all electrochemical impulses in the central nervous system just as clearly as we can in principle chart the course of the electrical impulses in the computer.

Consider now some human subject engaged in thought. For simplicity's sake we consider this subject to be engaged in a simple logical argument, or perhaps in the solution of a chess problem. We then plot all the electrochemical impulses that take place in the brain during the solution of the problem, and we isolate and set aside those impulses that subserve routine sensory and motor functions. We are left then with an analyzed bundle of ordered impulses that forms the physical counterpart of the problem.

It would appear that if physicalism is to stand, we must be able to see, by an analysis of these physical events taken in themselves, why the person gives the answer he does give, and why it is (as we shall assume) the correct one. Just as with the machine, we must be able to see why the significance of the succession of physiological steps both leads to and justifies the conclusion. If we can not do so, then we have come upon a fundamental difference between artificial and human intelligence.

This is not the place to discuss in detail the difference between artificial and human intelligence. It would appear, however, that there are important differences. Although Wooldridge's book is full of examples of analogies between computer operations and certain operations of the central nervous system, these have largely to do with the adjustment of sensory mechanisms and motor control. There are certainly now no examples of brain mechanisms the analysis of which would both show us how a human being solved some simple conceptual problem and justify the correctness of the solution at the same time. But for the moment my concern is merely to point out what a perfected

210

physiology must look like if the analogy with machines is to be sustained.

For physicalism to be persuasive it is not enough to know in detail the physical correlate of every conscious act and the physical correlate of coming into consciousness "out of" the unconscious. What is needed is that our knowledge of the physiology should enable us to determine not what the subject is thinking but whether what he is thinking is valid, or, more precisely, whether the steps taken by the nervous system are valid. We should be able to say, "His neural structure reached the conclusion by way of the following steps. Each of the steps is sound. Therefore the conclusion is sound." We should, that is, be able to eliminate consciousness and consider only input, steps, and output and still say (as we can with machines) that the reasoning is sound. Each step, as a physical process, would be understandable in $C \rightarrow E$ terms as in the case of the computer, and we should have invoked in addition only the significance of the steps to ourselves the observers (and not to the subject) to assure ourselves that the reasoning was sound.

It is not plausible that even if such a program were in principle sound it could ever be carried out; the practical difficulties seem so great as to be of quite a different order from any other scientific enterprise that can be imagined. If we conceive of it as going forward in spite of these difficulties and then breaking down at some point because of evidence decisively against this perfected materialist description, there will be some interesting consequences for the role of consciousness. If on the other hand we brush aside all difficulties and assume the program to be carried forward to a successful conclusion, we produce a "situation" whose logical structure may tell us even more interesting things about consciousness. Let us explore these possibilities in turn.

If it is not plausible that such a program could be carried out, it is plausible that its decisive failure would lie in the discovery that the consciousness of the subject played an indispensable role at some point. It can not be too much emphasized that it is a very strict program, and that recourse to an effective consciousness at this or that point in the explanation would vitiate the exclusively physicalist character of it. Suppose, for instance, that at some point in the research in support of this program some neural processes were discovered the whole significance of which seemed to be that they were associated with an effective conscious experience in the subject. It is important to be clear about what is meant by "effective conscious experience," but it is difficult to be clear about this matter. Our supposition has three parts, each of which is necessary to bring out this point. (*a*) Our hypothetical neural processes *lack meaning* in the sense of "meaning" appropriate to computers, in which, for instance, a set of relays or other electronic devices in a certain sequence of *on* and *off* positions might *mean* to the observer, the user, or the programmer of the computer a certain number in binary notation; or the passage of current through a set of devices making up a logical gate in the circuitry of the machine might *mean* some particular step in the proving of a theorem or the solving of a problem. (*b*) The neural events possess meaning in the sense that they have been shown to be the correlative of a conscious experience. (*c*) The experience, qua conscious, is effective in the reasoning of the agent. At the least, this means that in an explanation of his reasoning the materialist observer will find it necessary to employ such language as "the subject saw (or perceived, was aware of the fact, was conscious, noticed, observed, concluded) that if he took the pawn with his knight his queen would be vulnerable to his opponent's bishop," or "the subject saw that it followed from his premises that there should be smallpox antibodies in the blood sample," or "the subject concluded that the rate of inflation would not increase appreciably in the first quarter."

Two things should be added. Our physiologist does *not* read the meaning of the neural processes as a set of propositions to which he then adds "the subject saw that" or "the subject concluded that" and so on. The *meaning* of the neural process, on our hypothesis, is not "if the pawn is taken with the knight the queen becomes vulnerable to the bishop," but instead a conscious experience on the part of the subject that requires the investigator to use language like "the subject saw that if he took the pawn with his knight his queen would be vulnerable to his opponent's bishop." Nor does there seem any reason to suppose that his having to use such language would require some physical lacuna in the account of the neural processes going on at this time. The difficulty lies rather in the fact that to make sense out of his reasoning the neurophysiologist has had to employ a different language from the kind usual in a neurophysiological explanation. The neurophysiological account in itself would be as clear as any other; it would simply not yield as satisfactory an account of his reasoning. So also with the (as we assume) perfected neurophysiological account of his overt actions: there will be no anomaly because the subject fails to move his hand to take the pawn with the knight, but moves the queen instead.

In fact, no trouble arises at all unless our materialist, determined to make the evidence for the effectiveness of consciousness compatible with his materialist position in philosophy, sets about trying to show that the conscious experience, said in our supposition to be the correlative of a complex neural event, has a further relation to it that supports the claim that a neurophysiological explanation is not only complete in itself but explanatory as well of the conscious experience. It is to be hoped that he would not try to show consciousness to be an epiphenomenon or to demonstrate it to be identical with the correlative physical process, since the hypothesis we have taken for our example appears to exclude this. Probably he would try to show that the correlative neural event wholly caused the conscious experience, and that no conscious experience could legitimately be said to cause a physical event. His position would then be analogous to that of Culbertson, who, though he has taken the efficacity of consciousness seriously and has not been forced to it by the breakdown of an epiphenomenalist program, has nonetheless taken upon himself the burden of reconciling physicalism — the minimum feature of which is that consciousness is caused — with the usefulness of consciousness. It is not our job to find a sense of "cause" that will accomplish this for him.

Indeed it seems no sense would do: the conscious experience is to be wholly caused (in some sense) by the physical correlative; yet, being effective, it must be acknowledged to be effective in the minimum way associated with conscious experience — the calling forth of yet another conscious experience, as when, conscious of two propositions, I might then become conscious of another proposition as following from them; yet this next conscious experience must be caused by *its* physical correlative; which, on the other hand, also seems to have been indirectly called into being by the *first* conscious experience. This difficulty, be it noted, turns up even if our materialist manages to avoid invoking causation in the $C \rightarrow E$ sense. Once this sense is introduced, it brings with it the well-known hopeless logical tangles of Cartesian dualism, the chief of which is that of reintroducing into the order of physical causation the effectiveness of consciousness that our hypothesis credits it with, even though it also extrudes it from the neural sequence in holding it to be caused by the latter.

For my own part, I take it that a quite different framework, no Cartesian dualism but certainly no materialism either, is necessary to make sense out of the "relation" between a conscious experience and the neural events that in some sense support it and are made use of by it. In that framework, consciousness can not be said to be wholly caused in a $C \rightarrow E$ sense or in any other, no more than an act can be said to be wholly caused by its infrastructure. A consciousness that is not wholly caused by the physical events that subserve it, but is an aspect of the "real causality" that unifies the infrastructure to which those physical events belong, is sufficiently "related" to the physical events to be anomalous neither by an excessive detachment from, nor by an excessive involvement in, them.

These are important considerations, and it certainly seems likely that if the materialist program did break down decisively it would be in some such way. On the other hand, suppose it does not break down; suppose the goal had been reached, and in exactly the terms I stated with the help of the computer analogy. Will there not be something in the situation of our reaching that goal, and contemplating it, so contradictory that we can not find ourselves in it, no more than we can ever find ourselves contemplating a round square? Let us suppose that with the help of a perfected physiology a physicalist "demonstrates" that Newton's discoveries were made by an entirely computerlike process. On this supposition Newton was a computer whose print-out was the *Philosophiae Naturalis Principia Mathematica* precisely as we have it, but who at no moment in the working out of it depended in any way upon being aware of certain premises, being aware that any conclusions followed from them, or being aware of any definitions, any equivalences, or anything of that kind. Since not even a physicalist will ordinarily want to deny our Newton-computer awareness of some kind, we shall take the line Wooldridge suggested and assume that whatever awareness he did have was entirely useless to the course of his discoveries—that it was at best a symptom or display device indicative of the entirely physical processes that terminated in the print-out, or the write-out, of the *Principia*. We now make a further concession to the physicalist: although he knows, and we know, that conscious persons read and understand—or fail to understand—the *Principia*, we shall assume that the readers are also computers. Their reading, their private debate with Newton, in which they are, let us say, finally persuaded of the soundness of the *Principia*, also contains no awareness that does any useful job, and their print-outs, write-outs, or speak-outs are entirely computerlike.

But this whole line of speculation suddenly takes on an air of complete unreality even as I contemplate the skein of evidence that leads to this materialist theory of mind, with its infinite regress of computerlike activities. For it strikes me that I have seen, read, understood the evidence, which is to say that I am aware or conscious of it, together of course with the image that goes with it. Moreover, to say that it strikes me is to say that I am *aware of* the involvement of my *awareness* with the propounding and proof of the materialist thesis. In less paradoxical language, I am conscious of the fact that there is no way of stepping out of the circle of consciousness to confirm its supposedly

215

otiose character. And the more we reflect upon the nature of the circle the more this inability appears not so much a practical difficulty of a negative kind, but an aspect of a positive feature of consciousness. This brings with it a formidable logical difficulty for materialism: to the extent that we are aware of and understand the nature of this "circle" of consciousness we can not assert without contradiction the truth of the materialist theory of mind just sketched.

The image of a circle is a deceptive one, since consciousness is not a place to which we are confined. To say that I have seen, heard, read, understood the evidence for materialism (or for any other position) is to say that I am or could be aware or conscious of it, and is to say no more than that. But it is enough, since there is no other way in which the evidence is accessible. The point can be made without bringing in the metaphysical and epistemological presuppositions of Descartes, Berkeley, or, for that matter, Husserl. The point is not that we are conscious only of our own subjectivity or only of that miscellaneous gear the history of philosophy has furnished it with — essences, concepts, ideas, impressions, percepts, mental states, and all the rest of it. The point is that whatever we are conscious of declares the functional importance of the consciousness that has attained it, and declares it all the more to just the extent that we maintain that what we are conscious of is the flat, unqualified, and objective truth and to that extent independent of the consciousness by which it is known. Our hypothesis requires us to view the materialist's theory of mind as successful in the sense that all the evidence under review announces that subjectivity, consciousness, coming-into-consciousness is of no use whatever. The evidence purports to show that my being aware means at the most that the complex circuitry of the brain has processed and simplified a vast amount of information and "printed it out" in my speech or handwriting, and that my understanding (in the sense of being consciously aware of what is the case) is symptomatic rather than functional. Yet our assessment of the evidence is *from* subjectivity. The very conviction that it is objective is suffused with the subjectivity that formulates it. If it is said that the evidence is objective, and that the sense of the efficacy of our own subjectivity is precisely subjective, the materialist still does not escape the nub of the difficulty, for the very objective character imputed to the evidence is a function of the very subjectivity whose functional value the evidence calls in question. The very distinction between subjectivity and objectivity is a function of the subjectivity that entertains it. There simply is no other source for the normative notion "objectivity" than the subject that propounds it, so that it can scarcely invoke that standard of objectivity to question its own autonomy. And there is no other source for the pejorative judgment that some evidence or experience is subjective than the subject that propounds it.

The functional significance of consciousness pervades every attempt to discuss it, and its refusal to go away, as we shall see in the next chapter, is unaffected by our choice of a "realist" or an "idealist" epistemology. There is simply no stepping out of the circle of consciousness to confirm its supposedly otiose character. As we try to settle the status of that seemingly active labor whose seeming means, whose seeming fruit, is a coming-into-consciousness, we have no means at our disposal but that same seeming labor, no criterion but that same seeming fruit, that moment in which we see that such-and-such is the case. Suppose Newton to bombinate in write-outs; suppose Smith, when he expounds Newton to Jones, to fulminate print-outs or speak-outs; suppose Jones, when he is persuaded, to double-quick duck-speak an assent in which awareness plays no contributory role. But I, as I write these idle words, and you, gentle reader, as you take them in, are quite unable to hold fast to these suppositions. The very making of the supposition about Newton, Smith, and Jones is so dependent upon our own consciousness as to subvert its own content even as we make it. We make the judgment or assessment because we are aware, or conscious, of the steps Newton, Smith, and Jones have gone through, and because we are aware, or conscious, of the significance of these steps. We terminate the regress of supposed nonconscious "discourse" by our own response to it, a response so qualified by

217

the consciousness that makes it that we immediately become an exception to the generality we establish for observing their activity. We assert that mind-becoming-conscious plays no role in Newton, Jones, Smith, but the only reasons we can give for this assertion are reasons we become conscious of. Either Newton, Jones, and Smith operate differently from the way we do, or the supposition we have just made about them is false. Either way, we reinstate our own consciousness, so that we shall probably prefer to reinstate those of Newton, Smith, and Jones as well.

In an earlier article I called the situation that gives rise to this argument the consciousness-centered predicament. The predicament, though, is properly that of the materialist as he sets out to deny the efficacity of consciousness. Properly speaking, the conscious mind is a vantage point, the unique virtue of which is that *from* it one can reach out to things that are precisely not part of consciousness. For that reason I have labored to make it clear that the view expressed here is in no way tainted with Descartes' or Berkeley's supposition that our first certainties are about consciousness or its contents. I hope the reader will understand, then, that I am not saying that we are so enclosed in our own subjectivity as to make it a problem for us to pronounce upon an objective set of events. The point is a quite different one, one that is often overlooked in academic philosophy, either because its naïvety puts it beneath notice, or because the noticing of it would turn at least some learned disputes into idle games. It is that any determination of the nature of objectivity (reality, what is the case) in general, or any determination of the particulars within such a general framework, is an exercise on the part of a subject. Subjects attain or fail to attain objectivity; they are conscious of, aware of, what is the case, or they are aware of something else and take it to be what is the case. This is a hazard of subjectivity, but there seems no reason why this point should lead to an idealism, still less to a solipsism. It merely means that we can not consistently deny the functional relevance of subjectivity all the while we are hopelessly involved in it. Its functional presence qualifies alike its successful attainment of the truth and its unsuccessful preoccupation with itself or its own creations. My point, then, is not Berkeley's, and it leaves open the possibility of our determining objectivity to be anything whatsoever — so long as what we determine it to be does not make totally impossible the point of vantage from which we make that determination. "From" and "with" subjectivity we can manufacture and peruse computers, and can speculate in various ways about them; but "from" and "with" subjectivity is not in the least an enclosure or confinement within subjectivity: it is part of the finality and importance of subjectivity that truth seen "from" it may still be truth seen.

So the word "predicament" is not quite appropriate. It is a rhetorical flourish designed to point out that there is a genuine predicament for any philosophy of mind that, motivated by scientism, denies the efficacy of subjectivity. Viewed neutrally, it is merely a condition of the exercise in which a subject does precisely what subjects alone can do: becomes aware of, knows, pronounces upon, assesses other things, many of which are not subjects. We meet this "predicament" very often as we traverse the terrain of the debate about agency, mind, and body. We met it a little earlier when I observed in passing that it is the significance of a set of logical symbols on paper or of a set of physical steps in a machine that decides the soundness of the "reasoning" process in question. The determination of that significance is also endlessly regressive if a consciousness does not terminate it.

The predicament might well be called by other names. As the agent-centered predicament it gives rise to this line of argument: there is no way of disproving the "real causality" of agency except by exercising what presents itself in the very course of the proof as the "real causality" of agency; there is no way in which a proof becomes established as a proof except when agents exercise their seeming agency to accept it; it is therefore impossible to disprove the reality of agency. Alburey Castell has used a version of this argument to such good effect that there is very little that one can add to it.[27] Another familiar predicament, the language-centered one, leads back to the consciousness-centered one. It is a common observation that we can

219

only understand things as we articulate our understanding in language, and that our understanding of language itself must be articulated in language. It is less frequently noticed that living in a web of language is also living in a web of consciousness. A world in which one nonconscious computer was "read" by another, who reacted with a print-out that was "read" by another, who in turn reacted, etc., ad infinitum, is a world of highly ordered physical operations, but there is no language whatsoever in it. It is only because we make computers to "read" our language, or "read" languages intertranslatable with ours, and because somewhere, sometime, the results of computer activity are read and understood by conscious beings, that we are justified in using the word "language" about them at all.

If we were persuaded, either by the implausibility of the physiological goal of physicalism or by the sheer logic of the consciousness-centered predicament in which the physicalist is placed, that consciousness is an important part of the success of any human subject in solving a problem, making a discovery, or creating something of worth, we might return to physiology to pursue it free of the dominance of the machine image. In analyzing the physiological events in the brain we might no longer think of them as steps in the solution of a problem, but rather as part of the infrastructure that subserves an action one qualitative feature of which is the agent's consciousness, or more precisely his ability to bring things into consciousness; and the successive steps of the solution, or at least some of the chief of them, would then be regarded as owing their very existence to the fact that they *did* come into consciousness. Our problem might be no easier, for it would now be the old problem of the physical basis of consciousness, but then that might be nearer to the right problem than the other. On this hypothesis we might, incidentally, have fewer grounds for supposing that a set of problem-solving steps in a machine would produce consciousness in it. Consciousness would so imperiously present itself as at least a factor in the "real cause"as to make the notion that it can be wholly caused appear hopelessly naïve.

7

The Mind of the Prisoner. Part Two:
The Autonomy of
Mind-Becoming-Conscious

 WHATEVER MIND MAY BE, IT IS certainly active, and the being who "possesses" a mind is a restless, dynamic, and in some measure, always a dissatisfied one. No doubt in its movement it deploys an infrastructure of considerable complexity, but it need know nothing of that. What it can not do without is the completion of its movement in consciousness. Only then, in a moment of lucid possession of what lies before it, of what just a moment before might have troubled and puzzled it, does it find rest, although to be sure only a temporary one. All of us have known such moments, and the most one can do is call attention to them, and invite the unbeliever to exemplify the same movement by seeing one's point. The formula used in the last chapter, "mind-becomes-conscious," sums all this up, and in doing so expresses once again a conviction that for a long time now has been widespread in western philosophy: the conviction that, if consciousness is not the defining feature of mind, then it is at least an important one. So powerful is this conviction, despite all the obstacles that lie in the way of a precise understanding of the role of consciousness, that the great influence of behaviorism in the past half century may well be but an incident interrupting its steady development and clarification.

That we can not simply identify consciousness with

mind is clear from the fact that consciousness is also a state, a condition, or a mode of being. It is as variable as our mood, as our "state of mind," as the whole pattern of what I have called elsewhere our subjective dynamism; and it is therefore all too often the very antithesis of the state mind aspires to. When obscure, filled with confusion, error, and doubt, it is so far from being identical with mind that it forms rather an oppressive environment that the whole activity of mind is bent upon dissipating. The escape from it, though, is not to its opposite in the sense of the unconscious but to its own perfection, that is, to an intensified, heightened, and clarified consciousness. The being with a mind, finding himself unclear and confused, moves as best he can, when mind is ascendant in him, towards clarity and order. When he finds it, he is satisfied; or at least he is satisfied until he finds that the state thus reached is not so clear after all. The being with a mind is often mute, inarticulate, and inexpressive — merely a different way, maybe, of saying that he is unclear and confused; and, when mind is ascendant in him, he moves as best he can to express himself more adequately. The movement provoked by the dissatisfaction of mind, a dissatisfaction *in* consciousness and with what it is conscious *of*, is accurately enough described as one in which mind-becomes-conscious, but only if we take note of the fact that the consciousness towards which mind is moving is an ideal one: precisely the state of consciousness appropriate to mind. The desired state is one so suffused with clarity, so adequate to what is the case, that it approaches a transparency in which mind finds itself in the true presence of what it is trying to attend to. The failure of any real state of mind to match this ideal in all respects is plain enough, for even when on one level we have reached a state of mind in which we are tranquilly aware of something precisely as it is, as now, at this very moment, I seem to have attained a perfectly adequate consciousness of the tree outside my window; just then we can be, at another level, in complete puzzlement about it, torn between, say, the views of reductive and hierarchic science. The ideal movement of mind is towards consciousness of what is the case, of what, as Plato might have put it, is really real. Whether a movement seemingly so motivated is in principle completeable is a question we need not settle in order to make the claim about consciousness towards which we have been tending: that although it is by no means identical with mind, the nature of mind can not be clarified without adverting to consciousness. It is present in one way or another wherever we can trace any hint of mind — that appears to be the minimum concession we must make to Descartes and the whole idealistic tradition that builds upon him.

The reality of consciousness as a state, a condition, or a mode of being is that of subjectivity, a reality traditionally set in contrast with that of objectivity, and properly so, when the contrast is properly understood. As such it is a state mind never shakes off even in the most ideal forms of attention any of us know. On some blessed occasions the transparency of consciousness may be so limpid that what is the case wholly occupies us, but even then its crystalline character reflects back enough light so that we are aware of it. The very joy we take in some everyday thing of nature, like that tree outside the window, the very joy we take in seeing some difficult truth that had till then escaped us, is such a reflection; and that joy is so concrete a thing — even though all the while the thing seen, the truth understood, should seem uncolored by our wish or will, but attained just as they are — that the image of consciousness as ideally an utterly neutral medium suddenly seems false. It seems more accurate to say that mind, become-conscious-of these things just as they are, is nevertheless resonant with its thorough possession of them, and in this way proclaims its presence to itself as that of a concrete power. A power, though, whose presence does not in principle distort what it is directed upon, and in that limited sense a transparent one.

Sometimes consciousness is anything but transparent, anything but resonant with its attainment of what is the case, as when some affective reaction — it may be to what is or to what is not the case — is so full of fear, anxiety, repulsion, or confusion that the texture of consciousness itself is more manifest than what it is ostensibly directed towards. An opaque envelope either utterly distorts the object of attention or else itself so preoccupies us that we can not attend to what can be seen through it. Not that consciousness is opaque (subjective in a pejorative sense) only where feeling or emotion is negative. Even in affectively neutral error, mind's own activity is falsely creative and produces perceptual or conceptual interpretations that surround it like a wall or like the landscape of an alien country. Mind-becomes-conscious precisely of the wall, of the strange and incomprehensible landscape of its own making, and is troubled all the while by its inability to see what it wanted to see. Not resonant with the joy that attends its attainment of what is the case, it reverberates instead with a confusion, obscurity, or doubt that is nothing more than its own defective power, felt now as a hindrance. The extreme case is madness, where what slips through the slight residual transparency of consciousness is so transformed that reality and consciousness — with caution, and pending later clarification, let us call them the "objective" and "subjective" — fuse in one terrifying environment.

The complexity of the involvement of consciousness with mind is considerable: how inveterate, for instance, is the transparency of consciousness to the visible world, even though all the while we may be at a loss to interpret it soundly. The world of everyday in its visible aspects and in those intelligible aspects mediated by everyday language is ineluctably present all the while our own speculations and theory about it may surround us like a fog. We are no less conscious of the latter, though it is of our own making, than of the world of everyday. I am not suggesting that the world of everyday, once attained by mind, is a sufficient achievement. That mind should become more fully conscious of it by a more adequate exercise of powers usually called speculative, theoretic, or interpretative seems to me nearer the truth. I merely want to urge the point that sometimes mind, far from going on to become more thoroughly conscious of what in some measure it has already won possession of, may find itself quite cut off from its habitual possessions, and cut off by its consciousness of what are in fact merely its own artifacts.

But from all this there begins to emerge an ideal for mind

that is also an ideal for consciousness — or at least an ideal for the activity in which mind-becomes-conscious. It is ideally a self-transcendent activity in which mind completes itself by taking rational, articulate, and conscious possession of what is the case. This has often gone by the name of objectivity, and we may also call it by that name so long as we do not take it to be identical with the findings of a reductive science, but simply take it as a name for what is the case, what is true. Possessing this, the subject is the richer for also possessing, as it rejoices in the possession of what is other than itself, the very quality of its own creative and responsible activity. This is subjectivity in the positive sense: a creative activity that does not however create objectivity but discloses it, while disclosing at the same time its own proper nature and proper role with respect to objectivity. In transcending itself to become conscious of what is the case it also becomes conscious of what is the case about its own role.

When it fails of self-transcendence it is, however, the poorer for the way in which subjectivity now insinuates itself between itself and the object. Instead of becoming conscious of what is the case, it becomes obsessed with its own nature and with the objects itself has created. It becomes subjectivity in the pejorative sense: that which colors or distorts the objective. It is one of the intellectual ironies of the twentieth century that one of the artifacts of this crippled subjectivity is that false objectivity it has constructed by making an ideal out of the successful method of the natural sciences — a method in which such artifacts as theories, models, and the imposed standard of quantifiability play an obvious role. The irony is compounded because that kind of objectivity gets its force from the notion that it is precisely uncolored by subjectivity. The supreme irony, though, comes at a higher level of sophistication, in which it is maintained that subjectivity is in principle not capable of self-transcendence, and in which even scientific objectivity is taken to be a projection of subjective experience, though no less sacrosanct for the derivative role thus assigned to it. We shall meet one or two theories of this kind somewhat later in this chapter.

The activity in which mind-becomes-conscious — whether a

properly self-transcendent activity or an activity that terminates in its own creations — is always involved with the creation and use of symbols. That is an obscure word, "involves," but it is useless to pretend that we understand the precise role of symbols in the activity of mind. We are conscious, rationally conscious, with the help of symbols — of ordinary and technical language, of mathematics, of the arts — and though there may be a sense in which we can be conscious, behave intelligently, and maybe even think, without them, yet the emergence of well-deployed symbols seems to mark some special intensity and adequacy of consciousness. On the other hand, we are often conscious *of* them, and though they are the mind's creations, they are also sometimes its medium or environment, echoing in this way the ambiguous role of consciousness itself. Though we can deploy them, alter them, invent them, if not at will then at least in those fortunate moments when obscurity and inexpressiveness give way to clarity and articulation, we are often simply surrounded by them, as though by a baffling and even hostile environment, much as the texture of consciousness itself can sometimes seem so.

Mind, to its possessor, seems to move or develop, with an internal sense of effort, from conscious state to conscious state, and it is also conscious of the sense of the unsatisfactory character of the first state, of the effort to move out of it, of the satisfaction — sometimes — of arriving at the second state. The restlessness, the constant sense of effort, followed by momentary rest in a new achievement, suggests that we must regard any prior state, however naïve and habitual, however far back in genetic development, as itself an achievement of mind-becoming-conscious. The world of common sense, of ordinary language, the world that phenomenologists call the world of the natural standpoint, or, as in the later Husserl, the "life-world," thus also appears an achievement, a state of awareness, consciousness, apprehension, or understanding. This is but another way of reminding ourselves that objectivity, for all the desired independence from subjectivity conveyed by that word, is not given to subjectivity independently of its own activity. To the degree that mind-becoming-conscious is by definition subjectivity, it is precisely the disclosure, the making-present, of objectivity that is its achievement. Objectivity contains no warrant of its status that is totally independent of the pronouncement of the subjectivity that entertains it. On the other hand, it *is* independent to precisely the extent that we can regard the attainment of it as an achievement of the subject, for the warrant for its independent status is given by the autonomous yet responsible act-towards-consciousness that is mind. There is no other guarantee. It is not appropriate to say this with a sense of loss, as though there might have been some other assurance, one that might differ from this one in being untinged with subjectivity.

There is no assurance of objective status but the pronouncement of subjectivity. Yet the ideal intent of mind-becoming-conscious is that the attained objectivity should be nothing other than what is the case, should be in fact untinged by the subjectivity that pronounces upon it. The interdependence of objectivity and subjectivity lies in the activity of mind—in the fact that mind-becoming-conscious is the correlative of what is judged to be objective. The independence of objectivity lies in its being a goal of an ideal self-transcendence in which mind should become conscious of something and should, in its pronouncements about it, manage to be true to that and only to that.

2

Nothing is more puzzling than the role played in consciousness by linguistic and other symbols. And this puzzle is at its most tormenting when we are concerned to settle upon what state of consciousness—what state, if you prefer, of the subject—is most authentic, most objective, most likely to give us things as they are. One thing appears tolerably clear: there is no reason to suppose that authentic consciousness consists in a sensory-*cum*-bodily awareness that dispenses with symbols, and that is all the better for being mute and inarticulate. If some such state lies far back in maturation, ontogeny, and phylogeny, it is something we can not regain, nor would it help us if we could. For that which is authentic is not in principle accessible only to a mute embrace, nor do symbols necessarily stand in opposition to the directness of experiential awareness. Quite the reverse. They come into being as mediators of our understanding of the nonsymbolic world of men and trees and stones and houses, but an understanding of that sort is not in conflict with our direct consciousness or awareness of these things. An understanding mediated by symbols is ideally a heightened and intensified consciousness, and the deployment of symbols is not by definition the interposition between object and subject of a veil of concepts, ideas, essences, forms, or whatever else one wishes to call the entities that seem to accompany our use of symbols. Symbols do not hide, obscure, or distort whatever is primordial, reliable, and concrete in the nature of things — or, at least, if they sometimes do so, it is not because of some ineradicable defect in the nature of symbols themselves. Symbols may function precisely to disclose what is primordial and authentic in what the mind is directed upon. When it creates and uses symbols, it would have them ideally function as transparencies through which an "object" becomes more intensely present to mind, and present just as it is. It may well be that even the *general* character of symbols, so often considered to militate against our grasp of the particular, the individual, the existential, is not an ineradicable handicap: it may be that any "object" present to us "just as it is" is properly experienced and understood only if it is seen to possess something of the general, or universal, character that is usually attributed rather to the world of symbols "just as it is" and to the troublesome entities — concepts, universals, and the like — that are inevitably involved in our use of symbols.

To us, however it may be with the other animals, there is no primordial, reliable, authentic, experiential world that can profitably be opposed to the world as it is experienced in and with our use of symbols. We do not have recourse to an experiential world pure in the sense of being unqualified by symbolic activity, and can not therefore use it as a standard to criticize the adequacy of the world we are aware of and understand with the help of symbols. Conversely, there is no pure understanding of the world of concepts, universals, ideas, essences, forms, that is not also an experiential awareness colored by the role symbols play in mediating our sensory experience of the world about us. The contrast between the radically empirical and the radically rational is a false one, in that neither pole is attainable in an ideal state.

To put it another way, both poles when detached from each other are constructs, ideals devised for special purposes. Thus, forgetting that we live in a world our experience of which, no less than our understanding of which, is mediated by symbols, we may set up refined experiential criteria that, explicitly at least, do not bring in the whole character of that world. A light area seen against a dark ground, the coincidence of a needle with a calibration line on a dial, a track on a photographic plate, may be all the experiential warrant we need to bring some theory to the test. We may even pretend to be utterly noncommittal about the ontological status of the space in which the contrasted patches are seen, of the dial we read, of the track whose angle we measure: we may simply say that we are dealing with observations, thus leaving open the question whether experience ever gets us out of subjectivity. On the other hand, we may establish for special purposes rational criteria and rational constructs supposedly free of every taint of experiential interpretation. In logistic systems ideals like consistency and completeness can be pursued without regard to any interpretation of an experiential nature.

But in both cases the correlative commitments — in the first a rational, in the second an empirical one — have already been made, and are set aside as irrelevant to the game. The radical empiricist deploys language and a sophisticated understanding to make his point to sophisticated hearers. The radical rationalist uses ink on paper or chalk on blackboard. There is no harm whatever in all this, and much profit — so long as techniques of this kind are not used to establish a theory about the nature and

229

limits of the mind's intercourse with reality, about the vocabulary and syntax of a language towards which all scientific activity should aspire, about an ideal objectivity against which all other truth claims should be tested. Our symbols first of all grow out of and articulate the concrete world, so that we can experience it in the mode proper to mind. We, now, exploring mind-becoming-conscious, attempting to heighten our awareness and understanding of it, must not forget it. We can not let an ideal objectivity be defined for us by a "pure" version of experience or by a "pure" version of systematic order. Nor—what is more to the point, since the danger reaches far outside specialist circles—can we let science define an ideal objectivity for us in terms of the interplay between both "pure" criteria. We can not even begin to use such a version of objectivity except within a framework in which awareness and understanding are much more closely married than that.

3

Whatever mind is intent upon, the conscious state from which it moves towards a more satisfactory one is as much an achievement of mind-becoming-conscious as the state that displaces it will be. That is what it means to be a conscious being, and for us it is a condition from which there is no attractive escape in this life. On the other hand, it is not a condition to be deprecated, for while we never disembarrass ourselves of consciousness, and it is accordingly copresent with whatever we are conscious of, its whole mission is to disclose faithfully whatever it is directed upon. In principle it is always capable of renewing its efforts under the self-stimulus of the dissatisfaction that tells it that here and now, in this moment, it is still unfaithful to what it is trying to understand and thus be conscious of. But it is a faulty emphasis to suppose that it should aspire to so transparent a state as to deserve the name "nothing." Though mind's symbolic devices should be as transparent as may be, its sensory apparatus as undistorting as may be, the power that binds these media to their appropriate condition is the more present to itself ("subjective") the more successfully its labors are bent upon the disclosure of the "objective." This is because autonomy in possession of the "objective" is never possible without a reflective exercise that establishes the status of both subjective and objective: the perfection of mind-becoming-conscious develops *pari passu* with a self-knowledge in which mind-becomes-conscious of the power of mind itself.

The activity in which mind-becomes-conscious is no predicament except for a materialist bent on discrediting its efficacity or a physiologist bent on showing that it can be adequately understood only in terms of neural structures. For them, however, the predicament is real enough. They aspire to an ideal illumination about the "causes," or the irrelevance, of mind-becoming-conscious, and this could only consist in mind-becoming-conscious of those "causes" or of the reasons for that irrelevance. To say that that moment of illumination is caused is, I think, to say precisely that its content has not that truth, that objectivity, that *independence* of the subjectivity that attains it, that the materialist himself, as well as everyone else who tries to say something about mind, claims to have attained. And to say that it is irrelevant is to make us discard the illumination itself. There is no act so patently originative as that of mind-becoming-conscious, and even if it should turn out to fail utterly in giving an account of the infrastructure it commands, it still reveals to us as we exercise it the inadequacy of materialism for our own self-knowledge.

Some of the conditions of the reflexive act in which mind recognizes its own autonomy I have explored elsewhere under the heading *radically originative reflection,*[1] and I need not repeat them here. What was said there was directed, as this chapter will be, to showing that the recognition of its own autonomy by mind-becoming-conscious is anything but a solipsistic activity. The recognition neither begins with nor ends with consciousness only—not with its "internal" texture, not with its ideas, impressions, mental events, languages, symbols, or whatever other supposedly "internal" furniture might be proposed—but

231

with its capacity for getting at what is the case, with what an older terminology might have simply called the truth: the truth about that which is not itself, as well as the truth about its own capacities. And to say this, one merely adopts the implicit view of our capacities that lies behind every effort at philosophizing, and especially behind the claim of the tough-minded that they, at least, will contrive not to be deceived. The theme of this chapter develops under what I shall call the *practical postulate of the autonomy of mind:* mind, however it is constituted, can only act on the presumption that under some circumstances it can arrive at the truth, at what is the case. Rightly used, this is a powerful principle; it is also an inoffensive one, in the sense that no one who engages in philosophy can avoid exemplifying it. Here it is merely applied to the reflexive activity in which mind-completing-itself-in-consciousness seeks to understand and justify the nature and autonomy of that activity. The course this self-justification takes will I think show that, however "related" mind-becoming-conscious may be to a physical basis, it can not appropriately be regarded as wholly caused in either a $C \rightarrow E$ or any other sense. In that way this chapter prepares the ground for our return to the topic of originative action in the next one.

4

The emphasis on the functional importance of consciousness will inevitably remind the reader of Descartes, of the many revivals of a modified Cartesian outlook in this century, and perhaps even of some of the themes of absolute idealism. It is worth a short digression to make it clear that this part of our meditation has nothing in common with these views except its insistence on the inescapable autonomy of the activity in which mind-becomes-conscious. Good allies are hard to come by, and as all the views just mentioned lend a general support to the claim that this autonomy is real and is incompatible with materialism, it is both courteous and prudent to make common cause with them so far as that is possible. But there are differences, and at least one of them is a serious one: that the acceptance of a Cartesian starting point about the status of consciousness also places one in a consciousness-centered predicament, though a somewhat different one from that I have represented the materialist to be in. Those who are true inheritors of the Cartesian attitude towards consciousness do not inevitably deny the self-transcendence of consciousness, no more than Descartes himself did. But self-transcendence remains a problem for them as it was for him — something that needs to be established, and established by means of familiar and questionable ingenuities. They do not begin, as we are beginning here, with the view that mind-becoming-conscious is naturally self-transcendent.

Since Descartes convinced himself that he was more certain that he was a conscious, thinking thing than that he had a body, there has always existed an attractive, indeed a seductive, alternative to physicalism. Some features of it, though not the beginning in consciousness itself, go back at least to Plato, and even — what makes the task of distinguishing the view from that of this meditation all the more delicate — to the very dialogue from which I have taken Socrates' protest against materialism. These features are the dualistic ones, or at least those dualistic features that can be separated from a deliberate beginning with subjectivity. I ask the reader once again to remember that it was Socrates' protest I wanted, and not the whole of the Platonic philosophy. It is to Descartes, however, that we owe the formulation of it that has been most compelling to the modern mind. I shall not be concerned here with his dualism, whose materialist component has contributed so much to modern physicalisms, but only with what comes out of his claim that all certainties must rest finally upon the certainty that we are conscious.

Nor need the familiar story of the route Descartes took to this certainty detain us long. He does seem to have made it clear along the way that what we habitually and inveterately take for a certainty may be so in a sense no more significant than the habitual and inveterate attitude of which it is a function. He abandons many supposed certainties along the route to the one that eventually becomes his standard, but the most fundamental of these is the attitude of common sense, an attitude that is not only the one of the man in the street, but that of the scientist as well, for it is in that world that his theoretic activities must eventually be brought to account. If we did not, for the sake of the argument, take his dismissal of commonsense certainties seriously, we should not be disposed to entertain seriously his abandonment of other certainties along the route to the final one, for which *cogito ergo sum* is the usual formula. That first certainty abandoned, or held in abeyance, the whole scientific attitude goes with it.

In this sense, contemporary phenomenology, insofar as it "brackets," suspends, or holds in abeyance, the "natural standpoint," is thoroughly Cartesian. The certainties proposed instead by phenomenology are as varied as the movement itself, and in its recent interactions with existentialism and with linguistic philosophy it is a very varied movement indeed. Not all of them are Cartesian certainties, for many phenomenologists seem more concerned to employ consciousness scrupulously in order to let the true nature of all things reveal themselves to us than to insist upon the superior reality of consciousness itself. Thus, it does not distort the intent of some of them to say that whether it is a child, a flower, a number, a theory, time, an Aristotelian essence, a Platonic form, or the whole familiar world of common sense that is the object of our attention, it is our task to let the thing speak to our consciousness in its own terms. But insofar as the task requires us to come to terms with consciousness itself both in order to assure ourselves of our capacity to let things disclose themselves, or make their appearance, to us and to devise techniques to allow this capacity to be realized, we may say that it is also Cartesian in the certainty it adopts as its standard. Certain odd paradoxes can therefore crop up in phenomenological writing. Some of the most interesting work by this school has been upon the phenomenology of the body. Merleau-Ponty [2] and Straus,[3] for example, have contrived to let the whole phenomenon of embodiment disclose itself, so to speak, to consciousness; which thus, presiding au-

234

tonomously *as* consciousness, takes stock of precisely what it is to be also an *embodied* consciousness. Another paradox, which appears especially in phenomenological writing that owes something to Husserl's conception of the *Lebenswelt,* or life-world,[4] is the redemption of the commonsense world from the encroachments of science. According to Husserl, the presiding and autonomous consciousness, holding the commonsense world and science too in abeyance, founds for itself a true, or philosophical, science. From this vantage point it can return to defend the commonsense world and point out to the scientist that he misses much of its reality when he deals with it in terms of the abstractions of his science. In both cases, though, the emphasis on the nuances of embodiment and upon the nuances of our common world is an emphasis placed there by consciousness, which is thus the final arbiter both of itself and of other things.

Certainly Husserl felt that in this sense the Cartesian approach was the only one worthy of philosophy. In his later work, however, he frequently presses the Cartesian view of consciousness much further than Descartes would have done, who after all also believed in the independent reality of matter, or extended substance. In this extreme form phenomenology makes the following Cartesian points: (*a*) the self-assessment of consciousness yields us a prior certainty on the basis of which all other supposed certainties must be judged; (*b*) the world attended to by both common sense and the physical sciences must also submit to this judgement; and (*c*) therefore no approach based on the physical sciences can ever yield us a knowledge of consciousness more fundamental than its own self-assessment. But it also makes another point more reminiscent of idealistic metaphysics. Consciousness is, according to Husserl, always "consciousness-of" something, and this referential, or directed, character he calls intentionality. The life of consciousness, then, is an intentional life in the sense that it is "directed upon," or "intends" all its objects. But by this he does not merely mean, what common sense seems to tell us, that what consciousness is directed upon is independent of consciousness. Indeed, in his

Cartesianische Meditationen [5] the fundamental problem he is wrestling with towards the end is that of solipsism, that perennial danger to the soundness of all philosophies that do not begin with the assumption that consciousness is capable of attaining something utterly independent of itself. It is not surprising that in an article written in the twenties, published then only in a "translation" that was in effect a very compressed and sometimes inaccurate paraphrase, and only recently translated in full by Richard E. Palmer,[6] Husserl tells us that what we are *conscious of* is in fact an ontological function of consciousness itself. The very existence of our world consists in its relativity to consciousness, and the arguments by which he reaches this conclusion apply, he thinks, to any conceivable world. The consciousness, or subjectivity, he has in mind is not one's own particular consciousness, but a universal one. He calls this transcendental subjectivity, and maintains that, while it is different from the natural one, it is neither separated from the natural one (in the "natural" sense of *separated*) nor "bound up with it or intertwined with it in the usual sense of these words." [7] The term "transcendental," which he employs in a way that derives ultimately from Kant's views on the universally legislating and the "constitutive" character of subjectivity, but which he gives a much more ontological interpretation than Kant would have allowed, thus conveys a double sense of universality: (*a*) subjectivity in its intentional functioning lays down the structure of all experience and all worlds; and (*b*) it operates not as a particular and personal power, but as a general or universal one. The threat of "subjectivism," in the extreme sense of a radical solipsism, Husserl seeks to avoid by making the point—briefly in this article, at greater length in the tortuous later pages of the *Cartesianische Meditationen*—that what is at issue is in fact not a transcendental subjectivity in the sense of a transcendental I (or Ego) but rather a transcendental intersubjectivity, or transcendental We. Whether the movement to intersubjectivity is persuasive, considering the more or less Cartesian starting point from which he seeks to make it, seems to me doubtful. But, that question aside, there seems no doubt that transcendental subjectivity (or intersubjectivity) is made the ultimate ontological ground of his philosophy. "Transcendental intersubjectivity," he says, "is the concretely self-sufficient absolute ground of being, out of which everything transcendent (and, with it, everything of the real and what exists in the world) obtains its existential sense as the being of something that only in a relative and therewith incomplete sense is an existing thing, namely as the being of an intentional unity which in truth exists as the result of transcendental bestowal of sense, of harmonious confirmation, and from an habituality of lasting conviction that belongs to it by essential necessity." [8]

Pressed so far, the persuasiveness of the doctrine is diminished. Indeed, the whole idealistic tradition, from its roots in Descartes down through Husserl has not been widely persuasive in this century, or, at any rate, not in the English-speaking world. Existentialists like Heidegger and Sartre, who owe a general debt to idealism and a very particular one to Husserl, share in this implausibility. I shall not consider here the further development of Husserl's doctrine under the impetus of their characteristic existential concern for mankind as a being primarily practical and decision-making rather than theoretic. But in both cases the human body merely establishes the situation in which consciousness confronts its freedom and shapes its future. This in itself has a certain rough plausibility to it. But for both of them any scientific account of the body that might also be a partial account of the behavior of the total organism seems a large irrelevance. Sartre, for instance, by a development of a theme drawn from Hegel by way of Heidegger and an inversion of a theme drawn from Husserl, identifies consciousness with nothingness.[9] He then uses Hegel's terminology to identify it with perfect freedom: as *being-for-itself* it *is not* whatever it is conscious of, and this absence of a character of its own leaves it quite untouched by whatever causal laws should reign in the world of *being-in-itself,* and indeed undetermined by its own past. Even if we are neither behaviorists nor physicalists, we may be prepared to acknowledge *some* connection between the electrochemical events in the brain and the act in which mind completes itself in conscious understanding. But Sartre's doctrine does not appear to permit us to regard scientific accounts of such events as illuminating in any way the problem of consciousness.

An interest in the autonomy of mind-becoming-conscious need not follow Descartes in his assumption that the first certainties of a conscious being concern consciousness itself, an assumption which leads, by way of an argument that need not concern us here, to the dualism that makes him the philosophical ancestor not only of modern idealism but of modern materialism as well. Nor need we press the idealistic component of his doctrine in the direction in which Husserl and Sartre pressed it. But if we make common cause only with the theme of the autonomy of mind, it provides lessons it would be unwise to ignore. The central lesson for those interested in a better understanding of the mind-body issue is that the attitude of common sense and the related attitude of the physical scientist are attitudes taken up by a being whose understanding is completed in consciousness. The certainties and convictions of these attitudes are *his* certainties and convictions. He has other attitudes as well, and he also has the job of assessing all of them. In performing it he functions as what Socrates might have called a "real cause," and he is not in a position to give up this status even if he wants to. He may attach considerable importance to other attitudes, and may thus give considerable weight to explanations of mind that are devised from the point of view of them. Indeed, that we do attach considerable importance to explanations based on the methods of the physical sciences is what makes the full programs of many versions of phenomenology and existentialism so implausible. Being the creatures we are, we can not dispense with "causes without which the (real) cause cannot be the cause," and we can not dispense with trying to understand them. But as the attitudes are, from the point of view of the mind-becoming-conscious, attitudes that we have the inescapable responsibility of assessing, we need not find their correlative explanatory procedures utterly and definitively satisfying. For one thing, they do not seem competent to explain exhaustively the very activity we are now discussing: an assessment culminating in conscious understanding.

5

We now turn away from these extreme and, as it seems to me, self-defeating claims for the status of mind, and take up again the theme of the autonomy of mind completing itself in consciousness. I attend now to a great dark green oak with a summer rain streaming down on it and dripping from it. There is no sound but the sound the rain makes with its first drumming impact and the slower contrapuntal drip from leaf to leaf and so to the grass beneath. My senses and my whole sensibility are almost wholly taken up with the sight, which is so satisfying that I should be totally absorbed in it if I were not also trying to use it as an illustration.

It might not occur to me, if my state of mind were that of naïve common sense, to observe that I am *aware of* the tree or *conscious of* it. But then, although we are indeed interested in attending to the findings of common sense, and even of naïve common sense, we are also intent on attending to the autonomy of mind, so that these words, laden already with philosophy's interest not just in the tree but also in the act of attending to it, not just in seeming objectivity but also in the subjectivity that attains it, are fair enough. Having regard to the concreteness and apparent authenticity of our attention—a thing the sensuous and mildly poetic beginning was meant to bring out—we might also say that we have *experience of* the tree, meaning, I suppose, that it is present here and now, present to the mind very vividly by way of the senses and the general mediation of the body. No matter of mere concepts, ideas, theories this tree: nothing could be more real in the sense of an authentic, experiential presence. Yet understanding is continuous with this, and indeed I have called it to the reader's attention and to my own by a painstaking use of language. If I am in the world of sensation and call attention to the immediacy with which the tree takes up my whole bodily attention, I am also in a state of articulate and conceptual attention—the same mode of attention that not only uses but also creates linguistic symbols. And I can not find my way back from this attitude to some primordial experiential presence further back in the mists of phylogeny, ontogeny, and maturation. So that I am not in a position to find some more noncommittal, authentic, and certain mode of experience, of awareness, of consciousness to contrast with this equally conscious mode of understanding in which I use language as I talk about the tree. Nor can I find some more precise mode of attention, concerned perhaps with abstract objects, that can not be shown to be systematically related to acts of attention very like the one in which I attend to the tree.

Contemplating this example from the point of view of a mind intent on becoming articulately conscious of its own autonomy, one sees a good deal that is unsatisfactory about it. I represent it as mind-become-conscious of the tree, but neither the status of the tree nor that of the mind is certain, unless we return to a state of naïve common sense where questions about the autonomy of mind can not in principle arise. If we did understand the example though, did really understand it, we should then understand the autonomy of mind-becoming-conscious. What comes to the same thing, if mind-becomes-conscious of its autonomy, what is puzzling about the example would become clear. That is the point of the present exercise.

As we think about it, the example at once reveals the conventional dichotomy of object and subject, but at first in a vague form, with the two poles of it indeterminate. The use of the word "conscious," is, as noted just awhile ago, often symptomatic of an effort to distinguish one of the poles very precisely from the other; indeed, during the period in which it became common in ordinary speech and still more in philosophy, the word has often been used to call attention to the texture of subjectivity itself. Yet it does not seem possible to call attention to subjectivity in an utterly pure form. Just now, for instance, I spoke of being conscious *of the tree,* so that even if I had been trying to call attention to "subjectivity itself" I would have been doing so only by also calling attention to the object subjectivity was occupied with. To just the extent that I stress consciousness *of the tree* it even becomes difficult to attend merely to the qualitative nature of one's subjective response to it, as I was doing at the beginning of this example. Subjectivity as an "object" of our reflexive attention is deliberately neutralized, so far as concerns the tree, so that it may be wholly adequate to the tree — precisely *conscious of* it. The function or activity of attending to the tree is designedly a neutral or transparent one, and if consciousness of it is to be thought of as a state of being or a medium, it is authentically what it purports to be only when what is the case, what is real, what is true — in this case the tree — is attained by it. Certainly if the state of attending to the tree is what it purports to be, the tree (or some surrogate for it) is not *in* consciousness, but I, *here* in this room, am conscious of that old tree out *there* on the Bowdoin campus.

The dichotomy that appears every time we consider these matters is thus interpreted in this way: ideally the object, the tree, does not appear to me with any taint of subjectivity in it, even though subjectivity may qualify it in the sense that we can apprehend it only with the sensory modalities we are equipped with; my subjectivity, on the other hand, while it does not present itself to me as containing the tree but rather as having attained the tree as it is, is nonetheless colored by and qualified by that attainment. Whatever a scientific analysis of perception might say, to the subject intent upon it, the object is less colored by subjectivity than subjectivity is by the character of the object apprehended. It would only occur to a philosopher to suppose that subjectivity itself is an irremediable condition, state, function, or activity, forever cut off from what is truly the case, eternally condemned to concern itself not with reality as it is but only with its own texture. Notwithstanding that, the character of subjectivity is real enough and accessible enough to the subject, and only a tendentious philosophy would suppose that it is not.

I am conscious of the tree, and since my consciousness of it is in some measure articulate and rational, I have some under-

241

standing of it. Reflecting on this, I have distinguished both my own subjectivity and the independent reality, or objectivity, of the tree. It is not *in* my consciousness, it is not inferred *from* my consciousness, nor is it inferred from something else that is *in* my consciousness. On the other hand my consciousness is present to itself only as qualified by the tree and by other things of which it is conscious. That is not to say that subjectivity is present to itself indirectly; it merely means that it is not present in a pure form quite unqualified by this or that object of awareness. Although the object does not inevitably present itself as qualified by my subjectivity, my subjectivity is not present with the purity that sometimes characterizes the object, but is colored by its possession of the latter.

It may seem to the reader that this is most naïve of realisms: an objective world that is exactly what it seems to be, set in contrast with a mind quite capable of seeing it for what it is. Was not Descartes right, are not contemporary phenomenologists right, to reject so naïve a view in favor of an epistemological beginning not so plainly subject to error, delusion, and uncertainty as this one is? Closer inspection will reveal that it is anything but naïve, and if it is a realism of a kind, it is one arrived at only after considering the alternatives. Yes, to be sure, it may not be an oak, it may not be raining, I may be under the influence of a drug or subject to some systematic deception. But if now by some enlightened critic I were made to give up my description of what I see and give up also my grounds for holding my judgment in such matters to be reliable, my revised version of what I then took to be the case, and my revised version of a justification for taking some version or other of the facts to be reliable, would only repeat the pattern my critic had dismissed. That is, at some point I would either (*a*) have once more accepted some object or objects not *in* consciousness, not inferred *from* consciousness or from something else that is *in* consciousness; or (*b*) have accepted some version of the relation between mind and what it knows, or thinks it knows, and taken this version *to be what is the case.* And if it were indeed (*b*) that I accepted, I should than have attributed to my version of *what is the case about mind* all the independence of my subjectivity that I attributed awhile ago to the oak tree.

From all this, it appears that my reflection upon my awareness of the tree does not just disclose to me the fact that there is indeed an aged oak midway between my eye and the old granite walls of Memorial Hall. That oak, I take it, is indeed independent of my consciousness, but what reflection discloses is not that alone, but also the autonomy of mind-becoming-conscious, an autonomy that always prevails, since it will reign over any practical correction ("that is a reflection in the window of a picture that is in fact behind you") or any philosophical correction ("that is merely a set of subjective impressions") that forces me to revise my basic approach to epistemology. There is no more naïve realism here than there was in Descartes' rejection of everyday certainties or Husserl's rejection of the natural standpoint. But on the other hand there is an insistence that the self-transcendence of subjectivity is there from the beginning. It is the business of mind to become conscious of what is other than itself. It can not infer this capacity from more primal certainties, and if it sets about a task that it takes to be that one, it will never have done with it, even though its capacity to settle upon even a supposed starting point — something or other that is the case and about which mind must suppose itself to be self-transcendent — means that the task really need not have been undertaken.

Theories of knowledge that hold subjectivity to be thoroughly enclosed within itself reveal, in the truth claims made for the theory itself, a hidden belief in the self-transcendence of subjectivity. For all practical purposes this is a belief in the autonomy of mind-becoming-conscious. An extreme case is the theory put forward on several occasions in recent years by Eugene Wigner,[10] the physicist and Nobel laureate. It is not a new doctrine by any means, but as it purports to be an argument against materialism and is advanced by a prominent physicist, it has been welcomed by other scientists who share with Wigner a belief in the importance of subjectivity. Wigner's claim is that subjectivity is the primary reality, primary in the sense of being

243

the only one we can know directly, and that the objective world is a derivative reality, which we infer, or more properly construct, on the basis of our subjective experience. There is an obvious germ of truth in this, for the *scientific* image of the nature of things is in fact a construct founded upon our knowledge of the commonsense world. But this tells us nothing about the status of the commonsense world. Wigner claims that reality in general is such a construction, and a successful construction to the degree that it permits us to anticipate and control with its help the future character of our subjective experience. Superficially the position looks like Berkeley's, though without the theology, or indeed without any very searching examination of what "subjective reality" might mean beyond "subjective experience."

That same superficial resemblance to Berkeley is a familiar feature of many science-oriented epistemologies in this century. I suspect that in most such doctrines there is only as much of Berkeley as comes down through Hume as a legacy to the logical positivism that played so important a role between the two great wars. It may seem odd to represent the latter doctrine as a variety of idealism. The niceties of epistemology aside, it is probably not, for the methodology it advocates suggests the suppressed conviction that there *is* a real nonsubjective world against which our constructions prove themselves, even though it is inaccessible to us. At any rate, there is a practical alignment of this form of "idealism" with materialism, since only an ideal science is regarded as truly cognitive. It may be that Wigner's "idealism" is of this kind too, but I do not wish to press that point. All I want, in the first place, is the radical contrast between his point of view and the "naïvely" realistic example of myself looking at the oak; and, in the second place, the hidden agreement between the view I have expressed about the autonomy of mind-becoming-conscious and the theory in which Wigner, on the basis of his analysis of the procedures of science, lays down his distinction between the two kinds of realities. For Wigner takes this distinction to be a real one, to be what is the case about our cognitive faculties. The primacy of subjectivity, the secondary nature of an inferred or constructed reality, is not taken to be a distinction that merely exists *in* a subjectivity. So far from being a product of the subjectivity that attends to it or entertains it, it is represented as so independent of that coloring as to furnish an appropriate interpretation for the whole interpersonal world in which science is carried on. Being, as he supposes, conscious of the true status of subjectivity, Wigner takes himself to be free from that undesirable kind of subjectivity that would characterize a variety of mistaken views: naïve realism, naïve materialism, a belief in the reality of Platonic Forms—indeed, any other view that supposes, as Wigner (on the explicit level) does not, that subjectivity is able to attain directly realities other than itself. In an obvious sense—the sense in which he takes subjective reality to be the only one directly attainable—he has accepted the autonomy of mind-becoming-conscious; although it is less obvious, he has also implicitly taken it for granted that its activity is a self-transcendent one.

These criticisms, however, apply to Wigner's position only insofar as it appears to make claims about the status of subjectivity that commit him to an idealist ontology or at least to an idealist epistemology. He has elsewhere made the point that quantum theory is best interpreted as dealing not with physical realities (a concept he must naturally regard as a questionable one) but with possible observations—"probability connections between the outcomes of observations"; and that some apparent anomalies in quantum theory become less offensive on this interpretation.[11] And he takes this interpretation of one branch of science to be generalizable to the procedures of physics in general. One can accept this, while noting that it does not warrant our interpreting human observations in general (whether sophisticated ones or the more primitive ones upon which these depend) in terms of an idealist metaphysics or epistemology. It is one thing to say that mathematical physics correlates observations; it is another thing to say that in any observation what is observed is a subjective reality. And indeed towards the end of the paper just now referred to, Wigner

245

appears to be aware that a methodology restricting itself to a concern with observations can not itself settle the status of observations.

Beginning with a materialist metaphysics and theory of knowledge, Democritus was long ago led to conclude that a subjectivity "caused" by the movement of atoms was so lacking in self-transcendence as to be unable to maintain the truth of materialism. Beginning from quite different premises, Berkeley maintained that the priority of the subjective made it impossible for us even to give a coherent account of the nature of material, much less demonstrate its existence. This agreement of mighty opposites, an agreement well known to sophisticated materialists, has not prevented some of them from trying to defend materialism on the basis of a theory of knowledge that assumes the priority and the lack of self-transcendence of subjectivity. A theory of this kind, more unambiguously dedicated to a scientific materialism than Wigner's, has been set down in some detail by Arturo Rosenblueth, an associate of Norbert Wiener's in the early days of cybernetics, and a leading figure in the investigation of the central nervous system with the help of the computer analogy.[12]

Rosenblueth maintains that there is a unidirectional causal chain running from the material universe through receptor sense organs and thence, by way of afferent neural impulses, to the brain, where there take place "central neuronal events" that are correlated with "mental events."[13] He understands this causal chain to consist entirely of physical events, and this means that he is not claiming that the central neuronal events at the end of the causal chain cause the mental events. The word "correlated" as applied to those mental events is thus to be taken seriously: they do not occur *after* the central neuronal events they are correlated with, but are understood to be merely another aspect of the very same events whose physical aspect we attend to when we call them central neuronal events. By the same token, mental events do not cause physical events. Rosenblueth, in fact, makes it quite clear that he thinks that any causal chain consists only of physical events, and he goes so far

246

as to insist that a mental event can not even cause another mental event.

In considering the character of the sequence of physical events leading up to the central neuronal events, Rosenblueth, like Wooldridge, makes much of the fact that the afferent impulses reaching the brain are not specific for the several sensory modalities, but are encoded in terms of the timing and frequency of impulses that are in other respects identical. A coding of this kind might seem insufficient to provide the qualitative differences that distinguish, say, the mental event of being aware of an odor from that of being aware of a color. But Rosenblueth also takes it for granted that the spatiotemporal forms of the central neuronal events, which involve the differing spatial dispositions of the neurons of the olfactory and visual areas of the cortex, contribute to the completeness and adequacy of the code. He points out, for instance, that the complex neuronal event that takes place in the several layers of the visual cortex as the last step in the causal chain of visual perception is isomorphic with the physical features of the visual field with which it is connected by the afferent nerves. But he thinks this isomorphism is not merely a spatial one: he insists that it also involves the temporal relations of the firing of the neurons that make up the central neuronal event, no less than the spatial dispositions of the neurons themselves. The temporal coding (timing and frequency) of the afferent nerve messages is thus held to be completed in the dynamics of the central neuronal events. The spatial disposition of the cells in the cortex plays an important role in these dynamics, but the important point is that the isomorphism between the physical events constituting the visual field and the central neuronal events is not merely a topological one but a spatiotemporal one.[14]

Having begun with the idea of an *encoding*, Rosenblueth is led naturally to the idea of a *decoding*. A structural isomorphism of physical events is preserved throughout the "causally linked chain *material universe* → *receptors* → *coded afferent messages* → *central neuronal and correlated mental events*," and those mental events are said to consist in a "conscious decoding" of the central neuronal

247

events, and thus to provide us with the means—the only means
—of *constructing* a material universe isomorphic with the original.[15] By this active image of decoding Rosenblueth appears to
assign a kind of efficacity to consciousness. Indeed, elsewhere
he goes out of his way to point out that conscious behavior
differs from nonconscious and that conscious, or mental, experience has a survival value.[16] Through much of the book he uses
dualistic language: we have already noticed that he distinguishes
material, or physical, events from mental events, and in one
place he even says that the experimental scientist must adopt
a dualistic attitude.[17]

But the word "dualism" is to be understood in a Pickwick-
ian sense. For one thing, the efficacity of consciousness is not
really taken seriously, since it must be interpreted in accordance
with the demands of what, as Rosenblueth tells us, is an identity
theory of the two-aspect kind. According to that theory, the
mental processes making up consciousness and the neuronal
processes with which they are correlated are "two aspects of a
single event," but the mental aspect is given so little weight that
mental processes are said to play no causal role whatever, causality being both physical and deterministic.[18] Thus, while sensations, or perceptions, are causally related to events in the
material universe in the sense that they are correlated with central neuronal events that are at the end of a causal chain that
begins in the material world, they are not themselves links in
any causal chain, since causal chains are constituted exclusively
by material events.[19] For another thing, consciousness is *not*
regarded as self-transcendent by Rosenblueth, and the image
of decoding must not be taken to imply that he believes that
consciousness gives us, simply by virtue of what it is, a reality
that is distinct from itself. For Rosenblueth, intent as he is upon
establishing the doctrine that material causality is fundamental,
consciousness is a genuine predicament rather than a point of
vantage. The only things we are directly aware of, he tells us,
are mental events, and everything else is mere construction. His
starting point, he says, is that of Descartes, and he even accepts
the arguments of Berkeley.[20] What he does not appear to have

noticed is that those arguments can not be used to demonstrate that material causality is fundamental in the sense that he intends. At the least, if he accepts Berkeley's arguments he must also accept Berkeley's redefinition of "material" in terms of an idealistic framework: the very notions "material," "physical event," and so on can be no more than constructions — constructions in the sense of being ways of characterizing certain patterns of mental events. If he proceeds in this way he can then, by making appropriate adjustments, relive — if that should seem profitable — the history of philosophy from Berkeley through Hume to the logical positivism that was so powerful in the twenties and thirties of this century. But I do not think that this would entitle him to the robust metaphysical materialism embodied in his paradigm causal chain that "produces" consciousness as a simultaneous correlate of central neuronal events linked with the material world.

We can not suppose that Rosenblueth, Wigner, or indeed anyone else who holds that the only things we are aware of are mental events, the only reality directly accessible a subjective one, would accept the formula "mind-becoming-conscious" that I have been using. In that sense an autonomy growing out of a reflection upon that activity and its self-transcendence is not open to them. But it does not seem to do violence to what they are saying if we suppose them to believe that in the course of developing their theories they have become conscious of what is the case about objectivity, subjectivity, material events, mental events, causality, isomorphism, and so on. They are either claiming that they see what is the case about the status of mind in the nature of things or, at the very least, that they see what is the case about the structure of the theories I have just sketched. There is thus a self-transcendence implicitly ascribed to the subjectivity they profess to begin with. No doubt the structure of their theories forbids this possibility, but that is a problem for them and not for us.

The autonomy of mind-becoming-conscious is in effect the autonomy of subjectivity, but it is an autonomy properly directed *towards* objectivity — not in the conventional sense of the world view of science, but objectivity in the sense of what is the case, what is true. Any act of perception, attention, or understanding ideally takes the form of a movement towards an ideal transparency in which not itself but what is the case (what is real, true, objective) should appear. Yet as we saw earlier it is also a state, condition, or environment, detectable to the attentive reflexive eye at all times. I suggested that it was the qualification, or coloring, of subjectivity by the nature of what we attend to that makes it apparent to us as a state—a state that in some situations can paradoxically seem like a confining environment to that same subjectivity. That is only part of the truth about the accessibility of subjectivity to us, for our sensory modalities select only certain features of the object for our attention, and we are moreover aware of the mediating role that the senses, and, through them, the body in general, play. It is true that mind, once it has become conscious of the role of senses and body, treats them as objective: they are as much "what is the case" as anything else. But just because it is seen to be the case that the senses mediate our intercourse with objects, that mediation also colors the interior, or lived, quality of conscious. Subjectivity for that reason always has an ambiguity to it: it is the less transparent to us, the less capable of grasping with unambiguous neutrality whatever it attends to, just because what *can* be objects to it—body and senses—nonetheless mediate our intercourse with other objects. Subjectivity, insofar as experienced by the subject together with whatever else it experiences by virtue of it, is colored not only by its objects but by those mediating features as well. The body's mediation can in certain circumstances become oppressively present—as for instance when we are in pain—lending a character to subjectivity so definite that it acts more as a tormenting environment than as an ideal transparency.

Whether it is exact to say of such circumstances that subjectivity is more aware of itself than of the truth, I do not know. But whenever the truth-seeking function fails, it is usually because subjectivity itself interposes something between itself and the object. Instead of disclosing to us what is the case, part of

250

it declines into an opaque medium that makes the object less accessible. Pain is an extreme case. The opaque medium may also consist of unclear or inappropriate symbols, a poorly constructed theory, some sensory illusion, or just a poorly constructed sentence. But whatever it may be, the other part of subjectivity attends to this medium as though it were the reality it was intent on seeing. What mind, or subjectivity (sense *1*) ideally aims at goes by the name of objectivity, its failing by the name of subjectivity (sense *2*), though it is never an irremediable failing.

6

It would be a good thing if all philosophic meditations had the dramatic impact of Descartes', which seems to have been compressed into a relatively short period of time. This one, though brought to its final form in a few months, has in the working out of it taken a much longer time. I wanted to return to our oak tree and consider the source of the overpowering authenticity the sight of it had for me, but I am now in a quite different place, with things around me of equal authenticity. It will be convenient to use these things as an example, rather than the memory of the oak — the more so as our reflection will reveal that the authority for acquiescing in the authenticity of either oak or what is now before me does not lie merely in the innocent contemplation of them.

I sit in the *altana*—a kind of great airy gazebo—at the top of a tall old Tuscan villa half way up Monte Pilli, one of the larger hills looking down on Florence from the east. Because it is a broad-based hill with a gentle slope, and because the *altana* sits above all the trees that surround the house, the sky is enormous, and one looks down not just over the city, but over all the country round about. Though it is a setting of considerable beauty and power, it is not my purpose to describe it, but only to make it clear that its authenticity is impressive, combining the splendor of the countryside, still considerable even in this age, with all the tradition of an ancient culture. One's temptation to subject the whole scene to a reductive analysis of any kind, let alone a Laplacean one, is nil. It is early May, and just below me —I am high enough so that I can look down upon them—there are several horse chestnuts in full bloom, their profusion of creamy white candelabras now more than usually radiant as they refract the sun going down behind them. They are those very great-rooted blossomers Yeats took as an image of authentic being. To think of them in terms of a reductive analysis of the kind so often discussed in this book seems to be to miss something of urgent importance about them. To think of them as inhabiting my subjectivity (as "in" my consciousness), or as inferred or constructed on the basis of what inhabits it, seems also to miss the point of them.

With this innocent contemplation and acceptance of authenticity goes an equally innocent acceptance of the authenticity of the mind that contemplates the trees. We have no more thought of applying reductive analysis to it than to the trees, for to take them as authentic is precisely to take as authentic its own function—that activity of subjectivity in which it completes itself in what is *not* itself; in which it achieves awareness of the trees rather than of itself; in which (to hazard once again a word grown almost useless through its employment in the involutions of post-Kantian idealism, existentialism, and phenomenology) subjectivity transcends itself; in which (to return to the language of this chapter) mind-has-become-conscious-of the trees. Trees, though, even in their glory, are not the highest image of authenticity we can find. The friends of Socrates in prison must have found in his actions on that last day an even more potent image. There too mind-become-conscious had its own authenticity innocently taken for granted. In innocently affirming the matter of urgent importance that they saw in the actions of their friend, they no less innocently affirmed the capacity of their minds to transcend themselves to achieve awareness of him just as he was.

The appeal to innocence does not in itself yield the authority we are looking for. There are materialist accounts of great power—of Socrates, of these trees, of the mind itself that confronts them. Where is the authority for resisting them, for maintaining that, whatever clarification they bring in certain directions, they are beside the point? The question reminds us that just now we are not contemplating the trees and Socrates in all innocence. We have been proposing a way of understanding Socrates and ourselves in terms of a "relation" between action and infrastructure, and a way of understanding the trees that is, at the least, congruent with that "relation." The reader may in the end conclude that this view is wrongheaded, but he will probably not want to call it innocent or naïve.

The only authority we can find does not entirely set aside the innocent attitude in which the authenticity of the tree, of Socrates ("objects") and of the mind that attains them ("subject") is taken for granted. The only authority we can find is one like that the reader and I now exercise together as, well beyond epistemological innocence, we reflect upon the nature and role of that innocence. In one sense the innocence is set aside, for we no longer rely on it. In another sense it is not, for reflection is but an intensified and non-naïve use of the attention that was once more innocently and directly preoccupied with the trees and with Socrates, and indirectly (but just as innocently) with the mind itself. It is radically originative in the sense that it completes itself in becoming-conscious-of—that is, in originating awareness and understanding of—the role of mind in its innocent employment. Precisely *that* reflective awareness and understanding was lacking in the innocent employment. But this new awareness/understanding has as part of its "content" the prior achievement of innocence, namely, the self-transcendence of mind to attain its object; and as another part of its "content" it has the paradoxical self-transcendence of mind in its reflective employment, that is, its capacity to attain "what is the case" about itself. The internal resonance of the innocent act, a resonance that both "empirically" and "rationally" proclaims its own self-transcendence, its own attainment of trees and of Socrates in prison, is thus repeated in a higher form in the reflective act, a form that both confirms the innocent act and the reflective one. More simply, mind-becomes-conscious of its own self-transcendence and in doing so authenticates and preserves every-thing that was worth saving in the innocent act itself. The "cir-cle" implicit in all this can not be broken out of, but this indi-cates no defect in mind, since there are no intelligible alternatives to it. To set against it we have only the impossible objectives of extreme empiricism and extreme rationalism: on the one hand an object "given" and not attained by mind's-hav-ing-become-conscious of it; on the other an object that either *is* subjectivity or is inferred from or constructed by or con-stituted by subjectivity. Against all this we offer instead the au-thority of innocence regained in reflection: mind-become-con-scious-of its own self-transcendence.

This authority is absolute in the sense that there is no other that does not presuppose it. We sometimes *seem* to be making some other appeal — to the laws of nature, to the combination of rational and empirical criteria that make up the scientific method, to some philosophic doctrine or other, as, for instance, the one that occupies us in this book, that of originative action — but if mind can not in radically originative reflection become-conscious-of its own self-trancendence, its own capacity to become-conscious-of that which is distinct from itself, none of these other appeals would be effective.

It will be obvious that the authority of this kind of reflection restores the authenticity of our epistemologically innocent ap-prehension of the trees or of Socrates in prison, restores it at least within the scope of the relatively modest claims an appre-hension of that kind makes. Common sense is nonreductive, but it does not pretend to plumb all the depths of what it takes to be authentic. In now confirming its own first innocence, mind realizes that in common sense it indeed attained at least as much of the object as it was then bent on attaining, and it therefore lays down the requirement that its findings in the domain of science and philosophy should not displace but merely deepen those first findings. Although the autonomous reflective gesture propounds in itself no metaphysics, it demands that the oak on the Bowdoin campus, the chestnut trees now seen from the *altana,* and Socrates seen by his friends in prison rubbing his ankles to restore circulation after the removal of the fetters, should be accepted as irreducible; and that all of these things, when attended to more intensely and more profoundly, should be seen in a manner congruent with that irreducibility. The same thing holds for any more adequate apprehension of mind itself. This last requirement by no means vindicates the adequacy of the view of originative action when applied to the mind, but it does guarantee that any account accepted as adequate should be congruent with the irreducibility of the innocent act of mind, whose authenticity is confirmed in radically originative reflection.

In this atmosphere the bland assumption that the proceedings of the physical sciences, which have been methodologically reductive, *define* a reasonable account of the trees, of Socrates, and of mind, no longer operates. Even the so-called secondary qualities of my sensory apprehension of the trees, for so long taken by the reductive approach to be "subjective" in some pejorative sense, now appear as authentic characteristics of what has been attained by mind-become-conscious of what is before it. The chestnut tree in its life-garment of green and creamy white is in this atmosphere something triumphantly attained by mind rather than something constituted out of itself in response to data that either "in themselves" or in relation to a more "objective" approach are indicators of a quite different reality. That we should not know it as we do if we had different sensory modalities is true but irrelevant, for those we are in fact equipped with are not, just because they are selective, doomed to miss what is authentic in the tree or to impose or project upon it what is somehow alien to it. To the living reality that is the tree, though not to the individual "particles" that play an infra-structurelike role in relation to its irreducible nature, belongs that vibrant garment some of whose splendor mind-becomes-conscious-of through the medium of sensation.

7

Some working physiologists have been more sensitive to the irreducible and autonomous character of the activity in which mind-becomes-conscious of what is the case than many of the philosophers who wish to make philosophy an extension of the attitude of the physical sciences. I suspect that this is due to the influence of the great physiologist Sherrington, whose work set the example for much of what is most creative in current neurophysiology. He was himself sensitive not only to that character of mind, but also to the correlate irreducibility of that in the world about us that mind-becomes-conscious-of. Writing towards the end of his career, he summed up in this way a lifetime of meditation on the mystery of consciousness.

> The physical basis of mind encroaches more and more upon the study of mind, but there remain mental events which seem to lie beyond any physiology of the brain. When I turn my gaze skyward I see the flattened dome of sky and the sun's brilliant disc and a hundred other visible things underneath it. What are the steps which bring this about? A pencil of light from the sun enters the eye and is focused there on the retina. It gives rise to a change, which in turn travels to the nerve-layer at the top of the brain. The whole chain of these events, from the sun to the top of my brain, is physical. Each step is an electrical reaction. But now there succeeds a change wholly inexplicable by us. A visual scene presents itself to the mind; I *see* the dome of sky and the sun in it, and a hundred other visual things beside.[21]

To say, as Sherrington does, that consciousness is inexplicable is not to say that the methods of physiology do not explain something about it. Sherrington was quite aware that physiology contributed to the explanation of consciousness at least in the sense that an understanding of an infrastructure is a factor in the understanding of the originative act that is "related" to it. Indeed a perfected explanation of that kind will probably draw heavily on lines of investigation begun by him. What, then, is he getting at when he calls it inexplicable?

What he is getting at is sometimes obscured by the fact that he expresses himself in terms drawn from an epistemology inconsistent with his insight: after the passage just quoted, for instance, he goes on to say that we perceive a "picture" of the world around us. I hope it will not seem an impertinence to interpret him as trying to call attention to these two points, which appear to be in conflict but are not when they are sufficiently clarified. (*1*) On the one hand consciousness is an achievement of self-trancendence, in which the subject, far from being condemned to contemplate his own subjectivity, can in principle attain things as they are. (*2*) On the other hand, all study of the physical basis of consciousness is in the predicament of being consciousness-centered: it can thus explain neither the special "internal" quality of being-conscious nor the miracle in which mind-becomes-conscious of what is the case. Mind, though (as we suppose) self-transcendent, is nonetheless still *conscious* mind, and the consciousness-centered predicament of the physiologist consists in this: that the most he can hope to do is to establish an exact correlation between certain physical events in the nervous system and certain experiences, thoughts, operations, or insights that are reported to him by the conscious subject. From this predicament there is no escape. There are other ways of studying intelligent *behavior*, but there is no other way of studying *consciousness*. We may, then, represent Sherrington as saying that consciousness is not reducible to the physical events that subserve it, in this sense, that the laws in terms of which we understand the physical events do not in themselves enable us to understand the emergence of consciousness. But by "emergence of consciousness" we mean to call attention to two things: (*a*) the "interior" quality of subjectivity, what it is to be conscious, to be aware, to feel, etc.—a thing we could scarely call attention to if subjectivity were not in principle capable of a reflexive turn, and susceptible at the same time to the vice of self-enclosure; (*b*) the self-transcendence of subjectivity, in which it both attains that which is distinct from itself and is aware that that is its vocation and responsibility.

The stock response to a claim of this kind from the point of view of scientism seems to misunderstand both these points. It takes it for granted that the correlation of a set of physical events is a sufficient explanation of the emergence of consciousness in sense (*a*), since this method of correlation is typical of the scientific explanation of qualities in general. If we can understand color by separating white light into its components with the help of a prism and then correlating light of a certain wave length with each shade of color, why should we try to understand the emergence of consciousness in a more profound way? Can we not think of it too as a "quality" correlated with a very complex physical event? Yet the correlations upon which this suggestion rests are made only with the help of a conscious subject, for unless some conscious experience is taken as a point of reference no physical laws about light could possibly predict that the experience of color would be precisely what it is. The difficulty with (*a*) exists no matter what ontological status we give subjects on the one hand or qualities on the other. The point is that methodologically the procedure by which we make correlations of this kind is based upon taking consciousness for granted as a *general* thing and then altering its *particular* texture, and that this trick can not be repeated for the emergence of consciousness itself even if we should suppose consciousness to be entirely self-contained (or self-confined). There is no sense in which *consciousness* can emerge in such a consciousness in the way in which redness or greenness can emerge in it.

As for point (*b*), the stock response indicates unawareness of the real claims made for self-transcendence. What has to be accounted for is not just the interior, lived, experienced, texture of subjectivity, but also the fact that subjectivity, while remaining precisely that, nonetheless escapes from those confines to possess something other than itself. Can one possibly treat a "quality" that is in point of fact *self-transcendence* as though it were what the epistemological tradition that lies behind the stock response once called a secondary quality—as though it were somehow on the same level as the colors, sounds, odors it apprehends? The primary evasion built into the notion that consciousness is merely an emergent property of material events assumes (when convenient) precisely that about consciousness. That assumption of course carries with it the second assumption

258

that there are primary, or objective, qualities—size, shape, mass, velocity—all the quantifiable qualities. And this latter assumption is not tenable without upsetting that first convenient assumption, since it is the assumption that consciousness is *sometimes* self-transcendent. To prevent the collapse of the strategy there is a secondary evasion: all qualities, indeed all findings of consciousness are held to be "secondary" in the sense that consciousness is *never* self-transcendent. We are back with some variety of Berkeley's position—the position exemplified by Rosenblueth's doctrine or (though not without self-doubts) by Wigner. The tertiary evasion—it is, one suspects, an evasion in which the evader deceives himself—is the failure to announce that at least one "quality" of consciousness is self-transcendent: that in which the philosopher of science conceives of and assents to the doctrine he puts before us.

There is one point we must concede to the view that consciousness is an emergent property or quality of physical events, to be dealt with as any other quality might be. That is the innocuous point that the status of the qualitative and the status of subjectivity are indeed intimately related. But the governing matter in interpreting this truth is the status of subjectivity. If we settle that, we may also be able to settle the status of qualities —whether so-called primary and objective ones or so-called secondary and subjective ones. But we prejudge the whole issue if we accept a physicalist explanation of the significance of either or both kinds, and then use this to try to settle the status of the subjectivity upon which the apprehension of qualities of any kind depends.

The self-transcendence of subjectivity, the self-transcendence of mind-becoming-conscious, is something that at some point every science, every methodological study, every man in his ordinary occasions, and every philosopher must acknowledge. Not a self-transcendence at all times and in all respects, but a self-transcendence that is always in principle possible. It is something that makes it quite impossible to dismiss our ordinary assessment of the world in all its qualitative richness as somehow more illusory, more "subjective" (in the pejorative

259

sense) than a reductive analysis. But the point can be made at a deeper level than that of the status of the qualitative, as our long tussle with reductionism throughout this meditation should by now have made clear. It is expressible also in terms of the status of the entities to which in our commonsense mood we attribute these qualities. A blossom, a leaf, a plant, a butterfly, a man: there are important correlations between the quantitative features of these things and our direct and concrete apprehension of them with mind-becoming-conscious. The genetic code of the chromosome material will differ for these various creatures as the wave length of light differs for various colors. But there, in all its concreteness, is the apprehended living form—blossom, leaf, or man. From the vantage point of the autonomy of consciousness we have no grounds whatever for assigning to the physicist's account of these things a more ultimate status than the direct assessment of mind-becoming-conscious. Seen from one point of view, consciousness is just one of these many features of the world for which a physicalist explanation is inadequate; its especial "interior," lived quality is no more satisfactorily accounted for in that way than is the total agency of an animal. Shift the angle of sight just a trifle, however, and it is seen to have a unique role: that lived quality, that subjectivity so primordial that there is nothing in terms of which one can define it, is nonetheless the autonomous power that can attain what is the case about the world and about itself; it is the power by means of which we assess these other features and may well judge them to be irreducible, and even a dogmatic materialism accepts this autonomy in principle. How, then, can we accept an account of its physical basis as a completely adequate account of mind-becoming-conscious itself?

When Sherrington goes on to say, "I perceive a picture of the world around me," he falls into the language of an epistemology that is probably inadequate, and is certainly inconsistent with the most striking of his insights: I am *conscious of* a world —a world that can not be set aside as "merely" what a physicalist account would make of it. It is a world that displays itself in a complex hierarchy of entities and their correlate complex hierarchy of levels of operation, or powers. We can attend not only to the entities and powers of the atomic and subatomic level but also to the complex entities and powers of plants, animals, and man. The autonomy of our assessment of these things gives us no warrant for setting it aside in favor of another assessment based on another view, equally dependent on the autonomy of mind-becoming-conscious, that sees them as reducible to more basic entities in $C \rightarrow E$ connection under law. Still less can we set aside as a mere product of physical events the act of mind-becoming-conscious upon which every assessment of things or theories depends. Consciousness is surely in a sense "produced" by its physical basis, just as any complex entity or any complex level of operation is in a sense "produced" by levels below it. But the qualification "in a sense" is an important one. It suggests to us that a recognition of mind-becoming-conscious as an aspect of originative action may in itself be a mode of explanation complementary to that of science. From this point of view the study of the physical basis of consciousness is the study of the infrastructure of a certain kind of originative action.

8

The autonomy of mind-becoming-conscious may be attained and enjoyed independently of physiological studies and even in complete ignorance of the workings of the central nervous system. To say this is not to claim that physiology is irrelevant. On the contrary, this approach to the mind-body problem suggests the following working hypothesis for neurophysiological investigations. (a) Progress in knowledge of the brain, and especially of the neocortex, will reveal large regions of intense neural activity that can not be interpreted by an external observer as the physical equivalents of steps in logical or conceptual problems in the way in which the electronic events in a computer can be so interpreted. The inference from a physical state to a logical state can not in principle be made, although

261

it is called for in the case of the computer by the very nature of the device.

(*b*) *By consulting the subject* it may, however, be found that certain physiological states are the correlates of certain particular activities in which mind-becomes-conscious. If so, it might one day be possible to make an inference from a given neural event to such a proposition as "The subject sees (concludes) that S," where S is some step in the solution of a problem; from another neural event to such propositions as "The subject understands C" or "The subject understands T," where C and T are respectively a concept and a theory; from yet another event to "The subject is conscious (aware) of O and understands it to be an O," where O is some physical object or complex of objects present to the subject by way of his senses. It should be emphasized that some such expression as "the subject sees (concludes, understands, is aware, etc.)" is absolutely essential if the external observer is to give a correct interpretation of the physiological events. We miss the point entirely if we suppose the interpretation to be merely "S," "C," "T," or "O." And in any case the business of interpretation is quite different here from what it is in the case of the computer. There we can say that the physical state "means" the logical state in the sense (sense 1) that it is a physical instantiation of it. But in the case of our subject the physiological state (we now assume) supports, in a manner proper to an infrastructure, the movement of mind-to-consciousness, and it "means" the latter only in the sense (sense 2) that it might possibly warrant an inference to it. If the physiologist, enlightened by what the subject had told him, tries to interpret the succession of physiological states as the physical counterpart of a succession of logical states, he will not be able to do so, for he has no right to impute a meaning in one sense (sense 1) on the basis of the meaning in another sense (sense 2) he has found with the help of the subject. Not only does a physical event that is the physical basis of mind-becoming-conscious of S not mean "S" in the sense (sense 1) in which the physical state of the computer means, or signifies, its logical state; it does not even mean "mind-becoming-conscious-of S"

in *that* sense (sense *1*) of "mean." It is simply the physical basis of it. Having made that point, we are not obliged to say exactly how a *lack* of that computerlike meaning (or significance) on the part of the physiological events would reveal itself to the external observer.

(*c*) The physiological events, although they are the physical basis of mind-becoming-conscious (of a world of physical objects, of meanings, concepts, steps in problems, reasons, orders, coherences, consistencies, rules, and a host of other things mind seems to its "possessor" to deal in), do not wholly cause mind's-becoming-conscious, either in a $C \rightarrow E$ sense or in any other sense that might be advanced. The physical events of this kind, although never occurring without mind-becoming-conscious as their correlate, are as much accounted for by mind-becoming-conscious as it is accounted for by their occurrence. It would follow that the inventiveness of mind-becoming-conscious would also be an inventiveness in the domain of the neurophysiological events that form its basis. This would mean—and this is a plausible sense in which the lack of computerlike significance in the physiological events would reveal itself—that even with the help of the subject our external observer would never be able to hit upon a code for translating the structure of physiological events into conscious experience that would render him independent of future help by the subject. Whatever past correlations might have told him, some fresh insight on the part of the subject would confront him with a physiological pattern for which he had no precedent, so that by merely referring to his code he would not be in a position to read off from the physiology everything the subject was thinking, but would once again have to ask him.

9

When the principle of the autonomy of mind-becoming-conscious is expressed in this way, it becomes plainer than before that the activity of mind can be adequately understood only if the explanation calls attention to the activity itself. Rationalists have traditionally indicated the autonomous and self-explanatory character of mind with the help of the doctrine of innateness. Though heavy with metaphor, the doctrine still has its uses, and I shall try to give it an acceptable and illuminating sense here. The sense I have in mind differs in some important respects from most of the traditional senses, but it probably has more in common with them than with the sense of innateness Chomsky has recently advanced. His sense is dealt with briefly in the following section.

When the doctrine of innateness was widely influential, in a form to which Plato, Augustine, Descartes, and Leibniz were the chief contributors, discussion of it was based too trustfully on the distinction between sensations and ideas and the related distinction between truths arising out of experience and truths that were independent of experience. Sensations and truths dependent upon sense experience were a posteriori and thus by definition not innate. Ideas, or at least "adequate" ideas, or concepts, which could plausibly be said to be independent of sense experience, were candidates for innateness. Truths—in effect complexes of ideas—that were independent of sense experience and thus a priori, like those of mathematics and logic, were also sometimes said to be innate. In short, the role of sensations has usually been decisive in deciding whether an idea or a truth was innate. There is, to be sure, a tradition going back to Plato that gives sensory incitement a role in the emergence of an innate idea into conscious attention, and this tradition is very much alive in seventeenth century rationalism. But this incitement is an anomaly and a puzzle in systems that give mind as much independence of body as the great rationalisms do. Since I am assuming here that an originative action in which mind-becomes-conscious is "related" to the infrastructure it unifies, there is not that kind of independence. To mark this decisive difference from the rationalist sense of innateness I shall say that mind-becoming-conscious is characterized by act-innateness.

Despite this difference, which yields us a more modest sense of innateness than, say, Plato's or Descartes', the doctrine of act-innateness goes well beyond their claims in a certain direction, since it brings under its scope not just universal concepts and a priori truths, but even the particular and a posteriori awareness that mingles with our articulate understanding of the tree before us, and is indeed the basis for it. Act-innateness cuts across the distinction between a priori and a posteriori knowledge, and one's linguistically articulated awareness of the tree is regarded as an achievement of an innate capacity no less than would one's awareness of, say, the logical truth called *modus ponens.* The distinction between the one a posteriori and the other a priori item of knowledge is seen to lie rather in the nature of the things attended to than in the mind's capacity itself. Attending in one way, one sees the chestnut trees below the *altana;* attending in another way—not to a different world, but to the same world of the little park with its ilex, cypress, and chestnut—and one is aware of that important logical truth that qualifies the world. Consciousness, so understood, is a power, now turned this way, now that; now idling and receptive, now intense and active; now a general activity engaged with the most particular of all things—an object present to our senses—now a general activity intent upon a general feature of things—conformity with logic—that pervades all such particulars. The act-innateness lies in the fact that awareness of whatever sort can not be understood as caused by the neural excitations that subserve it. Yet the role given to the infrastructure in this unfolding from "within" the act its possession of what is so patently offered to it from "without" allows us to say this without depriving the a posteriori of its rightful status, as the extreme claims made for the innateness of the sensory in Leibniz's doctrine of preestablished harmony do.

In another context, I called the exercise of this autonomous capacity recognition, a term deliberately chosen to chime with Plato's *anamnēsis,* yet suggesting no such dualistic independence of the body as that term does in the *Phaedo* and elsewhere in Plato, where the body at best reminds the soul of Forms it possesses in another existence, but rather the mind's meeting,

265

through the body, of things — including things like the trees — that are at once independent of it, given to it from outside itself, and yet familiar, attainable, and assimilable. Here in this context the term "act-innate" allows us to couple two distinct and seemingly incompatible features in mutual support. The word "act" reminds us that there is a role played by the infrastructure in what is achieved, and that in some cases the neural activity thus referred to includes sensory support of the kind usually referred to as empirical. Its qualification by the word "innate" calls attention to the fact that in the case of mind the originative and so to speak "creative" character of the act must be compatible, despite the surface emphasis on novelty, with the theme of ancient and familiar possession if we are to suppose that the act is self-transcendent to attain what is other than itself. For the physical happenings that make up the infrastructure are radically different from those trees the possession of which they mediate, even though they may be isomorphic with them. What is originated in the act, what is therefore not "caused" by the infrastructure, is not something novel and created, but something disclosed. In a word, the power of an act to transcend itself, to attain the other, is act-innate in the sense that the infrastructure is not, except as unified in the act, adequate to account for it. This, no doubt, is what moves phenomenologists to think of the power of the mind as *constitutive* — a term too "idealistic" for the present context. Innateness is a metaphor meant to combine the otherness, the independent reality, of what is attained, with its attainment by the act, which, in no sense "receiving" it from outside, in that sense has "innate" possession of it. Part of what is originated in the act is *consciousness-of-the-trees:* it is not caused by the trees; nor is it caused by a complex of physical events, including neural events, although these play a role in contributing, as an infrastructure, to the act that unifies them. The response to the tree, though it takes place in and with the temporally ordered regional mappings in the cortex, is not a response to those events, but rather to the trees — to the great tree streaming in the rain, which was not then in my cortex but out there on the Bowdoin campus, to the chestnuts below the *altana,* which are not now in my cortex but out there on this little shoulder of Monte Pilli. The response to the trees is originated in the act itself and yet does not complete itself in some creative surrogate for them, but in the trees themselves. No cortical events, no physical events isomorphic with them but taking place in the sensory field, and no features of subjectivity itself — ideas, impressions, mental events, or whatever — make sense out of the self-transcendence in which subjectivity becomes aware of what is the case. And this self-transcendence, I must remind the reader, is taken for granted by every materialist who claims his doctrine to be true.

It is often assumed, even by physiologists who are sensitive to the importance of consciousness, that there is a one-to-one correspondence between the features of conscious experience and the spatiotemporal features of a complex neural event in the brain. This should be distinguished from the related assumption of an isomorphism between the physical events making up the sensory field and the physical events in the brain. Yet if mind-becoming-conscious is an instance of act-innateness, there may be no one-to-one correspondence of that first kind. That subjectivity should attain anything at all that is neither a feature of its own nature nor created by its own nature — anything at all that is the case, that is true — is so miraculous a self-transcendence that it surely in some sense transcends the physical events that support it. For whatever isomorphism may be preserved between the complete reality of the tree and those events that make up (say) the visual field, between the visual field and the events in the brain, consciousness does not deal finally with this isomorphism as it is in the brain, but rather *by means of this isomorphism* with the tree itself. However profound the preserved isomorphism, the tree as known, the tree as what-is-the-case, is not that set of neural events. In transcending itself, mind-becoming-conscious transcends also the neural events that support it, to attain what-is-the-case. And this transcendence would be little more miraculous for having been accomplished on the basis of a much less detailed one-to-one isomorphism between neural events

267

and the features of consciousness than is generally supposed.

The example that has occupied us for awhile—the tree in New England and those here in Tuscany—is high in sensory features, and if even there that detailed correspondence is at least open to question, it is much more questionable when we are dealing with activities of mind that are predominantly conceptual, theoretic, systematic. Can an external observer in principle describe, even with the help of the subject, neural events in one-to-one correspondence with each concept understood, each point taken, each inference drawn, each inconsistency rejected? Maybe so and maybe not. And meanwhile it is probably unwise to neglect other possibilities that might also furnish a guide to experiment. Mind, when it becomes conscious in this way, and conscious of these features of reality, may function as a very general power, and some of the neural events that subserve this kind of function may themselves be general, general in the sense that all of their properties support the intensity of consciousness, while none of them support the consciousness of some particular item in its field of concern. This general activity might then focus now here, now there, in the fields of perception, association, and memory, by drawing upon neural happenings of more particular import. But even particular and localized neural happenings like those that support sight and hearing might turn out to be less detailed and to contribute less to the rich and concrete particularity of our awareness than physiologists generally suppose. Instead, they might merely incite this more generalized psychic life to originate or unfold its own very particularized and concrete awareness in response to them. These expressions "originate" and "unfold" invite misunderstanding insofar as they seem to suggest that any awareness is "part" of the subjectivity that originates or unfolds it, and is thus out of touch with what it intends to be directed upon. Let me be quite plain, then, about the sweeping claim that I am making for act-innateness: what is originated by an act of mind in the unifying "relation" to its neural infrastructure can in principle be faithful to what is both distinct from subjectivity and distinct from the infrastructure.

10

Act-innateness should be distinguished from another sense of innateness made current in linguistics by Noam Chomsky in the course of the development of his claim that the grammatical laws of all languages are instantiations of a universal grammar. According to this theory, if we penetrate the surface structure of any statement in any language we shall find a deep structure whose laws are those of a universal grammar, which is thus innate in all language users. Though Chomsky sees affinities between this theory and the Cartesian tradition of innate ideas,[22] some of the things he has said about the sense in which such a universal grammar might be innate suggest that he has in mind a physicalistic rather than a Cartesian sense of innateness. The foundation of Descartes' sense of innateness lies in his claim that thinking substance is utterly immaterial, and the material substance correlated with it in his dualism is not in the least the carrier of innateness, though the paradoxical doctrine of interaction permits him to suppose that it can be the sensory "occasion" that brings to full consciousness what is innate in thinking substance. As Chomsky develops the idea of deep structure in a strictly linguistic context, it is clear that it is a *formal structure* or an *abstract structure*. But when he speculates about how this structure might be innate in the human mind, he uses language that suggests that it may be carried by a *physical structure*. Expressions like "innate mechanisms," "innate cognitive mechanism," "built-in structures," and "preset" turn up from time to time in his writing.[23] And though he seems to be aware that a programmed computer is anything but an appropriate example of Cartesian innateness, he is nonetheless willing to use it to show that innateness is a comprehensible notion.

> There is nothing incomprehensible in the view that stimulation provides the occasion for the mind to apply certain innate interpretive principles, certain concepts that proceed from "the power of understanding" itself, from the faculty of thinking rather than

269

from external objects directly. To take an example from Descartes (*Reply to Objections,* V):

> When first in infancy we see a triangular figure depicted on paper, this figure cannot show us how a real triangle ought to be conceived, in the way in which geometricians consider it, because the true triangle is contained in this figure, just as the statue of Mercury is contained in a rough block of wood. But because we already possess within us the idea of a true triangle, and it can be more easily conceived by our mind than the more complex figure of the triangle drawn on paper, we, therefore, when we see the composite figure, apprehend not it itself, but rather the authentic triangle.

> In this sense the idea of a triangle is innate. Surely the notion is comprehensible; there would be no difficulty, for example, in programing a computer to react to stimuli along these lines (though this would not satisfy Descartes, for other reasons). Similarly, there is no difficulty in principle in programing a computer with a schematism that sharply restricts the form of a generative grammar, with an evaluation procedure for grammars of the given form, with a technique for determining whether given data is compatible with a grammar of the given form, with a fixed substructure of entities (such as distinctive features), rules, and principles, and so on—in short, with a universal grammar of the sort that has been proposed in recent years. For reasons that I have already mentioned, I believe that these proposals can be properly regarded as a further development of classical rationalist doctrine, as an elaboration of some of its main ideas regarding language and mind.[24]

There is nothing about this example that is Cartesian, or, more generally, rationalist, except the suggestion that a physical stimulus can be the occasion for the emergence of what is innate.

Though Chomsky usually assumes that physiology will one day uncover biological mechanisms in which the deep structure of language will be found to be encoded, his stubborn adherence to the name of Descartes, despite fierce criticism from extreme empiricists, and his openmindedness about the controversy between hierarchic and reductionist science suggest that he may in the end develop a doctrine of innateness more compatible with the Cartesian tradition than is the passage just quoted. Nonetheless, his influence has made current a doctrine of innateness that we may call (physical) *structure-innateness* and distinguish from *act-innateness*. Presumably a deep-structure rule in accordance with which we form the surface structure of any language we speak [25] would be laid down in a physical neural structure in a way analogous to the way in which a logical rule followed by a computer is laid down in the electrical circuitry of a logic gate or gates. Such a sense of preprogrammed innateness is so wide that any physical structure that plays a role in our mental capacities would also be brought under it. It would apply not only to presumably a priori matters like rules and laws but also to a posteriori matters like sense perception. The neural connections from retina to the visual areas of the cortex would be no less innate than the neural structure — whatever it turned out to be — that laid down the universal grammar of our languages. Convinced that whatever was innate in mind was innate only in this sense, we might also expect to find that when in some particular instance a subject reasoned in accordance with a logical law like *modus ponens,* his reasoning consisted in the passage of a neural impulse through neural logical gates very like the electronic logical gates that make it possible for a computer to "reason" in accordance with *modus ponens.* For a mind whose capacities were innate in this sense, consciousness need not be invoked as an operative principle, although I do not suggest that Chomsky has explicitly set out to deny the efficacy of consciousness. It is at any rate a kind of innateness very far from what Descartes intended and very far from the "real causality" that Socrates wished to see attributed to mind.

It will be obvious that the notion of *act-innateness* is compatible with the notion of *structure-innateness* by virtue of the fact that the act in which mind-becomes-conscious unifies a spatiotemporal infrastructure some important features of which are given by the structural stabilities of the central nervous system. At least the two notions are compatible if that of structure-innateness is not extended to include the claim that coming-into-consciousness is nonfunctional, or epiphenomenal. It is essential to the notion of act-innateness that mind-becoming-conscious (in a self-transcendent sense) is an important aspect of the human agent's "real causality." Acceptance of act-innateness as a working hypothesis in physiological investigation means that there is no expectation that circuitry will be found that makes mind-becoming-conscious dispensable, merely symptomatic, or epiphenomenal. It is, however, compatible with the expectation that in due course neurophysiology will find circuitries and storage devices that will make it clearer how so general a power operates in so localized a fashion with such virtuosity. We may expect to find in much greater detail the topography of cortical excitations in which sensation is mapped, to begin to understand precisely what the physical correlate of a memory is, to discover in detail the neural channels by which an excitation in one region brings about an excitation in another region, to begin to see how consciousness remains free for new and important tasks by bringing about circuit patterns to which certain of its prior achievements are relegated. But we do not expect to find circuitry that makes consciousness seem useless, and we do not expect to circumvent the consciousness-centered predicament by showing how consciousness can be "caused." On this view, what is act-innate in mind is precisely its power to bring into consciousness both the particular and the general aspects of reality and to do so by utilizing the incitements of the myriad tentacles to the world that terminate in the knotted intricacy of the central nervous system. Its intricacy is presumably physically closed—a loop or loop of loops, a circuit or circuit of circuits in which all sensory channels end. But in another sense it is open at all points, open both to incite, and be incited by, the general power that is thus given a local habitation and a name.

If we think of act-innateness as in principle the power of bringing something into consciousness by means of a physical happening that is merely a partial incitement, we entertain a conception at once commonplace and extremely subtle. We attribute to mind a power of *becoming aware of what is the case.* What could be more commonplace? But the real incitement—an incitement in the sense that it is what mind is directed upon with the help of the physical incitement—now becomes reality itself—that is, what is really the case. And that mind should respond to this incitement by a self-transcendence that attains what is the case is a subtlety beyond explanation in that any explanation whatever must always presuppose it.

8

Mind, Action, and Infrastructure

 WE RETURN NOW FOR AWHILE TO the topic of originative action. Evidently if there are in fact originative actions the movement in which mind-becomes-conscious may qualify them. And there may also be originative actions in which that movement plays so large a role that it would be appropriate to call them actions on the part of the mind. This point may be made clearer if we make rather free use of the distinction between practical and theoretic that we inherit from Greek philosophy. Let us call a supposed originative action in which the subject is primarily concerned in the doing or the making of something a *practical* one. When Socrates rubs his legs to restore the circulation after the fetters have been removed he is performing a practical action. In fact, very many of the actions he performed on the last day are practical actions in that sense, even though most of them are sub-acts of an act that essentially consists in the refusal to perform another practical act—that of escaping. Standing fast in prison is a practical act, and many of its sub-acts are also practical acts. Practical though they are, mind-becoming-conscious evidently plays a key role in them. They are actions that are taken deliberately, and rational reflection and discourse play a large role in them; indeed we have only to look again at the passage from the *Phaedo* in which this meditation began to see at once that a certain view of the

274

nature of reality and of human life dominates them. But besides practical actions qualified by mind in this way there are also cases in which mind-becoming-conscious may itself be an instance of originative action, and these we may call *theoretic* originative actions. Socrates managing to express some elusive point for himself as well as for his hearers may be said to be acting chiefly theoretically. There are many other instances of at least a rough contrast with the practical: a scientist hitting upon some original theory; a scientist overcoming some obscurity in the interpretation of an experiment; a man sitting quietly working out a mathematical problem; even a child who suddenly grasps the meaning of some word or sentence that had puzzled him; all these are cases in point. The contrast between practical and theoretic originative actions is by no means an absolute one: consider, for instance, how even the most theoretic actions in which mind-becomes-conscious of some truth or other are hopelessly intertwined with the practical actions of speaking and writing, or with those odd "actions" in which, without actually writing or speaking, we find ourselves entertaining some formulation of a truth either in words or in imagined symbols.

If mind-becoming-conscious can qualify an action, if in some cases it can *be* an action, it is not at all clear that the category of action can do complete justice to the wonder of subjectivity. As I write now, engaged in what, for all its shortcomings, is intended to be an action in which my mind-should-become-conscious of the truth of certain matters that have heretofore remained obscure for it, there remains as a steady and relatively unchanged background to it the world of the chestnut trees. I have represented my awareness of it as an achievement of mind-become-conscious now grown habitual, but if it is an achievement it is one I can not escape from. There lies that world whose space the swifts, those subtle geometers, climbing, hovering, darting in swift rushes down through the garden, articulate with the living curves of their flight, and my awareness of it does not take place in an originative action of precisely the same order as the one in which I now try to express

275

myself. Nonetheless, the theme of originative action may be of considerable help in understanding any movement in which mind-becomes-conscious, against the background of the world of the chestnut trees and the swifts, of what until that moment it had not been conscious of, or at least had not attended to. This class of activities of the mind is quite large, comprising at one extreme mere shifts in our attention and at the other the most momentous insights and discoveries. The interpretation of these activities in terms of originative action carries with it the obligation, however, to show that what scientists now understand about the brain can be interpreted in a way consistent with the theme of originative action.

It seems to be beyond doubt that of all the more or less stable physical structures of the human body the brain is the chief organ of governance and control. If there are indeed originative actions, their infrastructures are made up not just of stable physical structures like the brain but of dynamic patterns that pervade them and maybe dominate them. At the least, the total dynamic pattern—precisely that of the act itself—must be an act-temporal one. But we saw earlier that if the possession of the total spatially organized structure of the body by an act-temporal pattern takes place at all, it probably is accomplished through the mediation of some infrastructure levels made up of dynamic sub-patterns that are also act-temporal. In this chapter we shall be asking whether the stable structure called the brain is so organized that it can indeed be dominated by dynamic patterns having an act-temporal character consistent with their unification in the power of an originative action.

2

If the concept of originative action is a sound one, it is of especial value in illuminating those dynamic features of subjectivity in which mind-becomes-conscious of what it had not theretofore been clear about. No doubt the fundamental explanatory dichotomy that we must use in such an interpretation

—the unity of the originative act contrasted with the spatiotemporal multiplicity of its infrastructure—is full of difficulties. But it has the advantage that it is not a radical dualism of the kind so readily generated when these issues are discussed in terms of the familiar contrast of mind and body, consciousness and brain, spirit and matter, and so on. The dichotomy of act and infrastructure is overcome as soon as it is stated, for it is held to consist in a "relation," itself *sui generis* and not to be further explained, in which the originative act unifies the multiplicity of the infrastructure. It is one instance of the fundamental contrast between the One and the Many that runs through the whole of nature, being exemplified in any object, concrete or abstract, that we can attend to, and being exercised as well in any act of attention or intelligence. And whatever that contrast may be, it is a unity-*in*-multiplicity that is quite at odds with dualisms of the kind that have so often been found to be logically objectionable.

From this point of view it becomes clear that when we recognize, attend to, or take account of, some originative act, what we are recognizing is a unification-of-a-multiplicity. And though this is not the place to press the point, our recognition itself is (*1*) the unification of its own infrastructure; (*2*) the "unification" of what might otherwise have been understood as the multiple data in the recognized act; (*3*) the acknowledgment that this "unification" is not constitutive, not a constructive synthesis, not a projection, but the self-transcending attainment on the part of mind of what is the case.

Some examples of theoretic acts thus recognized by the reader and myself as we consider these matters are these: (*a*) mind-becomes-conscious of the meaning of some complex sentence; (*b*) mind-becomes-conscious of some inconsistency in an argument; (*c*) mind-becomes-conscious of the correct interpretation of some physical phenomenon (as, for instance, that radiation takes place in discrete quanta or that gravity varies inversely with the square of the distance). The act "itself" is an affair of macroscopic unity, identifiable by some such formula as "Russell saw that the concept of the class of all classes not

277

members of themselves led to a contradiction." It is on the basis of our recognition of this macroscopic unity that we are able to identify elements of the infrastructure, for instance, the firing of a certain neuron in the course of the act. And in order to identify further elements of that infrastructure — whether successive levels in a hierarchic analysis or successive individual units within some particular level — we must continue to keep the total macroscopic unity of the act in mind. The macroscopic unity of the act is decisive in other respects as well. We can not, for instance, identify the act either with consciousness or with some unequivocally mental event distinct from the macroscopic unity of the act itself. The equivocal "dichotomy" of an *act* that is the unification of an *infrastructure* suppresses the superficially clear, unambiguous, but untenable dichotomy of consciousness and brain, or mental event and physical event. Nor does a dichotomy of consciousness and its infrastructure arise. Though consciousness is relevant to our understanding of the act, we do not identify the act *as* consciousness nor indeed as an act *of* consciousness. The act is *seeing that particular inconsistency*, or *having that particular insight*, or *seeing that particular point*, and the identification of any of these is by way of its macroscopic unity, which includes a progression-to-consciousness but is by no means identical with consciousness.

The familiar paradoxes of interactionism, which arise from considering consciousness (or mind) as an entity, state, or mode of being complete in itself yet somehow engaged in an interplay with a physical entity, state, or mode of being equally complete in itself, are thus avoided. We do not find ourselves engaged in the impossible task of establishing a $C \rightarrow E$ relation between consciousness and its physical correlate that is at the same time *not* a $C \rightarrow E$ relation. Nor does a despair born of that enterprise lead us to say instead that consciousness is flatly identical with its physical correlate.

An objectionable dualism of that kind is persistent, and it plagues even some of the more imaginative attempts by scientists to clarify the presumed efficacity of consciousness, or, as I have preferred to say, of mind-becoming-conscious. We noticed earlier what logical havoc that dualism raised with Culbertson's attempt to defend the usefulness of consciousness within a materialistic framework. And it was presumably MacKay's awareness of that kind of difficulty that led him to suppose that whatever case he might make out for the efficacy of consciousness would have to be made in terms of an identity theory committed to physical determinism—a supposition that confined him to giving instead, or so it seems to some observers, an account of the *feeling* that consciousness is efficacious. But the persistence of a dualism couched in terms of consciousness and brain causes difficulties even when a defense of consciousness is coupled with an anti-reductionism adventurous enough to look for alternatives to the orthodoxy of materialism. One of the more interesting defenses of this kind has been advanced within recent years by R. W. Sperry, whose work in neurophysiology has been widely influential. He is best known for his ingenious investigation of the consequences of the partial or entire severing of the corpus callosum, the main direct cortical link between the two halves of the brain.[1] It is curious that the influence of this work has by no means been unequivocally anti-materialistic. One interpretation of the behavior of the creatures thus altered (usually cats) is that two distinct consciousnesses inhabit the two separated cerebral halves, and this has naturally enough lent some support to the view that consciousness is only an epiphenomenon of underlying neural events. Interpretation of the data is naturally complicated by the fact that the two cerebral halves continue to be connected by way of the deeper subcortical structures of the brain. In any case the altered cats continue to display residual integrative powers. As for those men who, because of the injuries of war or accident or because of therapeutic surgery, have had part or all of the cortical connection severed, their powers of integration are sometimes remarkable, especially after the passage of time. Sperry has therefore not been led to epiphenomenalism on the basis of his experimental achievements. No doubt his recent position on consciousness also takes account of many other kinds of experimental work, since he has been active in scientific meetings designed precisely to arrive at an understanding of consciousness on the basis of many different kinds of work going forward not only in neurophysiology but in related disciplines as well.

At any rate, Sperry has recently questioned the prevailing view of consciousness in twentieth century science.[2] "It has long been the custom in brain research," he says, "to dispense with consciousness as just an 'inner aspect' of the brain process, or as some kind of parallel passive 'epiphenomenon' or 'paraphenomenon' or other impotent by-product, or even to regard it as merely an artifact of semantics, a pseudoproblem." In opposition to this view he offers the postulate that "the conscious phenomena of subjective experience do interact on the brain process exerting an active causal influence," an influence he calls "a directive role in determining the flow pattern of cerebral excitation." If we interpret Sperry as supposing this causal influence and direction to be of a $C \rightarrow E$ nature, there will be formidable difficulties of the kind that the long and exhaustive criticism of Cartesian interactionism has made familiar. In the same passage Sperry does indeed use the word "interact" in connection with this causal influence, but he also uses language that suggests a more profound and more difficult mutual involvement, noting that his interpretation "would make consciousness an integral part of the brain process itself and an essential constituent of the action."

Most of Sperry's discussion in that article of the relation between consciousness and the brain is cast in causal language, but avoids the language of Cartesian interactionism in favor of language popular in anti-reductionist circles. The term "holism," presumably coined by the statesman-philosopher J. C. Smuts in his *Holism and Evolution* (1926), and recently revived and given a wider currency by Arthur Koestler,[3] is frequently employed. "Compared to the elemental physiological and molecular properties," Sperry continues, "the conscious properties of the brain process are more molar and holistic in nature. They encompass and transcend the details of nerve impulse traffic in the cerebral networks in the same way that the properties of the organism transcend the properties of its cells, or the properties of the molecule transcend the properties of its atomic components, and so on." There are difficulties nonetheless, though I point them out in a cooperative spirit, since I am in agreement with what I think Sperry is getting at. For one thing, the holistic properties are said to have an active causal influence, but no alternative to the $C \rightarrow E$ sense of causality is provided, so that one is tempted to think in terms of the interactionism that must surely be excluded. Thus, the passage goes on in this way: "Just as the holistic properties of the organism have causal effects that determine the course and fate of its constituent cells and molecules, so in the same way, the conscious properties of cerebral activity are conceived to have analogous causal effects in brain function that control subset events in the flow pattern of neural excitation. In this holistic sense the present proposal may be said to place mind over matter, but not as any disembodied or supernatural agent."

If we try to conceive of these holistic "causal effects" in $C \rightarrow E$ terms we are at once in logical trouble. In that kind of analysis an event in "consciousness" causes an event later in linear time in "the flow pattern of brain excitation"; and that in turn causes a still later event in consciousness; meanwhile, the very efficacity attributed to consciousness suggests that it will itself, perhaps, have given rise to, or contributed to, another event in consciousness. All the familiar Cartesian difficulties assail us, including the familiar one that consciousness would "interfere" with the laws of the physical realm. Sperry's intent is obviously not Cartesian, nor has he set out in any explicit defense of $C \rightarrow E$ causality. He goes on immediately to deny any such interference, and to say that ordinary biological laws for the transmission of nerve impulses are in no way violated by the activity of consciousness, and, indeed, that these holistic causal influences can be disregarded by the electrophysiologist dealing in "analytic neurophysiology." But the difficulty arises again when Sperry notices that the electrophysiologist must nevertheless worry about these matters if he wishes "to explain how a sensation or a percept is *produced,* or how the *subsequent* volitional response is *generated*" (italics mine). The electrophysiologist venturing on such matters, I would contend, must explain as a philosopher explains, and not as a physiologist explains. One of the things he must provide is a sense of causality adequate to cope with "influences" of this kind. The doctrine of "real causality" developed in chapters 4 and 5 is designed to do this, but only by absorbing the category of causality in that of originative action, and—as we shall see in the next chapter—absorbing that category in turn into that of the ontic power of the agent to whom we ascribe the originative action.

The reader may by now find the reiteration of the phrase "mind-becoming-conscious" tedious. It has the advantage, though, that it reminds us that consciousness is an aspect of a dynamic ontological level of considerable richness. The unity of an action may be characterized by awareness, understanding, and reflexivity, but the outcome of the movement is the growth and enhancement of those features of it. The unifying "relation" of the action to its infrastructure is our basic explanatory category and not simply consciousness as a supposedly complete entity or ontological level. To make our basic contrast between *consciousness* and *neural events* as Sperry and many other physiologists do is to find oneself compelled to lean over backwards so as not to suggest that consciousness, regarded as somehow already complete and effective, is an illegitimate intruder in physical affairs. On the one hand the temptation is to make it seem an emergent property of any very complex neural pattern. After observing that "the individual nerve impulses and associated elementary excitatory events are obliged to operate within larger circuit-system configurations of which they as individuals are only a part," Sperry goes on to make a point that exemplifies that temptation. "These larger functional entities," he says, "have their own dynamics in cerebral activity with their own qualities and properties. They interact causally with one another at their own level as entities. *It is the emergent dynamic properties of certain of these higher specialized cerebral processes that are interpreted to be the substance of consciousness*" (italics mine).

On the other hand, to make it plain that consciousness is indeed physically efficacious, one tends to talk about it as though it *were* precisely a very complex physical event. In the following passage Sperry leans in that direction. "The subjective mental phenomena are conceived to influence and to govern the flow of nerve impulse traffic by virtue of their encompassing emergent properties. Individual nerve impulses and other excitatory components of a cerebral activity pattern are simply carried along or shunted this way and that by the prevailing overall dynamics of the whole active process (in principle—just as drops of water are carried along by a local eddy in a stream or the way the molecules and atoms of a wheel are carried along when it rolls down hill, regardless of whether the individual molecules and atoms happen to like it or not)."

His intent, though, is plainly to keep a balance between these two emphases, and this passage follows immediately. "Obviously, it also works the other way around, that is, the conscious properties of cerebral patterns are directly dependent on the action of the component neural elements. Thus, a mutual interdependence is recognized between the sustaining physico-chemical processes and the enveloping conscious qualities. The neurophysiology, in other words, controls the mental effects, and the mental properties in turn control the neurophysiology. One should remember in this connection, however, that the conscious phenomena are in a position of higher command, as it were, located at the top of the organizational hierarchy."

I have the utmost sympathy for anyone who tries this kind of tightrope walk, since I have had to teeter almost as perilously in my earlier discussions of the "relation" between the unity of an originative act and the multiplicity of the infrastructure. But if we consider the enhancement of consciousness to be an aspect of an originative action of mind, we have, I think, a clearer way of expressing the desired notion of a dynamic and ordering control that is nevertheless in interdependence with what is controlled. When we attend to an action like that ascribed to Russell, or an act like that in which Planck saw, on the basis of the evidence, that radiation must take place in discrete quanta, we identify a power-unity in terms of its macroscopic features, but the formula in which we sum up our recognition leaves out a good deal of the qualitative richness of the act. That qualitative richness is not, however, lost to us. Without forsaking the unity of the act in favor of an analysis of it into a multiplicity that properly belongs to the infrastructure rather than the act, we can turn our attention to the qualitative richness as well. When we do, it seems clear enough that the act-temporal unity completes itself in the enhancement of the consciousness of the agent. We can thus give consciousness a key role without thinking of it as an utterly distinct state, entity, or mode of being that is in $C \rightarrow E$ concourse with an equally distinct set of neural events. One must concede that the finality and authenticity of the power-unity thus identified by its macroscopic features is not provable except in the circular sense that the identification is made by what itself purports to be an originative act congruent with the first one. In this meditation I represent the reader and myself as engaged in such an originative act.

Sperry says as much as can be said about these matters without the introduction of a general view of action and its relation to causality—a general view of the class to which the doctrine of originative action belongs. "Individual nerve impulses and other excitatory components of a cerebral activity pattern are simply carried along or shunted this way and that by the prevailing overall dynamics of the whole active process," a whole active process of which he is struggling to insist that consciousness is a part. We see what he is driving at, even though the language he is employing—"carried along or shunted this way and that"—carries overtones of an inappropriate $C \rightarrow E$ causality with it. His difficulty is understandable: where the physical processes underlying all acts of the mind we know of are under discussion it is hard to make sense of them without employing the sense of causality that has, after all, historically developed *pari passu* with the exact study of physical processes. To say that the concept of originative action gives us a more natural way of talking about the "relation" between mind and its physical basis than the language Sperry is employing is to offer a criticism, but the very criticism is a concession that Sperry's views offer much support and encouragement to the ideas being developed in this meditation.

3

The status of the stable structural properties of the infra-structure—and where an act of mind is at issue, that is to say the status of the relatively stable physical structure that is the central nervous system—is a problem for the doctrine of originative action. If, for instance, physical nature were so con-stituted that the exact physical state of the central nervous sys-tem at time t_1 were precisely definable and in principle capable of being established, and if from that state a master physicist-physiologist could predict the physical state of it at time t_2, there would be good grounds for supposing that the central nervous system operates deterministically.

The view seems orthodox among neurophysiologists that that is exactly how nature *is* constituted. Sperry's views on this matter may be an exception, though I am not certain about this: some remarks he has made in more or less informal discussions at scientific meetings suggest that he has not made up his mind one way or the other. Among general biologists, Paul A. Weiss and some of his anti-reductionist allies may also hold that predictability in that sense is not possible in principle. On the other hand, we did notice in our discussion of the concept of the laws of nature that most anti-reductionists may be inter-preted as believing that although the laws of physics as now known permit no such predictability, there may be hierarchic laws which when perfected might permit it. In any case we shall probably not be far wrong if we suppose that for most physiolo-gists a later brain state is in principle predictable from an earlier one. An exception is often made in favor of the merely statistical predictions that physicists must make do with at that microevent level where quantum theory operates and the indeterminacy principle comes into play. If discrete electrons or photons are emitted from a suitable source and are permitted entry into a chamber by way of an opening small enough for disturbances in accordance with the indeterminacy principle to take place, it then becomes impossible to predict the exact point of arrival on the opposite wall of the chamber of any particular electron or photon, although the distribution of points of arrival of a suitably large number of them over a certain area will be uniform and thus statistically predictable. This flaw in the otherwise supposedly flawless Laplacean determinism of the texture of nature is often seized upon by neurophysiologists who wish to build upon it a case for the efficacity of what I have called mind-becoming-conscious. They themselves tend to speak instead of mind, consciousness, and will, and in some discussions of these matters these three words (and sometimes other related words) are used so loosely that they seem to be interchangeable. In this section I shall follow that practice so as to stay as close as I can to the spirit of their views.

It will be clear to the reader that if the texture of nature is such that originative actions can operate within it, revealing in their infrastructures some of the same act-temporality I attribute to the acts themselves, then nature has no such general Laplacean predictability. There would therefore be no need to build one's case upon a single exception to it. It will nevertheless be interesting to look at some of the suggestions of this kind that have been made, because, if the situation were indeed as these physiologists have supposed it to be, the efficacity of consciousness, mind, or will could only make itself felt by way of a "relation" to these small-scale events that had some resemblance to the "relation" between an originative act and its infrastructure.

The chief objections to building a case for freedom upon the indeterminacy principle have been clear from the time the suggestions were first made, and indeed Eddington, who was certainly among the first to see this possibility in the indeterminacy principle, was also clear about the objections to it.[4] Schrödinger's voice—a voice very eloquent in his old age on questions where philosophy and science meet—has, however, been the most influential one among the scientists who have argued against it.[5] There are three chief objections. (*1*) To build a case of this kind upon a random happening is to take away freedom and responsibility from the very mind, consciousness, or will to which you are trying to ascribe it: the will (for instance) seems no active agent if in fact it is carried along, diverted, or otherwise qualified by events for which there are no reasons. (2) In any case, since in long enough runs a statistical determinism prevails, the neural events will turn out to be just as much determined in their group functioning as they would be if the entire situation were neo-Laplacean, as the strong deterministic interpretation of statistical microevent determinism supposes it to be. (See chapter 2, section 1.) (3) The events are in themselves of too small a scale to be effective. If, for instance, you wish to show that the firing of a given nerve at a given point in time is due to one of these small-scale happenings (which is in turn, on this hypothesis, due to mind, will, or consciousness), you must also show that the energy required to trigger the nerve can in principle be small enough so that the very small energies that prevail at the level of the indeterminacy principle can be effective. Yet this does not seem to be the case.

The first and the second objections somewhat miss the point being urged by physiologists interested in making use of the indeterminacy principle. As to the first one, they do not pin their hopes precisely on some particular happening regarded as indeterminate in the sense of being random, chancy, or without reason. They see rather in a group of such happenings, determinate as a group, but indeterminate in their particulars, an openness to a determination of another kind. Thus, if, on their hypothesis, the particular movement of some electron played a key role in a moment of reasonable consciousness or in some free volition, it would not be because the movement of that particular electron was "without reason" but rather because the sum of the "reasons" for its particular movement included the determination exercised by mind, consciousness, or will. The purely physical determination of the behavior of a group of electrons leaves open the possibility of an enormous variety of particular patterns that would conform to it, and into the particular pattern that in this case, according to the hypothesis, will or mind intervenes in, there enters precisely the further determination that is will, mind, or consciousness. That this further determination can not be an additional physical force operative in a $C \rightarrow E$

sense they are well aware.[6] They do not, that is, claim that at the level of these minute delicacies nature stands in some sort of equipoise, so that a minuscule amount of energy contributed by the breath of consciousness, will, or mind, a breath so delicate as to be *almost* immaterial, would be sufficient to sway it. They therefore avoid the trap Descartes falls into when he seems to suppose that thinking substance, gathering its force at the pineal gland, might summon enough energy so that, if it did not move the delicately poised material reality of the "animal spirits," it might at least alter their course. They are, I think, perfectly aware that the determination exercised by mind, consciousness, or will can not be in the form of matter or energy. That the determination must nevertheless determine a physical reality is plain enough, and if we suppose them to be saying that this further determination consists of factors that are closer to being lawlike than they are to being matter or energy, we shall be closer to doing them justice. Though I am not aware that they make the point in precisely this way, what they are driving at is consistent with what anti-reductionists have to say about "higher-level" laws. It is also consistent with the claim I have repeatedly made for the resemblance between the way in which an originative act might pervade an infrastructure and the way in which a law might pervade it.

The second objection seems to say that a statistical determinism of a large number of microevents based on a genuine ontological indeterminism of particular microevents (weak deterministic interpretation of statistical determinism) is practically no different from one in which the indeterminism of particular microevents is merely a function of the limitations of our measuring techniques (strong deterministic interpretation of statistical determinism). In either case there is a *macroevent* determinism, and, since neural events are of the order of macroevents, that is all we need to consider. Against this version of the objection it should be said, in the first place, that the physiologists against whom it is directed hold the view that there is a genuine indeterminism of particular microevents, and, in the second place, that they claim that mind, will, or consciousness can so possess the particulars of it that the determinate macro-event that emerges shall be a function not only of the individual *indeterminate* microevent particulars but also of the *determining,* or *ordering,* power of mind, will, or consciousness. The physiologists weaken their case somewhat by referring to the neural macroevent that is hypothetically the result of all this as indeterminate, which of course it is not. But the second objection has a further force that is not countered by this rebuttal, for the objection may also be interpreted to mean that a statistical law applicable to a certain group of happenings expresses certain limits upon the indeterminations that can exist within that group. As the parameters of the happenings we are talking about are very small, the second objection would on this interpretation mean that the long-run statistical determinism of a large number of microevents made it impossible for a particular pattern of minuscule individually indeterminate events to be an effective vehicle for the intervention of mind, will, or consciousness in neural networks, even though the particular microevent pattern should (*ex hypothesi*) have been determined by mind, will, or consciousness. The second objection then, at its most effective, is really another form of the third.

The third objection is a serious one. Physiologists who are attempting to exploit the indeterminacy of the very small suppose that multitudes of such happenings can somehow be amplified to produce what they confusingly call a secondary indeterminism at the level of single neuron cells. The spontaneous discharge of neurons (that is, their discharge in a rhythm in some measure independent of particular environmental stimuli) plays, it is clear, an important role in the central nervous system, and if it could be shown that some factors in the brain operated to bring certain cells at certain times in the course of this spontaneous discharge into so delicate a state of energy balance that an event at the size where the indeterminacy principle operates would be sufficient to make them fire, then their firing would be indeterminate in a sense that was a function of the underlying indeterminacy of the very small-scale events.

J. C. Eccles has been the leading proponent of this view

289

among neurophysiologists. He has been very concerned to show how a factor he calls sometimes mind, sometimes conscious mind, and sometimes will, can play a role in neural-net physical events. The efficacy of consciousness, perceiving, and willing is associated, he thinks, with the fact that in the intense dynamic activity of the awake brain a considerable portion of its neurons are in such a critically poised state of excitation that it is problematical whether or not they will fire.[7] This intense activity is spontaneous, but only in the limited sense that it is not caused by a sensory stimulus but is an internally generated state of readiness to respond. (The spontaneous activity would thus be an example of the reign of deterministic laws, provided we could abstract from the possible effects on it of microevent indeterminacy.) The poise, which must be sufficiently delicate so that microevents at the level of the indeterminacy principle can trigger it, is understood to be essential to "brain receiving from conscious mind in a willed action and in turn transmitting to mind in conscious experience." Thus, when in sensation an additional spatiotemporal pattern is superimposed on the attentive background activity in which the poised neurons are involved, a wave front of great complexity is formed, and this is the correlate of subjective experience. In this wave front there is thus, by definition, a measure of indetermination. Similarly, one gathers, "conscious mind in a willed action" generates as a function of the same indetermination a wave front that issues in motor responses. Eccles has also remarked [8] that synapses operate by the discharge of the transmitter contained in only one or two of the synaptic vesicles, whose mass is so small as to bring them, and thus in principle the firing of a nerve, within range of microphysical indetermination.

A. O. Gomes has made calculations that tend, he thinks, to support the view that the amplification of discrete, indeterminate events into events of the relevant magnitude is possible. He has also more recently offered an ingenious electronic model for the coupling of indeterminate microevents with a determinate ordering system of larger size in such a way that the output of the total system shall be both ordered and indeterminate.[9]

290

He does not intend this as a model for the operation of consciousness, but wishes to make rather the supporting point that indeterminate microevents can be magnified to produce macroevents that are also indeterminate. The ordered character of the physical gadget Gomes suggests is a function of its physical structure. It is not, I take it, to be understood as a paradigm of the ordering that could be performed by way of will, mind, or consciousness, but merely as an example of the coupling of *some* order with macroevent indeterminacy. Some of the examples he gives suggest, however, that he tends to think of the "wired-in" features of the central nervous system as the entire source of order in such systems. Since, considered just as wired systems, these would be deterministic, their coupling with microevents of an indeterminate sort would be open to Schrödinger's objection: the indeterminate microevent, instead of being under the control of an act-temporal ordering, would be responsible for the particular pattern of impulses that went through the otherwise deterministic neural network. But this may be an inadvertence, and it is perhaps fairest to remember that Gomes in the essay in question has not taken on the job of finding a possible physical description for consciousness, mind, or will, but has simply set out to show that there can be ordered systems that are not deterministic.

The attempt to find, within a framework in which the generally deterministic character of nature is assumed, some indeterministic features of the central nervous system that can provide an entry into nature of the freedom we associate with mind, consciousness, and will, has also turned to statistical fluctuations of a larger sort: the thermodynamic fluctuations around delicately poised neurons. The purely scientific uncertainties that, at this writing, still prevail in this whole matter of the relation between cell-level events and events of a much smaller size can be seen from the fact that, despite the differences in scale between thermodynamic fluctuations and energy fluctuations of the scale appropriate to the indeterminacy principle, it is apparently no easier to settle the question whether the first kind are large enough to do the job than the question whether the second kind are large enough. In the case of thermodynamic fluctuations there is an additional perplexity, for while they are statistical — temperature is a measure of the mean behavior of populations of molecules — it is usually assumed that the movement of a single molecule is deterministic, and that in principle one could follow the career of a single particle in a way in which one can not in some circumstances follow the career of a single electron with an associated wave function. That thermodynamic fluctuations are offered as an example of indeterminism may reflect a suspicion that the many statistical regularities governing the behavior of items of a much higher order of magnitude than that of electrons and photons indicate other respects, besides the indeterminacy principle, in which nature is not deterministic in the extreme Laplacean sense.

The question remains obscure, and this present brief survey is designed to show only: (*1*) that there is significant physiological opinion to the effect that, while nature is generally deterministic, some curious circumstances may conspire to make the central nervous system an exception; (*2*) that among these same physiologists something sometimes called mind, sometimes consciousness, sometimes will, is understood to be not merely epiphenomenal, but to be capable of ordering the operation of organisms through the medium of this indeterminacy.

4

The view of nature expressed in the theme of originative action is not deterministic. I need not rehearse at this point the many respects in which it offers an alternative to determinism, while still managing to account for the many massive regularities of nature, and indeed for the several features of nature that are deterministic in a narrow mechanical sense. It is enough to remind the reader that in chapters 4 and 5 human action was interpreted in terms of (*a*) the levels of the originative action itself; (*b*) a subordinate level or several subordinate levels whose units, while not strictly speaking originative acts, are act-temporal and in that sense participate in the unity of the originative

292

act itself; (c) an indeterminate number of levels that are highly routine and repetitive, and in some cases simply mechanical, but that nonetheless reveal a temporal significance that participates in the unity of the act-temporal "gestures" that, in a sense both ontogenetic and phylogenetic, gave rise to them. We are therefore not obliged to show that an indeterminism at the quantum level is of sufficient magnitude for certain amplifying devices to transform it into an indeterminism at a higher level. Within the hierarchy of the infrastructure of an originative act *any* level exhibits some indeterminism with respect to the further determinations supplied by higher levels. It is true that we took the indetermination at the quantum level as an occasion for interpreting any "entity" at that level as a succession of act-temporal units, but we understood that characteristic of microevents to be but one instance of a much more general feature of nature.

The interpretation of scientific findings, either by scientists operating philosophically or by philosophers who are scientific amateurs, holds many problems. Not the least is that interpretation, which takes up time — and the more time as science itself, growing more specialized and more cooperative in its pursuit of particular issues, pours out a flood of findings to be interpreted — lags behind discoveries. At this writing it would appear that the question whether microevent indeterminacy is of sufficient magnitude so that what *did* happen indeterminately at that level could trigger happenings at the macroevent level is a still unsettled one. The answer to it appears to be a matter for calculation and experiment: that is, it is a scientific question. But the way it is posed even at this point assumes one matter to be settled, and that matter *is* open to interpretation. As the question is posed, the assumption appears to be that the higher level in which the amplification of microevent indeterminism *might* be felt is in itself determinate. And this is understood to mean that a given total state of the higher level is in principle predictable from an earlier state. The image is that of small indeterminately based events triggering, by way of the energy they supply at critical points — perhaps synaptic vesicles, certain delicately poised neural systems that, in their behavior *as determinately wired neural nets,* operate determinately. What obscures this point is that the intervention of the microevents takes place, on the hypothesis, at very many points in the system. Except for this feature, the intricate wiring system consisting of excitatory and inhibitory connecting points is usually understood to be, if not static, then at least deterministic in the laws governing such synaptic growth and change as does take place. And though the numerous microevents that intervene are assumed to be indeterministic, their intervention in the macrosystem of the neural net is understood to be by way of triggering energy changes, and is thus a $C \rightarrow E$ one. If this should be the *only* genuine indeterminism operative in the macrosystem, there are obviously puzzles. The chief one would appear to be that the efficacy of mind (or will, or consciousness) would appear to consist not in its direct possession of the neural events, but in its possession of the microevents that trigger them.

From the point of view of originative action, it is nevertheless encouraging that so many physiologists have thought they saw in the macroevent activity of the brain sufficient indetermination to suggest a correlate determination by mind, consciousness, or will. If this should seem likely to them within a generally deterministic outlook, how much more likely is the efficacy of mind-becoming-conscious when we regard the neural net, not as merely inheriting an indeterminism that belongs of right only to the lowest level of its infrastructure, but as pervaded by an indeterminism that belongs to it precisely *as* a neural net, precisely *as* a certain level of an infrastructure many, if not all, levels of which have their own appropriate indeterminations.

I do not mean to suggest that neurophysiologists accept dogmatically the thesis that any indetermination of the neural net must be a function of microevent indeterminacy. Among the neurophysiologists who are willing to entertain the possibility of the efficacy of mind, consciousness, or will we can certainly count Eccles, Gomes, and Sperry; so far as I can judge, V. B. Mountcastle and W. Penfield also lean in this direction.[10] Their position does indeed require a correlate indetermination of some sort in the neural net, but the conviction that there *is* such an indetermination seems more powerful than the conviction

294

that it must be traced to an amplification of microevent effects. Certainly Sperry's language often carries him well beyond any reliance on the indeterminacy principle alone, and indeed he seems to make common cause with the hierarchical views of order advocated by such anti-reductionists as Paul A. Weiss and Michael Polanyi, in which it is understood that any given level is indeterminate with respect to the determination of the level above. Sperry speaks, for instance, of "conscious properties of cerebral activity," which control "subset events in the flow pattern of neural excitation," and seems to assume some degree of indeterminateness in the subsets — an indeterminateness certainly not specifically ascribed to the amplification of microevent indeterminateness — that leaves them open to such control. From the point of view of originative action we should have to speak of this indeterminateness in terms of what the subset events *might* have been in the absence of the exercise of that particular control, for, if we were capable of analyzing any such subset event after its completion, we should certainly find it determinate enough. Sperry, writing in this vein, suggests a view of the central nervous system even more hospitable to an interpretation by way of originative action than do, say, Eccles and Gomes.

The emotional tie between science and determinism is naturally very strong. Indeed we can not take it for granted that just because a scientist advocates a hierarchical system of order, rather than one based on the dominance of reductionistic physical laws, he is necessarily thinking in anti-determinist categories. I noted earlier that the idea that nature is ordered in a hierarchical way, with higher levels of law determining what is left open by lower levels of laws, does not exclude the possibility that the total system is law-determined in a sense that would be recognizably deterministic. Certainly the intervention of the efficacy of mind (as distinct from higher level neural-net physical laws) in such a hierarchical system would be problematic. That is one reason why I have developed the present view of the efficacy of mind in terms of the dominance of an infrastructure by originative acts and by analogous act-temporal units rather than by general higher level laws. The discussion of the idea of the laws of nature in chapter 2 is relevant to this point.

5

The theme of originative action receives additional support from another, though no doubt related, tendency in recent neurophysiology. There is a growing realization that the total operation of a neural network is time-bound and that there are, moreover, "parts" of the total dynamism—distinguishable regional and functional sub-patterns—that are themselves time-bound. V. B. Mountcastle points out that till now physiological studies have mainly added to our knowledge of the "anatomical substratum for function," which he calls "static properties," but goes on to draw encouragement from a trend away from this. "The tide of experiment," he says, "moves towards an elucidation of the time-dependent, dynamic aspects of cortical function." [11] This is especially important, he thinks, for higher-order aspects of cortical function. Some evidence for this has already been introduced in chapter 6, where it was also pointed out that time-bound patterns are also given weight in the parallel computer-oriented investigation of Culbertson.

I am not aware that there is as yet any clear realization in these circles that the interpretation of any spatiotemporal neural-net unit as time-bound in any nontrivial sense requires more than the observation that the full development of the pattern takes up a certain amount of the time that clocks measure. A thought, an action; the development of an organelle, a cell, or an embryo; indeed the whole sweep of a human life; are all of them probably time-bound. But to make sense of this matter we shall have to approach it with an attitude towards time, causality, and law different from the one that prevails in philosophy of science today. If we are able to identify any complex spatiotemporal configuration of firing and silent neurons, that configuration will be time-bound in at least the trivial sense that we *have* identified it as a pattern and it *has* taken a certain amount of time to run its course. Within the configuration there will be many

$C \rightarrow E$ relations of excitation and inhibition between the component neurons, but the mere fact that we have identified the larger pattern, and that it did take a certain amount of time, does not in itself suggest that those individual $C \rightarrow E$ events are in any sense under the constraint (or determination) of the larger pattern. Indeed most physiologists would probably want to say that the only determinants upon those events were (1) the usual laws of nature and (2) the complex spatial organization of the neural net itself. And they would probably not want to say any more than this even if they were able to express mathematically the complete nature of the spatiotemporal configurations laid down by those two determinants. If one wants to say that structure is not decisive but that the overall dynamism is decisive, one is obliged to suggest how that dynamism can be effective in a way that is not *merely* a function of the structure. The brain no doubt does function as a very complex dynamism in which not only the position of a given firing neuron is decisive, but also the temporal relations of its firing to the firing of large numbers of other neurons, and the temporal relations between the firing of the sub-pattern within which it fires to the firing of many other sub-patterns. But this could be true even if the nature of the structure and the nature of the stimulus were completely decisive as indeed they are decisive, *mutatis mutandis,* in the case of a computer. Perhaps Mountcastle would be content with a sense of "time-bound" that was merely a function of structure, but the contrast he makes suggests that he is reaching for a deeper sense.

A deeper and nontrivial sense of "time-bound" that suggests itself is one in which the total spatiotemporal pattern is not merely a summation of particular sub-patterns and particular firings as these are laid down by existing structures, but a unit that exercises a reciprocal determination upon the particular spatiotemporal happenings that make it up. It goes without saying that the complex structures involved would play an important role in this, but they would not play the only role. All this, however, puts us in the odd position of saying that a spatiotemporal pattern that at a given time t is incomplete is nonetheless, *as complete,* a partial determinant of a component event at a certain point in the structure at that same time *t*. If we consider the total pattern precisely as a physical spatiotemporal pattern this seems impossible. It is still odd and unusual to ascribe the time-bound nature of the total pattern to the unification of a spatiotemporal multiplicity by an originative act that possesses it, but it does not seem a physical impossibility. The pervasion of the spatiotemporal region by the act, though a dynamic one, bears to the identifiable physical entities of the region a "relation" more like a law than like the physical events it pervades. At least we do not think of the act as a complete spatiotemporal event effective, *as complete,* before its completion.

The suggestion, then, is that the act-temporality of an originative act gives us a sense in which the total dynamisms of the brain are time-bound in a sense not fully accounted for by the brain's structure. The unity of sub-patterns within that total dynamism can then be similarly interpreted: they are themselves time-bound by act-temporal units that "participate" in the unity of the originative act. This would be consistent with our earlier speculation that in the upper reaches of the many levels of an infrastructure of an originative act there are units that display an act-temporality analogous to that of the act itself. The reality of nested dynamic units that are in *some* sense—perhaps only the trivial one—time-bound seems consistent with the assumptions of the more advanced kind of neurophysiological science. That these nested dynamisms are time-bound in the nontrivial sense of act-temporality seems consistent with the further aspirations of some leading neurophysiologists, if not with their explicit assumptions, for it clearly suggests how mind-becoming-conscious could be effective in the physical dynamisms it possesses.

6

We are now in a position to say something more about the nature of the indeterminations that we might expect to find in the structure and function of the brain if we are to suppose that

Socrates is capable of originative action in both the practical and the theoretic senses introduced at the beginning of the chapter. It may help to remind the reader that we are dealing with practical actions in which mind-becoming-conscious plays an important role and also with theoretic ones in which it plays the principal role. Both kinds of action are qualified by that feature we have in mind when we speak of will, volition, or intention, though no doubt that is more obvious in the case of practical actions. We shall not however try to isolate any entity, function, or mental event that might be called by one or another of those names, since the category of action is meant to absorb that category or categories. Will, then, becomes a qualitative feature of action. Though important, it is only one among many qualitative features, some important, some trivial. The complex attitude towards what Socrates called the Form of the Good, an attitude of reverent attention that surely qualifies much of what he does in his last days, is another such qualitative feature, one which, because it is nothing if not intentional and willing, colors and is colored by the one we call will. But the qualitative complexity of any act, even the most negligible, can be considerable. We can not dismiss any velleity, any nuance of emotion, valuation, or motivation: all may qualify the act and all have accordingly some correlate or other in the infrastructure.

The story goes well beyond the brain, and includes every shade of bodily set, organic and muscular tone, glandular response. Even if we confine ouselves to those portions of the infrastructure that concern only the brain, the story is only beginning to unfold. It is not the business of philosophy to try to tell it, even at secondhand, but it seems fair to say that whether the story is told firsthand by those who are actually doing the neurological research or secondhand by one of several skilled masters of the exacting art of *haute vulgarisation,* the way in which (in our language) the many layers and regions of a spatiotemporal infrastructure contribute to the qualitative richness of an originative act remains very obscure. It is true that there is general agreement that the neocortex is essential to our higher intellectual faculties, that the deeper and older regions of the brain are important in emotions and in the control of routine and automatic bodily functions, but even an observation like that must be qualified. It is true also that in many regions of the brain highly localized neuron clusters can be seen to have an importance for sight, speech, sexual pleasure, anger, but just *how* they fit into the totality of the infrastructure remains very unclear.

A less arrogant group of scientists than the leading neuro-physiologists would be hard to find. It may be that the complexities of the brain and the incredibly delicate experimental techniques that are needed to make it yield up even its smallest secrets make for modesty. None of them would be offended at the remark that, for all the rapid advances of the last ten years, the present knowledge of the brain is an unusual mixture of exactness and complete ignorance. On the one hand it is possible to isolate single cortical cells that respond to afferent impulses coming from two or three sensory modalities, or to show graphically the effects in the brain-waves of an attentive subject of a sensory stimulus of a highly precise and localized nature. On the other hand it seems impossible to say whether the highest level of integration and control and the most important level for conscious experience and for the efficacy of mind-becoming-conscious is in the cortex or deep in one of the older subcortical regions. It is even impossible to say whether it is in fact a property of the total system, involving both the cortex and impulses coursing back and forth between its various regions and such deeper levels as the reticular formation, or whether it can be more or less localized.

It seems to be generally agreed that, setting this last question aside, there is in the attentive subject (to whom we confine our discussion) a very generalized pattern of intense activity of an overall nature that goes on in some independence of any particular sensory stimulus and also in some independence of whatever particular spatiotemporal patterns might be ascribed — either on the basis of the doctrine of originative action or on that of the views of, say, Eccles or Sperry — to the efficacy of mind-becoming-conscious. Indeed to the outsider there are

300

strong suggestions that we are dealing with a highly complex spatiotemporal physical reality that bears some resemblance to the carrier wave of radio transmission. This underlying regularity is then further complicated by the superposition upon it of other spatiotemporal "wave" patterns that we can ascribe to particular sensory stimuli, to the response that converts the stimuli into sensory experience, and to the efficacy that, on our hypothesis, we assume mind-becoming-conscious to have. Unlike the radio wave, the underlying "carrier" spatiotemporal pattern can not be isolated in a pure or even a relatively pure form, for the attentive subject, so soon as he is attentive, is attentive to something, expectant of something, and, maybe, intent on something.

It should be said at once that even if there should be a rhythmic carrier wave whose underlying regularity is complicated both by environmental stimuli and by the responsive activity of feeling, valuation, and mind-becoming-conscious, this image drawn from communication devices is not really of much help to us. Such a complex spatiotemporal "wave" pattern is by definition loaded with "information"—both in the sense of sensory information and in the sense of the creative response to it. But unlike the information-loaded waves of radio, television, and the like, there is not in this case any *independent* consciousness to take stock of what information is carried by it. In the present case mind-becoming-conscious possesses or inhabits the wave, and why it should, and how it should, remain mysteries probably outside the range of empirical investigation (which is by definition confined in the consciousness-centered predicament) though not, I think, outside the range of philosophical interpretation.

Tied into this total activity, which we here take to be a major component in the infrastructure of any act involving mind, there are any number of subroutines concerned with routine functions like the control of heart, breathing, glandular function, and so on. Other subroutines of a servomechanical sort will be involved with the control of routine motor functions such as those in which Socrates rubs his ankles or raises the cup to his

301

lips. And there will be all the complications so airily subsumed above under the heading of sensory stimulus, for even if, as the thesis of mind-becoming-conscious supposes, not all functions of mind can be understood in terms of information processing, it is perfectly clear that in the sensory channels, at the least, a good deal of information processing goes on before a signal, perhaps by now considerably simplified, reaches some location like that of the visual cortex. All this activity will contribute to the unimaginable complexity of the spatiotemporal neural-event configuration that accompanies, and is here regarded as part of the infrastructure of, a practical or theoretical originative action.

Assume now that within such a spatiotemporal configuration there is a time-bound pattern of neural activity that is essential to the infrastructure of some particular action of Socrates — say the one in which he raises the cup to his lips or the one in which he says his last words to Crito. Since it is probable that in the second of those acts he was trying to make a quite subtle point, led us use that one, since the aspect of mind-becoming-conscious will be more prominent in it. Consider now some single cortical neuron, A, that plays a role in this pattern by firing at a certain point and thus, by way of numerous intermediaries, exercising after a short interval a $C \rightarrow E$ influence on another cortical neuron B at some distance from it. Both neurons may have been firing regularly as part of the overall background activity, but our assumption is that in *these* firings they are concerned in the additional complications proper to the infrastructure of the act we are now considering. After a further brief interval, but still within the infrastructure of the same act, A fires again. This time its firing has a somewhat different set of temporal and spatial relations to the neurons that contribute in a $C \rightarrow E$ way to its firing, and one of the $C \rightarrow E$ factors contributing to its new setting will be the previous firing of B. In other words, A fires twice in a complex loop, and, by way of B, exercises a $C \rightarrow E$ influence on its own second firing.

Even if we assume that this is an originative act and that its temporality is act-temporal, shall we be able to find any indeter-

302

mination in this analysis of the infrastructure? I think not. Act-temporality requires that, when A fires the first time, the act within which it fires is at the same "instant" involved with and bearing upon the conditions around B: that is to say that the act has a *spatial*"reach." Its involvement with both A and B concerns not only the firing of A but also, and at that same "instant," the arrival at B of the impulse that is then originating at A and is to traverse several intermediaries to contribute to the firing of B: that is to say that the act has a *temporal* "reach," and that that "instant" is an abstraction. In telic language — and it should be plain enough that the notion "time-bound" has appropriate affinities with what is sound in telic language — at the firing of A, the act is preparing B for the reception of the impulse from A; while at B it is retaining the contribution of A, which consists, so far as concerns the act, in more than simply the indirect excitement of B by A. Exactly the same points can be made about the completion of the pattern, by way of the firing of B, to include the second firing of A; that is, we can consider in a somewhat analogous way the relation between the first firing of A and the second — its indirect self-excitation. But where is the indetermination in all this? If we assess the first firing of A in terms of the $C \rightarrow E$ forces that bear upon it and the known laws (of whatever level, and whatever status) that govern those forces, we shall find no absence of determination. Our causal account will be as complete as the relevant laws and the parameters permit.

Even if (following Eccles and Gomes) we were to find an increment of energy of microevent size at a synaptic vesicle, and could show that the energy balance of the cell had been delicate enough so that that event was crucial to A's first firing, this in itself would be a determination with respect to A. Though in principle the arrival of that particular bundle of energy at just that point had not been predictable, its impact upon A is clearly a $C \rightarrow E$ one. So for the forces bearing upon B, either at the time A first fires or at the time when B itself fires. And so again for all the events around A as it recovers, and the events bearing upon it when it fires for the second time. There is then *no*

303

indetermination with respect to any events at the level of the cells. But this is not inconsistent with the possession of the total spatiotemporal pattern by an originative act, since this is precisely what the idea of originative act calls for. There may or may not be a role played by events taking place at the level for which quantum theory is relevant; the applicability of the act-temporality of originative action would be the same in either case.

What the doctrine of originative action calls for is that, considered in abstraction from the action in question, the complex multiplicity of the infrastructure should be indeterminate. But, in the circumstances of precisely that action, the infrastructure is unified by the action that is thus "related" to it. And this means that what was indeterminate and determinable in the infrastructure is now determinate. The act-temporality of the originative act is the reason why that spatial region is possessed by just that spatiotemporal pattern of neural activity and no other. The action determines what was determinable; its absence would be the presence of some other action or else the presence (in passivity) of multiple units proper to some level below that of action. And in either of *those* cases a $C \rightarrow E$ analysis after the event would yield a perfectly determinate physical system. The presence of indetermination in nature does not in principle require the presence of anomalies in it.

On this interpretation of the determination exercised by the power of an originative act, any given infrastructure level will be indeterminate in relation to the one above. Whatever role microevent indeterminacy may play, we have therefore no reason to assign it a unique role. Perhaps it is amplifiable in a way that permits it to play a significant $C \rightarrow E$ role in the firing of neurons; perhaps not; only experiment and calculation will settle this. If it is a real ontological indeterminacy in a sense not completely defined by the measurement dichotomy laid down by Heisenberg, then the principle of the indetermination of *any* infrastructure level merely calls for it to be determined by the supervention of the next higher level.

One criterion for indeterminacy of this sort is the inability of science to calculate the particular point of impact of some particular electron. But by this criterion there are notable indeterminacies at many levels. Returning to our cells A and B in our highly complex "loop" of neurons, it is certainly not in practice predictable at the time A fires that B will fire; or at least it is not predictable precisely when B will fire and in precisely what spatiotemporal connections with precisely what neurons. That is to say that the total spatiotemporal pattern in which A and B are engaged is not in practice predictable from what is known of the total state of the system at the time A fires. It is usual for those who accept the general determinism of nature (with the usual qualification about microevents) to suppose that this is just a matter of the extreme complexity of the neural networks involved, and the total impossibility of determining any but a very few parameters. Thus, MacKay says, in the informal atmosphere of a discussion at the end of a remarkable study week, "Let us ask then about the predictions of physiology in relation to free action. The scientific 'check' written by theoretical physiology (at least pre-Heisenberg) says, in general, that for any action, whether we call it free or not, given the external and internal data, observers can in principle write a detailed prediction of the action. In this *general* form I see no grounds for objection in our experience." [12] MacKay is talking about the predictability of action, and, in the present context at least, we are concerned about the predictability of an infrastructure pattern. But it seems quite clear that he takes the claim to apply there too. A little later he goes on to say, "neurophysiology in principle regards itself as based on physics, and in pre-Heisenberg physics, at least, there *existed* a determinative specification for any configuration in the future, whether people knew it or not." [13] It is just the dogma of "in principle" predictability I am challenging. Even in the more controlled and isolated proceedings of physics and chemistry there are, along with the numerous predictions that could pass, though not without challenge, as deterministic ones, a great many more merely statistical predictions besides those at the level of microevents. Indeed there are so many that it would be dogmatic to suppose that all of them are in principle reducible to (Laplacean) deterministic ones. If ever there are laws found that will predict the firing-rhythm of the individual neurons in a network of cortical neurons of any size, it is a safe bet that they will be statistical ones. And it is dogmatic to suppose that these predictions are mere practical alternatives for Laplacean predictions that can "in principle" be made.

It seems a safer bet that the total pattern in which two well-separated neurons fire while subserving the speech-act in which Socrates addresses his last words to Crito would be predictable only in the odd circumstances in which the scientist not only had at his command a perfected physiology and God-like measurement techniques but also knew in advance at time t_1 what Socrates was about to say and would have said by time t_2. If this should be true, incidentally, when it was also true that there was no *in principle* physical predictability of the total physical state, it would show identity theorists to be at the very antipodes of the truth. On this assumption, though not attempting the impossible task of disentangling the act from the infrastructure to which it is "related," one nevertheless takes it to be at least as illuminating to say that Socrates' uttering those words "really caused" that spatiotemporal pattern in the neural net as to say that the spatiotemporal pattern caused his utterance. This is, naturally, consistent with the remarks in chapters 4 and 5 about the *asymmetrical* "identity" of an act with its infrastructure.

It is probably true that many statistical laws besides those of quantum theory are not deterministic laws *manquées* but are statistical in principle. The presence of statistical laws at some level—say that of organelles in a cell or that of the behavior of individual neurons—would then be prima facie indicators of the possibility of the supervention of determinations consisting of the unifying presence of higher levels in "relation" to those lower ones. The vague notion that an indeterminism in any level is unreal unless some anomaly can be discovered in it can thus be dismissed. So can the dogmatic assumption that the massive regularities of nature imply that (setting aside microevent indeterminacy) nature is predictable in the sense that any state of any system at time t_1 will in principle yield us the state of that system at time t_2.

The assumption that a physical analysis of what happens in

and around neurons A and B during the last speech of Socrates will reveal no physical anomalies contributes nothing whatever to a rehabilitation of the Laplacean (or, considering the exception of microevents, quasi-Laplacean) dogma. Nor does the reality of free will, of the efficacy of mind, of originative action, require any anomalies. What they do require is the assumption that the truly time-bound is not merely something that takes a certain amount of the time of physics to happen, but something whose temporality is act-temporal: a unity whose power is felt throughout the whole of a spatiotemporal "region." And under these conditions the determinateness in a $C \rightarrow E$ sense of any unit caught in the grip of that power is just what one would expect, just as one expects a planet caught in the grip of gravity to behave determinately in respect of its relations to other massy bodies.

In this sense, the instinct of Michael Polanyi, who has long argued that any superordinate level merely sets the boundary conditions under which the laws appropriate to lower levels operate, is surely sound, though his claim has not been widely accepted.[14] It is interesting to note that MacKay, in the second of the two remarks just quoted, was responding to the distinguished ethologist W. H. Thorpe, who had thought that MacKay *might* have been making a point like Polanyi's. MacKay takes care to show that he was not. And the point he goes on to make rejects the "in principle" indetermination of some parameters. If the doctrine of originative action is taken seriously, the boundary conditions around A and B during the course of that speech act are understood to be functions of the fact that Socrates is making to Crito just that subtle point he did make. If he had made another point, the boundary conditions, or parameters, that a physiologist might measure would have been different. In either case there would be a complete $C \rightarrow E$ account, provided that one does not mean by "complete account" that the whole spatiotemporal event was in principle predictable on the basis of the parameters throughout the system at the time of A's first firing.

9

From Act to Agent: Ontic Power

 THE READER WILL RECALL THAT when we began our discussion of originative acts in chapter 3, the status of the agent to whom we attributed them remained very obscure. We spoke of the acts as acts of Socrates, but this commonsense attribution left both the status of the agent and the status of the acts vague in at least the sense that it did not take us beyond common sense. In section 7 of chapter 3 I made a set of assumptions about originative acts that—so it seemed to me—gave some hope, provided they proved sound, of clarifying the nature of the agent. Let me repeat them here in abbreviated form: (*a*) no originative act is caused in a $C \rightarrow E$ sense by a prior act of the agent; (*b*) none is *wholly* caused (in any sense of "cause") by virtue of a network of $C \rightarrow E$ relations within its infrastructure; (*c*) an originative act that embraces sub-acts will not simply be a collective designation for the group of sub-acts but will have at least those originative properties we ascribe to each member of that group; (*d*) an originative act may always ramify in further originative sub-acts, and indeed it may be impossible to identify utterly simple originative acts, although presumably they do exist; (*e*) in principle, a new originative act may begin at any time; it may or may not be subordinate to some other originative act, and it may itself ramify in further sub-acts.

Chapters 4 and 5 were concerned, among other things,

with justifying assumptions (*a*) and (*b*), since those assumptions describe in compressed form the notion of an originative act. It is the other assumptions that gave some hope of clarifying the status of the agent. I expressed this by observing that if an act ramifies in sub-acts that it unifies, then the act will stand to each of its sub-acts much as an agent would stand to a set of successive acts we attributed to him as to an entity with an ontological status more fundamental than the acts themselves. Thus, if the whole life of Socrates should, on assumptions (*c*), (*d*), and (*e*), appear to be a single originative "act" whose seamless unity was asymmetrically identical with a vast number of distinguishable originative sub-acts, we should be justified in taking that as a warrant for moving from the category "act" to the category "agent" and thus to the category "entity" as well. To repeat an earlier formula: the ontological feat of an originative act ramifying in sub-acts that are themselves originative acts is appropriately attributable to a subject-entity whom we appropriately call an agent.

If assumptions (*c*), (*d*), and (*e*) are sound, we need not be satisfied with an act-ontology in which the name "Socrates" is merely a name for a succession of related acts. It is true that we began with a view of Socrates sufficiently close to common sense that we attributed acts to him. Indeed we had no other way of grasping the nature of act than by such an attribution. From the beginning the notions "act" and "agent" have been interdependent, and if we have succeeded in bringing into view and recognizing the nature of the one, that is only because we are at the same time bringing into view and recognizing the nature of the other. In that sense our meditation has been circular. But since our initial understanding of the agent to whom we ascribed the acts was vague, we were in some danger of resolving him into a series of acts, much as Hume, beginning with a common-sense understanding of the self, resolved it into a series of impressions and then found the series inadequate to provide a thoroughgoing rational ground for the idea of the self. On our present view, that sort of resolution of the self depends upon an illegitimate detachment of the notion of an impression from that of the self, or subject, a detachment we have not made in the case of the notions of agent and act. If we keep the two notions together, any clarification of the one affects the other.

So now, with the help of the extended discussion of the "relation" between an originative act and its infrastructure in chapters 4 and 5 we are in a position to justify the view of originative acts and their sub-acts summarized in assumptions (*c*), (*d*), and (*e*). We can use this in turn to justify the view that Socrates is a subject, entity, or being, who is an agent; and that as an agent he transcends his individual acts. The word "transcend" has so many senses that it may be well to say that I shall take this to mean only (*1*) that the category "entity" is more fundamental than the category "act"; (*2*) that the originative character of the acts is compatible with the claim that the acts originate in an entity; (*3*) that the entity is continuous although his acts are distinct units; (*4*) that his self-identity can not be adequately understood solely in terms of the inheritance by a given act of characteristics from earlier acts. If what follows is persuasive, we shall indeed — as suggested in chapter 3 — have ascribed to the agent "some of the features commonly looked for in an agent and fewer of the deficiencies he has in accounts that must construct him out of atomic units — memories, impressions, events, bodily states, or whatever — that are taken to be more patently authentic than the agent himself."

2

Throughout the discussion of originative acts in chapters 4 and 5 I spoke only — unless by inadvertence — of the power of the act (rather than the power of the agent) as pervading its infrastructure. The point of this was that we should not be drawing upon what was merely vague in the notion of agent as we tried to recognize the nature of his action. The only "transcendence" of the multiplicity of the infrastructure we attributed to the act was therefore a modest and unobjectionable

310

one: we thought of it as pervading the infrastructure as the bond that unified it. This is another way of saying that the unifying power of the act is asymmetrically identical with the multiplicity of the infrastructure; that it is the "true cause" of the complex of $C \rightarrow E$ relations that can be found in the infrastructure; that the "relation" between the One of the act and the Many of the infrastructure is *sui generis*. A transcendence of this kind does not require us to locate the act "above" the infrastructure as an ontological item thoroughly distinct from it. The act endures through and completes itself in its own time unit, and its self-completion is the giving of a pattern to that infrastructure, but when that pattern is completed the act is "gone": it does not endure after the pattern, nor is it elsewhere than in the pattern. Its transcendence consists solely in its being, qua power, distinguishable from the mere multiplicity of the context it pervades and unites, as an electromagnetic field that was maintained only during an experiment on the behavior of charged particles within it might still be distinguished from the behavior of those particles.

This modest sense of transcendence has an interesting consequence for our earlier and more tentative treatment of the idea that an originative act may embrace sub-acts that are originative. Consider again the diagrams of figures *3*, *4*, and *5*. I repeat here figure *5*, in which *S–1* is the whole pattern of action described as "the unity of Socrates' total action in defending himself at his trial, refusing to escape, conversing with his friends on the last day, calmly taking the hemlock, and then lying

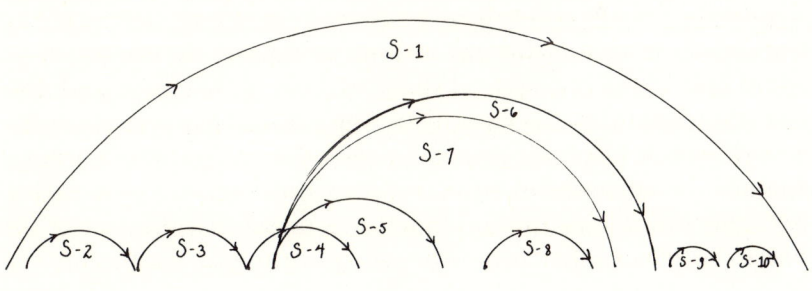

down to let it have its way with him." The interesting consequence is that although all of the units labeled *S–1* through *S–10*
are on the same ontological level, in that we ascribe to each the
status of an originative act, any superordinate act among them
stands in much the same "relation" to its sub-acts as an originative act is said to stand in to the multiple components of its
infrastructure. Thus *S–1* is one indivisible time-unit over against
the multiple discrete time-units *S–2* through *S–10,* and it binds
them together not only in the sense that they would be different
if it were different, but also in the sense that their total significance is the significance of the pattern given them by *S–1,* rather
than the significance of a simple series of discrete acts. And the
same thing can be said about the "relation" between *S–6* (which
happens to be a sub-act of *S–1)* and the group *S–4, S–5, S–7,*
and *S–8* that form *its* sub-acts.

In short, if we can regard the power of an originative act
as being present throughout the total spatiotemporal multiplicity of its infrastructure, we can also regard the power of a
superordinate act like *S–1* as being present throughout the
whole multiplicity of sub-acts, *S–2* through *S–10,* running from
Socrates' defense at the trial to the uncovering of his face to
speak to Crito. We can therefore regard a superordinate originative act as transcending its sub-acts in the same unobjectionable
sense put forward in the case of the "relation" between an
originative act and its infrastructure. And the "relation" between the act and its sub-acts will show an especially striking
resemblance to the "relation" between any originative act and
whatever act-temporal units are to be found in its infrastructure.

The line of our argument now begins to return upon itself.
Up until now the account of originative acts was vulnerable to
the objection that it did not require us to ascribe the act to an
agent having the ontological status of a being, or entity, and thus
did not warrant our assigning an ontological status to an entity
called Socrates. A critic might concede the unity of the temporal
span of the act and the unity of the spatial region it was said to
pervade, but might contend that it was no more indicative of the
presence of an agent than the unity we might discern in any

physical happening. Rather than bringing in an agent, he might say, we would do better to attribute whatever unity we find to what Bohm called "inherent and essential aspects of what things are," aspects perhaps better expressed in terms of laws of nature than of agents.

We may begin to close our circle with this simple but momentous observation: the concept of an originative act that may either ramify in sub-acts or be brought under originative acts of still greater scope is tantamount to the concept of an agent. For the acts were taken to be originative in the sense that they accounted for themselves in a way that no $C \rightarrow E$ account in terms of their infrastructures could do, and yet it now turns out that, multiple and independent as they are, they all originate in the same ontological "source." We are, to be sure, by no means clear about what we mean by the word "source" when we use it thus, but at least this much is clear: even if the several sub-acts are, as we suppose, discrete exercises of originative power, they can not be totally and radically independent of one another and still be regarded as sub-acts of the same originative act. And the "relation" between any originative act and its infrastructure is ample warrant for the claim that an originative act may unify a set of originative sub-acts. The several sub-acts express in their multiplicity the unity of the superordinate act, and in that sense they are severally partial expressions of what it expresses more completely. Each of them is therefore in part accounted for by the same superordinate originative act. Not, however, completely accounted for: it is not claimed that they originate "out of" the superordinate act, since in other circumstances any of the sub-acts could have been performed independently of the superordinate one. It is merely claimed that in the origination of the superordinate act and of the several sub-acts there is something in common.

No doubt this principle must be pressed further before the agent is clearly in view, but it discloses already some of the features one might expect to find in one agent expressing himself in many acts. I think that if we do press further we shall make evident an agent who is as substantial as it is sensible to look

313

for—for there are no doubt many senses of "substantial" that are so far from the original dynamic overtones of the word *ou-sia*[1] as to stultify this or any discussion of agents and acts. Certainly some of the well-known demands for a relative continuity of the agent are already satisfied. The time of a superordinate act, for instance, is utterly continuous over against the discontinuous successiveness of its sub-acts: despite the fact that the superordinate act is by definition a paradigm of becoming, it remains the same act, having the same act-temporality, throughout the whole of its span, while within this enframing environment its sub-acts succeed each other. Furthermore any superordinate originative act, however evanescent in itself, may always be subsumed under another, so long as that puzzling commonsense entity called Socrates endures. Act *S–5*, for instance (the speech about pleasure and pain), while it could have been an independent act, not necessarily found together with acts like *S–6* and *S–7*, is here indeed found with them and subsumed under them. In fact, a superordinate act can begin anywhere in the history of a commonsense entity like Socrates, and it will have something of its originative character in common with the sub-acts it transcends, and something of it in common with any originative act by which it is transcended. In that sense they will have the same "source." And this will apply to any superordinate act, however prolonged it may be and however much it may ramify in sub-acts. The principle that establishes the possibility of such a superordinate act requires the possibility that it should be transcended at any time. And while this situation continues—and in principle it will continue as long as common sense can identify that entity called Socrates—there is an act-source transcendent of all the originative acts so considered. Let us simply identify this source with the agent to whom common sense ascribes the acts.

This ontological commitment does not require us to isolate the agent either within or above the whole of a superordinate act as a self-contained and complete entity "from which" the whole act flows, no more than we could have separated an act from its infrastructure or a superordinate act from its sub-acts.

His transcendence is not of that sort. He becomes in his acts: but his becoming is the unifying power in each of his acts and the unification of all of them, just as we earlier identified the becoming of an originative act as the unification of an infrastructure. It should be noticed that no attempt has been made to identify utterly simple acts. It may be impossible to do this: it is only a traditional reliance upon atomisms that makes it seem reasonable to begin a discussion of action by identifying utterly simple acts. Indeed, as we move now towards a better understanding of the category of agent, and accordingly, of the category of entity (or being), it appears to be so much more fundamental than the category of action that we can hazard the conjecture that the simplicity of an act is always relative to the agent: the act of forming a given letter with a pen may be simple with respect to its emergence from the superordinate act of writing a word; but in another context, say, one in which it was my intent to illustrate the notion of a curved line segment, I might be said to perform another simple act which would be identical with a part of the simple act of writing a letter.

If the account so far suggests, then, that because an agent becomes in virtue of his acts, he is merely their outcome, it is defective. It is probably closer to the truth to say that the acts bear the mark of the developing entity out of which they spring, and that the internal continuity, external discontinuity, of them is characteristic of the entity that performs them. An act wells up out of an entity, since it is but one unit in which his being expresses itself. And the entity's first mark is that of unity: over against the potential multiplicity of his acts his unity is absolute. It is no less bound upon the wheel of becoming for all that: in any single act it "expresses" itself, that is, exercises power to "come into being"; before any succeeding act it stands poised, enriched with what it has "brought into being," for yet another moment in its *genesis eis ousian;* and the whole train of its acts is as much a "coming into being" as any one of them is. But the unity of a being runs through all of it. Because of it, none of its acts is a mere multiplicity, however much it may ramify in sub-acts at the same ontological level or in act-temporal powers

315

at subordinate levels. And because of it, no train of its acts is a mere multiplicity in which one act merely inherits something from an utterly distinct predecessor. In any such train it is one being that "becomes."

It follows that no act of an agent operates in a $C \rightarrow E$ fashion to produce his next act. Rather, by its mastery of subordinate powers, it helps establish an environment for his next act. That way of putting it, however, is abstract, for the being of the agent is neither wholly separate from his acts nor wholly separate from the infrastructure of each of them. It is therefore just as accurate to say that an agent, considered qua entity, upon completion of an act "retains" what it has "brought into being," even though the retention may be expressed in a structural stability in the infrastructure. This "retention" contributes to its "poise" before a succeeding act. The "becoming" of the agent is thus "simultaneous" with his acts, and, although the entity and the acts are on the same ontological level, this "simultaneity" is analogous to the "simultaneous relations" between any one act and its subordinate powers.

3

Acts and sub-acts are alike in being acts of the agent: in our discussion of them we consider no other ontological level. Socrates reaches down to rub his ankle, and all the while he also performs all the sub-acts that ingenuity might discern within that act. Meanwhile the act of rubbing his ankle has been but an incident in the long, sustained, and immensely important act of both professing and exemplifying his view of the nature of man. The fact that one of the acts is of shorter duration than the others blurs the issue somewhat. An agent realizes himself, expresses himself, "comes into being" more or less profoundly in this or that act, and often, it may be, an act of telling importance comes almost unlooked for, and not, as was the case in the taking of the hemlock, as the climax of a number of sub-acts that have deliberately prepared for it. But at any rate the acts of an agent may differ profoundly in their ontological intensity, and this is enough to remind us that the categories "being" and "act," while they stand in mutual support, are profoundly different. The human agent, considered as a being, transcends the multiplicity of any set of his acts in a more profound sense of "transcend" than the one we noticed earlier. Considering the unity of an act over against the multiplicity of subordinate powers deployed in its infrastructure, we did not find it to be "elsewhere" than in the multiplicity it pervaded. Yet the human agent, all the while he links together a number of sub-acts in the unity of a superordinate act, may be profoundly "elsewhere" in the sense that he either withholds or is unable to express something of what he nevertheless in some sense "is." What is thus withheld or not expressed "is" in a less important sense than if it had reached expression in act; no doubt it helps little to say that it "is" only potentially, especially since its failure to reach enactment does not mean that the agent remains wholly potential but only that it is enacting other potentials. But as these may be potentials of less ontological significance, the point remains. And this "potential" dimension of the reality of the agent, however difficult it may be to understand and articulate in language, is enough to warn us that the category "act" is less fundamental than the category "being," even though the two categories stand in mutual support.

Perhaps much of this is true of whatever kind of agent we choose: presumably animals other than man, or some of them, can sometimes be considered as agents. But certainly it is so when we deal with the human agent. At best, its levels of peak activity are intermittent. For most of us most of the time it is well below what we know it ought to be, and for this reason, if for no other, any doctrine of agency must in the long run aspire to more than an adequate theory of causality. A flick of the finger, a tennis stroke, a gesture of affection, a few halting or a few magisterial steps in a dance, the falling into place of a line in a poem, the formulation of a decisive experiment in physics, the sustained labor over years on the Sistine ceiling, the making of a difficult moral decision: in all of them something of an agent

317

comes into being, yet they differ profoundly in ontological and moral importance. Sometimes the paradoxes of a being that must *become* to *be* are especially poignant, as in that most significant of Socrates' acts, the sustained one in which his coming into being is also dying into being. But it is always the unity of the being out of which the unities that are his acts flow.

Having used features of agency to reach this point, we shall do well to take careful note of it. The structure of act is conferred on it by the structure of the being of the agent, and we do not by any means exhaust our understanding of his being by contemplating him as agent. The reader must already have felt some discomfort when I stretched the ordinary sense of the word "act" somewhat to speak of an argument developed by Socrates as an *act* of his. We should have to stretch it out of all recognition to account for the times in any man's life that are times of rest, of suffering, of passivity, or at least of receptivity. And these any adequate account of the entity Socrates must provide for.

It does not do too much violence to the relation between the categories "being" ("entity") and "act" to say that each of the acts participates in the unity of Socrates' being, and that each derives the unity it confers upon its multiplicity of subordinate powers from that "source." As Socrates acts in our paradigm case to unify in his moral gesture the movements of nerves, bones, and muscles that would otherwise take him to Boeotia, his gesture bears a family resemblance to other gestures he has made. This act, prior ones, and successive ones all spring from the same unity. There is, on the other hand, something irreducibly multiple about the notion "act," for all that I have been mainly interested in the unity of a single act. Any agent may express himself in an indefinite number of them. And these may ramify indefinitely in sub-acts. It is out of our being that we act, out of our being, paradoxically, that we exercise *genesis eis ousian.*

If there is a metaphysical scandal in thus endowing the entity we call the agent with an ontological transcendence of the acts he originates, it is trivial in comparison with the one we must now touch upon. If the being of an agent—that is, his status qua entity—is an absolute unity over against the indefinite multiplicity of the acts in which he "becomes," or "comes into being," that unity is not absolutely private to him. Any thoroughgoing scrutiny of the agent as the "source" of originative acts in the long run commits us to the view that all such "act-sources" have a common source. It is the scandal of an absolute "act-source," which, in terms of our shift from the category of act to that of entity, can only be read as an entity-source. And this we recognize as that ultimate metaphysical scandal, Being Absolute. But, as any contemporary reader knows, the word "absolute" is disreputable and to be avoided, and so we shall simply speak of Being, allowing the device of capitalization to indicate that whatever we mean by it, we do not wish to see it confused with the being of Socrates, or the being of the reader, or the being of myself. It would be surprising if the theme of unity-in-a-multiplicity introduced in our paradigm case of the originative act could be carried as far as we have carried it and then give way to a multiplicity of agents constituting a radical pluralism of act-sources. It is true that Socrates was indeed the man whose career we find rehearsed briefly in the *Apology* and who lived through the last day that has concerned us here. But if we think of him as an act-source exhaustively defined by just those acts he gave rise to and radically sundered as a source from all the other act-sources he tries to make common cause with, then we introduce another metaphysical scandal—the scandal of so-called originative acts springing from the radical fatality of a wholly discrete and particular "thisness," or *haecceitas*.[2] And that one might be worse than the one it is designed to avoid.

Words defeat us here, and at need we are driven into formulations that have no doubt been used in an obscurantist spirit in our times: the agent, qua entity, "comes into his being," but he also "comes out of Being." And it is more than a rhetorical flourish to capitalize the word now. The unity of each of an agent's acts is a shared one: his acts participate in his unity. And his unity in turn, his power, his order, is also a shared one: it participates in, is a partial expression of, the unity of Being. We come into our being by coming out of Being; but also by acting for Being, by standing firm upon its ground, by giving up our individual, our particular being for it—that is, by going "back into Being," by trusting, as Socrates did, that any particular unity will be "retained" by it, even as we "retain" each of our acts. Here words slide and slip, decay with imprecision. But we must try to use them to make points of this sort. Many of the gnomic formulas that have been used from the pre-Socratics onward will do service, so long as we turn to them only at need, and do not mumble them over in a hieratic privacy that simply generates variants of the same cipher. We come into our being by coming out of Being. The mystery of the One in the Many, of a Being that both *is* and *becomes* as One in Many, is irremovable. The present account is merely an attempt to give it a habitation in that most familiar of all things, our own agency, which, without that inhabitant, seems but an illusion even as we enact it. Certainly Socrates supposed his own being to be a participation in Being, although he expressed his conviction in terms of a doctrine of Forms that this meditation does not draw upon. If we transpose into our own terms his convictions about his own immortality and how its fate was dependent upon his continued attention to the Form of the Good and his acknowledgment of its power, we can conclude that he regarded his own particularity as an ambiguous thing. That he was just that bald, snub-nosed, popeyed person who had just that history for which he is revered, goes without saying. But if he had discussed these matters in terms of a vocabulary of agents and acts, he would surely have agreed that his status as a particular act-source was dependent upon an utterly common entity-source, and that though he had tried to express that source in his own acts, he had not achieved more than a partial similitude of it. His reflection upon the universality of what we here call an entity-source and upon the character of all possible participations in it was no doubt faulty, as our own must be in its quite different way. But he was probably well aware of it. He gave up his life in the conviction that it was not entirely his own, but he is hardly likely to have missed the point that his expression of this conviction in terms of the logical paradoxes of immortality and reincarnation was a defective one.

4

For those who find a radical pluralism of agents rationally satisfying, the introduction of the theme of Being at this point will seem unnecessary, imprudent, and obscure. I should therefore say at once that I do not regard it as a speculative frill, but as an essential element in our meditation, in which it has in fact been implicit from the beginning. To make this point clear we shall now turn to consider in a little more detail the circularity of our meditation. There are in fact two major circles, neither of which is a vicious one, since the argument is not a deductive one. (*1*) The first concerns the theme of agent and act, and as it has already been discussed in the first section of this chapter and touched upon at several points earlier, little need be said now. Perplexed by the agent himself, finding that for all our concentration upon him his nature was far from evident to us, we tried to make it more evident by looking intensely at the acts that, to common sense at least, appeared to be his. It was our attention, and not a deductive argument that moved in a circle, from agent to act and back to agent again; and as it moved its focus, it moved also in the sense of increasing the adequacy of its disclosure of both agent and act.

(*2*) The other circle concerns the relation between the theme of act and agent and the capacity of our minds to disclose and authenticate that theme. I have dealt with that capacity in two related ways in this meditation. (*a*) One of them draws upon the notion of recognition, which I have given a developed technical sense elsewhere, and of which I have made some use in this meditation. (*b*) The other, though closely related to this, was devised to bring out the important role of consciousness in rationality, and much of chapters 7 and 8 was given over to it. It made use of the theme of mind-becoming-conscious, and made the claim that mind-becoming-conscious is in principle capable of self-transcendence, a point which is central to the idea of recognition as well. The nature of the circle can be indicated readily enough: an exercise of rationality (understood in both of these ways) is an originative act, and it is an originative act of this kind that we must perforce rely on to authenticate the nature of agents and originative acts.

Let us now see how the investigation of rationality in either of these ways (*a*) and (*b*) leads us inevitably to the universal, or general, status of the activity of mind, and how the nature of what it discloses requires the theme of Being. We shall then be able to use that theme to so illuminate the status of the agent as a being, or entity, as to clear up certain puzzles about the infrastructure that were left up in the air in chapters 4 and 5.

(*a*) Recognition has both an empirical and a rational component, although any attempt to detach one of these components from the other must falsify both of them. Thus, the recognition of originative action is both a way of being aware of, or experiencing, action and a way of understanding it: the particularity of the action is experienced not just by our sensory powers but by our sensory powers pervaded by our rationality. And rationality is concerned both with unity and generality: it grasps the unity of what in other circumstances might have been a multiplicity of sensory particulars, and it grasps also whatever in that unity is not to be understood in terms of its uniqueness and particularity—in short it is concerned with what is also general or universal in that unity. To link experience and rationality in this way is not to say that if we confine our attention to the sensory particulars of a given act our experience of them now will be in any way different from what it was before. But whatever we do when we experience an act, it is surely different from experiencing sensory particulars; and if we have really made the nature of act more evident, our experience of the act will have altered. To say this is merely to say that experience in the sense of awareness is suffused by the intelligence that directs it: we experience the particular originative act—say the uncovering of his face by Socrates—but we also experience this particular *as an originative act*. Our experience, that is, is suffused with a general grasp not just of this act but of the nature of act. It begs the question to say that we have suddenly shifted our ground and are now in fact considering the component of rationality—that we are now merely bringing the particular act under the newly offered concept of originative act; because the concept has not been contrived in some theoretic isolation from experience, but has grown in and with the experiential awareness of what is before us.

The meditation, then, purports to intensify our understanding of action in and with an intensification of our awareness of action. Our method is therefore rational, but does not consist in the construction of theories to be tested against an independent experience; it is empirical, but does not consist in an attention to an experience supposed to be ineluctably given to us; it is language-bound, but does not consist in attending *to* our language but rather attending *with* it as we creatively deploy it. No doubt at the purely sensory level there is much in an experience that must remain ineluctably the same, but our experience in the broader sense of evidential awareness is also a function of our rationality. Thus it was a group of horse chestnut trees I experienced below the *altana,* and not a set of discrete and multiple impressions, or sense data, although I could have experienced severally such items if I chose to focus my attention on them. Experience of this sort is a function of our language, our categories, our symbols. It is a premise of this meditation that we still deal creatively with these creations of ours, and that there is an intimate connection between this creativity and our experience that is missed when we suppose ourselves to be merely interpreting with their aid an experience that remains obdurately the same in its texture as we interpret it.

Such metaphors as sight, disclosure, keeping in view, and so on are therefore appropriate here. If the intelligibility of action should be heightened by this meditation it would be because action itself were more clearly "seen." This would mean that the character of the infrastructure were also more clearly "seen." The combined distinction and interdependence of action and infrastructure is a subtle matter, difficult to disclose and, once disclosed, difficult to keep in view. While it is seen, however, no account, however exhaustive, of the causal relations within the infrastructure of an act of this kind will be acceptable as an adequate account of the act itself.

(*b*) In dealing with the theme of mind-becoming-conscious and its self-transcendence we do not leave the theme of recognition. Not all the occasions in which mind-becomes-conscious are recognitions in the technical sense of that word, but in all recognitions mind does indeed become conscious of what is recognized, and in all of them subjectivity becomes rationally aware of what is the case, where what is the case is neither constructed by subjectivity nor constituted by it. This self-transcendence is of considerable complexity and we can discern at least four kinds of transcendence that are either contributory to it or ingredient in it.

(*i*) If we correctly recognize some item as a unity, then its unity transcends the multiplicity of the items that we recognize as contributing to that unity. Thus some unit like the oak tree on the Bowdoin campus or one of the chestnut trees below the *altana* can also be regarded as a multiplicity of items — of leaves, twigs, and branches; of shapes and colors; or even (given a certain kind of attention) of cells. The particular kind of multiplicity discerned will depend upon the kind of discriminatory attitude that is brought to the analysis of the tree. It is a mistake, I think, to suppose that at the basis of any recognition of a unity like the tree, or any resolution of it into a multiplicity, lies some purely sensory multiplicity like the sensuous manifold Kant had in mind. Given a certain attitude of attention, one could resolve one's awareness of the tree into such a sensuous manifold, but, considering the union of awareness and understanding we are assuming to exist in recognition, such a multiplicity has no primordial evidential status: indeed, when we attend to any such sensory item our recognition of it may include the recognition that its status is less fundamental than the entity on or within which we find it, as for instance, when we recognize a certain color patch as belonging to the surface of the tree. We shall not attempt to settle just now the ontological and epistemological status of all the diverse multiplicities ingenuity might find within our recognition of a tree. The only point that concerns us now is that, when mind-becomes-conscious of a tree, any such multiplicity is transcended in the recognition of it as a unity. The self-transcendence of mind transcends any potential multiplicity in its field of attention. The recognition on our part of an originative act that might yield upon analysis a multiplicity of $C \rightarrow E$ relations is a special case of this transcendence.

(*ii*) Any act in which mind-becomes-conscious (and hence any recognition) transcends the multiplicity of its infrastructure, and therefore the multiplicity of both the structural components of, and the happenings in, the central nervous system. The self-transcendence of mind depends upon a transcendence of its infrastructure.

(*iii*) Any recognition transcends the particular subjectivity in which it takes place. The self-transcendence of mind is nothing more than its being aware of and understanding what is the case, or what is true. Seen from one angle that is a mere truism, but from another angle, one from which one takes seriously expressions like "true" and "what is the case," it is a definition of immense importance, since it signalizes the inappropriateness of conceiving of mind or subjectivity as a confinement within whatever subjective state, event, or mode of being it happens to be expressing itself in. If, for instance, Socrates is aware of and understands that Phaedo is in the prison with him, and if that is indeed the case, the functioning of Socrates' mind can not unambiguously be identified with a wholly particular subjective state, event, or mode of being thought of as in principle cut off from whatever is nonsubjective. Granted that it is indeed the case that Phaedo is there, the particular subjective state, or state of mind, in which Socrates affirms it to be so is by definition not *merely* particular, since its particular psychological, mental, subjective character is *also* the entertainment of a quite different particular: the particularity of Phaedo's being there in prison with him. This "double" particularity of subjectivity is something we are all on some occasion or other familiar with. It is at least one of the things we mean by the self-transcendence of subjectivity. But something more than a double particularity of a subject and an attained object is involved, for the entertainment of something understood to be true carries with it the assumption that it holds for other particular minds as well: that it is in principle coercive of rationality in general. Socrates, aware and understanding what is the case, and aware also of what this means, is not merely the particular subjectivity of Socrates: he is a transcendental subjectivity as well. I do not mean to introduce what James called a characterless witness to any mental content, with everything Socratic being reckoned with the content; I mean to make the simpler point that subjectivity, when it is aware of and understands what is the case, can not understand itself adequately in terms of a mere unique particularity, but requires the category of generality as well. It is no exaggeration, no straining after some peculiarly nonexperiential and metaphysical assertion, to claim that, when Socrates understands what is the case, it is not just Socrates who does so, but mind-in-Socrates. The impersonal qualifies any achievement of rationality, however personal it may also be, and it qualifies it experientially as well as "rationally."

(iv) Any act of mind-becoming-conscious, and therefore any recognition, transcends the particularity of whatever "object" it is aware of and understands. This type of transcendence is signalized, but not fully clarified, by the conceptual element in our recognition of any object, any truth, any originative act, any entity. The connection with the conceptual is what leads Platonists, who also wish to make this point, to claim that the true reality of particulars lies in the Forms. But what we understand and are aware of is not only a particular brought under a concept: it is the particular so qualified by generality that we can not even take it for granted that we can attach any clear meaning to the notion of a wholly discrete, wholly unique particular. It is not just a particular I see, but an oak tree; and not just an oak tree, but a tree, and not just a tree but an entity. It is not just Socrates I see, but a man, and an entity. It is an originative action of his that I contemplate, but not just *this* one, but this *originative action*. But this supposed progress from the wholly particular up through the realm of general concepts or forms obscures the fact that the first particular, in which such a progress begins, is itself so qualified by the general power on which it depends and of which it is an expression that Being itself is present in the presence of any such "particular."

The last two senses of transcendence, (*iii*) and (*iv*), are the crucial ones: any act in which mind-becomes-conscious transcends the particularity of the subjectivity in which it takes place and it transcends also the particularity of any objectivity it entertains. It does not matter which of these we emphasize, since in either case we encounter Being, in the one case expressing itself in subjectivity, in the other expressing itself in objectivity. Being qualifies each particular entity and each particular act of intelligence, and not just as an empty and abstract notion we might reach at the limit of abstraction, but as a general, or common, power. Our investigation has repeatedly made use of the idea of a power ramifying in a multiplicity to which it is "related." But any such originative act and any entity can itself be regarded as one of a multiplicity, and all of them are no less "related" to a One whose power ramifies in all multiplicities.

5

The argument so far purports to advance our recognition of originative acts and their infrastructures, but only by also advancing our recognition of agents and their infrastructures. The latter recognition carries with it the recognition that the agent is an entity having an ontological status more fundamental than the acts that flow from him. The category of entity — more properly, the category "an entity," or "a being" — is so general, however, that there is nothing that can not be brought under its scope; we shall therefore confine ourselves here to what I shall call fundamental entities. The most general characteristic of a fundamental entity is that it is an act-temporal power-unit that expresses itself through a spatiotemporal region which is thus given unity. This highly abstract statement is meant to take account of the fact that there are some fundamental entities that are simple in the sense that their unity is not expressed in an infrastructure consisting of discrete units: at any rate, the quantum principle makes this plausible. Whitehead's "actual entities" are all of this simple character,[3] but this atomic restriction compels him to give entities like Socrates the derivative ontological status of "societies" of such "actual entities." Our own position, based as it is on our attention to Socrates, is that he too is a fundamental entity, but of the hierarchical kind that expresses itself in an infrastructure of discrete units some members of which are also fundamental entities. It would in fact appear that most fundamental entities are of this complex type. Our highly abstract statement of the most general characteristic of a fundamental entity should therefore be reformulated in this way to take account of the complex ones: the spatiotemporal region to which they give unity is analyzable into a multiplicity of subordinate fundamental entities. We should therefore expect to find in the infrastructure of Socrates, besides the presumably simple ones forming its base, a number of levels made up of complex fundamental entities of a lower order than Socrates himself.

Provided we can interpret a seemingly enduring entity like an electron as the repeated exercise of act-temporal power in discrete spatiotemporal power-units, and the scientific model of elementary "particles" seems open to such an interpretation, the atom can be regarded as a higher order succession of act-temporal units binding in their power infrastructures of simpler "particles." The rhythmic reiteration of pattern that is an elementary "particle" would then have as its correlative the reiterated power that binds it in the more complex dance of the atom. This entails interpreting the atom not as a single enduring fundamental entity but a succession of them. The molecular level is open to the same interpretation. The prominence of the spatial order displayed by molecules and atoms works against this, but as we shall see soon enough, on this interpretation an enduring spatial order is regarded as derivative from act-temporal power. Above the level of the molecule the cell presents itself as one obvious candidate for the status of fundamental entity. I think we can accord it that status only with important qualifications, but let us overlook that issue for the moment. If we do, we emerge with a highly simplified new monadology— Socrates, his cells, molecules, atoms, and simple "particles"— in which the preestablished harmony is replaced by true power "relations" between a superordinate monad and its subordinates, power "relations" that would be the ontological basis for the One-Many "relation" of originative acts.

It is far too tidy and simple a picture, and it will not stand up to close examination, but there is some truth in it, and some principles that can be extracted from it will apply also to the more complicated reality of Socrates. Let us work with it for awhile.

It is essential to the idea of a fundamental entity that it should stand in a succession of similar entities. Entity gives rise to entity, and this principle operates at every infrastructure level that itself consists of fundamental entities. At the level of Socrates the relation parent-offspring exemplifies this principle; at the cellular level, cell-division exemplifies it; and if we construe enduring "entities" like molecules, atoms, and subatomic "particles" as reiterated trains of fundamental entities, each expressing itself in a discrete spatiotemporal power-pattern, then these levels also exemplify it.

But to say that entity gives rise to entity is not quite accurate. Certainly the relation between parent and child is not a $C \rightarrow E$ one, if only for the reason that the capacity for originative action we attribute to an entity like Socrates is at odds with this kind of succession; and presumably some similar reservation must be made in the case of the succession at every infrastructure level that consists of fundamental entities, down to the succession of simple spatiotemporal power patterns at our lowest level. A succession of this kind at the lowest level has been attributed to "creativity" by Whitehead, but this notion, which I have criticized elsewhere, holds many difficulties, the chief of which for our present purposes is that it implies a quite radical pluralism of powers that it seems to me is not tenable. An alter-

329

native view, applicable to all levels, and equally dismissive of a $C \to E$ affiliation, will be advanced shortly. For the moment, though, we have this picture: if a fundamental entity like Socrates possessed an infrastructure made up entirely of a hierarchy of subordinate fundamental entities, then at each level there would be fundamental entities succeeding each other in relationships that were not $C \to E$ ones. Each entity, qua fundamental entity, would thus be originative, or act-temporal, and originative action at the Socratic level would be based upon this.

It is obvious that in any such complex fundamental entity there would be a massive principle of inheritance at work, even though each unit at each level would "give rise to" successors in a non-$C \to E$ sense. Thus each entity at each level, including Socrates, will have an infrastructure for which he is not entirely responsible, seeing that entities at every one of the levels will succeed each other without regard to the power of the superordinate entity. Yet that same principle insures that each entity at each level, once again including Socrates, will be originative, or act-temporal. Socrates' inheritance of elements that then enter into his infrastructure is the inheritance of originative, or act-temporal, units; and he himself can make use of such an inheritance only because of his own act-temporal status. As we shall see, however, the principle of inheritance that operates in a fundamental entity like Socrates is much more complex than this.

Though it is probably easier to give an example of a fundamental entity than to define it, we are in a position to list some of its characteristics in an informal way. It is a power-unit that is by definition originative, and a minimum condition of this notion is that it is not caused in a $C \to E$ sense by any entity it succeeds, despite the massive inheritance it may receive. In principle the notion of inheritance and the notion of infrastructure are correlates, with the reservation, however, that an infrastructure is not merely an assemblage of act-temporal units, but an ordered one brought about by the superordinate entity. That is to say that an infrastructure includes, but is not identical with, an inheritance. The power of a fundamental entity is expressed

330

in a becoming that is act-temporal and, if the entity is complex, the power is felt throughout the spatiotemporal manifold of its infrastructure. The infrastructure of a complex fundamental entity will "contain" other fundamental entities, though in the case of a fundamental entity like Socrates, that is not all it will "contain." Any fundamental entity that has an infrastructure will be "related" to it in a way analogous to the "relation" between an originative act and its infrastructure: it will therefore be a One asymmetrically identical with the Many of the infrastructure. It will not escape the reader that I am trying to give the category of fundamental entity at least as wide an extension as the category of substance once had. But I am trying to preserve the dynamic and individual note originally proper to the category of *ousia,* though long since lost in the vicissitudes the successor term "substance"—it is too far from the original to deserve to be called a translation—has suffered.

Continuing for awhile with our too-simple new monadology, we may observe that although all fundamental entities form a multiplicity of discrete units, the multiplicity is not a radical pluralism. Each unit of it is a union of particular and general, and the nature of this union is not successfully expressed in the observation that each of the particulars can be brought under a number of general concepts or subsumed in a variety of classes. Insofar as each of them exemplifies power, each such instance of power is a *participant power.* It hardly need be added that by making this point I am not simply saying that each of these instances of power can be brought under the general term "power." If the power of the fundamental entity Socrates pervades his infrastructure it is no doubt distinguishable from the power of Crito considered as pervading *his* infrastructure. But the distinction is made only if we ignore the inadequacy of the notion of particularity to characterize the exercise of power on the part of a fundamental entity. The term "participant power" is intended to call attention to this point. It is a commonplace of philosophy to think of *particulars* as participating in concepts, universals, or Platonic Forms, which by contrast are understood to be *general.* But to express the contrast

331

between particular and general in this way is to fail to notice the ontological mystery of the concrete particular whose very particularity includes a union with and dependence upon a general, common, or universal power.

The move I made awhile ago from the being of an individual to the Being he participates in expressed this same point is more conventional language. The power exercised by any fundamental entity is not unambiguously "its own." The unity by virtue of which a fundamental entity pervades its infrastructure is also not unambiguously "its own": it is a common one, and in ordering the infrastructure it exercises in a particular instance a common formative power. Though fundamental entities constitute a multiplicity of unities—a Many made up of "ones"—it is not a pure multiplicity, and the "ones" are not utterly discrete, but power instances of a common One. That is one reason why in recognizing them we do not function as utterly discrete rational units: our reason is also an instance—a power instance—of a common One. Our world is interpersonal not just because a multiplicity of distinct persons has wrought it, but also because neither rationality nor its object can be adequately characterized in terms of utter particularity.

Let us call the power exercised by the unity of any fundamental entity in its "relation" of asymmetrical identity with its infrastructure *supervening, or governing, ontic power;* and the power exercised by any entity of the infrastructure in contributing to its superordinate entity *conditioning ontic power.*[4] Ontic power will naturally be *participant power* in the sense just developed. Supervening ontic power is the more fundamental, since the capacity of any (complex) entity for exercising conditioning ontic power must obviously be derivative from the supervening ontic power it exercises in "relation" to its own infrastructure. In the case of simple fundamental entities we shall not use the expression "supervening"; we shall simply say that they have ontic power, and that in virtue of it they can exercise conditioning ontic power within entities of higher order.

By virtue of their supervening ontic power, fundamental entities are also capable of exercising *causal power.* Any exact sense we give the word "cause" in $C \rightarrow E$ analysis will properly be derivative from the causal power of fundamental entities. Let us, however, defer consideration of it until section 9.

Not all fundamental entities are capable of originative action, but all, it would appear, have two characteristics that are necessary conditions for the emergence of originative action in the higher fundamental entities. We have already touched upon them in the discussion of succession and inheritance in this section: their becoming is act-temporal, and it is originative in the sense that the supervening ontic power of any unit is never wholly derived from a predecessor. Whether we deal with living fundamental entities affiliated in the parent-offspring relation, or with the serial order of fundamental entities that in their patterned coming-to-be sustain the enduring "entity" we call an electron, the point is essential to the idea of a fundamental entity. No act-temporal unit in the electron-succession is wholly caused in a $C \rightarrow E$ sense by its predecessors. Similarly, *mutatis mutandis,* Socrates is not wholly caused by his parents or even by the whole biological chain of his ancestry. A fundamental entity can no more be wholly accounted for by its predecessors than an originative act can be wholly caused by prior acts or by a series of events not having the status of an act.

Nevertheless, the problem of inheritance is a difficult one, and, especially in the case of Socrates, it raises problems that can not be dealt with in terms of this simple new monadology, even though the general principles so far enunciated will be found to be applicable to the more complicated case of Socrates himself.

6

The most casual inspection of the infrastructure of Socrates shows it to comprise many entities that are not fundamental. His very cells, at first glance such obvious candidates for that status, offer immediate problems. It is true that he began his career as a one-celled entity, and that life itself began in that way. More generally, it is true that there are many one-celled organisms that themselves do not belong to the infrastructure of some higher-order fundamental entity, and in that sense exist "in themselves." Nevertheless, in the differentiation of cells in the course of the development of his body, most of the cells became so specialized that they are not viable except within his body or within an artificial environment that closely resembles it. Other entities having some of the characteristics of fundamental entities must be disqualified for similar reasons. Thus, although at infrastructure levels higher than that of the cells, organs like brain, heart, eye, and liver display impressive credentials; and although at lower levels so do cell-nuclei and organelles; yet the need for a specialized environment is even clearer in all those cases than in the case of the cells.

It would therefore appear that the infrastructure of any higher-order fundamental entity contains many entities that express the unity of the fundamental entity without themselves having that same status in an unambiguous way. We may attribute act-temporality to many or most of them, but the act-temporality will simply be a participation in, or partial expression of, that of the superordinate entity. They are thus participant powers. Each such unit belongs to a level—that of organ, of cell, of organelle, etc.—and these levels are general, not just in the obvious sense that they can be brought under general concepts, but in the sense that each occupant participates equally in the fundamental entity to whose infrastructure it belongs. It is worth noting that the entity in which they participate—in this case Socrates—is itself a participant power. This is consistent with the imperfect but nonetheless real rehearsal of phylogeny in ontogeny: the very growth of an individual fundamental entity bears witness to an aspect of generality that is always present, and the very foundations of the individuality of Socrates are laid down by an act-temporal power that is not merely his own. There is a counterpart principle in phylogenetics that is more speculative: if in the course of the life of Socrates the DNA material in his germ cells were to be altered in a way that could not be brought under the usual rubrics of neo-Darwinian evolutionary theory, the alteration would be attributable to Socrates, but only in the sense that, even at his most individual, he is a participant, and therefore under one aspect a general, power. No doubt he himself would not accept this deviation from his view of the Forms, but the notion that power can be general, or common, or One, though ramifying in a multiplicity of particular fundamental entities, permits us to conceive of reality in terms of a hierarchy of general levels without postulating a realm of general forms as their ontological basis. Though we began our meditation with a passage from Plato, we have been under no obligation to defend the status he gives the Forms.

There are other obstacles to dealing with Socrates exhaustively in terms of a new monadology. If he is a fundamental entity whose infrastructure consists in great part of a hierarchy of act-temporal subordinate entities, he also has many features that can readily be interpreted in terms of a kind of mechanism that is usually opposed to the telic, and is certainly on the face of it at odds with act-temporality. Because it seems to me that the idea of a machine when construed in any sense close to the normal or even technical use of the word "machine" is nothing if not telic, I shall call these features spatiomechanical. A spatiomechanism is that abstract feature of a machine we get when we attend to it without considering either the origin and design of the machine or the origin of any motion (or other energy impulse) within it. It consists of persistent units disposed in a persistent spatial order, the nature of the units and their order being such that (a) the movement of one unit can be transmitted to others in accordance with the order or (b) impulses of other sorts can be transmitted through the structure in accordance with the order.

If we neglect the watchmaker and the origin of the energy in the watch, it is a spatiomechanism. With similar reservations, so is a computer. But so also are the human skeleton, the circulatory system, the heart, and a great many of the other components of the human body. So also are the various servomechanisms we tried to reconcile with originative action in chapter

335

5. These, incidentally, introduce yet another complication into any attempt at a new monadology, for even if they do, as I suggested there, bear the image of the act-temporal gesture (ontogenetic and phylogenetic) that made them, they are certainly not fundamental entities or even act-temporal entities that are not fundamental. They are units in which several organs and other structures cooperate: bone, muscle, nerve, hand, eye, brain are linked together for even the simplest tasks, and the servomechanical units form a shifting pattern in which linkages are established for some tasks and relinquished for others. Given the act of abstraction that permits us to attend to them, all these spatiomechanisms are passive structures through which $C \rightarrow E$ impulses move, their pathways being determined by what we may sum up in the commonsense notion of shape.

Not only can we find any number of such spatiomechanisms in Socrates' infrastructure in addition to many units having some claim to act-temporality, but we find besides many spatiomechanical features within supposed act-temporal units and many spatiomechanical relations between them. Thus, if we assume a cell to be an act-temporal entity, the impact of two macromolecules within it is spatiomechanical, and so too is the very confinement of a large molecular population within a membrane. So, for that matter, is the very contact of cell with cell within the confines of an organ. There are so many features that, taken one by one, appear to be spatiomechanical that the counter-image of himself to which Socrates opposed "real (or true) causality" is a powerful one.

The spatiomechanical image becomes even more persuasive as we turn to the matter of inheritance. The simple image of a fundamental entity inheriting an infrastructure without detriment to its act-temporal status depends upon the claim that each level of its infrastructure consists of a succession of entities that are *also* act-temporal, and on the face of it this does not seem to be strictly true. The simple monadic image is thus less plausible. Some of the most important elements of Socrates' infrastructure are, as we saw, not fundamental entities — his organs, for instance — and even if they are act-temporal, their de-

336

velopment and their phylogenetic stability is nonetheless under the control (so, at any rate, a reductionist would put it) of the DNA macromolecule in the nucleus of the germ cell.

Though we may insist that Socrates' biological inheritance did not "cause" the whole of his career in a $C \to E$ sense, the role of DNA in inheritance gives some support to the view that an adequate explanation of his development can be given in terms of $C \to E$ causality and the laws of nature. A macromolecule of DNA in the fertilized egg sums up the nature of the influence of predecessors in the case of entities like Socrates, except for the character of the environment supplied for the developing embryo—a notable exception to be sure. The role of the stable structure of the macromolecule might well seem to be not so much an augmentation of $C \to E$ causality and law as a special case of it. Not only is there a massive inheritance of spatiomechanical features, but besides, the very principle of inheritance itself has profound spatiomechanical features. The function of the DNA macromolecule is to take part, by virtue of its very structure, in a set of interactions between other stable physical structures; and these interactions, considered one by one, have surprising analogies with the very naïve description of mechanical operations given in the speech of Socrates that furnishes our text. From this perspective, recourse to the idea of fundamental entities possessing ontic power seems superfluous.

7

Against these difficulties we may bring the following principles.

(1) Far from being in conflict with the idea of act-temporality, some spatial order is required by it, since act-temporality is exercised throughout a spatial region in the course of its coming-to-be. Thus, if a complex organism is an act-temporal power, its cellular level will consist of the development of a spatial arrangement of cells and then the persistence of this

arrangement for a certain time. Nor is the *persistence* of a spatial order in itself any evidence that it is the *mere* persistence of a *merely* passive structure of the kind called for by the abstract notion of spatiomechanism. For if the units of the cellular level are act-temporal, as our hypothesis requires, the successiveness of generations of them will yield a persistent spatial order. Such a persistent order would then be ontologically dependent upon the act-temporality of the superordinate organism and the act-temporality of the generation of superordinate cells. In principle, then, *some* persistence of spatial order is called for by the idea of a hierarchy consisting *entirely* of act-temporal units, and the massive stability of the molecular level, and in particular the massive stability of the macromolecule of DNA, does not in itself demonstrate that the molecular level is not act-temporal. We have left open the question whether the power that binds together the components of molecules is act-temporal. If it is, the persistence of a molecule would be dependent upon a succession of periodic power-units, and we should be interpreting a single molecule as a succession of act-temporal units, in much the same way we have interpreted a single electron as a succession of act-temporal units. If molecules are not act-temporal, but instead merely persistent, merely passive, spatial structures, whose most basic infrastructure units alone are act-temporal, then they may be the closest thing in nature to the spatiomechanical ideal: passive participants in $C \rightarrow E$ transactions and combinations, passive transmitters of $C \rightarrow E$ impulses. The same considerations, naturally, apply to the atomic level as well. But even if molecules and atoms are ideal spatiomechanisms, they may still enter into and be utilized by higher-order act-temporal units. We may even think of act-temporality as exploiting such ideal spatiomechanisms, if they do indeed exist in nature.

(2) There may be no pure spatiomechanisms in nature. In any case, most spatiomechanical features found in an entity like Socrates seem to be in ontological dependence upon units that can be construed as act-temporal. (*a*) They may be abstractions from a total concrete reality that is act-temporal, as when we

regard a cell merely as a stable spatial order. (*b*) They may be found within act-temporal units, as a DNA macromolecule belongs to the infrastructure of a cell. (*c*) They may be made up of act-temporal units, as the complex biological servomechanism Socrates uses to raise the cup to his lip is made up of cells.

(*3*) A meaningful order originated by an act-temporal power in its "relation" to an infrastructure may be preserved in a spatial order through the succession, within the infrastructure, of generations of act-temporal units. In that sense both phylogenetic stability and phylogenetic change are functions of the act-temporality of the ontogeny and mature activity of the individual that is "related" to the infrastructure. It should be recalled, however, that we are interpreting individual act-temporal units as participant powers.

(*4*) One highly complex and meaningful spatial order that may be regarded as an achievement (both ontogenetic and phylogenetic) of act-temporality is the one that includes the macroscopic order of the body, the microscopic order of DNA, and also the relation between those two orders by virtue of which the structure of the body represents itself in the structure of the DNA and the structure of the DNA represents itself in the body. This relation is one of *mutual* encoding, and *mutual* representation, but it is also a relation that is an effective one in the sense that the *total* spatial order that includes the macroscopic and microscopic orders governs $C \rightarrow E$ relations effective in the succession of one organism by one inheritor. In other words, the total spatial order that includes both (*a*) the general strategy of stabilizing one level by using the stability of another level as a code and (*b*) the particular macrostructure of a particular organism and the particular microstructure that encodes it, is attributed to act-temporality. It will follow that an account of either ontogeny or phylogeny exclusively in terms of changes in DNA that are attributed exclusively to non-act-temporal sources will be highly abstract.

(*5*) When it is abstracted from the total act-temporal context in which it is found, any spatial structure, however ordered and indeed telic its origin, however much it may be subject to some higher level control (as, say, a biological servomechanism employed in an originative act) will display transmitted motions (or transmitted impulses) understandable in part in terms of $C \rightarrow E$ relations within a passive structure. Bone x moves bone y; neuron x contributes to the firing of neuron y; structural fit of macromolecule to macromolecule is effective in the building of a protein. No conclusions contrary to an overriding act-temporality can be drawn from such an abstraction, for any ontic power expresses itself in an infrastructure that upon analysis discloses a set of genuine $C \rightarrow E$ relations.

(6) What is inherited, and only inherited, belongs to the infrastructure of an act-temporal unit. Structures thus inherited are interpretable in terms of conditioning ontic power. A macromolecule of DNA, for instance, constitutes one element in the multiple infrastructure elements of a cell, and therefore one element in the multiplicity of the infrastructure of the fundamental entity to which the cell belongs.

The theme of persistent spatial order is therefore not to be identified with the spatiomechanical abstraction I have constructed in terms of inertness, passivity, and $C \rightarrow E$ relations. Its positive aspect is that it is an achievement of act-temporality, and that it preserves, in a purely spatial order, whatever can be so preserved of the spatiotemporal order in which an ontic power comes-to-be. An order of this kind does not merely bear the mark of act-temporality, but also frees the ontic power for further achievements. In some cases the achievement of a given order will be of significance chiefly for the growth and development of the individual, and the persistence of the structure will also be chiefly individual. Thus Socrates may well produce some structural changes in his brain as a correlate of some thought or decision, or some structural changes in receptor and motor mechanisms as a correlate of lifelong repetitions of originative acts of a physical kind. Later repetition of similar thoughts, decisions, and physical acts will be facilitated, but will be no less a function of his act-temporality, and the range of act-temporal possibilities open to him will at the same time be increased. Such individual achievements will however be based upon a massive inheritance. Those particular brain changes, perhaps a correlate of the originative acts of his last days, were possible because of the inheritance of a general brain structure that some authorities would claim to be little altered since the appearance of *Homo sapiens*. And an even stronger case can be made out for the biological servomechanism into which he might have introduced particular refinements as a correlate of his military service as a youth. Yet these inherited structures will bear the image not only of the myriad successive act-temporal units within whose framework they were gradually laid down, but also of the particular ontic-power — that of Socrates — in whose ontogeny they were in this case rehearsed. And they will bear the image too of the multitude of act-temporal units — cells and those of lower order — that, linked in a spatial order, sustain them.

The mark of act-temporality in a spatial structure, we saw in chapter 5, was its capacity to give, by virtue of a total spatial structure, a total temporal order to a set of $C \rightarrow E$ transactions. We used this point there to show that an originative act could include in its infrastructure, without detriment to its act-temporality, a structural feature of seemingly spatiomechanical import. The reader will remember that we interpreted these structures in a way that we may now systematize as follows. (*a*) The sequence of movements or impulses through the structure, though they are in part functions of the structure, are controlled by the enframing temporality of the superordinate act: Socrates *uses* servomechanisms in raising the cup to his lips. (*b*) Although each movement within the servomechanical structure itself when isolated from its context can be regarded as a $C \rightarrow E$ movement in a spatiomechanism, the total spatial pattern determines a total temporal sequence, and it is the total sequence that is effective in raising the cup to the lips or in performing analogous tasks. A happening in one part of the structure at time t_1 is thus related not just to a happening at time t_2 in some adjacent part with which it is in immediate $C \rightarrow E$ relation, but also to other happenings in other parts of the structure at the same time t_1. The relation is a significant or meaningful one, and the significance is displayed when causal chains beginning in two distinct places at time t_1 converge in some third place at, say, time t_6. It will of course be possible to analyze the total pattern into an indefinite number of such chains depending upon what location and what time we choose. Although we should not want to assign a temporal "reach" to any of these distinct events, which might in some cases be as passive as the movement of a toothed wheel by a cog, the structure as a whole defines a temporal unit the totality of which resembles the reach of act-temporality. (c) The origin of the temporally significant structure was attributed to an act-temporal phylogenetic gesture. The gesture is made by a succession of act-temporal units, any one of which may contribute to its elaboration and the preservation of it, just as any one of them is responsible for some particular reiteration of the significant structure. It may be noticed in passing that some particular phylogenetic contribution to the gradual refinement· of an inherited structure like a servomechanism may be irrelevant to the subsequent career of a particular fundamental entity, even though its preceding career may be one of the factors responsible for the changes in the genetic material that is the correlative of its stability. It is one feature of a participant power that it may be the carrier of a significance that transcends it. On a thoroughly telic interpretation, any act-temporal power would be the bearer both of what has been called an external teleology and of what has been called an internal teleology.

8

If structures that have superficial spatiomechanical features may be act-temporal in origin, nowhere is this more evident than in the very "mechanism" that mediates reiteration. Regard any organism as a stable macroscopic spatial structure whose genetic heritage is passed on by virtue of a component microscopic structure that encapsulates its order, and we must regard the total spatial order that includes the reciprocal relation between the macroscopic and microscopic as a highly significant one. It contains more than a code; it contains also the whole strategy of coding, caught up and spatialized in the totality of the body.

342

We must live with the logical consequences of the coding image: we are dealing with an order so meaningful that it carries both a general strategy and a particular application of it. The suppression of this burden of significance in favor of the spatiomechanical features of the structure that carries it is a special instance of that odd distortion by which machines, those most telic and purpose-laden objects, have been taken to be the very antithesis of the telic. I have tried to replace one of the polar terms of this antithesis with the abstraction "spatiomechanism," from which the theme of purpose and meaning, so proper to machines, has been removed. But the distortion encapsulated in the opposition "mechanical" and "telic" is probably irremediable.

The strategy of coding, the particular coding relation between that particular macroscopic body and that particular bit of DNA, is nothing if not telic and meaningful. The notions "telic" and "meaningful" (or "significant") are in mutual support: if a significant structure mediates a process, the process is *ipso facto* telic; and if a structure is indeed significant it is the outcome of a telic process. If we assume a nonanthropomorphic sense for "code" and "significant," there will be a sense of "telic" equally free of the notion of conscious human purpose. In this book the idea of act-temporality has been offered as such a sense, and human purposive acts have been understood to be a special case of an act-temporality that is widely distributed in nature. Significance, stabilized in a structure of spatially disposed units, is the result of an ordering, and one of the things signified by it is the ordering phylogenetic gesture that brought it about. An ontogenetic gesture isomorphic with that one now makes use of it. In the language of this meditation we may say that, whether we are considering a mature organism in which there is a reciprocal relationship between macroscopic body and microscopic DNA, or an earlier state in which the code is present but the body not fully developed, the spatially persistent structure that carries both the strategy of coding and the particular code is to be reckoned with the infrastructure of the ontic power that makes use of it.

A macromolecule of DNA in the single cell from which

Socrates developed is a coded structure, and the significance, or meaning, of the code is disclosed in the order of his development. The distinction between governing and conditioning ontic power permits us to interpret this order as contributory to, rather than utterly productive of, his development; and the reciprocal of this is that the same coded structure — coded in the double sense that it embodies both the strategy of coding and a particular code — is an order achieved by the act-temporality in which the ontic power of his ancestry expresses itself. A coded contribution has as its counterpart an encoding achievement, and this carries with it the logical consequence that the ontic power of Socrates is in principle capable of an encoding achievement. This interpretation requires us to consider the original macromolecule in the one-celled Socrates as a stable physical structure forming part of his infrastructure. As such it is capable of contributing to his development only what an infrastructure contributes. The macromolecule and its successors, though they will have histories amenable to $C \rightarrow E$ analysis, will in the development of the entity Socrates play the role of conditioning ontic powers; furthermore any subunit revealed in the $C \rightarrow E$ analysis of any such macromolecule will play the role of a conditioning ontic power with respect to the macromolecule itself. The sequence of operations "triggered" by the macromolecule, a sequence which, by its spatiomechanical feature, seems to make ontic power a superfluous notion, is in this perspective understood to be possible only under the act-temporality — a kind of law-in-becoming — of the supervening ontic power that goes by the name of Socrates. This means that much in the infrastructure of Socrates is inherited, but it also means that it is only inherited qua infrastructure, and that the inheritance can only be made use of by an enframing governing ontic power. The corollary of this is that what is here inherited was once laid down by a governing ontic power — a participant power and therefore in principle always of both ontogenetic and phylogenetic import. And indeed DNA, controlling as it does a succession of operations whose temporal ordering is vital to the outcome, reflects in its very structure the act-temporality of the ontic power that has gradually shaped it.

To say all this is not to deny for a moment that the contribution of the infrastructure is a profound one: the ontic power of Socrates pervades with act-temporality a spatial region that includes but is not limited to the coded structure of the macromolecule, but it is on the other hand so "related" to the multiplicity of that region as to be identical with it, even if the identity is that vital asymmetrical one by which the One expresses itself in the Many. It is essential to this polarity of a contributory (or a received) order and a governing (or achieved) order that the received DNA represents an achievement of predecessors; but it follows from this that in principle the achieved order of Socrates may in some respects be stabilized in the DNA he leaves behind him. The oddness of this claim from the point of view of genetic and evolutionary doctrine is somewhat mitigated by the fact that we are interpreting the ontic power both of Socrates and of each of his predecessors to be a participant power. What the ontic power of Socrates might contribute to the modification of received DNA might in any case be of more narrow biological import, irrelevant to his moral achievement, and often in any case literally without issue. The phylogenetic influence of a participant power transcends that in him that makes him a *particular* participant power. Whatever subsequent developments in evolutionary theory may bring, we may continue to suppose that the primary influence of Socrates on the race lies in his words and deeds.

But the principle of the openness of DNA to the encodings of ontic power is not a negligible one, and it is not lightly to be dismissed, despite the contrary dogmas of current evolutionary theory. It is orthodox genetics and orthodox neo-Darwinian evolutionary theory to suppose that the role of DNA, here represented as playing the contributory role of a conditioning ontic power, is in fact a controlling one. It is also assumed that it will be transmitted unaltered to the germ cells, there to exercise a different control on successors only in virtue of natural selection operating together with two factors both of which are usually brought under the rubric of chance: (*a*) mutations in a DNA macromolecule; (*b*) combinatory possibilities of the union of DNA material from both parents in a fertilized egg-cell. The reciprocal of the notion of a coded order that controls (in our view, contributes or conditions), namely an achieved order that encodes, is thus denied. And it is denied with respect both to Socrates' ancestry collectively and severally and to himself: neither encapsulates, or encodes, in the structural stability of DNA, any order achieved in the exercise of ontic power. DNA is insulated from the development it controls, and the development, in that sense not "creative," could not in any case have repercussions on the DNA.

This dogma has remained without serious challenge for a long while, since the only alternative has seemed to be a return to some version of the views of Lamarck, which are understood to be scientifically disreputable. Recently, however, some scientists whose devotion to experimental and theoretic rigor is beyond reproach have been exploring alternative views. It is no doubt too early to say whether some future theory along lines worked out by Waddington and others will replace neo-Darwinian orthodoxy.[5] Insofar as alternatives of this kind suggest the possibility of an ontogenetic biological "field" in which the successors of the DNA macromolecule that helps establish that field are themselves altered, it is more open to interpretation in terms of ontic power than the orthodox view is. Supervening ontic power, as the "source" from which originative action springs, is understood to be a "field" spatiotemporal in nature —a law-in-becoming pervasive of a region the units of which are subject to the unifying power thus "related" to them. An order pervasive in this sense is an achieved one despite the received order it incorporates, and it may well stabilize itself, in subtle ways not yet clearly understood, by encoding alterations in the DNA material in the course of the myriad reiterations of the spatiotemporal patterns of genetic material that take place in the full sweep of the infrastructure. No more than for originative action does this suggestion require that an analysis of successive generations of genetic material within the field of an ontic power should reveal any physical anomalies or indeed any physical steps that can not be understood, when taken severally, in a $C \rightarrow E$ sense. Recourse to the metaphor of code implies that one takes this to be in principle possible for Socrates, for each of his predecessors, and for each of his successors. As participant powers, all of them are in any case of both ontogenetic and phylogenetic import.

9

By virtue of its governing, or supervening, ontic power a fundamental entity exercises conditioning ontic power on a superordinate ontic power. But governing ontic power is also the source of causal power, and any exact sense we give the word "cause" in $C \rightarrow E$ analysis will be clear only if we can derive it from causal power. As the term implies, causal power is more appropriate to the working rather than to the official view of $C \rightarrow E$ analysis. It would follow that the official view, which is surely important for the many useful kinds of analysis that do not make explicit use of the idea of power, would then be derivative by abstraction from the working view. I have no intention of attempting that last derivation here, but if this is the appropriate order of derivation, it would be inappropriate to appeal to some form of the official view — even those who use it constantly will agree that it is not as clear as one would like it to be — in a criticism of this, or indeed any other similar effort, to give the idea of causality a foundation in metaphysics.

Any exact sense we might give the term "causal power" and thus any exact sense we might give the no doubt too commonsensical working view of the $C \rightarrow E$ relation will depend upon the exactness with which we can discriminate any particular fundamental entity and distinguish its causal concourse with other entities from its own "relation" to its infrastructure and from its own infrastructure role in some entity of higher rank. It is not surprising, therefore, that the clearest example of causal power we can give is that of our own agency. If I pick up a ball and throw it, I act originatively. Socrates acts originatively in raising the cup to his lips. Taking for granted the interdependence of agent and infrastructure, I can also say that I caused the ball, he the cup, to move; or that we exercised causal power on ball and cup respectively. Other cases are clear enough, though most, to the degree that they lack this note of origination, will have something of passivity in them, and the power they exercise will be in part transmissive, as when a cell, carried in a stream of blood, might collide with another cell, thus exercising causal power on it. This and many other examples of this sort make it clear that entities that are (on our hypothesis) act-temporal may bring causal power to a $C \rightarrow E$ transaction that will have many features in common with the spatiomechanical abstraction.

If we turn away from entities that are fundamental, we find that our examples, clear enough for common sense, have nonetheless some obscurity in them. Those commonsense entities the ball and the cup, upon which causal power was exercised, according to our examples, can themselves operate as causes: the ball may break a window, the cup may fall to the ground and leave an indentation. If they are not fundamental entities we shall presumably have to attribute to them the derivative causal power proper to entities that are assemblages of fundamental and act-temporal entities. It is of course open to us to interpret them as assemblages of this kind, and the interpretation makes as much sense as other metaphysical interpretations of the commonsense entities physics deals with in a quite different way. But if we wish to ground a causal power of this kind upon the causal power of the fundamental entities of which ball and cup are presumably composed, there will be many complications. It is not that the component entities do not afford examples of causal power. They do so in abundance, provided, that is, that they are indeed fundamental entities. Thus, if a subatomic particle is a fundamental entity, it seems tolerably clear that when one such particle deflects another upon collision with it, we can reasonably speak of both colliding entities as causal powers. But what exactly we are designating by the term "entity" is not so clear. Evidently they are vibratory "entities" of some kind, and we have been willing enough in this meditation to consider them, and, provisionally, even atoms and molecules, as successions of act-temporal entities. But if they are more appropriately considered successions of entities, then we must suppose that the causal power of the periodic components is somehow summated in the succession. Probably, though, this problem need not detain us, since it is one that turns up in the case of any complex entity, though in a slightly different form. Thus if one attributes causal power to a cell, one must nonetheless remember that its infrastructure will have those same vibratory "entities" as its base: in that sense the causal power of the cell would in part be a summation of the distinct powers of that succession of "entities." A more general statement of this point is that causal powers enter into $C \rightarrow E$ relations in ways that on first glance seem to approximate the spatiomechanical ideal, but on closer inspection display characteristics that remind us of their act-temporal basis.

It need hardly be said that the causal power illustrated by our simple examples exhibits a temporal order of the sort expected. The cause precedes the effect, and, to just the extent that we consider only the aspect of causal power, the temporal order need not have act-temporality attributed to it. The cause, furthermore, is sufficient for the effect and in that sense explains it; explains it, however, only if we take for granted the conditions that permit the causal power to make itself felt. These conditions will partly be expressed in terms of the laws that reign within the context in which the causal power is felt, as for instance the laws of Newton are conditions of my throwing the ball. If the causal power produces an effect within the infrastructure of a superordinate ontic power, as for instance, in the impact of two macromolecules within a cell, then the ontic power of the superordinate will form part of those conditions. The reader will remember that I spoke of the unifying power "relation" of the superordinate to its infrastructure as a "law-in-becoming." The conditions that reign in a given context may also be described, though not exhaustively, in terms of all the other $C \rightarrow E$ relations between causal powers that may be found in the region of the one we are considering. But if the context in question is the infrastructure of an act-temporal unity, such an analysis in terms of a summation of $C \rightarrow E$ relations would simply mask the fact that they belonged to a total act-temporal pattern.

There are difficulties enough, but it would appear that with ingenuity and industry a persuasive account of causal power can be constructed on the basis of the idea of ontic power. A developed account of that sort would give us a clearer understanding of our right to use the working view of $C \rightarrow E$ analysis as well as of the limits within which it can profitably be used. This would be an achievement of some importance, since analysis of this kind is essential not only to our everyday activities but also to science, insofar as science is tied, as it surely is at some crucial points, to the world of common sense.

As to the official view, it can probably be shown to be an abstraction from the working one, an abstraction that, in the interests of certain goals, dispenses with the idea of power; deals exclusively in terms of events or states in the highly abstract sense discussed in chapter 4; concerns itself with relations between events in that sense, rather than between entities or between states or events defined in terms of entities; and may even, in the interest of a comprehensive metric, dispense altogether with the idea of becoming. It would, for all its abstractness, still be an abstraction from the idea of causal power, and could therefore furnish no valid basis for a criticism of that idea. It is no reflection on the legitimacy of the working view of the $C \rightarrow E$ relation that we can not arrive at it by a logical process that takes the official view to be more fundamental.

If we derive the $C \rightarrow E$ relation, which in both its versions seems so central to science, from the idea of ontic power, we shall be in a position to reinterpret many of the findings of science in terms of the paradigm of agent and action, surely a more acceptable alternative than interpreting ourselves in terms of a paradigm which, as Socrates saw so long ago, does our agency much violence. I do not think by this device we shall escape from the ancient antinomy of freedom and necessity. The burden of habit, circumstance, environment, of the body itself, is no less when we interpret it in terms of the "relation" between the agent and his infrastructure than when we interpret it in terms of a more reductionist philosophy of science. But it is a different kind of burden, one rather of tragedy than of mechanism. It is tragic, for instance, that our attempts at self-recognition are subject to the infrastructures these attempts are deployed in, which impose limitations no less exigent for not being completely mechanical. Self-knowledge at best flickers intermittently, hindered by the very individuality it is directed upon. It is no less tragic when successful, for when a recognition of what we are possesses the rhythm of the neural volley, uses the complexity of an infrastructure to transcend the particularity of it in the rare way we call truth, that very recognition makes us feel imprisoned by that particularity and not entirely native to it. Regarded in terms of act and infrastructure, the seeing of any truth, however trivial, is always "innate," yet always colored by the infrastructure within which it plays. In the kind of truth called self-recognition, though, what is thus "innate" confronts itself as estranged in the very infrastructure in which it realizes itself. It is the universal caught in the particular; or, in the technical language invoked earlier, we may say that the recognition comes as an expression of "inherent and essential aspects of what things are" — the source of any individual freedom worth troubling about, and yet the expression of a necessity that is anything but private to the particular entity in whom it arises. So with any act of which such insight might be an aspect. Though shaped in the coming-to-be of Socrates or of any unsung prisoner of our own times who stood fast in less dignified circumstances, it is colored by those same ambiguities of "innateness." Socrates, no less perplexed by them than we are, could at least be clear, as he spoke of immortality, reincarnation, and all those related matters that ramify in so many logical tangles, that his action concerned more than his own particularity. But insight, art, and action rising thus to the level of moral gesture are marked by a freedom difficult to distinguish from inevitability. In that sense the necessities that have been looked for with the help of $C \to E$ analysis under the laws of nature reappear, though no doubt now transformed, in the beings upon whose ontic power we seek to ground causal analysis.

351

Notes

Index

Notes

Chapter 1
The Prisoner's Views on Action and Causality

1. *Phaedo,* 98–99, trans. F. J. Church (New York: Liberal Arts Press, 1951), pp. 51–52.

2. A. M. Turing, "Computing Machinery and Intelligence," *Mind* 59, no. 236 (1950): 433–60. Reprinted in *Minds and Machines,* edited by Alan Ross Anderson (Englewood Cliffs, N. J.: Prentice-Hall, 1964), pp. 4–30.

3. J. T. Culbertson, *The Minds of Robots* (Urbana: University of Illinois Press, 1963).

4. See especially Noam Chomsky, "A Review of B. F. Skinner's *Verbal Behavior,*" *Language* 35, no. 1 (1959): 26–28.

5. B. F. Skinner, *Beyond Freedom and Dignity* (New York: Alfred A. Knopf, 1971).

6. For a representative group of essays in action theory see Alan R. White, ed., *The Philosophy of Action* (London: Oxford University Press, 1968).

7. For a friendly account, see Richard Rorty's introduction to *The Linguistic Turn,* edited by Richard Rorty (Chicago: University of Chicago Press, 1967). For a less friendly one, see my "To Live at Ease Ever After," *Sewanee Review* 66, no. 2 (1958): 229–51.

8. Jerome A. Shaffer, "Recent Work on the Mind-Body Problem," *American Philosophical Quarterly* 2, no. 2 (1965): 98.

9. E. H. Madden, "A Third View of Causality," *Review of Metaphysics* 23, no. 1 (1969): 67–84.

10. Bertrand Russell, "On the Notion of Cause," *Proceedings of the Aristotelian Society,* 1912–13, pp. 1–26. Reprinted in Bertrand Russell, *Mysticism and Logic* (London: Longmans, Green and Co., 1918), pp. 180–208.

11. David Bohm, *Causality and Chance in Modern Physics* (London: Routledge and Kegan Paul, 1957), pp. 1–2.

12. For a clear and detailed statement of the conditions that must be met if one science is to be reduced to another, see Ernest Nagel, *The Structure of Science* (New York: Harcourt, Brace & World, 1961). Chapter 11, "The Reduction of Theories," and chapter 12, "Mechanistic Explanation and Organismic Biology," are especially important.

13. I first heard of these matters at the Conference on the Hydrogen Bond in Biological Systems, held by the Department of Chemistry, Bowdoin College, January 11–12, 1971. I am grateful to my colleague Professor Dana W. Mayo, chairman of that department, for his helpful explanations and for supplying me with the following list

of relevant articles. He is not, of course, responsible for the interpretation I give this matter in the example in the text.

Bertil Jacobson, "On the Interpretation of Dielectric Constants of Aqueous Macromolecular Solutions. Hydration of Macromolecules," *J. Am. Chem. Soc.* 77, no. 11 (1955): 2919–26.

Michael Falk, Karl A. Hartman, Jr., and R. C. Lord, "Hydration of Deoxyribonucleic Acid. I. A Gravemetric Study," *J. Am. Chem. Soc.* 84, no. 20 (1962): 3843–46.

Michael Falk, Karl A. Hartman, Jr., and R. C. Lord, "Hydration of Deoxyribonucleic Acid. II. An Infrared Study," *J. Am. Chem. Soc.* 85, no. 4 (1963): 387–91.

Michael Falk, Karl A. Hartman, Jr., and R. C. Lord, "Hydration of Deoxyribonucleic Acid. III. A Spectroscopic Study of the Effect of Hydration on the Structure of Deoxyribonucleic Acid," *J. Am. Chem. Soc.* 85, no. 4 (1963): 391–94.

R. C. Lord, and G. J. Thomas, Jr., "Raman Spectral Studies of Nucleic Acids and Related Molecules. I. Ribonucleic Acid Derivatives," *Spectrochim. Acta* 23A, no. 9 (1967): 2551–91.

R. C. Lord, and G. J. Thomas, Jr., "Raman Studies of Nucleic Acids. II. Aqueous Purine and Pyrimidine Mixtures," *Biochem. Biophys. Acta* 142, no. 1 (1967): 1–11.

The theory was first proposed in the first article and modified, with respect to the extensivenss of the "iceberg" effect, in the following ones.

Chapter 2
Action, Entities, and the Laws of Nature

1. An example of a weak deterministic interpretation of a statistical microevent determinism is the one worked out by Arturo Rosenblueth and Norbert Wiener in 1950, and summarized in Rosenblueth's *Mind and Brain: A Philosophy of Science* (Cambridge: M.I.T. Press, 1970), pp. 74–77. It strikes me, however, that the notion "degrees of causation," which is central to that interpretation, is not really compatible with the notion of a complete determinism, whether microevent or macroevent. Rosenblueth, however, calls his philosophy of science a deterministic one. He does not, surprisingly, exploit the principle of "degrees of causation" in the interest of demonstrating the efficacy of consciousness. His views are dealt with in more detail in chapter 6.

2. Especially Maine de Biran, Boutroux, Bergson, and Whitehead. The clearest expression of this point of view is Whitehead's claim that the laws of nature change from cosmic epoch to cosmic epoch. See Alfred North Whitehead, *Process and Reality* (New York: Macmillan Co., 1929), as indexed under "cosmic epoch."

3. See Adolf Grünbaum, "The Status of Temporal Becoming," in *The Philosophy of Time,* edited by Richard M. Gale (New York: Doubleday & Co., 1967), pp. 322–53.

4. Essays by some of the leading figures in the anti-reductionist movement will be found in two recent collections: Arthur Koestler and J. R. Smythies, eds., *Beyond Reductionism: New Perspectives in the Life Sciences* (London: Hutchinson & Co., 1969); Marjorie Grene, ed., *The Anatomy of Knowledge* (London: Routledge & Kegan Paul, 1969).

5. Arthur O. Lovejoy, *The Great Chain of Being* (Cambridge, Mass.: Harvard University Press, 1936).

6. Paul A. Weiss, "The Living System: Determinism Stratified," in *Beyond Reductionism,* edited by Arthur Koestler and J. R. Smythies, pp. 3–55. See especially pp. 28–40.

7. Roger W. Sperry, "A Modified Concept of Consciousness," *Psychological Review* 76, no. 6 (1969): 532–36.

8. Weiss, "The Living System," pp. 28–32.

9. Ibid., p. 10 *n.*

10. Erwin Schrödinger, *What Is Life? The Physical Aspect of of the Living Cell* (Cambridge: At the University Press, 1944); idem, *Science and Humanism: Physics in Our Time* (Cambridge: At the University Press, 1951). Note especially the note of mysticism towards the end of the former.

11. Weiss, "The Living System," p. 22.

Chapter 3
The Originative Acts of the Prisoner

1. Some support to this view is given by the work of Sperry, discussed briefly in chapter 2. We return to Sperry's work in chapter 8, and there other supporting evidence is given.

2. For instance, Dean E. Wooldridge, *The Machinery of the Brain* (New York: McGraw-Hill Book Co., 1963). See the discussion of that book in chapter 6.

3. Arthur Koestler cites some remarkable evidence, based on work by Baerends and Hingston, of improvisation by wasps confronted with problems outside their normal routines. *The Ghost in the Machine* (New York: Macmillan Co., 1968), p. 106.

4. Edward Pols, *The Recognition of Reason* (Carbondale: Southern Illinois University Press, 1963).

5. See for instance, the articles in John O'Connor, ed., *Modern Materialism: Readings on Mind-Body Identity* (New York: Harcourt, Brace & World, 1969). See also D. M. Armstrong, *A Materialist Theory of the Mind* (London: Routledge & Kegan Paul, 1968).

6. Arthur C. Danto, "Basic Actions," *American Philosophical Quarterly* 2, no. 2 (1965): 141–48.

Chapter 4
The Originative Act and Its Infrastructure

1. For the spirit of this view of time see two essays by Adolf Grünbaum, "The Status of Temporal Becoming" and "Modern Science and Zeno's Paradoxes of Motion," both in *The Philosophy of Time*, edited by Richard M. Gale.

2. "*Quid est ergo tempus? Si nemo ex me quaerat, scio; si quaerenti explicare velim, nescio. . . .*" *Confessions*, bk. 11, ch. 14.

3. Grünbaum, "Modern Science and Zeno's Paradoxes of Motion," p. 438.

4. Because of the obvious resemblances to some features of Whitehead's epochal theory, it may be well to emphasize the differences between act-temporality and epochal time. (*a*) The chief difference is that on the present view the quantum of action is not invariable and not restricted, as it is with Whitehead, to the smallest possible unit. It should be remembered, although it is often forgotten by those who are drawn to Whitehead's doctrine because of the hope it seems to offer for traditional humanistic

attitudes, that in his doctrine all identifiable actions, processes, and entities—and this includes entities as small as electrons—are "societies" or "routes" of minuscule events not in principle observable, and that the "self-creation" of these minute "actual entities" is the only possible locus of action. Each discrete moment of becoming, then, is extremely small. On the conception of time appropriate to the idea of originative action, each action of an entity and each entity considered as a source of many actions makes its discrete contribution to time. As these actions and these entities vary enormously in the time associated with their realizations, their discrete contributions to time vary enormously too. (*b*) For Whitehead the continuity of time is derivative from epochal acts of becoming—there is no "continuity of becoming" but only a "becoming of continuity." Towards the end of section 5 of this chapter I also derive the continuous aspect of time from a large number of discrete units. There is an important difference, however. Whitehead seems to be chiefly concerned to establish an epistemological basis for the time measured in physics—what I call linear time. As he interprets the continuity of time, however, it occasionally appears to be not only an ontological derivative but perhaps also an abstraction—something we encounter only when we measure and perhaps therefore partly a result of our measuring techniques. I wish to bring out, as the end of section 5 I hope makes clear, that the continuity of time, though ontologically derivative from discrete time-units, is no less concrete than the latter. (*c*) The units of act-temporality are not primarily "feeling" units, although they may involve feeling, but power units. On the present view, then, an entity does not simply "enjoy" a quantum of time, but rather enacts its time in the exercise of power. It thus contributes to a general temporal environment as well as to a general environment of power. (*d*) Whitehead uses the image of an epoch, or arrest, for his least quantum of temporality. Despite his assurance that actual entities undergo an internal adventure of becoming, the image is a static one, and its static character is reinforced by many passages in which he discusses the subjective aim of an actual entity in such a way as to suggest that there is something not quite authentic about the successiveness of the various phases of an actual entity. One is at least tempted to think of these "phases" as "all-at-once" and to suppose that the "duration" of an actual entity is reducible to a matter of logical relations. No doubt Whitehead would repudiate such a Leibnizian view of time, but it is not clear that he has completely avoided it. On the present view the enactment of time is by way of a quantum, but temporality is of the essence of that quantum, and "earlier" and "later" have a thoroughly nonderivative sense.

5. Though there are obvious differences, this point has resemblances to Polanyi's claim that higher-level laws set the boundary conditions upon which lower-level laws are effective. This view is discussed further in chapter 8, section 6.

Chapter 5
The Hierarchy of the Infrastructure

1. M. L. Colonnier, "Structural Design of the Neocortex," in *Brain and Conscious Experience,* edited by J. C. Eccles (New York: Springer-Verlag, 1966); J. C. Eccles, "Cerebral Synaptic Mechanisms," ibid.

2. See chapters 6, 7, and 8.

3. B. Libet, "Brain Stimulation and Conscious Experience," in *Brain and Conscious Experience,* edited by J. C. Eccles.

4. J. C. Eccles, "Conscious Experience and Memory," in *Brain and Conscious Experience,* edited by J. C. Eccles. See especially pp. 319–21.

5. C. S. Sherrington, *The Integrative Action of the Nervous System* (Cambridge: At the University Press, 1905, rev. 1947).

Chapter 6
The Mind of the Prisoner. Part One

1. Eccles, "Conscious Experience and Memory." The relevant papers by Hydén are cited in the bibliography at the end of Eccles's article.

2. Wooldridge, *The Machinery of the Brain,* p. 235.

3. John B. Watson, *Behaviorism,* rev. ed. (New York: W. W. Norton, 1952).

4. *Mind* 59, no. 236 (1950): 433–60. Reprinted in *Minds and Machines,* edited by Alan Ross Anderson, pp. 4–30.

5. *Mind* 62, no. 246 (1953): 230–40. Reprinted in *Minds and Machines,* edited by Alan Ross Anderson, pp. 31–42.

6. Sidney Hook, ed., *Dimensions of Mind* (New York: Macmillan Co., Collier Books, 1961), p. 132.

7. Culbertson, *The Minds of Robots.*

8. Ibid., pp. 76–78.   9. Ibid., p. 385.   10. Ibid., p. 78.

11. Ibid., pp. 385–86. See also p. 78.   12. Ibid., p. 78.

13. See O'Connor, *Modern Materialism;* and also see Armstrong, *A Materialist Theory of the Mind.*

14. D. M. MacKay, "Cerebral Organization and the Conscious Control of Action," in *Brain and Conscious Experience,* edited by J. C. Eccles. See p. 423.

15. Ibid., p. 435.   16. Ibid., p. 433.   17. Ibid.

18. Second edition (Cambridge: At the University Press, 1950). See also Eccles, "Conscious Experience and Memory," especially pp. 319–21.

19. Wooldridge, *The Machinery of the Brain,* p. vi.

20. Ibid., p. 219.   21. Ibid., p. 220.   22. Ibid.

23. Ibid., p. 229.   24. Ibid., pp. 235–36, 239–41.

25. J. R. Lucas, "Minds, Machines, and Gödel," in *Minds and Machines,* edited by Alan Ross Anderson, p. 44.

26. MacKay, "Cerebral Organization and the Conscious Control of Action."

27. Alburey Castell, *The Self in Philosophy* (New York: Macmillan Co., 1965).

Chapter 7
The Mind of the Prisoner. Part Two

1. *The Recognition of Reason.* See especially chapter 4.

2. M. Merleau-Ponty, *The Phenomenology of Perception,* trans. Colin Smith (London: Routledge & Kegan Paul; New York: Humanities Press, 1962).

3. Erwin W. Straus, *Primary World of Senses* (New York: Free Press, 1963); idem, *Phenomenological Psychology* (New York: Basic Books, 1966); idem, *Phenomenology: Pure and Applied* (Pittsburgh: Duquesne University Press, 1964).

4. Edmund Husserl, *The Crisis of European Sciences and Transcendental Phenomenology: An Introduction to Phenomenological Philosophy,* trans. D. Carr (Evanston, Ill.: Northwestern University Press, 1970).

5. Edmund Husserl, *Cartesian Meditations: An Introduction to Phenomenology,* trans. Dorion Cairns (The Hague: Martinus Nijhoff, 1960).

6. " 'Phenomenology' Edmund Husserl's Article for the *Encyclopedia Britannica* (1927): New Complete Translation by Richard E. Palmer," *Journal of the British Society for Phenomenology* 2 (May 1971): 77–90.

7. Ibid., p. 86.   8. Ibid.

9. Jean-Paul Sartre, *Being and Nothingness,* trans. H. Barnes (New York: Philosophical Library, 1956).

10. Eugene Wigner, "Two Kinds of Reality," *Symmetries and Reflections* (Bloomington: Indiana University Press, 1967).

11. Eugene Wigner, "Epistemology of Quantum Mechanics: Its Appraisal and Demands," in *The Anatomy of Knowledge,* edited by Marjorie Grene.

12. Rosenblueth, *Mind and Brain.*

13. Ibid., pp. 51–52.   14. Ibid., p. 64.   15. Ibid., p. 52.

16. Ibid., p. 26.   17. Ibid., pp. 10, 114.   18. Ibid., pp. 114–15.

19. Ibid., pp. 69, 85.   20. Ibid., pp. 114, 70.

21. C. S. Sherrington, Introduction to *The Physical Basis of Mind,* edited by P. Laslett (Oxford: Basil Blackwell, 1950), p. 3.

22. Noam Chomsky, *Cartesian Linguistics: A Chapter in the History of Rationalist Thought* (New York: Harper & Row, Publishers, 1966).

23. Noam Chomsky, *Language and Mind* (Harcourt, Brace & World, 1968). See especially pp. 72–73, 76, 78, 80, 83–84.

24. Ibid., pp. 72–73.

25. I trust it is clear that my use of Chomsky's notion of deep structure as an example does not mean that I am prepared to accept it as an account of the nature of human language.

Chapter 8
Mind, Action, and Infrastructure

1. Roger W. Sperry, "Brain Bisection and Mechanisms of Consciousness," in *Brain and Conscious Experience,* edited by J. C. Eccles. Some of Sperry's earlier essays are listed at the end of the article.

2. Sperry, "A Modified Concept of Consciousness."

3. Arthur Koestler, "The Concept of the Holon," in *Beyond Reductionism,* edited by Arthur Koestler and J. R. Smythies.

4. A. S. Eddington, *The Nature of the Physical World* (New York: Macmillan Co., 1928). See especially pp. 310–15.

5. Schrödinger, *Science and Humanism.* See especially pp. 58–64.

6. Note, for instance, this remark made by A. O. Gomes during an informal discussion among a group of leading neurophysiologists many of whom are prepared to consider the possibility that an indeterminacy at the level of particular microevents plays a role in the efficacy of what they call mind, will, or consciousness. The discussion took

place after the reading of a paper by Gomes. "There are so many different ways of maintaining a statistical regularity, because the selection to be effected by the will is a selection on a field where no physical factor could achieve it, that is, where no physical factors can be determinatingly at work—although it is a physical field. It is not only that the will would not require physical energy to achieve its presumable influence on the microphysical level of the nervous system; physical energy could not effect any influence of that kind—this is what physics itself assures us" (immediately following A. O. Gomes, "The Brain-Consciousness Problem in Contemporary Scientific Research," in *Brain and Conscious Experience,* edited by J. C. Eccles, p. 466).

7. J. C. Eccles, *The Neurophysiological Basis of Mind: The Principles of Neurophysiology* (Oxford: Clarendon Press, 1953); cited in his "Conscious Experience and Memory," see especially pp. 326–27; see also "Final Discussion," in *Brain and Conscious Experience,* edited idem, pp. 566–74, especially p. 567.

8. *Brain and Conscious Experience,* edited by J. C. Eccles, p. 467, in a discussion following A. O. Gomes, "The Brain-Consciousness Problem."

9. A. O. Gomes, "The Brain-Consciousness Problem," especially pp. 449–55.

10. See both their essays in *Brain and Conscious Experience,* edited by J. C. Eccles, as well as their remarks in several discussion sections.

11. Ibid., p. 549.   12. Ibid., p. 568.   13. Ibid., p. 572.

14. Michael Polanyi has discussed this point about boundary conditions on many occasions. One of his clearest statements of it is in his "Life Transcending Physics and Chemistry," *Chemical and Engineering News* 45 (August 21, 1967): 55–66.

Chapter 9
From Act to Agent

1. The use of the word "substance" to cope with matters of the kind discussed here is unfortunate. Behind the word lies the Greek word "*ousia,*" whose overtones are certainly blurred when we translate it as "substance." It is a feminine participial form of the verb "to be," and it can be more happily rendered, especially when we are talking about individuals, as "a being" or "an entity." In Greek some inflectional form of this word turns up in many circumstances in which the English "real," "being," or "entity" is called for: it lies behind such Platonic expressions as "really real," "coming into being," and even the word "real" in "real cause." When Aristotle uses the word in his search for what really deserves to be called *ousia,* he is in fact looking for a very fundamental kind of being or entity. The use of the word "substance" in this search causes a good deal of trouble, since its literal sense is "that which stands under." That literal sense carries over into the Cartesian notions of thinking substance and material (extended) substance. The idea of a fundamental being, or entity, is thus distorted by translation into the idea of an underlying, permanent, homogeneous stuff: we think of consciousness as something at once diversified by and hidden by particular thoughts, feelings, and volitions; and of material substance as something at once diversified by and hidden by the sensory qualities in terms of which we apprehend it.

Some of this distortion we owe to terminological wrangles about the Trinity in early Christianity. The mature Trinitarian doctrine is that God is one divine *ousia* in three divine *hypostases,* and in Latin this becomes one divine *substantia* in three divine *personae.*

Yet *substantia,* while a poor translation of *ousia,* is a good one for *hypostasis.* Aristotle himself furnishes some of the overtones that make for this odd result. He uses, for instance, *hypokeimenon* (that which *lies* under), which is a near equivalent of *substantia,* sometimes to refer to matter as that which persists through changes and sometimes to refer to an individual entity—a man, for instance—as something permanent underlying the changes it undergoes. Our Latin-based "subject" is the equivalent of "*hypokeimenon,*" and it often turns up in the literature in place of "substance." Whatever else it means, the word "substance" still carries this force of permanence in change. But, then, so does the word "entity," which surely produces less confusion.

2. I have in mind the problems of predestination in Leibniz, who of course uses the term *haecceitas* about his monads.

3. See my *Whitehead's Metaphysics: A Critical Examination of Process and Reality* (Carbondale: Southern Illinois University Press, 1967).

4. In an earlier discussion of these matters I spoke of the contribution of the lower levels to the higher levels simultaneous with it as "causal power." This produced a mistaken emphasis: the contribution of the lower levels surely also deserves to be called ontic. This modification allows me to save the term "causal power" for another use, which is introduced a few lines further on. See my *The Recognition of Reason.*

5. C. H. Waddington, "The Theory of Evolution Today," in *Beyond Reductionism,* edited by Arthur Koestler and J. R. Smythies.

Index

Aberrations: physical, 204
Action theory: and ordinary language, 12–16; Socratic, 37
Action-unit, 174
Activity: consciousness as, 180
Act-ontology, 100, 101
Act-source: common, 319; mentioned, 319, 320
Act-temporality: and the infrastructure of originative acts, 118–19, 135–36, 204, 292; and continuous aspect of time, 120–21; and mechanism, 150–51, 336, 337, 338, 339; and central nervous system, 152–53, 157, 276, 298; and indeterminacy, 152, 291, 303; and act of attention, 154–57; and meaning of structurally-based routines, 155–57; and computers, 157; and consciousness, 157, 284; and C → E causality, 341; and coding, 342, 343, 344; and ontic power, 345; and causal power, 348, 349; mentioned, 102, 104, 107, 111–17, 114, 153, 174–75, 314, 328, 330, 334
Act-temporal units: in infrastructure, 143, 159; in brain, 161–68
Actual entities: Whitehead's doctrine of, 118, 134, 328, 358
Affect: realm of, 183
Agent: "real causality" of, 4, 219; and materialism, 8; ontological status of, 73, 94, 101; and analysis, 91, 93; category of, 94; and C → E analysis, 110; and synthesizing intelligence, 193; and originative acts, 308–51
Agent-ontology, 101
Aitia, 2, 72
Analysis: linguistic, 11–16, 93; and originative acts, 91, 92, 93, 102; of agent, 92, 93; and multiplicity, 92; elec-tronic versus mathematical, 209; La-placean, 252; reductive, 252
—causal (C → E): Humean, or official version of, 109; and mathematical version of temporal continuum, 116; and act-temporal simultaneity, 130; and continuous aspect of time, 131; of infra-structure, 205; and ontic power, 344; and necessity, 351
Analytical Engine: Babbage's, 188
Anamnesis: Plato's doctrine of, 265
Anaxagoras, 1, 3, 6, 7
Animal spirits: Descartes' doctrine of, 265
Anisotropic character of time, 113
Anomalies: physical, 307
Antinomy: Kantian, 36, 350
Anti-reductionism: and hydrogen bond-ing of water and DNA, 24–26; in science, 37, 38; and determinism in cen-tral nervous system, 285. See also Hierar-chic science
Apology (Plato), 319
Aristotle: on hierarchy (scale of nature), 38; on form and matter, 123; on sub-stance, 361, 362
Armstrong, D. M., 359
Asclepius, 165
Atomism (Democritus): and self-tran-scendence of mind, 246
Attention, 154–57
Augustine, St.: on time, 111, 357n2; on innateness, 264
Awareness: and originative action, 160; its efficacity, 215–16; and symbols, 229; and understanding, 253, 326; eviden-tial, 323; mentioned, 182, 239

Babbage, Charles: his Analytical Engine, 188

Becoming: and static interpretation of temporality, 33, 34; and laws of nature, 34; and mathematical version of temporal continuum, 115; and being, 318; and act-temporality, 330; mentioned, 350, 351, 358

Behaviorism, 7, 187, 190–91, 192, 193, 237, 257, 359

Being: and laws of nature, 34; Parmenides on, 121; -for-itself, 237; -in-itself, 237; and acts, 315; and agent, 315, 318, category of, and act, 317; and becoming, 318; absolute, 319; and particularity, 327; mentioned, 321, 361n1

Being and Nothingness (Sartre), 360

Bergson, Henri, 111, 356

Berkeley, George: metaphysical presuppositions of, 216, 218; on subjectivity, 244, 246; on materialism, 246; his idealism, 248–49

Beyond Freedom and Dignity (Skinner), 355

Body: as part of infrastructure of an originative act, 104; role of, in subjectivity, 250

Body-mind problem. *See* Mind-body problem

Bohm, David, 21, 313, 355

Boundary conditions: and power, 164; and laws of nature, 170; and C → E causality, 307; and originative act, 307; Polanyi on, 307, 361

Boutroux, E. E. M., 356

Bowdoin College: Conference on the Hydrogen Bond in Biological Systems, 355–56

Bracketing: phenomenological, 234

Brain: act-temporality in, 161–68, 172, 276; and computer model, 185–220. *See also* Central nervous system; Circuits, neural; Cortex, cerebral; Neocortex

Bruner, Jerome G., 38

Carrier wave, 301

Cartesian. *See* Descartes, René

Cartesian Linguistics (Chomsky), 360

Cartesian Meditations (Husserl), 236, 360

Castell, Alburey, 359

Causal chains, 247–48

Causality: pre-philosophic meaning of *aitia* in Greek, 2, 72; reasons contrasted with, 3–4, 35, 36, 52–53, 70, 73; conditioning, 5; and action theory, 12, 13; and laws of nature, 15–23; and interpretation of time as static, 33; final, 114, 115; formal, 114, 115; and consciousness, 186–87, 214; material, 248; and metaphysics, 347

—C → E: as interpretation of "causes without which the (real) cause cannot be the cause," 9, 10, 13, 70–72, 74, 238; and power and necessity, 17, 18; official version of, 17–19, 116, 170, 350; and laws of nature, 18, 21–22, 35, 41, 50, 60, 108; working version of, 19–20, 79, 169, 187, 350; and prediction, 20, 33, 204, 205, 285–86, 305, 307; in infrastructure of originative acts, 35, 69, 71, 105, 139, 143, 168–72, 184; and biological parameters, 51; and levels of hierarchic order, 61, 62–63; and "real (true) causality" of originative acts, 70–71, 199, 308; derivative ontological status of, 71, 91, 100, 107, 347–51; and power of acts, 73, 76, 85, 86; and mechanism, 79, 80, 335, 336, 340; and act-dynamism, 89; and temporality of events, 109–10; and final and formal causality, 114, 115; and act-temporality, 115, 168–72, 174, 302, 303, 341; and mathematical version of temporal continuum, 116; and spatio-temporal "reach" of originative acts, 126, 127, 129–30; and coded structures, 147–49; in brain, 152–53, 211; and routines or sub-programs, 154–56; and consciousness, 178, 207, 231, 232, 272; in computers, 187, 209; and Descartes' interactionism, 189–90; and mind-body problem, 189–90, 214, 278, 280–81, 284; and Descartes' dualism, 214; Rosenblueth on, 247–48; and indeterminacy, 287–88, 294; and time-bound patterns, 296, 297, 307; and "relation" of agent and acts, 316; and recognition of originative acts, 324; and fundamental entities, 330; and causal power, 333, 347, 348, 349; and role of DNA in inheritance, 337; and ontic power, 344, 350; and evolution, 346; mentioned, 16–21

—"real" (or "true"): Socrates' views on, 3–4, 176; and "causes without which the (real) cause cannot be the cause," 3–5, 71–72; and science, 8; and the infrastructure of originative acts, 35, 132, 306; and originative acts, 37, 105; and definition of irreducibility, 41; and hierarchic science, 51, 52, 59–67; and reasons, 52–53; and levels of hierarchic order, 64–65; and C → E causality, 85, 86, 130; and temporality of events, 110; and subjectivity, 160; and mind, 160, 184, 271; and mechanism, 168; and agency, 184, 219; and consciousness, 214, 220; and spatiomechanisms, 336; mentioned, 3–4, 36, 70–71, 94, 101, 238, 361

Causality and Chance in Modern Physics (Bohm), 355

Causal power: and C → E causality, 347, 348, 349, 350; and ontic power, 347, 348, 362

Cell: as member of a hierarchic level, 44; as dynamic unit, 82, 83; level of, its interpretation in hierarchic science, 57, 58, 60; as nested dynamism, 94

Central nervous system: structure versus act-temporality in, 119; indeterministic features of, 291. *See also* Brain; Circuits, neural; Cortex, cerebral; Neocortex

Central state materialism, 197

Cerebellum, 165

Certainty: Descartes on, 233–34, 238; mentioned, 243

Chance: and neo-Darwinian theory of evolution, 39; and indeterminacy principle, 287

Choice, 109

Chomsky, Noam: and innateness, 264, 267, 270; mentioned, 335, 360

Circuits, neural: and act-temporality, 118, 152–53; as coded structures, 147; spatiotemporal patterns in, 167, 296; determinacy and indeterminacy in, 293–94

Circularity, 321, 322

Coding: in meaningful control structures, 145–49; genetic, 147; in neural processes, 247, 263; mutual, in physical structures, 339, 342; strategy of, 342–43; as an achievement of act-temporality, 344; and ontic power, 346

Colonnier, M. L., 358

Common power, 327

Common sense: and ordinary language, 13–16; and acts, 91, 93; and phenomenology, 235; and science, 350

Commonsense world, 244

Computers: and thought, 7, 9, 185–220 passim; question of consciousness in, 10, 188–220; mechanical programs and

sub-programs in, 88, 151; indeterministic, 152; and act-temporality, 156; and symbolic logic, 184; as model for brain, 185–220; C → E causality within, 187; digital (discrete state) type, 192, 205–6; electronic versus mathematical analysis of, 209; logical versus machine state of, 209; logical gates in, 271

Concepts: and consciousness, 182; and generality, 326

Conditioning ontic power, 340, 344, 346, 347

Confessions (St. Augustine), 357

Consciousness: and act-temporality, 157; and originative acts, 160–61; Descartes on certainties of, 177–78; as a medium, 181, 182; and conceptual understanding, 182; and power, 182; whether caused, 186–87, 198, 207; whether present in machines, 187–206; epiphenomenalistic, 196; whether efficacious, 197, 198, 199, 203; and aberration in physical principles, 204; mentioned, 179–84

Constitutive: consciousness as, 236; mind as, 266; activity of mind, 277

Constructibility, rational: of acts and entities, 102

Continuum: temporal, 33, 110, 115–16

Control structures: meaningful, 157

Corpus callosum: Sperry's work on, 279

Correlation of consciousness and physical events, 257–58

Cortex, cerebral: as infrastructure component, 74; structure versus act-temporality in, 119; and indeterminism, 152, 285–96 passim; and quality of subjectivity, 165; visual, 247; regional mappings in, 266

Cosmic epochs, 356n2

Creativity: Whitehead on, 329

Crisis of European Sciences and Transcendental Phenomenology (Husserl), 360

Criteria: rational and empirical, 229, 254

Crito (Plato's *Phaedo*), 103, 122, 150, 159, 161, 165, 170, 173, 302, 306, 331

Culbertson, J. T.: his views on consciousness in computers and other robots, 10, 195–202; on temporal integration (time-bound patterns) in central nervous system, 163, 296; on causal transmission in machines and brains, 199–202; physicalism of, 207; on efficacity of consciousness, 213, 279; mentioned, 205, 206, 355, 359

Danto, Arthur, 357
Decoding of central neuronal events (Rosenblueth), 247–48. *See also* Coding
Dedekind partition, 115
Deep structure, 360
Denseness of mathematical version of temporal continuum, 115
Descartes, René: on thinking substance (thinking being), 160, 179, 188, 189, 191, 233–34; and consciousness (subjectivity, mentality), 177–78, 232, 233, 246; dualism of, 184, 233; interactionism of, 189–90, 191, 204, 205, 288; on extended substance, 189, 191, 235; and behaviorism, 191; metaphysical presuppositions of, 216, 218; and idealism, 223, 237, 238; philosophical starting point of, 242, 243, 248; and philosophical meditation, 251; on innateness, 264, 265, 269, 270; on animal spirits, 288
Determination: and hierarchic levels, 44–48; by mind, will, or consciousness, 289
Determinism: Laplacean, 19, 31, 32, 204, 205; and laws of nature, 30, 36; of microevents, strong interpretation of, 31; neo-Laplacean, 31, 32; of microevents, weak interpretation of, 31, 356n*1;* classical, 34; statistical, 34, 288, 289, 306, 356n*1;* and Kant's views on free causality of will, 59; and science, 170, 295; and central nervous system, 199, 285–86; of macroevents, 288, 293, 356n*1;* and molecular movements, 292
DNA: its hydrogen bonds with water, 24, 25, 41, 44, 355–56; and hierarchy, 61, 75; as structural unit, 85, 128, 145; as code-bearing structure, 145–48; 343–45; and neo-Darwinian theory of evolution, 334; and C → E causality, 337, 338, 339. *See also* Coding
Double-aspect theory of mind-body relation, 198, 248. *See also* Mind-body problem
Dualism, 184, 197, 205, 214, 233, 248, 279. *See also* Interactionism; Mind-body problem
Durée: Bergsonian, 111
Dynamic units, 82, 83, 84, 86. *See also* Nested dynamisms

Eccles, J. C.: on hierarchy, 38; on indeterminacy principle and mind, 289–90; on efficacity of mind, 294, 295; mentioned, 300, 303, 359, 361
Eddington, A. S., 286, 360
Efficacity of mind or consciousness, 197, 198, 203, 207, 211–13, 215–16, 248, 279, 281, 282, 294, 295, 356n*1*
Ego: and consciousness, 180; transcendental, 236
Einstein, Albert, 31, 34
Electroencephalograph, 161
Electron, 58, 153
Emergence: and consciousness, 282
Emotion: and older regions of brain, 299–300
Empirical, 229, 253, 254
Encoding. *See* Coding
Entity: and consciousness, 278; continuity of, 310; agent as, 310, 318; Socrates' status as, 312, 314; as act "source," 314; -source, 320; fundamental, 327–35, 336, 337, 348, 349; enduring, 328; actual, Whitehead's doctrine of, 328; and substance, 362
Epiphenomenalism, 187, 188, 191, 193, 195, 196, 203, 206, 207, 213, 279
Epistemology, 242, 257
Epochal theory of time: Whitehead's, 111, 118–19, 357–58
Essence, 229, 234
Events: and causes, 13; temporality of, 107–10, 108, 113, 138; neural, 167, 246, 247, 281, 282; mental, 197, 246, 247, 278, 325; physical, 278
Evolution: theory of, 7, 39, 334–35, 345–46, 362
Existentialism, 237
Experience, 230, 239, 322–23
Explanation: based on acts, 11, 12, 13, 27, 54–55; scientific, 14, 102; neurophysiological, 211–14

Falk, Michael, 356
Feeling: Whitehead's doctrine of, 358
Formal logical system, 209
Form of the Good: Plato's doctrine of the, 5, 176, 299, 320
Forms: Platonic, 5, 70, 71, 176, 233, 234, 245, 265, 299, 320, 326, 331, 335
Freedom and necessity, 36, 59, 350, 351
Freud, Sigmund, 179

Fundamental entities, 327–35, 336, 337, 348, 349

Generality: and mind, 208; and power, 327; and particularity, 331, 332. *See also* Common power; Universality; Universals

Ghost in the Machine, The (Koestler), 357

Gomes, A. O.: on indeterminacy principle and mind, 290–91, 303, 360–61; on efficacity of mind, 294, 295

Governing (supervening) ontic power, 344, 346, 347

Grammar: generative, 270

Great Chain of Being, The (Lovejoy), 356

Grünbaum, Adolf, 115, 356, 357

Haecceitas, 319, 362

Harmony: preestablished, 265, 329

Hartman, Karl A. Jr., 356

Hegel, G. W. F., 237

Heidegger, Martin, 111, 237

Heisenberg, Werner, 304, 305

Hierarchic science, 39–68

Holism, 280, 281

Holism and Evolution (Smuts), 280

Hume, David: on causality, 17–20; on free will, 20, 86; and logical positivism, 244, 249; on the self, 309–10

Husserl, Edmund: metaphysical presuppositions of, 216; on the life-world, 226, 235; idealism of, 237, 238; and natural standpoint, 243; mentioned, 179, 360

Hydén, H., 186

Hydrogen bond, 24–26, 41, 44, 45, 128

Hydrogen Bond in Biological Systems, Conference on (Bowdoin College), 355–56

Hypokeimenon, 362

Hypostasis, 361–62

Hypothalamus, 165

Idealism, 232–39, 243–50, 266

Identity, asymmetrical: of originative acts and their sub-acts, 99; of originative acts and their infrastructures, 105, 106, 107, 123, 140, 163, 174, 184, 306, 310

Identity, mind-body: theory of, 94, 105, 173, 206–7, 210, 248, 355n5

Imitation game: Turing's, 192

Indeterminary principle, 32, 152, 285–92, 293, 294, 295, 360–61n6

Indetermination in hierarchic levels, 44–48

Information, 145–49, 301

Innateness: traditional doctrine of, 264; and acts (act-innateness), 264–68, 269, 271–73, 351; and structures (structure-innateness), 269–71

Integrative Action of the Nervous System, The (Sherrington), 201, 359

Intentionality, 160, 235–36

Interactionism: Descartes' doctrine of, 189–90, 204, 205, 280, 281; Culbertson on, 196, 197, 198

Intersubjectivity: transcendental, 236, 237

Isomorphism, 112, 247, 267

Jacobson, Bertil, 356

James, William: his view of time, 111, 118, 157; on consciousness, 180, 182; on transcendental subjectivity, 326

Joyce, James, 179

Jung, C. G., 179

Kant, Immanuel: on causality, 19–20, 36, 59, 79; on freedom, 36, 59: on transcendental nature of subjectivity, 236; on sensuous manifold, 324

Koestler, Arthur, 280, 356, 357

Lamarck, J. B. P. A. de: 346

Language: common, everyday, or ordinary, 11–16; of science, 14, 15; and codes, 147; and consciousness, 219–20; and experience, 323. *See also* Symbols

Language and Mind (Chomsky), 360

Laplace, Pierre Simon de: 19, 32, 34, 171, 199, 204, 205, 252, 292, 305, 306, 307

Laws of nature: and causality, 15–23, 28–34, 36, 39; and reductionism, 25, 35, 37, 76, 90; ontological status of, 29–34, 35, 60; hierarchic, 37, 39–68 passim, 75, 76, 90, 131, 285, 295, 296; and originative acts, 102; and boundary conditions, 164

Lebenswelt. See Life-world

Leibniz, G. W., 38, 42, 123, 264, 362

Levels: hierarchy of: in the infrastructure of originative acts, 133, 134, 135, 136, 140–75 passim; mentioned, 41, 44–48, 51, 261, 312, 316, 328

Libet, B., 358

Life-world: Husserl's doctrine of, 226, 235,

Linguistic Turn, The (Rorty), 355

Logic: of ordinary language, 15; symbolic, and computers, 184
Logical positivism, 56, 244, 249
Lord, R. C., 356
Lovejoy, Arthur O., 39, 356
Lucas, J. R., 209, 359

Machinery of the Brain, The (Wooldridge), 202–6, 359
Machines: whether consciousness present in, 187–206; analogies with brain, 202–6, 359
MacKay, D. M., 198, 207, 209, 279, 305, 307, 359
Macroevents: determinism versus indeterminism of, 32, 289, 290–91
Madden, S. H., 18, 355
Maine de Biran, M. F. P. G., 356
Manifold: sensuous, 93, 324; spatiotemporal, 103
Man on His Nature (Sherrington), 201
Materialism, 6–9, 19, 22, 30, 33, 50, 57, 71, 74, 94, 176–220, 246, 249
Materialist Theory of the Mind, A (Armstrong), 359
Meaning: in structures, 145–49, 155–57; in brains and machines, 208–9; of neural processes, 208, 212, 262–63. *See also* Coding
Mechanics: laws of, 16, 22, 204
Mechanism, 6, 88, 94, 137, 150–51, 153, 168, 187, 202, 206, 335, 343
Mediation within infrastructure, 134, 136, 143, 153, 167, 173, 276
Meditations (Descartes), 160, 251
Medium: consciousness as a, 181, 182, 223, 224
Memory, 186
Mental events. *See* Events
Merleau-Ponty, M., 234, 359
Metaorganizing system in brain, 198
Metaphysics, 8, 56, 70, 71, 347
Microdeterminacy, 47, 48
Microevent indeterminism, 31, 32, 288–92, 293, 294, 295
Mind and Brain: A Philosophy of Science (Rosenblueth), 356, 360
Mind-body problem, 186, 192, 196, 198, 206, 243–49, 278
Minds of Robots, The (Culbertson), 195, 355, 359
Mitochondrion, 61, 62, 76, 178
Monadology, 329, 331, 333, 335

Monads, 123, 362
Moore, G. E., 14
Mountcastle, V. B., 294, 296
Multiplicity: of acts, 69–100 passim, 315, 317; of infrastructure, 92, 93, 101–75 passim, 277, 298, 310; and unity, 92, 101–75 passim, 298, 308–51 passim; and recognition, 324, 325
Mutation, 345
Mysticism, 14

Nagel, Ernest, 355
Naturalism, 6
Natural standpoint, 234, 243
Nature of the Physical World, The (Eddington), 360
Necessity, 17, 18, 350, 351. *See also* Determinism
Neocortex, 261, 299
Neo-Darwinian. *See* Evolution
Nested dynamisms, 89, 94, 107, 123, 124, 298
Neural nets. *See* Circuits, neural
Neurons: as infrastructure component, 143, 144, 172; and act-temporality, 154–55, 159, 167; adjustable thresholds in, 186; electronic, 206; and indeterminacy principle, 288–92
Neurophysiological Basis of Mind, The (Eccles), 361
Neurophysiology, 261, 280–84
Newton, Isaac, 215–18, 349

Object, 240–42, 326
Objectivity, 183, 217, 218, 219, 223, 224, 225, 226, 227, 231, 249, 251, 253–55
Observations, 245–46
Ontic power, 282, 332, 337, 347, 348
Ontogeny, 228, 339, 347
Ontology: and hierarchic science, 65–68; and status of acts and agents, 94, 98–100, 107, 308–51
Organ, 57, 82, 83
Organelle, 22, 57, 58, 61
Ousia, 314, 331, 261n*1*

Palmer, Richard E., 236, 360
Parmenides, 121
Participant power, 331, 332, 334, 335, 339, 342, 344, 345
Participation, 298, 320, 334
Particularity, 288, 320, 326, 327, 331, 332, 351, 355
Partition: Dedekind, 115

Index

Patterns: spatiotemporal, 120, 205, 247, 283, 296–98, 301, 329, 346
Penfield, W., 294
Persona, 361
Phaedo (Plato), 5, 176, 179, 184, 265, 274, 325, 355
Phenomenological Psychology (Straus), 359
Phenomenology, 226, 242
Phenomenology: Pure and Applied (Straus), 359
Phenomenology of Perception, The (Merleau-Ponty), 359
Phylogeny, 158, 228, 339, 342, 347
Physical basis of consciousness, 256–63
Physicalism, 6, 187, 196, 198, 202, 206, 207, 210, 211, 213, 237
Picture theory, 257
Planck, Max, 31, 283
Plato: on the really real, 8, 176, 222–23, 233, 265; on innateness, 264, 265; mentioned, 1–3, 5, 70, 72, 96, 233, 265. *See also* Forms
Pluralism, 319, 321, 331
Point-instants, 115, 127
Polanyi, Michael, 38, 295, 307, 361
Positivism, logical, 56, 244, 249
Postulate, practical, of autonomy of mind, 232
Power: and causality (C → E), 17, 18, 73, 76, 85, 86, 90, 350; of originative acts, 36, 91, 102, 111–14, 125–33, 140, 150, 153, 163, 164, 172, 173–75, 310, 312, 313, 316, 329, 342; of agent, 90, 309–51 passim; and act-temporality, 111–14, 131, 140, 153, 163, 173, 342; as pervading spatiotemporal region, 125–33, 172, 174–75, 329; and the infrastructure, 136, 143, 173, 316; ontic, 282, 332, 337, 347, 348; common, or general, 327; and fundamental entities, 328, 331, 332; participant, 331, 334, 335, 339, 342, 344, 345; causal, 347, 348; mentioned, 5, 94, 143, 182, 187, 261, 289
Power-units, 106, 161–63, 283, 328, 338
Practical acts, 69, 274–75
Predicament: consciousness-centered, 218, 233, 257, 301
Predictability, 20, 204, 205, 285–86, 305, 307
Present, 111, 112
Pre-Socratics, 320
Primary World of Senses (Straus), 359
Proust, Marcel, 179

Qualities: secondary, 255, 258, 260
Quantum level of infrastructure, 125, 293
Quantum mechanics, 25, 26

Randomness, 152, 287
Rationalism, 229, 264, 270
Rationality, 91, 229, 230, 321, 322, 323
"Reach," spatiotemporal: of act-temporality, 111–14, 150, 169, 342; of originative acts, 124, 133, 174–75
Realism: epistemological, 242, 245
Really real: Plato's doctrine of the, 8, 361n*1*
Reasons and causes, 3–4, 35, 36, 52–53, 70, 73
Recognition, 93, 94, 103, 277, 278, 321, 322–26, 351
Recognition of Reason, The (Pols) 357, 359, 362
Reductionism, 23, 24–26, 39, 68, 169, 187, 254, 255, 280, 351, 355n*12*
Reflection: radically originative, 231, 253, 254
Reflex arc, 172
Reflexivity of subjectivity (mind, consciousness), 231, 258
Regularities, 48, 49, 292
Reincarnation, 351
"Relation": of originative acts to sub-acts, 94–100, 308–51 passim; asymmetric power, 135, 136; of mind and its physical basis, 232, 284
— of originative act to its infrastructure: and consciousness, 177, 178; and mind-body problem, 278; mentioned, 101, 102, 106, 107, 111, 114, 122, 140, 150, 163, 174, 183, 184, 214, 253, 268, 282, 283, 286, 306, 310, 312, 350
Relations: between acts in a series, 95–100; significant temporal, 155–56
Relativity: theory of, 29
Representation: mutual, 339
RNA, 75, 146, 147
Robots, 188–206
Rorty, Richard, 355
Rosenblueth, Arturo, 240, 246, 356, 360
Routine: neuromuscular, 154–55
Russell, Bertrand, 21, 283, 355

Sartre, Jean-Paul, 237, 238, 360
Schrödinger, Erwin, 56, 286, 291, 357, 360

369

Index

Science: and language, 14–15; reduction-ist, 23, 24–26, 39, 68, 169, 187, 254, 255, 280, 351, 355n*12;* hierarchic (anti-reductionist), 40, 41–68, 53, 54, 56, 57, 68, 69, 82; administrative sub-categori-zation of, 53; and determinism, 170, 295; and phenomenology, 235

Science and Humanism (Schrödinger), 360

Scientism, 6, 14, 257

Scriven, Michael, 193–95

Self, 180

Self-awareness (consciousness), 179, 180

Self-creation, Whitehead's doctrine of, 358

Self in Philosophy, The (Castell), 359

Self-knowledge, 351

Self-transcendence: of mind (subjectivity, consciousness), 225, 233, 243, 246, 248, 252, 254, 257–60, 267, 273, 277, 321, 324, 325–26

Sense data, 323

Sensory modalities, 250

Servomechanisms, 145, 301, 335, 341, 342

Shaffer, J. A., 17, 355

Sherrington, C. S., 162, 200, 256–57, 260, 359, 360

Simplicity. *See* Unity

Simultaneity: act-temporal, 105, 124–33, 173, 175, 316

Skinner, B. F., 10, 355

Smuts, J. C., 280

Smythies, J. R., 356

Societies: Whitehead's doctrine of, 328, 358

Socrates: speech from Plato's *Phaedo,* 1–3; views on action, cause, materialism, etc., 1–5, 5–27 passim, 37, 69–72, 80, 87, 89, 233, 271, 351; actions or remarks, 34–35, 38, 39, 51, 52, 54–55, 59–67, 79, 85, 86, 87, 90, 91, 92, 94–100, 101, 105, 109, 121, 122, 123, 127, 130, 131, 132, 133, 142, 150, 151, 160, 161, 165, 170, 173, 174, 178, 179, 183, 238, 254, 274–75, 299, 306, 307, 308–51 passim

Source: ontological, 313; of acts (act-source), 319, 320

Spatiomechanisms, 335–43, 348, 349

Spatiotemporal patterns, 120, 205, 247, 283, 296–98, 301, 329, 346

Sperry, Roger W.: on hierarchies, 38, 42, 43; on temporal integration in nervous system, 163; his work on corpus cal-losum, 279; on mind-body problem, 280–84; and efficacity of mind, 294, 300; his articles, 357, 360

Starting point: epistemological, 233, 236, 242, 243, 248

State: consciousness as a, 180, 182, 223, 226, 278; total, of physical system, 204; logical versus machine, in computers, 209; subjective, 325

Straus, Erwin W., 234, 359

Structure: in infrastructure of originative acts, 74–77, 76–81, 103, 104; C → E causality in, 76–81, 88, 144, 184, 208; its ontological dependence on dynamic units, 81, 82, 86; inheritance of, 85; and mechanism, 88, 94; and act-temporality, 120, 128–29, 168; code-bearing, 145–49, 342–43; meaningful control, 146, 341; telic, 173; deep, in language, 269; as problem for originative act, 285; mutual coding in, 342–43

Sub-acts, 69, 97–100, 101, 308–11, 313, 316

Subject: and consciousness, 180, 258, 262; and object, 240–42, 326

Subjective aim: Whitehead's doctrine of, 358

Subjectivism, 236

Subjectivity: and originative action, 160, 165, 275; Descartes on certainties of, 178; and objectivity, 183, 217, 218, 219, 223, 224, 225, 226, 227, 231, 249, 251, 253, 255; and consciousness, 222, 224; Husserl on transcendental and constitu-tive character of, 236; as state or func-tion, 241–42; Wigner on 243–46; and doctrine of Democritus, 246; self-tran-scendence of, 252, 254, 257–60, 267; reflexivity of, 258; efficacity of, 283; transcended by recognition, 325; James on transcendental, 326

Substance: thinking, Descartes' doctrine of, 160, 179, 189, 191, 233–34, 365; and consciousness, 180; extended, Des-cartes' doctrine of, 189, 191, 235, 361; mentioned, 314, 331, 361–62

Substantia, 361–62

Supervening (governing) ontic power, 344, 346, 347

Symbols, 182, 226–30, 240, 323

Symmetries and Reflections (Wigner), 360

Synapse, 159, 293, 303–4

Synthesis, 92, 93, 102

370

Systems: formal logical, 209; physical, ordered but not deterministic, 291
Systole, 158, 159

Teleology, 147, 173, 335, 342, 343
Temporal continuum, 33, 100, 115–16
Temporality: linear, of events, 33, 107–10, 138, 173; of multiplicity of the infrastructure, 136. *See also* Act-temporality; Becoming; *Durée;* Time; Time-bound units
Thalamus, 165
Theoretic action, 274–75, 277
Thermodynamic fluctuations, 291–92
Thinking being (substance): Descartes' doctrine of, 160, 179, 188, 189, 191, 233–34
Thomas, G. J., Jr., 356
Thorpe, W. H., 307
Time: linear interpretation of, 107–10, 138, 173; James' theory of, 111, 118, 157; Whitehead's epochal theory of, 111, 118–19, 357–58; St. Augustine on, 111, 357n2; continuous aspect of, 120–21, 131, 137. *See also* Act-temporality; Becoming; *Durée;* Time-bound units
Time-bound units, 157, 158–59, 163, 173, 302–7
Transcendence: of infrastructure by originative act, 310, 311, 325, 351; of sub-acts by originative act, 312; of acts by agent, 314, 315, 317; of multiplicity by recognition, 325; of particularity by recognition, 325–27. *See also* Self-transcendence
Transcendental subjectivity, 236, 326
Transmission: causal (CT), Culbertson on, 200–201. *See also* Causality, C → E
Transparency of consciousness, 223, 230
Trinity: doctrine of the, 301n1
Turing, A. M., 9, 192–93, 195, 335, 355

Understanding and awareness, 239, 253, 326

Unity: of originative acts, 101–75 passim, 277, 319; act-temporal, 140, 143, 159, 161–68, 284, 293, 330; of agent, 308–51 passim; of being, 319, 320; and recognition, 324, 325; of fundamental entities, 334
Universality, 319, 320. *See also* Common power; Generality; Universals
Universals, 229, 331, 351. *See also* Common power; Generality; Universality

Variables: intervening, 191
Vesicles: synaptic, and indeterminary principle, 293, 303–4
Vitalism, 191
Volition, 109

Waddington, C. H., 346, 362
Wasps: and programmed behavior, 89–90, 357n3
Watson, J. B., 190–91, 359
Wiener, Norbert, 246
Weiss, Paul A.: views on hierarchy in organisms, 41–48, 52, 61, 63–64; on determination and indetermination, 47, 48, 285, 295; on administrative organization for science, 53–54; works, 356, 357
What Is Life? The Physical Aspect of the Living Cell (Schrödinger), 357
Whitehead, Alfred North: on epochal theory of time, 111, 118–19, 357–58; on actual entities, 118, 134, 328; on societies, 328; on creativity, 329; on laws of nature, 356; mentioned, 168
Wigner, Eugene, 243–46, 249, 360
Will, 59, 299
Wittgenstein, Ludwig, 14
Wooldridge, Dean E., 202–6, 210, 247, 359
Woolf, Virginia, 179
World-line, 200

Yeats, William Butler, 252

371